D1001444

Building Service-Aware Networks

The Next-Generation WAN/MAN

Muhammad Afaq Khan, CCIE No. 9070

Cisco Press

800 East 96th Street

Indianapolis, IN 46240

Building Service-Aware Networks:
The Next-Generation WAN/MAN

Muhammad Afaq Khan

Published by
Cisco Press
800 East 96th Street
Indianapolis, IN 46240 USA

Printed in the United States of America

First Printing September 2009

Library of Congress Cataloging-in-Publication Data:

Library of Congress Cataloging-in-Publication data is on file.

ISBN-13: 978-1-58705-788-5

ISBN-10: 1-58705-788-3

Warning and Disclaimer

This book is designed to provide information about enterprise WAN/MAN network architectures: design, selecting and qualifying, deploying, and troubleshooting the router. Every effort has been made to make this book as complete and as accurate as possible, but no warranty or fitness is implied.

The information is provided on an "as is" basis. The author, Cisco Press, and Cisco Systems, Inc. shall have neither liability nor responsibility to any person or entity with respect to any loss or damages arising from the information contained in this book or from the use of the discs or programs that may accompany it.

The opinions expressed in this book belong to the author and are not necessarily those of Cisco Systems, Inc.

Trademark Acknowledgments

All terms mentioned in this book that are known to be trademarks or service marks have been appropriately capitalized. Cisco Press or Cisco Systems, Inc., cannot attest to the accuracy of this information. Use of a term in this book should not be regarded as affecting the validity of any trademark or service mark.

Corporate and Government Sales

The publisher offers excellent discounts on this book when ordered in quantity for bulk purchases or special sales, which may include electronic versions and/or custom covers and content particular to your business, training goals, marketing focus, and branding interests. For more information, please contact: U.S. Corporate and Government Sales 1-800-382-3419 corpsales@pearsontechgroup.com

For sales outside the United States please contact: International Sales international@pearsoned.com

Feedback Information

At Cisco Press, our goal is to create in-depth technical books of the highest quality and value. Each book is crafted with care and precision, undergoing rigorous development that involves the unique expertise of members from the professional technical community.

Readers' feedback is a natural continuation of this process. If you have any comments regarding how we could improve the quality of this book, or otherwise alter it to better suit your needs, you can contact us through email at feedback@ciscopress.com. Please make sure to include the book title and ISBN in your message.

We greatly appreciate your assistance.

Publisher: Paul Boger

Associate Publisher: Dave Dusthimer

Executive Editor: Brett Bartow

Managing Editor: Patrick Kanouse

Senior Development Editor: Christopher Cleveland

Senior Project Editor: Tonya Simpson

Editorial Assistant: Vanessa Evans

Indexer: Ken Johnson

Cisco Representative: Erik Ullanderson

Cisco Press Program Manager: Anand Sundaram

Technical Editors: Partha Palanisamy, Lakshmi Sharma

Copy Editor: Keith Cline

Proofreader: Apostrophe Editing Services

Book Designer: Louisa Adair

Composition: Mark Shirar

About the Author

Muhammad Afaq Khan, CCIE No. 9070, attended the NED University of Engineering and Technology, Karachi, Pakistan, where he earned his bachelor's degree in computer systems. After finishing at NEDUET, Afaq worked for various start-ups as a C/C++/Web programmer. From 2001 to date, Afaq has been with Cisco both in post-sales technical support and technical/product marketing roles. Currently, Afaq works as a senior technical marketing engineer for the Cisco Edge Routing Business Unit, focusing on both inbound and outbound marketing for Cisco ASR 1000 series routers. Afaq is also a sought-after speaker at the Cisco WW Networkers event and many other similar technical seminars. He holds three CCIEs in the areas of routing, security, and service provider technologies. He also holds multiple patents in the area of computer networking. Afaq lives with his wife and son in Santa Clara, California.

Dedications

First, I'd like to thank God for enabling me to complete this project.

This book is dedicated to my father, Muhammad Shoaib Khan, and my mother, Fahmeeda Sultana, for providing guidance and education.

Khadija and Usman, my lovely wife and son, without their support and patience this wouldn't have been possible!

Saira, Faiza, Najia, and Ishtiaq—my lovely siblings, for always being there for me!

Thank you all for making me complete.

Acknowledgments

I want to give special recognition to Lakshmi Sharma and Partha Palanisamy for their expert technical knowledge provided as part of the editing of this book. They both are good friends. I also want to extend thanks to my entire Edge Routing Business Unit marketing and engineering teams for professional guidance, support, and indirectly contributing to this book.

A big thank you goes out to the production team for this book. Brett Bartow, Christopher Cleveland, and Drew Cupp have been incredibly professional, thorough, and an absolute pleasure to work with. I couldn't have asked for a finer team.

Contents at a Glance

Introduction xix

Part I Overview of WAN Architectures

Chapter 1 Introduction to WAN Architectures 1

Chapter 2 Next-Generation WAN Architectures 17

Chapter 3 Selecting and Qualifying Enterprise Edge Platforms for Next-Generation WANs 29

Chapter 4 Sizing Up a Router 39

Part II ASR 1000 System Hardware, Software, and Configuration

Chapter 5 System Overview and Carrier-Class Attributes 43

Chapter 6 Cisco ASR 1000 Series Router Hardware and Software Details 71

Chapter 7 Cisco IOS XE Software Packaging, Releases, and Licensing 93

Chapter 8 Cisco ASR 1000 Initial Setup and Configuration 103

Chapter 9 In-Service Software Upgrade and Software Modularity 113

Part III System Management and Troubleshooting

Chapter 10 Using the ASR 1000 Embedded Graphical User Interface 141

Chapter 11 Understanding ASR 1000 System Troubleshooting and Error Messages 149

Part IV ASR 1000—Bringing Innovative Solutions to the Routing Industry

Chapter 12 IP Routing Use Cases 177

Chapter 13 IP Services Use Cases 205

Chapter 14 Security Services Use Cases 231

Chapter 15 WAN Optimization Services Use Cases 259

Chapter 16 Unified Communications Services Use Cases 269

Index 287

Contents

Introduction xix

Part I Overview of WAN Architectures

Chapter 1 Introduction to WAN Architectures 1

Introduction to WAN Solutions 1

Branch/Private WAN Aggregation Role 2

Basic Feature Requirements 5

Basic Service Level Agreement Requirements 5

Internet Edge Role 8

Basic Feature Requirements 9

Data Center Interconnect 10

Basic Feature Requirements 11

Large Branch WAN 12

Summary 15

Review Questions 15

Answers 15

Further Reading 16

Chapter 2 Next-Generation WAN Architectures 17

The Evolution of Next-Generation WAN Architectures 17

Business Drivers Behind WAN Evolution 18

Service Awareness and Integration 18

Infrastructure Consolidation 19

Segmentation/Virtualization 20

Security and Reliability 22

Bandwidth Commoditization 22

Carbon Footprint Reduction 23

Regulatory Compliance 24

Time to Adoption 24

Mean Time to Understanding and Troubleshooting 24

How the Changing Business Requirements Relate to Network Infrastructure 25

Summary 26

Review Questions 27

Answers 27

Further Reading 27

References 28

Chapter 3 Selecting and Qualifying Enterprise Edge Platforms for Next-Generation WANs 29

Essential Attributes of an Enterprise Edge Platform 29

Carrier-Class Routing 29

True Services Integration 29

Robust In-Built Quality of Service 30

Flexible System Architecture 30

Feature Velocity 31

Common Sharing and Sparing for Investment Protection 31

Interface Diversity and Density 31

Power and Space Friendly 31

Industry Standard Compliance 32

Qualifying the Enterprise WAN/MAN Edge Platform 32

Anatomy of a Test Plan 32

Test Scope and Objective 34

Test Setup and Topology 34

Test Resources 34

Test Approach and Methodology 35

Test Entry and Exit Criteria 35

Test Schedule 36

Test Results Reporting 36

Test Case Details 36

Summary 36

Chapter Review Questions 37

Answers 37

Further Reading 37

Chapter 4 Sizing Up a Router 39

What to Look for When Choosing a Router 39

Metrics for Benchmarking a Router 40

Routing-Plane Performance and Scale 41

Data-Plane Performance and Scale 41

Summary 42

Chapter Review Questions 42

Answers 42

Further Reading 42

Part II ASR 1000 System Hardware, Software, and Configuration

Chapter 5 System Overview and Carrier-Class Attributes 43

Introduction to ASR 1000 Series Routers 43

ASR 1000 Carrier-Class Attributes 46

Availability 46

Reliability 46

Scalability 48

Quality of Service 48

ROI and Investment Protection 49

ASR 1000 Applications 49

ASR 1000 Enterprise WAN Aggregation 49

Enterprise Internet Gateway 49

Enterprise Security Headend (Branch and Remote User Aggregation) 50

Service Provider Layer 3 VPN 51

Service Provider Layer 2 VPN 51

Broadband Aggregation, Including FTTH and DSL LNS, LAC, and PTA 53

High-End Customer Premises Equipment 54

Reinventing Enterprise Routing with the ASR 1000 56

Cisco QuantumFlow Processor and Embedded Services 56

True Carrier-Class Routing 57

Chassis Design and Modularity 57

Operating System Modularity 57

In-Service Software Upgrade 58

Separation of Planes 58

Dealing with Oversubscription 59

Integrated QoS 59

BITS Reference Clock 60

Nonstop Router Management 60

Breadth and Diversity of LAN/WAN Interfaces 60

Introducing ASR 1000 System Hardware Components 61

Chassis Options 61

Chassis Slots Naming and Numbering 62

Route Processor 62

Embedded Service Processor 63

SPA Interface Processor 63

Introducing ASR 1000 Software Components 63
IOS XE 63
RP Software 63
ESP Software 65
SIP Software 66
IOSD and Linux Kernel 67
System ROMMON 68
Basic Partitioning of the ASR 1000 System 68
Routing Plane 68
Data Plane 68
Input/Output Plane 68
Introduction to ASR 1000 System Redundancy and Modularity 68
Summary 69
Chapter Review Questions 69
Answers 70
Further Reading 70

Chapter 6 Cisco ASR 1000 Series Router Hardware and Software Details 71

Route Processor Overview 71
Route Processor Functional Elements 71
Front Panel 72
CPU, DRAM, Bootflash, Hard Disk Drive, and Interconnect Application-Specific Integrated Circuits 73
RP Initialization 75
RP Packet Handling 75
Hardware-Assisted Control-Plane Protection 78
Legacy Protocol Traffic 78
ESP Overview 79
ESP Functional Elements 79
ESP Initialization 81
ESP Packet Handling 81
ESP and Crypto Engine 82
SPA Interface Processor Overview 83
High-Level System Software Architecture 85
RP Software Details 85
RP Chassis Manager 85
RP Forwarding Manager 86

RP Interface Manager 86
ESP Software Details 86
QFP Software 86
ESP Forwarding Manager 86
ESP Chassis Manager 87
SIP Software Details 87
SIP Chassis Manager 87
SIP Interface Manager 87
SPA Drivers 87
Day in the Life of a Packet 88
Ingress Processing 88
Arrival Processing 88
Egress Processing 91
Summary 91
Review Questions 91
Answers 92
Further Reading 92

Chapter 7 Cisco IOS XE Software Packaging, Releases, and Licensing 93
Cisco IOS XE Software Overview 93
Cisco IOS XE Software Packaging 94
Software Redundancy 98
Cisco IOS XE Software Releases 99
Cisco IOS XE Software Licensing 100
Summary 100
Review Questions 101
Answers 101
Further Reading 102

Chapter 8 Cisco ASR 1000 Initial Setup and Configuration 103
Booting the ASR 1000 103
Initial Cisco ASR 1000 Configuration 107
Understanding the Cisco ASR 1000 File System Structure 109
Summary 110
Chapter Review Questions 110
Answers 111
Further Reading 111

Chapter 9 In-Service Software Upgrade and Software Modularity 113

Why ISSU Is Needed 113

Operational Benefits 113

Business Benefits 114

ASR 1000 ISSU Details 114

A Consolidated Package ISSU on a Fully Redundant 6RU 117

ISSU on 6RU System (with Dual RP and ESP) for IOSD Using Legacy `issu` Commands 118

Subpackage ISSU on a Fully Redundant 6RU 124

Upgrading SIP/SPA Subpackages 131

Upgrading the RP-Specific Subpackages on the Active RP 132

Upgrading the ESP Subpackage on the Standby RP (Formerly Active) 135

Running Dual IOSD on a 2 or 4RU System 137

Summary 138

Chapter Review Questions 138

Answers 138

Further Reading 139

Part III System Management and Troubleshooting

Chapter 10 Using the ASR 1000 Embedded Graphical User Interface 141

Introduction to the ASR 1000 Web GUI 141

Configuring the ASR 1000 GUI 142

Common Usage Examples 143

Summary 146

Review Questions 146

Answers 147

Further Reading 147

Chapter 11 Understanding ASR 1000 System Troubleshooting and Error Messages 149

Troubleshooting Methodology 149

ASR 1000–Specific Troubleshooting Commands 150

Troubleshooting System Hardware and Software 154

Displaying the Overall Processor and Memory Utilization on an ASR 1000 System 154

Displaying IPv4-Related Drops for the Active QFP 155

Displaying Overall QFP Memory Statistics for IRAM, DRAM, and SRAM Usage 156

Displaying QFP Memory Statistics on a Per-IOS Feature and Internal-Usage Basis 157
Tracking Control CPU Usage from the Linux Shell 161
Tracking a Command Output Repeatedly Using the `monitor` Command 162
Displaying the Status of Front-Panel LEDs Using the `show platform hardware` Command 163
Displaying the Status of SPAs in a SIP 163
Displaying Statistics for a Slot or SIP 164
Displaying Drop Statistics for All Interfaces in the System 164
Displaying the Interface-Level FIA for Both the Ingress and Egress Feature Set 165
Displaying System Components Such as RP, ESP, and SIP Insertion and Uptime 166
Displaying QFP PPE Utilization Information 167
Useful `debug` Commands 168
Troubleshooting IOS Features via Platform-Specific Commands 169
Common System Error Messages 174
Message: "Warning: Filesystem Is Not Clean" During RP Boot 174
Message: "%IOSXE-7-PLATFORM: F0: sntp: Resetting on Error x > y" 175
Message: "%ASR1000_PEM-3-PEMFAIL: The PEM in Slot 0 Is Switched Off or Encountering a Failure Condition" 175
Summary 175
Review Questions 176
Answers 176
Further Reading 176

Part IV ASR 1000—Bringing Innovative Solutions to the Routing Industry

Chapter 12 IP Routing Use Cases 177

Introduction to the Scalable and Modular Control Plane on the ASR 1000 177
NSF/SSO, NSR, Graceful Restart to Ensure Robust Routing 179
Use Case: Achieving High Availability Using NSF/SSO 179
Packet Capture Using Encapsulated Remote SPAN 184
Use Case: Ethernet Frame Capture and Transport Across a Layer 3 Cloud 184
Achieving Segmentation Using MPLS over GRE and MPLS VPNs over GRE Solutions 187
Use Case: Self-Managed MPLS and Enterprise Private WAN Segmentation 187

Scalable v4/VPNv4 Route Reflector 190

Use Case: Route Reflection 191

Scalable and Flexible Internet Edge 193

Use Case: Internet Gateway/Edge Router 193

Scalable Data Center Interconnect 195

Use Case: Encrypting Traffic over an EoMPLS Psuedowire at Layer 2 Using TrustSec 198

Summary 203

Chapter Review Questions 203

Answers 203

Further Reading 204

Chapter 13 IP Services Use Cases 205

Introduction to IOS IP Services on the ASR 1000 205

Scalable In-Built QoS Using QFP's Traffic Manager 206

Ingress SIP Buffering 207

Traffic Manager Packet Buffering 209

Unicast Packets 210

Multicast Packets 210

Punt Packet 210

Egress SIP Buffering 211

ESP Interconnect Scheduler Default Behavior (Aggregating All SIP Traffic) 213

ASR 1000 Traffic Manager Priority Queues 213

Scalable Hierarchical QoS and Metro-E Use Case 216

Scalable IPv4 and IPv6 Multicast Acceleration Using Cisco QuantumFlow Processor 219

Multicast High Availability on the ASR 1000 220

Multicast Replication on the ESP 221

Scalable In-Built Multigigabit NAT 221

High-Speed Logging Using NetFlow v9 Format for NAT and Firewall 223

Scalable In-Built Multigigabit NBAR and FPM 225

Summary 228

Chapter Review Questions 228

Answers 228

Further Reading 229

Chapter 14 Security Services Use Cases 231

Introduction to IOS Security Services on the Cisco ASR 1000 231

Secure Connectivity Solutions 232

Introduction to IPsec Solutions on the Cisco ASR 1000 232

IPsec Packet Flow (Ingress) 235

IPsec Packet Flow (Egress) 235

IPsec High-Availability Considerations 236

IPsec and Interaction with IP Multicast 236

Scalable Encryption with QoS Before/After Crypto Engine 237

Scalable DMVPN Hub and Spoke 239

Scalable GETVPN Group Member for Data Center and Large Branch Solutions 242

Cisco ASR 1000 GETVPN Solution Benefits 242

Cisco ASR 1000 GETVPN Solution Architecture Overview 242

GETVPN Configuration Overview 246

Cisco ASR 1000 Memory, Performance, and Scaling 247

Caveats and Limitations 248

Cisco ASR 1000 GETVPN Deployment Models 248

Troubleshooting GETVPN on Cisco ASR 1000 250

Integrated Threat Control Solutions 251

Introduction to Threat Control Solutions on the ASR 1000 251

Using In-Built Firewall High Availability 253

IOS Firewall Zone/Zone Pair Scale 253

Scalable Multigigabit Router Firewall at the Internet Edge: Use Case 254

Summary 256

Chapter Review Questions 256

Answers 256

Further Reading 257

Chapter 15 WAN Optimization Services Use Cases 259

Introduction to WAN Optimization Solutions on the Cisco ASR 1000 259

Using WCCPv2 for Web Caching 260

Interaction of WCCPv2 with Other IOS Features 261

WAN Optimization Through WAAS Integration 262

Campus WAN Headend Deployment 263

Branch Deployment 264

WAN Headend and IronPort's WSA Appliance 265

Troubleshooting WCCPv2 on Cisco ASR 1000 265
Voice Header Compression Using Cisco IOS cRTP 267
Chapter Review Questions 267
Answers 268
Further Reading 268

Chapter 16 Unified Communications Services Use Cases 269
Introduction to Unified WAN Solutions on Cisco ASR 1000 269
Using Integrated CUBE 271
CUBE (SP) Deployment Scenarios 274
SP-to-SP Peering 274
SP-to-Managed Enterprise and Residential SIP Trunking 275
Business-to-Business Telepresence 276
Troubleshooting CUBE 279
Using the WebEx Node Services Module 280
WebEx Node Deployment Architecture 282
Deployment Considerations 282
Installation Steps 283
Summary 285
Review Questions 285
Answers 286
Further Reading 286

Index 287

Icons Used in This Book

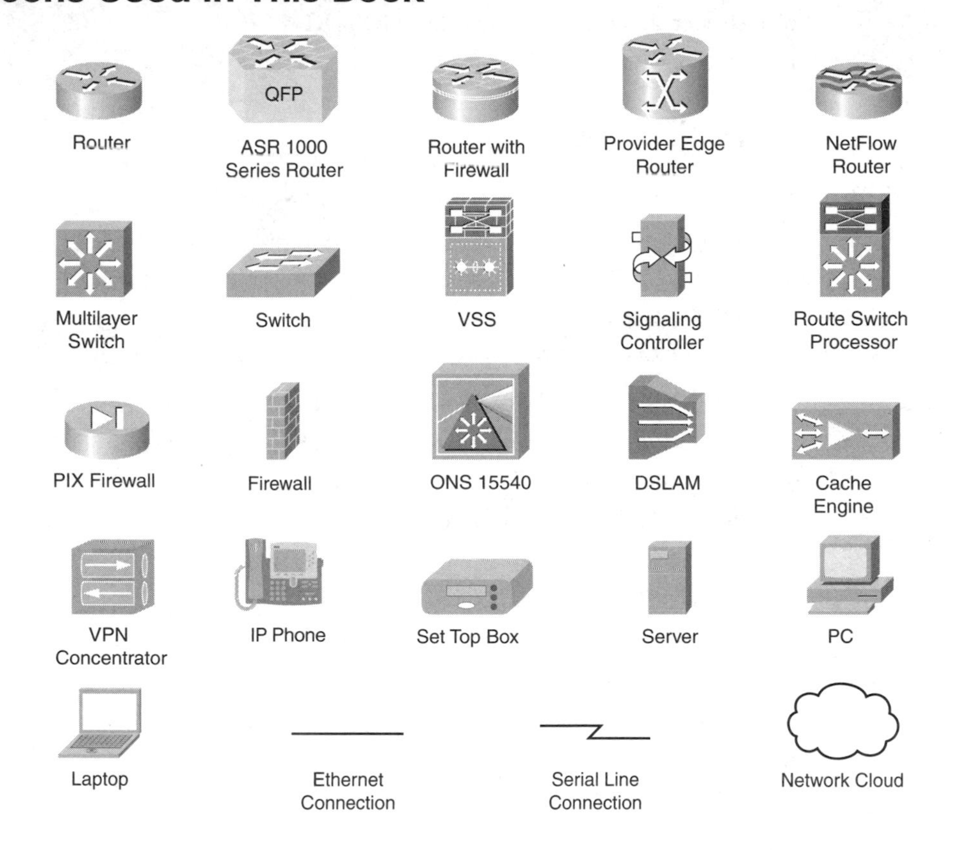

Command Syntax Conventions

The conventions used to present command syntax in this book are the same conventions used in the IOS Command Reference. The Command Reference describes these conventions as follows:

- **Boldface** indicates commands and keywords that are entered literally as shown. In actual configuration examples and output (not general command syntax), boldface indicates commands that are manually input by the user (such as a **show** command).
- *Italic* indicates arguments for which you supply actual values.
- Vertical bars (|) separate alternative, mutually exclusive elements.
- Square brackets ([ ]) indicate an optional element.
- Braces ({ }) indicate a required choice.
- Braces within brackets ([{ }]) indicate a required choice within an optional element.

Introduction

Both traditional WANs and next-generation WAN aggregation are an integral part of any network design. This is where you aggregate all your traffic coming from branches of all sizes. This place in the network, due to being the center of all traffic aggregation, becomes extremely crucial and must handle failures both from platform and network architecture perspectives. Therefore, just as we must understand WANs, emerging trends, and how those trends are creating newer requirements for WAN routing products, it is equally important to understand how to select, qualify, and adopt them into your network.

This book covers all topics related to WANs/MANs. It starts with an introduction to WAN/MAN architectures, followed by information specific to Cisco ASR 1000 series routers. The book concludes with five chapters of real-world use cases based on the ASR 1000 platform.

Goals and Methods

This book can help you understand existing and emerging WAN architectures, including the underlying business trends and how they are creating newer demands for the infrastructure. The hardware and software architectures of the Cisco ASR 1000 series routers are discussed as a perfect example of the modern infrastructure, and that concept is reinforced using various real-world use cases in the last five chapters of this book.

The book is organized into four parts. Part I discusses the WAN architectures, Part II introduces Cisco ASR 1000 series routers, Part III goes over system management and troubleshooting, and Part IV concludes the book with many real-world examples.

Who Should Read This Book?

This book does not focus on a single technical topic or area. Instead, it covers a variety of technical topics that are useful within the context of overall WAN/MAN architectures. This book introduces the reader to both the technical and business landscapes surrounding WAN/MAN technologies.

Other objectives, such as qualifying and sizing up routing equipment from any vendor or understanding various system architectural aspects of a modern system, can also be achieved by reading this book.

Hence, this book can serve well the needs of network engineers, architects, and network visionaries, those who must understand the changes happening within the WAN/MAN arena and the infrastructure design imperatives of next-generation WANs/MANs.

How This Book Is Organized

Although this book can be read cover to cover, it is designed to be flexible and enable you to easily move between chapters and sections of chapters to cover just the material that you want to focus on.

Part I covers the details of WAN/MAN architectures, changes that are happening, and the associated business drivers of those changes. It also covers the selection, qualification, and how to size up a routing device for a given deployment.

Part II discusses Cisco ASR 1000 series routers (including hardware/software architectures). Part II also covers IOS XE packaging, releases, initial setup, and extremely important topics such as in-service software upgrades (ISSU).

Part III focuses on system management and troubleshooting, including some common error messages that you may encounter during deployment.

Part IV delves deeper into actual deployment scenarios, via use cases. A wide variety of topics are covered, from pure routing/switching, IP services, WAN optimization using Web Cache Communication Protocol Version 2 (WCCPv2), and unified communication topics such as Cisco Unified Border Element (CUBE) and the WebEx Node module.

Chapters 1 to 16 cover the following topics:

- **Chapter 1, "Introduction to WAN Architectures,"** discusses various types of WAN architectures and associated infrastructure requirements to build them. Areas covered include branch WAN aggregation, private WAN aggregation, the Interenet edge, data center interconnect, and large branch WANs.

- **Chapter 2, "Next-Generation WAN Architectures,"** builds upon the basic ideas discussed in Chapter 1. It discusses the evolution of WAN architectures, and the drivers behind them, with references to various research done in the area. It also links these drivers to the newer demands that they are creating for the underlying routing network infrastructure.

- **Chapter 3, "Selecting and Qualifying Enterprise Edge Platforms for Next-Generation WANs,"** covers attributes of a next-generation enterprise WAN/MAN platform, to help you select the appropriate devices. It also discusses how to qualify a routing device by using a methodical approach and a test plan.

- **Chapter 4, "Sizing Up a Router,"** examines essential traits of a modern routing platform for WANs/MANs. It also includes benchmarks that prove useful for testing and sizing up a WAN router.

- **Chapter 5, "System Overview and Carrier-Class Attributes,"** introduces the architecture of Cisco ASR 1000 series routers. This includes an overview of both hardware and software of the platform.

- **Chapter 6, "Cisco ASR 1000 Series Router Hardware and Software Details,"** covers Cisco ASR 1000 series routers in detail. It delves into both hardware and software components and expands on the subject matter that was briefly discussed in Chapter 5.

- **Chapter 7, "Cisco IOS XE Software Packaging, Releases, and Licensing,"** covers the IOS XE operating system (its packaging, releases, and licensing) and examines the concept of software redudancy.
- **Chapter 8, "Cisco ASR 1000 Initial Setup and Configuration,"** goes over the initial ASR 1000 system setup and configuration. This chapter serves as a necessary introduction to prepare you for the use cases in Chapter 12 to Chapter 16.
- **Chapter 9, "In-Service Software Upgrade and Software Modularity,"** discusses only one topic: in-service software upgrades (including various booting options). It also examines the different levels of ISSU support available across various packages, IOS flavors, and ASR 1000 chassis.
- **Chapter 10, "Using the ASR 1000 Embedded Graphical User Interface,"** covers the ASR 1000-specific graphical user interface (GUI) and includes a few use cases.
- **Chapter 11, "Understanding ASR 1000 System Troubleshooting and Error Messages,"** covers basic troublshooting methodology. The focus of the chapter is on IOS and ASR 1000 **show** and **debug** commands. This chapter also examines some common error messages that you may encounter on ASR 1000.
- **Chapter 12, "IP Routing Use Cases,"** starts off the ASR 1000 use cases by using basic IP routing for example purposes. It discusses high availability (HA), route reflectors, and data center interconnect scenarios. These are explained using all relevant configuration snippets and **show** commands.
- **Chapter 13, "IP Services Use Cases,"** covers IOS services such as quality of service (QoS), Network Address Translation (NAT), multicast, NetFlow, and NetFlow event logging. These are explained using all relevant configuration snippets and **show** commands.
- **Chapter 14, "Security Services Use Cases,"** discusses IOS security services available in IOS XE. It uses various IPsec solutions such as Group Encrypted Transport VPNs (GET VPN), IOS zone-based firewalls, and their interaction with other features such as multicast and QoS.
- **Chapter 15, "WAN Optimization Services Use Cases,"** covers fundamental router-based WAN optimization solutions such as compressed Real-Time Protocol (cRTP) but also includes the integration with Cisco Wide Area Application Services (WAAS) and Iron Port's Web Security Appliances (WSA) with ASR 1000.
- **Chapter 16, "Unified Communication Services Use Cases,"** rounds off the discussion with Cisco unified communication. This chapter discusses the Cisco Unified Border Element (CUBE) SP (service provider) Edition and various associated use cases. It also discusses the Cisco WebEx Node module and provides complete integration details. Chapters 12 to 16 evidence how ASR 1000 offers flexiblibility without compromising scale and performance.

Chapter 1

Introduction to WAN Architectures

The WAN is a place in the network that aggregates various types, speeds, and links running a disparate set of protocols together crossing metropolitan, state, and even country boundaries. The largest example of a WAN is the Internet itself, which can be regarded as the public WAN. The primary purpose of a WAN is to connect users and applications connected to various LANs.

As evident from its definition, the WAN is the central point for all data aggregation coming from various places within an enterprise network. Because of this, it is important to understand not only how a WAN is constructed, but also the underlying business drivers that have been and continue to bring changes to this place in the network.

In this book, you study the variety of WANs as they exist today, business models, and the associated emerging trends and how they are giving birth to "next-generation" WAN. Once you have the first four chapters (or Part I) behind you, it should become evident that the core requirement to building such networks hinges on the usage of modern routing/switching infrastructure that is highly available, scalable, flexible, and above all, service rich.

This chapter describes the various types of WAN architectures and their various associated aspects.

Introduction to WAN Solutions

Thanks to an increasingly dispersed global work force, businesses rely on their WANs more than ever. So much so that business performance is now directly tied to how well quality, reliability, and security are implemented when it comes to communications between main and regional headquarters, branch offices, suppliers, partners, and customers. Because of the development of new IP services and applications such as VoIP, video, and mobile data connectivity, and because of remotely connected road warriors and the unification of both wired and wireless networks, the headend router must perform a wide variety of functions.

Depending on the connectivity, transport protocols, and whether the medium is private or public, several different varieties of WAN might be in play. The four main WAN types are as follows:

- Branch/private WAN aggregation
- Internet edge
- Data center interconnect
- Large branch WAN

The WAN aggregation role can also be subdivided into the following three categories, based on what is typically found in the enterprise networks:

- Basic WAN aggregation (explained in the following section)
- Secure WAN aggregation (add-on with solutions based on IPsec or Secure Sockets Layer virtual private networking [SSL VPN])
- Optimized WAN aggregation (add-on with solutions based on WAN optimization with Web Cache Communication Protocol Version 2/Policy Based Routing [WCCPv2/PBR] and Wide Area Application Services [WAAS])

Figure 1-1 shows various WAN options and puts them into perspective as to how they come together.

Branch/Private WAN Aggregation Role

Branch WAN aggregation is a way to connect and aggregate all the enterprise branches into the WAN core router, or headend. On the cloud-facing side, router interfaces use various physical transport options (as outlined in Table 1-1), whereas on the campus core side, the connection is Gigabit Ethernet (GE) or 10 Gigabit Ethernet (10 GigE) that is acting as the uplink for the campus core switches to the WAN. Leased lines are one of the most common ways (now more so Ethernet) of interfacing with the WAN cloud. IPsec tunnel termination and firewall functions are usually not collapsed in the WAN aggregation/edge router. This is usually implemented as classical hub-and-spoke design with traditional Layer 2 connectivity.

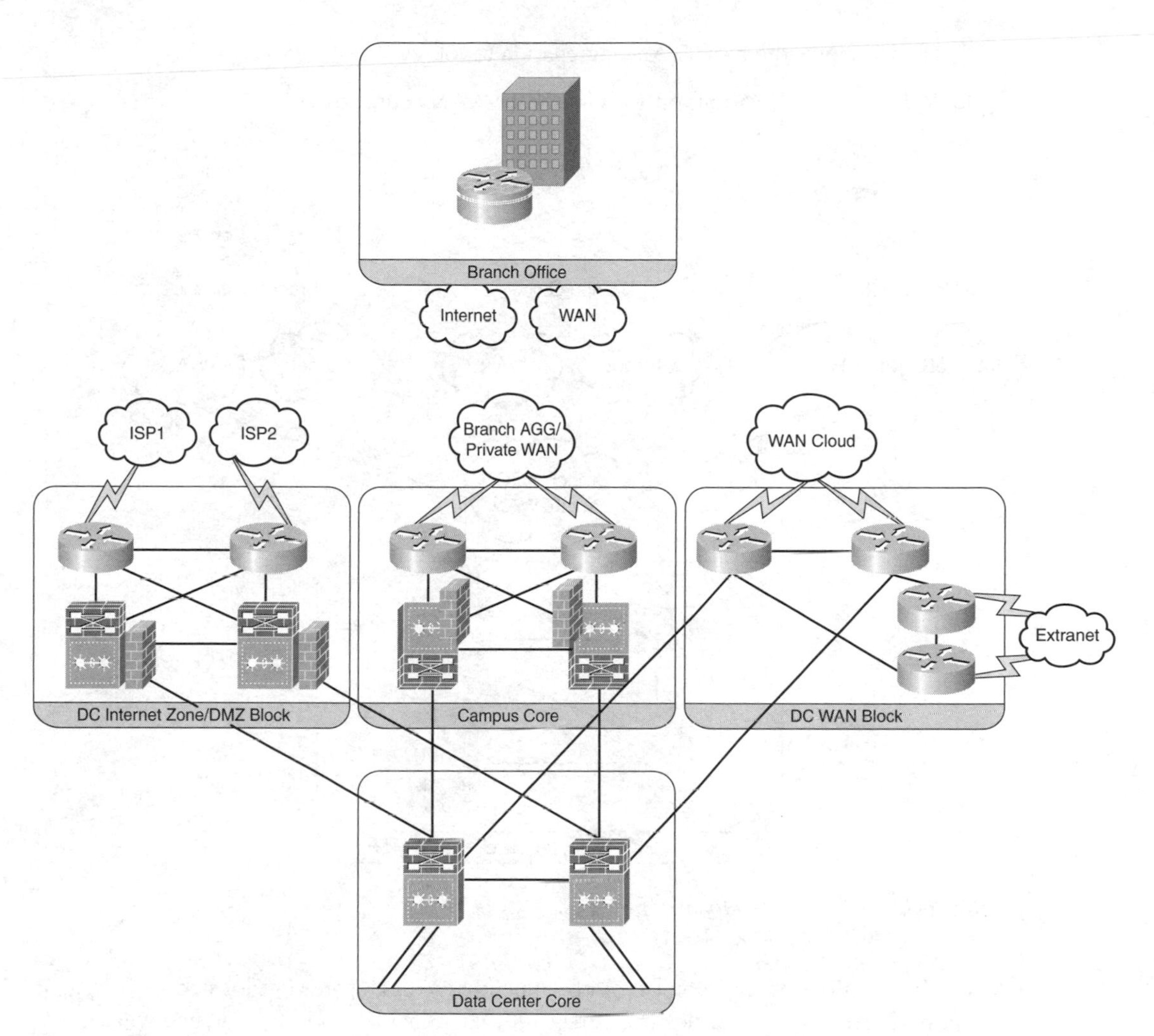

Figure 1-1 *WAN options.*

Figure 1-2 shows the basic WAN aggregation topology.

Table 1-1 shows the various options in use for WAN connectivity.

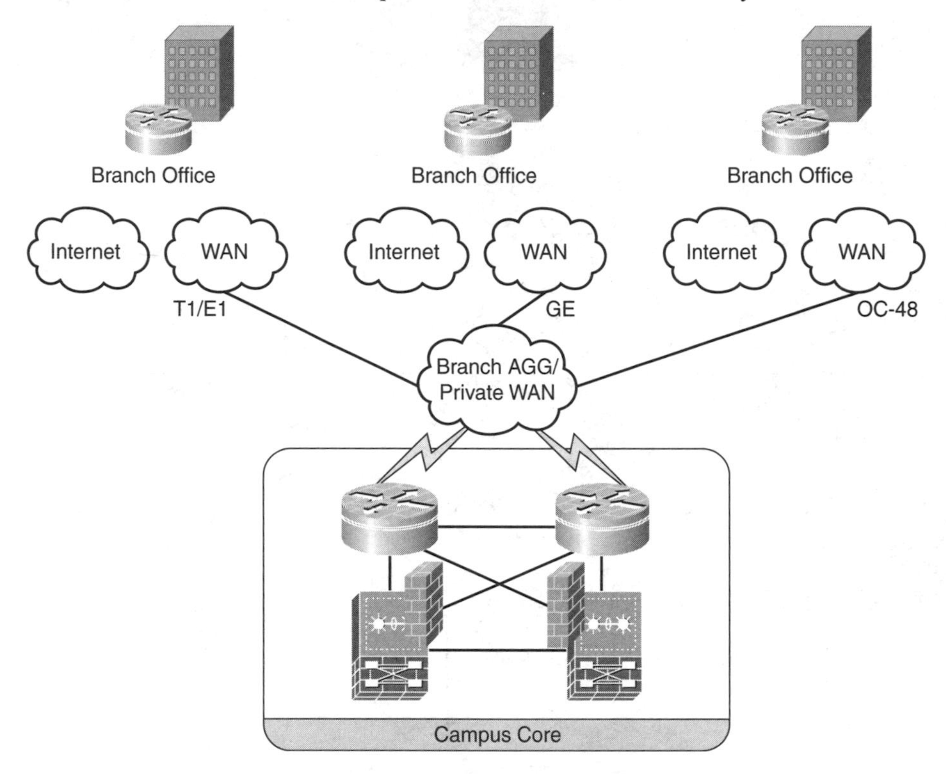

Figure 1-2 *WAN aggregation topology.*

> **Note** Metro Ethernet is gaining a lot of momentum to aggregate sites located in a given geographic area. This also scales well today with fractional GE and 10 GigE, and will scale even more with the newer standards of 40 and 100 Gbps already in the works at IEEE as P802.3ba, and the first drafts are already out

Table 1-1 *WAN Connectivity Options*

Types	Physical Transport	Pros	Cons	Typical Bandwidth	Protocol Encapsulations
Leased line	T1/E1, T3/E3	Private	Costly	1.544 to 45 Mbps	High-Level Data Control (HDLC), PPP
Circuit switching	Packet over SONET/SDH OC3/OC12/ OC192	Affordable	Less secure	155 Mbps to 10 Gbps	HDLC, PPP
Packet switching	T1/E1, T3/E3 (PVCs)	Affordable	Shared band-width	Up to 45 Mbps	Frame Relay
Cell relay	OC3/OC12/ OC48	Private	Higher per port cost	Up to 620 Mbps	ATM
Metro Ethernet	Ethernet, GE, 10 GigE	Affordable	Lacks inherent reliability	Up to 10 Gbps	Ethernet (Frac-GE, Frac-10 GigE)

Basic Feature Requirements

Table 1-2 outlines the basic requirements that a router must meet to be positioned as the WAN aggregation platform. Scale and performance for these services are driven based on how large the branch site concentration is for the given deployment. A platform with a separate control, data, and input/output plane is most preferred, for obvious reasons.

Basic Service Level Agreement Requirements

Table 1-3 outlines the usual service level agreement (SLA) requirements that need to be met for the converged WAN for voice, video, and data traffic types.

Traditional WANs (such as those based on Frame Relay) are assumed to be inherently secure, which is not the case (because providers do use shared physical infrastructure to carry this traffic). An MPLS VPN is another example where traffic is isolated (via Virtual Routing/Forwarding [VRF] instances and labels) but still share the same physical infrastructure while traversing the service provider cloud.

It is not uncommon to see some form of encryption used to achieve confidentiality, the drivers behind which could be company policy (such as any traffic leaving the premises must be encrypted) or regulatory compliance (such as with HIPAA or SOX).

Table 1-4 outlines the commonly used technologies to secure WAN traffic. Chapter 14, “Security Services Use Cases,” provides further detail.

Table 1-2 *Feature Matrix for WAN Aggregation Role*

Feature/Service	Feature/Service Details
IP routing (v4/v6)	Interior Gateway Protocol (IGP) and Border Gateway Protocol (BGP) with fast convergence, such as bidirectional failure detection (BFD) Policy Based Routing (PBR)
IP unicast and multicast	Protocol Independent Multicast(PIM) Sparse, Sparse-Dense Mode, Auto-Rendezvous Point (RP), Anycast-RP, Source Specific Multicast, Bidirectional PIM, Unicast Reverse Path Forwarding (uRPF)
NetFlow	v5, v9 NetFlow Data Export
Quality of Service (QoS)	Classification based on application traffic, protocol/port, access control lists (ACL) Marking Hierarchical QoS Class-based weighted fair queuing (WFQ), fair queuing, low-latency queuing (LLQ), weighted random early detection (WRED) Traffic policing Traffic shaping Link Fragmentation and Interleaving (LFI)
Compression	Real-Time Protocol (RTP) header compression for voice traffic
WCCP (Web Cache Control Protocol)	WCCPv2 for web cache engine and WAN optimization for data and video traffic
Multilink PPP (MLPPP)	MLPPP with LFI
Multiprotocol Label Switching (MPLS)	2547-based VPNs, Layer 2 VPNs
High availability (HA)	Intra- and Interbox HA

Note In a majority of the cases, the transport medium for secure connectivity solutions (as outlined in the table) is the public WAN Internet.

Table 1-3 *Typical SLA Targets*

Traffic Type/Application	SLA Target
VoIP	Interactive video Videoconferencing
Delay <= 50 ms	Jitter <= 5 ms Loss <= 1% Voice MOS (mean opinion score) >= 3.8
Video broadcast Video on Demand (VoD)	Delay <= 50 ms Loss <= 1%
Mission-critical WWW traffic Voice signaling	Response time <= 3 sec
Loss of service (RP convergence)	IGP <= 3 mins

Table 1-4 *High-Level Details of Secure WAN Technologies*

Secure WAN Technology	Details
Native IPsec (unicast and multicast)	IPsec using both encryption and a hashing algorithm. The virtual tunnel interface can be used for multicast traffic support.
Point-to-point (p2p) generic routing encapsulation (GRE) over IPsec (or p2p GRE inside IPsec)	IPsec with multicast and routing protocol support.
Dynamic Multipoint VPN (DM VPN)	Typically deployed over the public Internet infrastructure.
Remote-access VPNs	Soft IPsec/SSL VPN clients and small office/home office (SOHO; 8xx/18xx) router tunnel aggregation.
Group Encrypted Transport (GET VPN)	Tunnel-less encryption, best suited for private IP or MPLS clouds.

Internet Edge Role

The Internet edge is the boundary where an enterprise private network connects to the public Internet. In the simplest sense, the Internet edge device acts as the gateway for the inside network. Contrary to popular understanding, the Internet edge is not only just about accessing the Internet for web traffic for campus users.

The Internet edge serves various functions, including those outlined in Table 1-5.

Table 1-5 *Internet Edge Router Functionality*

Function	Details
Corporate Internet gateway for campus and data center	Users at the campus access the Internet to browse, email, and use instant messaging, and so on.
Corporate Internet gateway for branches	Users at the branches access the Internet to browse, email, and use instance messaging, and so on. This is to enforce a common set of policies across the enterprise at the burden of bringing all traffic to the headend.
Demilitarized zone (DMZ) services	Traditional FTP, Domain Name System (DNS), and Network Time Protocol (NTP) services located at the DMZ.
Teleworker (remote users)	Teleworkers or road warriors connect to corporate resources via the Internet through encrypted VPN technologies such as IPsec or SSL VPN soft or hard clients (such as Cisco 800 series routers).
Branch WAN backup	This serves as the backup or alternate connection for branch office routers to connect to the corporate headend via the public Internet. Commonly used technologies in this scenario are DM VPN, GRE over IPsec, or dynamic virtual tunnel interface (VTI)-based remote access.
Multi-Homing	This is where the Internet edge router connects directly to multiple SPs. This provides higher fault tolerance for brownouts and greater path selection with advanced routing techniques. This requires that the router be capable of supporting one or multiple copies of Internet routing table.

Figure 1-3 shows the Internet edge topology.

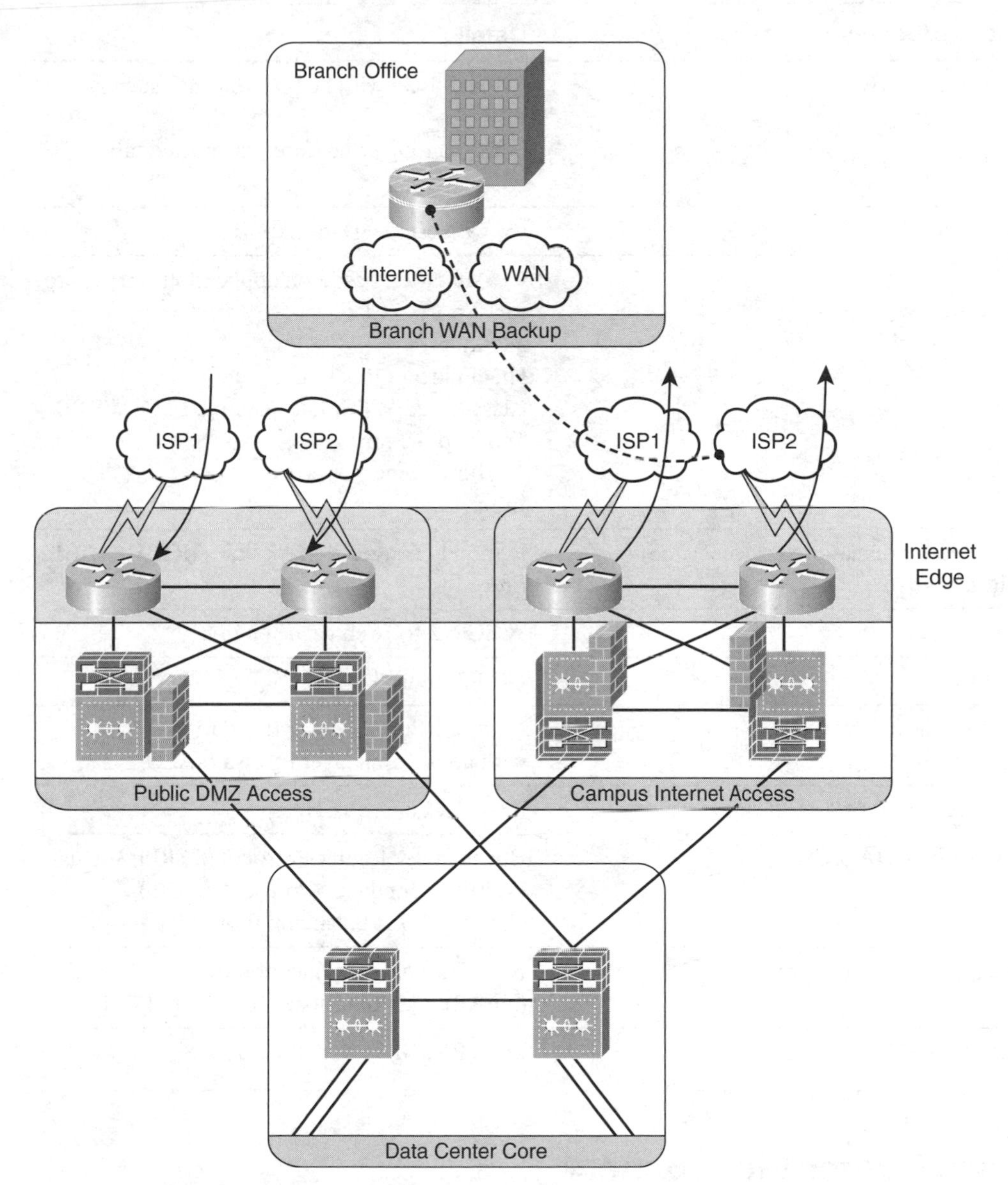

Figure 1-3 *WAN Internet edge topology.*

Basic Feature Requirements

The primary function of a device at the Internet edge is to act as the demarcation between the private (campus or data center) and public network (that is, the Internet). Features required in a single device depend on how the Internet edge is designed, although typically the basic features are those outlined in Table 1-6.

Table 1-6 *Internet Edge Network Device Feature Requirements*

Feature/Service	Details
IP routing (v4/v6)	IGP, and BGP with fast convergence such as BFD PBR Large routing scale (Internet routing table)
NetFlow	v5, v9 NetFlow Data Export
QoS	Classification based on application traffic, protocol/port, ACLs Marking Hierarchical QoS Class-based WFQ, fair queuing, LLQ, WRED Traffic policing Traffic shaping LFI
Distributed denial of service (DDoS) mitigation	Remotely triggered black holes (RTBH), rACL, firewall
WCCP	WCCPv2 for web cache engine
Firewall	L4–L7 firewall
Address translation	Network/Port Address Translation (NAT/PAT) with application layer gateway (ALG)
High Availability	Intra- and interbox HA
Box-to-box HA	Hot Standby Router Protocol (HSRP), Virtual Router Redundancy Protocol (VRRP), Gateway Load Balancing Protocol (GLBP)
Deep Packet Inspection	Network Based Application Recognition (NBAR), Flexible Packet Matching (FPM)
Secure WAN connectivity	DMVPN, GRE over IPsec, IPsec

Data Center Interconnect

Data center interconnect (DCI) is yet another WAN function where someone is trying to connect two data centers together via Layer 2 or 3 links. Layer 2 extensions are much more common because of their capability to take all Ethernet frames (or even dot1Q or QinQ [IEEE 802.1Q-in-Q VLAN]) as is across the data centers. This is usually done with some kind of pseudowire (for example, Ethernet over MPLS [EoMPLS] for two data centers, and Virtual Private LAN Service [VPLS] for multisite data center connectivity). Major drivers behind DCI are as follows:

- Data center consolidation and virtualization (VMWare VMotion)
- Disaster recovery or data center HA
- Geo-clustering, where clusters are connected across geographies
- Layer 2 extensions for any reason

Figure 1-4 shows the DCI topology

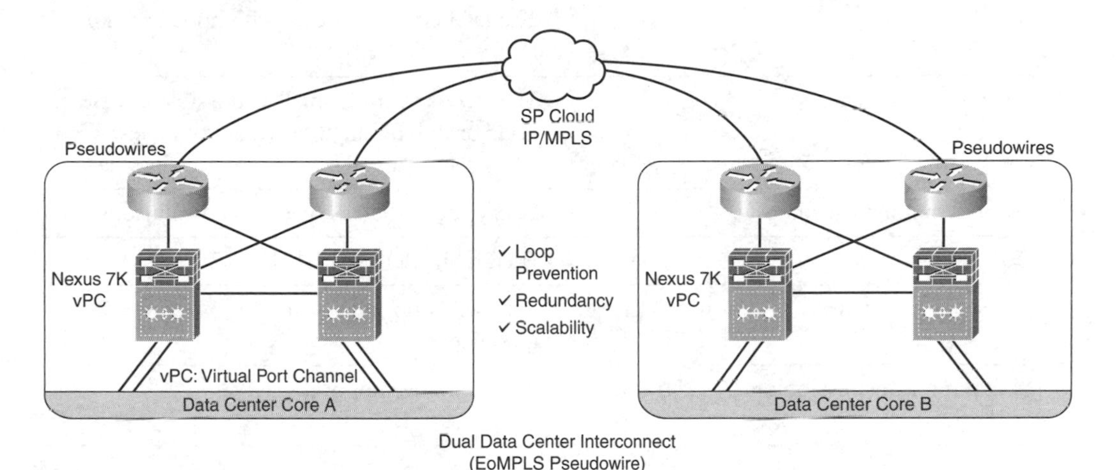

Figure 1-4 *WAN DCI topology.*

Basic Feature Requirements

The primary function of the edge device at the DCI is to extend VLANs across the data centers for the previously listed applications such as VMWare's VMotion or geo-clusters to function. Convergence and failover times for this type of connectivity are of extreme importance because the underlying assumptions from the application perspective usually require them to be on the same LAN.

Note Almost all the VMWare and IBM or Microsoft cluster architectures call for LAN connectivity as a baseline requirement. Hence, emulating LAN service while still connected via a WAN poses a lot of challenges for convergence (ideally within a few seconds).

Table 1-7 outlines the basic features and capabilities required for the DCI solution.

Table 1-7 *DCI Feature Requirements*

Feature	Details
Layer 2 extensions	Typically using pseudowires.
Spanning Tree Protocol (STP) isolation	Spanning-tree isolation is one of the must haves, where each DCI does not extend the STP to avoid any loop. Having redundant links functioning at the same time without STP in the core.
HA	The DCI edge must deal with node and link failures.
Faster convergence	This needs to be as small as possible in case of node or link failure. Ideally, anything less than a few seconds.
Secure communication	Encryption, such as IPsec-based solutions.
QoS	Hierarchical QoS for DCI.
WAN optimization	DCI WAN optimization using WAAS technologies.
Maximum transmission unit (MTU) requirements	Jumbo frame support.

The solution requirements in Table 1-7 call for an infrastructure that has the features outlined in Table 1-8.

Large Branch WAN

As universally understood, not all branches are equal. This is not only true for the size of branch (as in number of users or perhaps application servers residing at the branch) but also for how critical the branch is to the overall business function. Consider bank branches, for example. Not all branches provide the entire portfolio of services. In the real world, some provide only basic banking services, whereas others provide full-blown services, including home mortgage, small business loans, and investment services to commercial customers.

Table 1-8 *Router/Switch Feature Requirements Needed to Meet the DCI Solution Requirements*

Feature	Details
Layer 2 extensions	Using EoMPLS (p2p), or VPLS (point to multipoint).
STP isolation per data center	Capability to terminate the STP at the given data center itself. Redundant links functioning at the same can be provisioned using Cat 6500 Virtual Switching Systems / Multichassis Ethernet Channel (VSS/MEC) and/or Nexus 7K vPC (virtual port channel).
HA	Usage of redundant routers (ASR 1000, for example) or switches (6500/Nexus 7K).
Faster convergence	There are two broader approaches: EoMPLS remote port shutdown via laser off (supported on ASR 1000). Using Embedded Event Manager (EEM) or undirectional link detection (UDLD) on 6500, Nexus 7K, or ASR 1000.
Secure communication	GRE over IPsec solution, or Nexus TrustSec (Cisco TrustSec based on IEEE 802.1AE link-layer encryption).
QoS	Hierarchical QoS at the DCI edge.
WAN optimization	WAN optimization using WCCPv2 or PBR using existing Cisco WAAS appliances.
MTU requirements	Jumbo frames are supported on Cat 6500, Nexus 7K, and ASR 1000 GE / 10 GigE links.

Large branches (those that provide more services or services that are critical to the business, or in most cases both) tend to have slightly different requirements for a WAN infrastructure that connects them to the corporate backbone. Table 1-9 outlines the large branch WAN requirements.

Table 1-9 *Large Branch Office Deployment Requirements*

Requirements	Details
Larger bandwidth uplink	OC3, or even Metro Ethernet.
Ability to handle both WAN and Internet traffic	Because of the volume of traffic, large branches are connected directly to the Internet.
Multitenancy	Capability to support multiple departments or even customers or partners that use the common physical infrastructure along with employees.
QoS	Hierarchical QoS to support multiple levels of classes of service. Class-based WFQ, fair queuing, LLQ, WRED Traffic shaping.
Services requirements	Services such as NAT, firewall, and NetFlow at high speeds and scale.
HA	Intra and interbox HA supporting basic traffic forwarding and services.

Table 1-10 maps the requirements onto the infrastructure needed to support such requirements.

Table 1-10 *Large Branch Office Requirements/Traits*

Requirements	Infrastructure Traits to Meet Them
Larger bandwidth uplink	Interface diversity
Ability to handle both WAN and Internet traffic	Modular data and control plane to deal with the increasing set of requirements
Multitenancy	Capability to support virtualization of interfaces, services, and routing/forwarding tables
QoS	Flexible architecture being able to adopt to changing QoS requirements via software upgrade
Services requirements	Capability to support the existing and newer services with the existing hardware via software upgrades
HA	Inherently highly available system

Summary

This opening chapter covered the basic building blocks of WAN architectures:

- Branch aggregation
- Internet edge
- Data center interconnect
- Large branch office

Although the basic requirements are common across the various roles, they differ significantly enough that you need to understand how they are architected, deployed, and troubleshot. If there were one word to describe the hardware required to meet these needs, that word would be *flexibility*. Infrastructure needs to be very flexible in terms of feeds and speeds, scale and performance, service richness, and interface diversity (to name a few).

The next chapter covers the various business drivers, and the underlying technical requirements that they are generating. It concludes with an analysis of how these are driving requirements for next-generation WAN infrastructure.

Review Questions

1. What are the four usual WAN architectures?
2. What does optimized WAN mean?
3. What are the few fundamental requirements for WAN aggregation?
4. Why is service richness so important to enterprises?
5. Why would an enterprise connect directly to a service provider or be multihomed?
6. What are the core business drivers for DCI?

Answers

1. Usual WAN architectures typical in today's networks include the following:

   Branch and private WAN aggregation
   Internet edge
   Data center interconnect
   Large branch WAN

2. Optimization here refers to the capability of the network infrastructure to provide the voice, video, and data traffic optimization before it goes over the WAN links. This helps reduce the need for more bandwidth every time a new application is added to the network. Cisco WAAS and IOS provide such services.

3. WAN aggregation requires, at a minimum, infrastructure to support the following:

   Flexible routing/switching architecture that can evolve with the changing business requirements

   Capability to combine various types and speeds of interfaces into one common infrastructure

   Modular and highly available carrier-class design with the separation of control, data, and I/O planes

   Capability to add basic services without requiring new hardware

4. Service richness refers to an in structure (hardware and software) that can introduce a basic service and some of the advanced services into baseline hardware with simple software upgrades. Enterprises and their businesses thrive on applications, and that in turn requires network-based services for them to work on common physical infrastructure and with the ability for virtualization for today's typical multitenant requirements.

5. Enterprises connect to multiple Internet providers (or what is generally known as multihoming) for a few key reasons, including the following:

   Fault tolerance and resiliency to failure in one provider's network

   Granular routing control

   Path selection based on features such as performance-based routing or PfR

6. Core business drivers behind DCI include the following:

   Layer 2 extensions

   Data center consolidation

   Data center disaster recovery site

   Virtualization and clustering applications such as VMWare's VMotion

Further Reading

Introduction to WAN, document: http://tinyurl.com/6g8cym

Cisco Validated Designs, document: http://tinyurl.com/lnnyjt

Unified WAN Services, document: http://www.cisco.com/en/US/netsol/index.html

DC Interconnect, document: http://tinyurl.com/rclv2f

Chapter 2

Next-Generation WAN Architectures

As we all understand, words such as *next generation* and *emerging* are and will remain moving targets. Businesses are changing at a much faster pace, so too are the IT requirements servicing the entire enterprise. If you were to sum up all trends to define the next wave of IT spending, more than likely it will be about meeting "end-user preference and experience." Hence, it is likely that a major chunk of the IT spending (hardware, software, and services) will be about providing the infrastructure that can deliver that experience regardless of how the user is connected to the network.

WAN solutions covered in Chapter 1, "Introduction to WAN Architectures," serve as a baseline, so you can refer to them when going over the changing business environment and why it is important to understand them well before refreshing the existing or building newer WANs.

This chapter focuses on the changing or emerging requirements and how they relate to the newer demands that they are generating for underlying WAN infrastructure.

The Evolution of Next-Generation WAN Architectures

Next-generation enterprise architectures are evolving in response to the changing business needs and models. Major trends such as Web 2.0, Software as a Service (SaaS), an increase in the mobile workforce, an increasing presence of open source software, CO_2 footprint reduction initiatives, and many more trends will be driving the hardware and software application buying decisions by IT organizations worldwide.

Next-generation WAN architectures will focus more on the anytime, anywhere, anything mantra. More and more centralized resources or applications (as a result of data center consolidation) call for increased bandwidth needs and WAN optimization technologies to achieve the same response times as if the data were stored somewhere locally. Economies of such disrupting trends result in lower capital expenditures (CAPEX), even lower operational expenditures (OPEX) based on usage, and quicker return on investment.

Business Drivers Behind WAN Evolution

It is impossible to understand the changing requirements and demands for the WAN/MAN networking gear without first understanding the business drivers that are creating them in the first place.

The focus of this chapter remains on business requirements relevant to the evolution of the WAN itself and not the entire ecosystem. The latter is beyond the scope of the subject matter covered in this book.

The drivers of WAN evolution covered in the following sections by no means capture *all* IT trends. Rather, the discussion is an attempt to make you familiar with some of the top trends that are driving major changes and paradigm shifts within the enterprise IT related to networking and telecommunication devices.

Service Awareness and Integration

WAN infrastructures have long evolved from being just pushing the bits through them to delivering a plethora of services at the network edge. True integration of services in the same metal sheet as the router/switch itself is the new reality. Although there might still be good reasons to keep them separate (even when integrated options exist, such as high availability [HA], organization policy, or regulatory compliance), the new economies of using a single shared physical infrastructure is the order of the day.

A finding from premier global marketing research firm Interactive Data Corp (IDC) outlines that firewall and encrypted virtual private networks (VPN) top the list of services that are deployed today in the headend router, whereas wide-area application acceleration and WAN bandwidth management are among the top two areas that are under consideration for future deployment. Firewall function research further shows that 80 percent of the deployments are using firewall as an embedded function in the router today, 21 percent as the primary firewall and 59 percent as a secondary firewall.

Services that are offered integrated within the network fabric include security, data optimization, network monitoring, quality of service, and many more. Service-rich and -aware networking platforms not only allow the organizations to achieve lower total cost of ownership (TCO), because of lower CAPEX due to tighter integration and OPEX due to easier troubleshooting based on a common user interface, but also faster time to service delivery. The time it takes to deploy a given service (such as a firewall or VPN) is perhaps the single most inhibitor to service adoption in the enterprise; truck rolls or service adapter shipments for new services delivery are not desired. The integrated services also allow enterprises to provide better service level agreements (SLA) to their customers and partners, because services can be enabled with just a software upgrade within a relatively shorter time to qualification because there is no new hardware to qualify!

Figure 2-1 shows the Cisco ASR 1000 router and the type of services that are embedded on the QuantumFlow Processor (QFP).

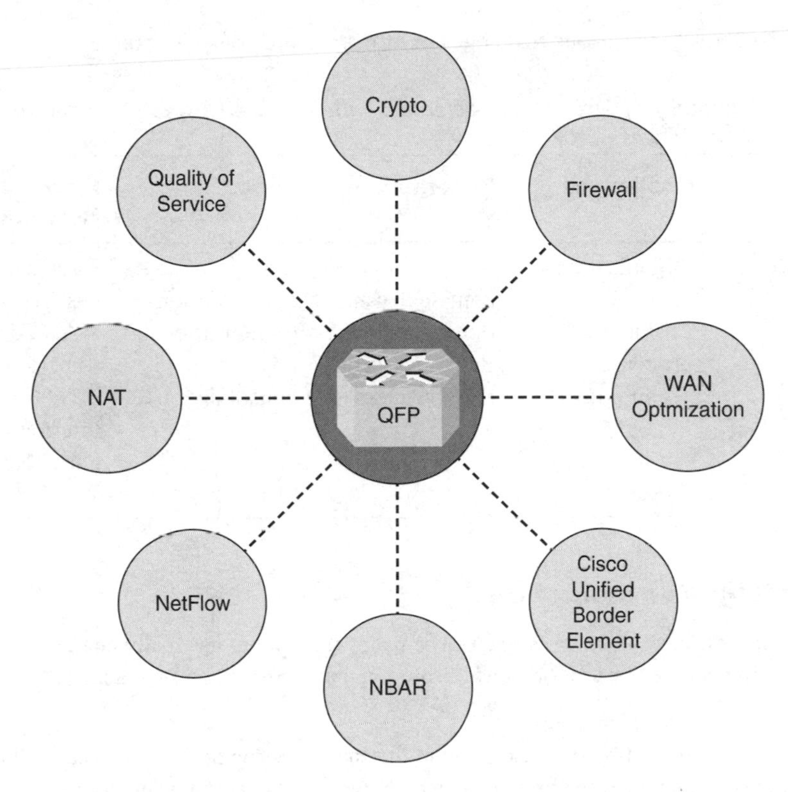

Figure 2-1 *Desired mix of services that should be available in the platform without the need for a services module.*

Infrastructure Consolidation

Infrastructure consolidation is mostly driven by the various factors such as enterprise-wide TCO reduction initiatives, ease of management and policy administration, and a common set of physical infrastructures. It also allows devices to be qualified faster (for repeat deployments) and simplifies device management using centralized monitoring systems.

IDC's research shows that the top three services and attributes that users intend to support on their WAN are as follows:

- Voice over IP
- Lower TCO
- Convergence of voice, video, and data.

Data centers and branches have seen a lot of consolidation in recent years, as application, database, and web servers have been consolidated into fewer locations for a given enterprise. Data center consolidation poses serious challenges for networking vendors and at the same time relies on cheaper and commoditized bandwidth (mostly over Ethernet links) to enterprises, especially within the metropolitan areas.

Table 2-1 shows the various challenges to infrastructure consolidation.

Table 2-1 *Summary of Drivers, Associated Challenges, and Types of Consolidation Desired for Given Places in the Network*

Drivers	Challenges	Benefits	Types	Places in the Network
Budget reduction Savings Efficiency	Organizational silos Business processes Technology	Reduction in complexity and operational cost Better focus on core business	Logical consolidation (organizational) Physical consolidation	Data center (servers, storage) WAN edge (functions such as VPN, firewall) Internet edge Large branch WAN

Segmentation/Virtualization

Segmentation/virtualization is one of the major trends that has really changed the way networking and server vendors have created and even marketed products over the past few years.

This is mostly driven by the increasing multitenant environments end to end, all the way from the data center to the branch. There are many other reasons, including compute/storage resource allocation per virtualized instance, driving better utilization of compute cycles present in a server, regulatory compliance, stricter SLAs per virtualized instance, and above all, cost-reduction measures. The Cisco Unified Computing System is a recent example of how computing, networking, and virtualization are coming together to simplify and integrate the various elements even further.

During a conference on virtualization, one of the IDC researchers described the current adoption rate for virtualization as "unprecedented in the history of emerging technologies."

IDC anticipates that growth will only accelerate, primarily driven by the underlying flexibility of virtualization technology. Whereas today the primary use case is infrastructure consolidation, new use cases are already evolving and taking hold. IDC foresees the following three growth phases to virtualization:

- **1.0—Encapsulation:** Greater flexibility to move data and isolate applications, capability to consolidate hardware to generate higher utilization levels. (This is becoming a mature market today.)
- **2.0—Application mobility:** Workload balancing, planned downtime, dynamic capacity. (This market is just beginning to take hold.)
- **3.0—Policy-based automation:** Enforcement of SLAs through automated capacity flexing, adaptive computing, making computing a variable cost to the business, and so on (growing closer as we approach the next-generation data center).

Another interesting statistic is that the take-up of virtualization is relatively evenly spread across the enterprise market. Forrester did a segmentation study ("Virtualization Goes Mainstream," 2006) and found these response rates for "currently using or piloting":

- Global 2000: 46%
- Very large: 39%
- Large: 28%
- Medium to large: 25%
- Medium: 25%

Which essentially points out that the adoption of virtualization is relatively evenly spread across the enterprise market.

Note For more information on virtualization, refer to the "References" section.

Figure 2-2 shows one single physical infrastructure partitioned into various virtual networks.

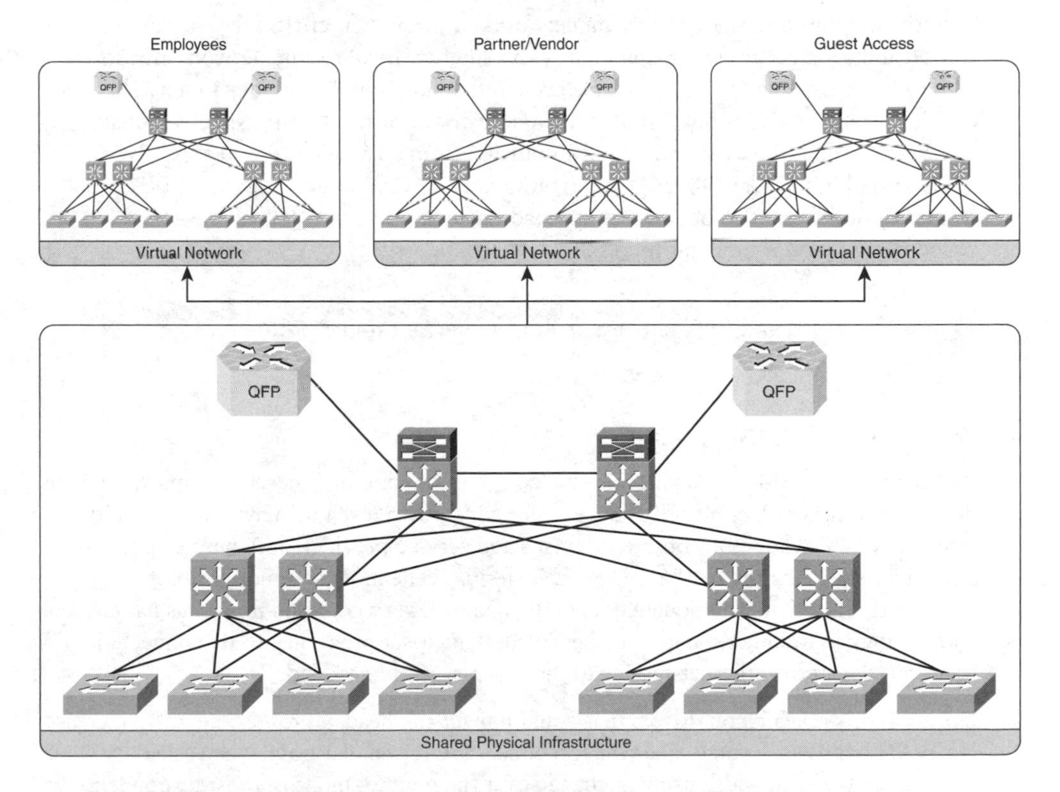

Figure 2-2 *Reference architecture for WAN edge, campus core, and distribution that is virtualized for employees, partners, and guest users.*

Security and Reliability

Security is no longer considered an add-on to existing networks; instead, it is to be part of the very fabric of the network infrastructure itself. Regulatory compliance, such as for Sarbanes-Oxley (SOX), Health Insurance Portability and Accountability Act (HIPPA), and Payment Card Industry (PCI), has also driven a lot of requirements in this area. Security overall can be divided into three major areas:

- Confidentiality, such as encrypted VPNs
- Threat control (Layers 4–7 services to protect user data transport, including application traffic and deep packet inspection [DPI])
- Infrastructure protection (from distributed denial of service [DDoS] and similar attacks)

IDC's research notes that the top concerns when making configuration changes to the headend router remain relevant to overall system reliability. Changing critical configuration causing postchange network slowdowns/failures, not being unable to restore service after planned downtime, and a change in one area having a negative impact on another area are among the top concerns identified during the survey.

As more and more businesses rely on networks to carry their critical day-to-day functions (think of a connected hospital), it is absolutely critical for the network infrastructure to be reliable and remain available even in the face of link or node failures. This is a problem that is usually solved both from a network infrastructure perspective (dual supervisors, dual power supplies, and so on) and from an architectural perspective (such as interbox high availability [HA], multipathing, Hot Standby Routing Protocol/Virtual Router Redundancy Protocol/Gateway Load Balancing Protocol [HSRP/VRRP/GLBP]-based design, and routing protocols).

Note HRSP, VRRP, and GLBP are examples of redundant router protocols.

Bandwidth Commoditization

Bandwidth commoditization is really the commoditization of Ethernet equipment, where per port along with per bit prices have really gone down (even for Layer 3 ports) in the past few years. As a result, both enterprises and service providers (SP) have stepped up and widened their Ethernet-based service offerings. The most common form of this is Metro Ethernet, with fractional GE and 10 Gigabit E very common now. This has caused a lot of bigger and high-speed branches located in closer proximity to be connected together via Metro Ethernet service to the campus WAN headend.

During IDC's research on drivers that could impact the headend router the most, increasing WAN bandwidth emerged as the top concern. On a similar note, when asked by what percentage the bandwidth use will change over the next 24 months, most respondents suggested 50 percent or more.

The Ethernet standard itself is evolving, and prestandards are already out for 40- and 100-Gbps bandwidth, which will revolutionize both LAN and WAN connectivity and soon will be available in commercial network equipment.

Carbon Footprint Reduction

The green initiative has gained a lot of momentum, and so audit standards based on such will likely follow in the future. Networking vendors might have to comply with certain standards before they can even be shortlisted for a Request For Proposal (RFP) process, for example.

Power and cooling requirements for large data centers are increasing substantially, and this is driving a huge requirement for "greener" networking gear. A moral aspect also drives this: to not damage the environment and to be more efficient with the given energy resources. Gartner mentions that green IT will reduce some risks, such as "failure to scale IT because you run out of power" and "taxes and penalties incurred because of failure to meet requirements around carbon emissions."

Gartner further discusses how to best measure power efficiency.

Table 2-2 shows the Gartner's estimate based on discussion with its clients.

Here, PUE (power-usage effectiveness) and DCiE (data center infrastructure efficiency) are related in the following manner:

DCiE = 1 / PUE

where

PUE = Total facility power / IT equipment power

DCiE = IT equipment power / Total facility power

This is likely to become a competitive advantages for networking vendors, especially for those selling to greenfield WANs and data center build-outs.

Table 2-2 *Power-Usage Effectiveness Values and Their Associated Grading in Terms of Efficiency*

PUE	DCiE (%)	Comments
1.3	77	Optimized design
1.6	62.5	Best practices
2.0	50	Some opportunity
3.0	33	Unmanaged

Note For more information on carbon footprint, refer to the "Further Reading" section.

Regulatory Compliance

One unique aspect of regulatory compliance is that regulations *must be* obeyed. Failure to obey them may tarnish a company's reputation, cause financial loss in litigation, and so on.

There are several areas of compliance for IT, but the areas most frequently discussed are as follows:

- Business processes
- General IT
- IT security
- Data storage
- IT applications

According to Gartner's research, businesses are likely to face increasing compliance scrutiny. Studies further suggest that there is a major disconnect between what companies report and what they could report. To complicate matters, midsize businesses face a number of challenges while building out their compliance strategies, including mandates, economies of scale, and corporate culture.

Time to Adoption

When enterprises are adopting a game-changing product into the network, the trade-off is usually the longer qualification cycle. This delays the return on investment for the CAPEX invested in procuring the product. Ideally, a product should borrow from the last generation as much as possible in terms of preserving the command-line interface (CLI) experience.

Mean Time to Understanding and Troubleshooting

Next-generation products should not increase the barrier to understanding the product and troubleshooting when it comes to failure analysis. If not planned accordingly, this can result in retraining staff, including but not limited to architecting, configuring, and troubleshooting of these devices. Availability to experienced post Sales support is a major plus and should be considered carefully while selecting the platform.

How the Changing Business Requirements Relate to Network Infrastructure

It is extremely important to not only understand the changing and emerging trends in businesses, but also their implications on how the networking gears need to evolve to effectively meet those requirements. Table 2-3 outlines these considerations.

Table 2-3 *Most Common Business Drivers and Their Associated Considerations for Network Equipment*

Business Drivers	Infrastructure Considerations
Service awareness and integration	Flexible system architecture that allows instant-on services delivery to meet the customer demands. Not just carrier-class routing, but also scalable and high-performance services (such as Network Address Translation [NAT], firewall, IPsec, Secure Sockets Layer [SSL] VPN, Session Border Controller (SBC), SaaS, and so on), ideally without requiring services modules. Not just a platform, but a platform family to support the scale with a unified sense of data-plane scale and performance.
Infrastructure consolidation	Highly modular and dense platform from control-, data-, and I/O-plane perspective to be able to support consolidation of various devices. Attractive price/performance point.
Segmentation/ virtualization	Support for virtualization of routing/switching and network-based services. Allocation and control of resource allocation per virtualized instance.
Security and reliability	Ability to provide native acceleration for IPsec/SSL VPN, integrated threat control, distributed denial of service (DDoS) mitigation using existing platform hardware. Inherent ability to deal with stress to control, data planes (ideally, without even user intervention). Because of the increasing amount of VoIP (Voice over IP) traffic, the average packet size in an enterprise is no longer an IMIX (Internet mix).
Bandwidth commoditization	Interface diversity to take full advantage of the SP's offerings (Ethernet, Packet over SONET [POS], or leased line at various speeds up to TENGE/OC-192). Ability to adopt newer standards (that is, a flexible system architecture that doesn't restrict adoption of emerging draft standards such as 40 Gb when more bandwidth is required).

continues

Table 2-3 *Most Common Business Drivers and Their Associated Considerations for Network Equipment*

Business Drivers	Infrastructure Considerations
Carbon footprint reduction	Proven green track record, ideally verified via some third-party validation process. Lower power and space footprint options without sacrificing the feature set. A single-RU (rack unit) device is ideal in such scenarios for both enterprise and managed SP service offerings.
Regulatory compliance	Proven track record via third-party validation process, and complete articulation in the product's literature about how to achieve regulatory compliance through. Low-level hardware and network operating system compliance, such as Federal Information Processing Standard (FIPS) or Common Criteria (CC).
Time to adoption	Literature that shows the expected time to adoption for the product from the vendor's perspective. Benchmarking the product with the previous generation and sharing other customer testimonials are key elements to prove that the product can be adopted quicker and with a clear understanding of any risk involved.
Mean time to understanding and troubleshooting	Product must share the front-end or CLI experience from previous generation product to ease configuration and troubleshooting management. Trained post-sales support staff should be able to support the product in case of failure and root cause analysis.

Summary

This chapter discussed the next-generation WAN architectures and the business drivers behind them. The chapter also outlined how these business drivers are creating and driving new benchmarks and requirements for the enterprise IT.

We consider architectures, topologies, and deployment guidelines in more detail starting in Chapter 12, "IP Routing Use Cases."

Review Questions

1. What are the four major trends influencing next-generation WAN architectures?
2. What are the four major business trends driving the new requirements for WAN/data center platform hardware and software?
3. Describe how service awareness and integration is changing the landscape as to how enterprise IT adopts a new platform?

Answers

1. The four major trends are as follows:

   Proliferation of Web 2.0 within the enterprises

   Ever-increasing mobile workforce

   Consolidation of data centers

   Software as a Service models

2. The four major business drivers are as follows:

   Service awareness and integration

   Infrastructure consolidation

   Segmentation/virtualization

   Regulatory compliance

3. TCO reduction, faster return on investment, instant service delivery without requiring truck rolls, power efficiency, and tighter SLAs are some of the trends that are driving requirements for service-rich platforms. One of the prime requirement for that is a custom-designed silicon that is scalable, high performance, and flexible to adapt to newer services without requiring a significant amount of microcode work.

Further Reading

Introduction to WAN Technologies, document: http://tinyurl.com/6g8cym

Cisco Validated Designs, document: http://tinyurl.com/lnnyjt

Unified WAN Services, document: http://www.cisco.com/en/US/netsol/index.html

Cisco ASR1000 Green Award, document: http://tinyurl.com/qhxada

Gartner's IT Predictions for 2009 and Beyond, document: http://tinyurl.com/r5ak3v

"42U's PUE and DCiE measurement and benchmarking for Data Center Efficiency," paper: http://www.42u.com/measurement/pue-dcie.htm

Compliance Home, regulatory compliance portal, Gartner: "Wall Street Meltdown Will Lead To More Regulatory Compliance," news: http://tinyurl.com/p97fjy

References

Germanow, A. (2008). "The Next-Generation Enterprise WAN Aggregation Router" [PDF]. Retrieved from Cisco.com: http://tinyurl.com/o94fyn

Metreweli, K. (2007). "Three Growth Phases to Virtualization" [Blog]. Retrieved from Tideway website: http://tinyurl.com/oj2neq

Reynolds, M. (2007). "Green IT—Scalability and Sustainability" [Powerpoint Slides]. Retrieved from Oregon Association of Government Information Technology Management website: http://tinyurl.com/q9v7le

Chapter 3

Selecting and Qualifying Enterprise Edge Platforms for Next-Generation WANs

Now that you have a baseline understanding of WAN solutions, the business trends, and how they relate to newer demands for infrastructure, this chapter focuses on the details of how to select and qualify such a platform while going through the Request For Information/Proposal (RFI/RFP) process. These could also be the questions that IT managers might ask a vendor during executive briefings or product overviews.

Essential Attributes of an Enterprise Edge Platform

Before a platform can be qualified, the essential requirements that exist for that role in the network must first be understood. In general, an edge platform draws the demarcation between a private and a public network. This device provides an entry point into the private network from an outside perspective. It often connects a private network to carrier and service provider networks.

The sections that follow review the essential traits of such routing devices.

Carrier-Class Routing

Carrier-class routing is the most discussed characteristic of modern system design. Carrier-class or grade systems are the ones that are extremely reliable and highly available both in hardware and software. The measure of reliability is usually the overall redundant system design with sub 50-ms failover times and availability in the nines. Meeting or exceeding the five nines (99.999%) is considered carrier grade. In-service software upgrade (ISSU), the capability to upgrade (or downgrade for that matter) pieces of system software, is also key to achieve higher uptime.

True Services Integration

This is the capability of the system to be able to natively accelerate and easily integrate key services such as the following:

- Network Address Translation (NAT)
- Firewall
- IPsec
- NetFlow
- Header compression
- Multicast replication
- Quality of service (QoS)
- Packet fragmentation and reassembly

Services integration comes in various shapes and forms, ranging from truly embedded in the host network processor to add-on modules. Systems that require service modules for basic services such as those listed tend to eat up the precious I/O slot density, increase the overall power budget, and come as a hidden cost that adds to the capital expenditures (CAPEX) over the life of the product.

Robust In-Built Quality of Service

QoS functions such as policing, shaping, queuing, and multiple scheduling hierarchies are in increasing demand. In today's world, where Ethernet has become the easiest and fastest way to get higher-bandwidth circuits in most parts of the world, QoS becomes even more important. Think of Metro Ethernet and how multitenancy and fractional Gigabit/10 Gigabit Ethernet require the hierarchical QoS capabilities at multiple gigabits. Usage of service modules to accelerate something that requires almost every packet to go through the extra pieces of silicon (that is, ASICs on a service module) introduces extra latency and queue limitations and makes the overall troubleshooting more cumbersome. Another side effect of service-module–based design (as opposed to a unified QoS acceleration model) is that the various limitations tend to change with each generation of the module.

Flexible System Architecture

Flexible system architecture is a more subtle aspect of system design, where an ideal system is a combination of hardness and softness in the platform. *Hardness* refers to hard-coded silicon that is good at performing certain tasks that usually do not evolve over time (such as various hash functions, encryption algorithms, policing, and so on). In contrast, *softness* refers to the use of network processors with flexible and extensible instruction sets (such as a majority of the feature applications—NAT, firewall, NetFlow, and so on). The former feature set doesn't change over time, and therefore it makes more sense to put those pieces in ASICs. The latter requires the flexibility that is usually the character trait of network processors. There is a traditional trade-off with the network processors, however, that has plagued them for a long time: speed versus flexibility. But, the modern custom silicon (along with some commodity processors), seems to have overcome that barrier for networking vendors, even up to 10 Gbps.

Another way to look at system architecture flexibility is the separation of various planes inside a routing system. In all modern designs, there must be at least a separation of the control, data, and I/O plane. Physical separation of these planes is ideal, because it not only enables to you reap the benefits of separation (where loading of one doesn't impact the other), but also enables you to upgrade them individually over the product lifetime (and can thus significantly lower the overall total cost of ownership [TCO]).

Feature Velocity

Feature velocity refers to the ability of the vendor to add features to the existing system hardware via software upgrades. At the core of it, from a vendor perspective, feature velocity relates to how easy it is to add more features in the existing silicon with the least amount of low-level programming. It is also reflected in a vendor's ability to have shorter software release cycles.

Network processor-based designs usually enjoy a higher degree of flexibility (as opposed to ASICs) due to a network friendly instruction set and being programmable in a high-level language.

Common Sharing and Sparing for Investment Protection

System investment protection refers to the ability to retain most of the hardware as is while adding newer control, data, or I/O planes to the system. The I/O plane is not only just about the capability to have more bits per second per slot, but also about the capability to support the existing or common interfaces across several routing products. It is much easier to standardize and build IT change management processes for shared I/O interfaces across systems than it is to keep track of several generations of Ethernet, optical, and leased-line interface cards.

Interface Diversity and Density

Interface diversity and density refers to the I/O plane's capability to support a variety of interfaces, such as Ethernet (10 Gigabit Ethernet, Gigabit Ethernet, Fast Ethernet), optical, high- and low-speed serial, and so on. Per slot, interface density plays an important role in defining the longevity aspect of the platform and its capability of meeting both existing and future demands within the same sheet of metal or chassis.

Power and Space Friendly

With the ongoing green initiative, enterprise IT managers are looking for a power- and space-friendly platform. Reasons include regulatory compliance and carbon footprint reduction (discussed in detail in Chapter 2, "Next-Generation WAN Architectures").

Power consumption can be measured in the form of total and typical power draw. Typical power draw is what an IT manager should be concerned with, because this is what the system will be using in the common operating scenarios. Power per bit/byte is another interesting way to look at the power usage.

The routing platform footprint is another important factor, especially in a collocated data center or managed service environment. Rack space is limited, and bits/sec per rack unit (RU) at times becomes the most definitive criterion.

Industry Standard Compliance

Industry standard compliance is yet another area that requires attention when building your next-generation network. All routing systems (and their associated services) must conform to the typical Internet Engineering Task Force (IETF), IEEE, or ITU-T standards. Adherence to standards proves the capability of the networking gear to work and interoperate in a multivendor scenario.

Other regulatory compliance criteria exist, too, from various standard bodies, such as Federal Information Processing Standard (FIPS) 140, or Common Criteria (CC) Evaluation Assurance Level (EAL). Network devices conforming to the standard bodies prove that they have gone through the rigorous processes set by these standards and meet the underlying hardware and software quality standards.

These are by no means the only attributes out there. These also continue to evolve; however, adherence to the criteria list of the various standards bodies should strongly be considered at the time of creating the RFI or RFP for vendors.

Qualifying the Enterprise WAN/MAN Edge Platform

Once the list of vendors and gear is narrowed down, it is perhaps the best time to kick off the qualification process. This can be done at the vendor's premises (proof of concept, or proving grounds lab) or at the customer's lab using various forms of loaners that might be available from the vendor.

The most basic requirement before qualification can be started is a clear understanding of what and how the desired solution needs to be tested. Both of these questions are best answered by a well-written test plan that outlines the requirements and how the select system needs to be benchmarked against them, with clear pass and fail criteria wherever applicable.

The sections that follow present and then drill down into the required items that should be present in a good qualification test plan.

Anatomy of a Test Plan

At a high level, the following can be used as a template before you set out to write a test plan:

- Test Scope and Objective

- Test Setup and Topology
- Test Resources
- Test Approach and Methodology
- Test Entry and Exit Criteria
- Test Schedule
- Test Results Reporting
- Test Cases Detail

Table 3-1 outlines the details of different test items.

Table 3-1 *New Product Qualification: Test Plan Components*

#	Items	Brief Description
1	Test Scope and Objective	Functions, performance, and scale that will be tested. It should also be noted what falls out of scope and will therefore not be tested.
2	Test Setup and Topology	Outlines the test topology and the overall end-to-end test setup.
3	Test Resources	Outlines what hardware and software is needed to complete the testing, including routers, switches, testing gear, interfaces, servers, human resources, and so on.
4	Test Approach and Methodology	Identifies the test setup, and each feature or requirement. This includes the positive, negative, stress, and longevity testing aspects.
5	Test Entry and Exit Criteria	Includes specific criteria for the product under test to pass or fail the test iteration. This is to ensure that all the tests are run; if not, this should include the reason for not having done so. Any caveats that are observed must be noted here, too.
6	Test Schedule	Identifies the start and end dates for the each test or set of tests.
7	Test Results Reporting	Includes reporting of test results (pass, fail for positive/negative functional tests, and data for performance/scale type tests). This should also include the output format for the test results documentation and archival policy to have a record of it.
8	Test Case Details	This is where the actual test case details are included. This is agreed-upon detail of each test that needs to be executed.

Now that you are familiar with the test plan high-level structure for new product qualification, the sections that follow provide more details with some examples to put all this into perspective.

Test Scope and Objective

This should identify all the items to be tested in the test plan, things such as the following:

- New features/functionality depending on the product.
- Stress to control, data, and I/O planes can also be used.
- If this is a follow-up to a previous test plan, it should clearly highlight what needs to be repeated and the previous outcome.

An example of this is "to identify the product adoption into Internet edge role in the network." For this, you need to line up features such as NAT, firewall, NetFlow, distributed denial of service (DDoS) mitigation, and related features.

Test Setup and Topology

This part of the test plan describes the hardware and software revisions and releases that should be used for the testing. The software recommendation should usually come from the vendor, and ideally should be something already in the public domain.

This also needs to have the end-to-end test topology diagram, showing exactly what roles the product under test will be used for within that setup. If multiple topologies are required, they should map back into "Test Cases Details" section.

Finally, this needs to include full details of the network operating system, microcode, ROMMON versions, and versions and names of any of the traffic generator or impairment device used.

Test Resources

This part of the test plan includes anything that needs to be procured, arranged, or scheduled for the entire test run. This will be the logical outcome of the test setup and topology.

Test Approach and Methodology

This part the test plan expands on the various types of testing that need to be performed, and the overall methodology used for each. Examples of these include the following:

- **Test types:** There can be three broader areas here:

  Functional: Includes the features and combination of those features that need to be tested in the product qualification.

  Scale: Refers to finding the breakpoint during the testing for scaling of a given feature based on the product's literature and requirement in the test plan. An example is the number of firewalls or NAT sessions.

  Performance: Refers to finding the breakpoint during the testing for performance, which is usually measured in packets/sec and bits/sec. The *non drop rate* (NDR) is a commonly used term in this context. NDR means testing the performance just before the point where the system under test starts dropping packets or reaches saturation.

- **Test methodology:** There can be four general test methodologies:

  Positive testing: This is where the product is tested based on the vendor's literature. Most of the test plan should focus on this testing, because passing this criteria determines the feasibility of a product's viability for a given role. Boundary testing is an important test case for this part of the test. This test focuses on testing the minimum and maximum numbers that the product supports for a given feature or configuration.

  Negative testing: This is where the product is tested in ways that are not officially supported or recommended by the customer. The goal here is to note the product response in these scenarios (because they might actually occur in a production environment as opposed to a controlled environment, such as a test lab). Sending crafted invalid packets to see how the system responds is an example of such testing.

  Stress testing: This is where the product is tested beyond the vendor's performance and scale datasheet numbers. The goal here is to note the product response in these scenarios (because they are likely to occur in a real-world environment). An example of this would be to apply more traffic than the system is advertised to withstand; this would be a data plane stress test.

  Load or longevity test: This involves running a positive test simulating some real-world events for a long duration to find out how the product progresses in terms of memory and CPU usage over time.

Test Entry and Exit Criteria

Under this part of the test plan, you define what a pass or failure is for each test case. If a test fails, the vendor should conduct a root cause analysis (unless the fail is purely cosmetic).

Test Schedule

This part the test plan pretty much defines the overall testing schedule. It includes the fallback or contingency plan in case the failure threshold is surpassed for the overall testing. The vendor should provide a plan to address the failure.

Test Results Reporting

Test results (including data that needs to be captured, such as with **show** commands) should be documented as agreed on by all parties. In general, the results should be mapped back to individual test cases so that you can quickly identify the affected areas. There should usually be some sort of high-level summary included in the test plan, as well.

Test Case Details

This is what constitutes most of the test plan. That is, it is the meat of the test plan itself. This part of the test plan consists of nothing but the details of all test iterations, with configuration snippets and the **show** commands required to validate that test for the product.

Summary

This chapter discussed some of the main attributes of an enterprise edge platform. The chapter also expanded that discussion into how you can qualify a new product, focusing on a routing device. The chapter examined how to construct such a test plan, and provides a template for this purpose. Although the test plan discussion remained focused on new product qualification, it can also be used to qualify a new feature (or combination of them) on an existing product.

To sum up Part I of this book (Chapters 1–4), you began with a review of the existing WAN/MAN architectures, and then learned about the recent and emerging trends based on observations and analyst predictions. Chapter 2 followed up by drilling down into how these trends create newer demands for the routing infrastructure and how IT managers need to spot them to be able to successfully identify their next-generation WAN/MAN buildup. This chapter explained how these new demands impact decisions about next-generation system architecture. The chapter then showed how to prove and measure them via a thorough test plan that helps narrow down the choices during the RFP process.

Part II builds on the foundation you've learned in this first part as it covers the ASR 1000 router family.

Chapter Review Questions

1. What are the four major attributes of a next-generation routing product?
2. What are the two essential parts of a good product qualification test plan?
3. What are the four common types of test methodologies used for routing product qualification?

Answers

1. The four major attributes of a next-generation routing product are as follows:

   True services integration

   Carrier-class routing

   Built-in QoS acceleration

   Flexible and future-ready system architecture

2. There are many important parts of a good product qualification test plan, but the most essential parts are the test case details and the reporting and capturing of the right data dimensions.
3. Four common test methodologies used for routing product qualification are positive, negative, stress, and load testing.

Further Reading

Testing Routing Protocol Convergence, document: http://tinyurl.com/7gkvh

Cisco Validated Designs, document: http://tinyurl.com/lnnyjt

Testing Routing and Switching, document: http://tinyurl.com/nawy3f

Testing Green Routing and Switching Devices, document: http://tinyurl.com/nfv5ax

"Miercom, Third-Party Testing Reports," test report: http://tinyurl.com/y65r4l

"Isocore, Third-Party Testing Reports," test report:
http://www.isocore.com/news/papers.htm

Chapter 4

Sizing Up a Router

This chapter explains what to look for in a given router deployment, based on the levels of performance and scale desired. This chapter also covers the various metrics that you can use to benchmark router performance and scale for the given application.

What to Look for When Choosing a Router

The role of a router is not as straightforward as it was a decade ago (that is, simply routing and switching traffic). The increasing number of IP services being integrated into routing systems introduces a lot of complexity when qualifying the system and understanding the value add.

Characteristic to consider when introducing a new router include the following:

- **Performance, scale, and high availability:** The platform should be able to support both current and future performance and scale requirements. High availability, in terms of software/hardware, is a must-have because of the increasing amount of latency-sensitive traffic types present in today's enterprise network.
- **Feature velocity (the pace at which new features are introduced):** Feature velocity really refers to the router vendor's ability to deliver newer features faster. The key to gauge this capability for a new router is to look into the hardware architecture and the software release cycles:

  You should look for a hardware architecture that is based on application-specific integrated circuit (ASIC) or network processors and that is easily programmable without running into any type of low-level resource crunch.

  Software cycles that follow strictly time-based releases are the best for successfully operating a given router in variety of roles.

- **Total cost of ownership (TCO):** This is one of the most difficult aspects to gauge about the new system. TCO is not really what you just pay upfront, but also includes both what you're going to spend on the system to add more services *and* recurring operational expenditures over time.
- **Longevity:** The system should have at least five to seven years of life in it. The longer the vendor is willing to stand behind the product, even after its end of sale, speaks volumes about the confidence they have in the system.
- **Return on investment (ROI):** This is yet another difficult-to-gauge aspect. In today's world, with infrastructure consolidation happening both at WAN aggregation and data centers, ROI calculation should include the capability of the platform to collapse various point devices in the network into the routing platform itself.
- **Introduction of newer services:** The system should not require additional hardware for every new service that needs to be added to the system, such as encryption, firewalls, NetFlow, Session Border Controller (SBC) or Cisco Unified Border Element (CUBE), and so on.
- **System qualification:** Easier and faster qualification of a system depends on how similar it is to what the vendor has already been offering in terms of look and feel. In an ideal world, existing scripts will continue to work with little to no modification.
- **Power and space footprints:** Given the benefits of being green in today's world, both power and space footprints are two of the most important aspects of a system.
- **Ease of use, troubleshooting, and training required:** This is one single aspect that can skew the TCO completely if not understood correctly at the time of platform qualification. The mean time to understanding should be small, and the vendor should have public-facing documents available for the platform.
- **Pre- and post-sales technical support:** Nothing is better than when you have an issue and you know that an experienced pre- and post-sales support team stands ready to take your call and work through your trouble ticket. This is true for both platform hardware and software support. This support might indirectly impact platform ROI and service availability.

Metrics for Benchmarking a Router

No single way exists to benchmark a router today, given the versatility of roles that a router might serve. One methodical way to benchmark is to break down the various aspects of a router's performance and scale into planes, as described in the following sections.

Routing-Plane Performance and Scale

Faster convergence for routing protocols is the single most useful metric for benchmarking a platform. One major benefit of the clear separation of the routing and data planes is a more agile routing plane. Different Interior Gateway Protocols (IGP) might have different metrics specific to the underlying algorithms. For the Open Shortest Path First (OSPF) Protocol, for example, you can benchmark the following:

- Convergence with an increasing number of routers in an area
- Shortest path first (SPF) calculation with an increasing number of routers in an area
- Route Processor (RP) CPU utilization with an increasing number of routers

You can also measure additional factors, including session setup rates for features such as calls per second for L2TP/PPP or Unified SBC/CUBE and IKE tunnels per second.

Data-Plane Performance and Scale

Benchmarking data-plane performance is about measuring the packets per second (forwarding potential of the router) and bits per second (bandwidth potential of the router). You can measure this both with or without services. During this testing, it is expected that performance might degrade as you add more services over the baseline packet-forwarding performance.

Scale, in the case of the data plane, will be testing a number of routes, Forwarding Information Base (FIB) entries, and so on. For services, a given service can be measured against several dimensions, such as the following:

- Total number of sessions (such as Network Address Translation [NAT], firewall, IPsec, Secure Sockets Layer virtual private network [SSL VPN], and so on).
- Sessions per second (such as NAT, firewall, IPsec, SBC, SSL VPN, and so on).
- Variation in sessions per second at various points and up to a maximum number of sessions.
- Duty cycle testing (that is, you configure a service and leave it running for a day or more). For such types of testing, make sure to note the CPU/memory usages before and after the test to spot any memory-leak situations.

Summary

This chapter briefly examined the various criteria to consider when selecting a router based on the known functional and performance requirements. You also learned that, generally, the best way to benchmark a router's performance and scale is to keep the control and data planes in perspective.

Chapter Review Questions

1. When benchmarking data-plane performance, what two significant dimensions should you use?
2. What are the usual dimensions to gauge service performance?

Answers

1. These two dimensions are packet per second (pps) and bits per second (bps).
2. Service performance varies, but in general you can use the total aggregate throughput (bits per second), the total number of concurrent sessions, and sessions per second to measure performance of a platform.

Further Reading

Router Benchmarking IETF Work Group, drafts: http://tinyurl.com/qonftr

ISOCORE Test reports, papers: http://www.isocore.com/news/papers.htm

Chapter 5

System Overview and Carrier-Class Attributes

This chapter provides foundational knowledge you need to understand about the ASR 1000 system hardware and software (before you investigate the configuration details in later chapters). Previous chapters discussed how various business trends are causing enterprise networks to change and how crucial it is to select the right platform for a WAN architecture. This chapter begins with an overview of the ASR 1000 series routers, including a look at various architectural and technological enhancements, and then discusses what makes this series a true carrier-class product. The chapter then finishes with a more detailed look at both hardware and software components.

Introduction to ASR 1000 Series Routers

The Cisco ASR 1000 series aggregation services routers are the Cisco next-generation, modular, service-rich routing platform designed with the flexibility to support 5- to 20-Gbps system bandwidth, high performance, and scalability higher than any other comparable product. The overall system architecture is common across all types of supported chassis.

With the introduction of the Cisco ASR 1000 series routers, Cisco is creating an entirely new price-for-performance class of routing product with an innovative set of capabilities to respond effectively and quickly to the changes within the service provider and enterprise networks (for example, video, Web 2.0, collaborative applications, and emerging requirements, all of which require a different type of aggregation or headend device).

Figure 5-1 shows three currently available ASR 1000 chassis options: ASR 1002, ASR 1004, and ASR 1006

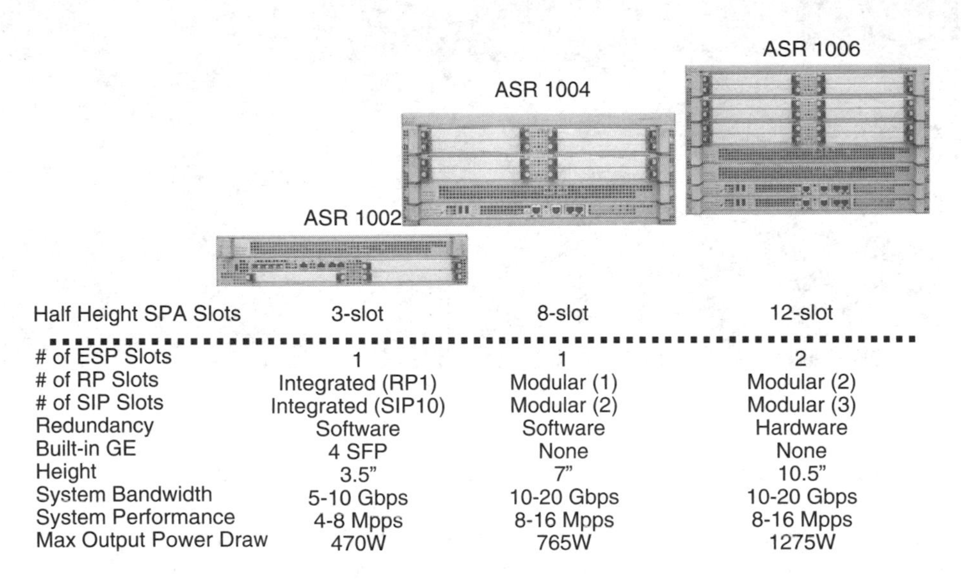

Half Height SPA Slots	3-slot	8-slot	12-slot
# of ESP Slots	1	1	2
# of RP Slots	Integrated (RP1)	Modular (1)	Modular (2)
# of SIP Slots	Integrated (SIP10)	Modular (2)	Modular (3)
Redundancy	Software	Software	Hardware
Built-in GE	4 SFP	None	None
Height	3.5"	7"	10.5"
System Bandwidth	5-10 Gbps	10-20 Gbps	10-20 Gbps
System Performance	4-8 Mpps	8-16 Mpps	8-16 Mpps
Max Output Power Draw	470W	765W	1275W

Figure 5-1 *Three available chassis options: ASR 1002, ASR 1004, and ASR 1006.*

Note ASR 1000 chassis are numbered by the rack-space units they take up. For example, ASR 1006 takes up six rack units. (One rack unit is equal to 1.75 inches.) On an ASR 1006, looking bottom up, the first two boards are system Route Processors (RP), the next two are forwarding processors (Embedded Service Processor [ESP]), and the last three are shared port adapter (SPA) Interface Processors (SIP). ASR 1002-F (as in Fixed) is a lowest-price entry option into the ASR 1000 family. It comes with fixed RP1, ESP 2.5 Gbps, and SIP10 into the two-rack unit chassis.

From the perspective of changing network architectures, the ASR 1000 series has the potential to provide the consolidation needed to unify various applications, platforms, and functions into one single device:

- **Convergence of features:** The Cisco ASR 1000 allows for an extreme degree of feature and application integration by way of Cisco QuantumFlow Processor (QFP). This series of platform is geared for deploying various applications in both enterprise and service provider (SP) marketplaces. For an enterprise environment, these applications include traditional WAN aggregation, next-generation WANs, Internet gateways, and the secure headend; for the SP, the feature set includes the broadband and edge market segments.
- **Convergence of platforms:** The Cisco ASR 1000 bridges the gap in the Cisco routing portfolio between the Cisco 7200VXR and 7600 series routers, by addressing

the 5-Gbps to 40-Gbps bandwidth requirements, along with services at those rates. Therefore, the convergence of various platforms is possible within a single device that may be used at various places in the network (for example, a router for the WAN edge [typically, as a 10- to 40-Gbps system] and at the WAN access layer [typically, as a 5- to 10-Gbps system]).

- **Convergence of network elements:** You can also use the Cisco ASR 1000 to consolidate diverse feature requirements that are instead usually met via a mix of routers and appliances, such as firewalls, IPsec termination, an Internet peering edge, and WAN aggregation. Some other platforms integrate features similarly, but by way of multiple service adapters that take up I/O slots and introduce various data planes into a single routing platform. Such an integration results not only in complicated configuration and troubleshooting of the accelerated features, but it also leads to hidden costs in the form of procuring these modules over time.

Figure 5-2 shows the flexibility and breadth of functions that can all be collapsed into a single ASR 1000 system (such as virtual private networking, firewalls, and application optimization).

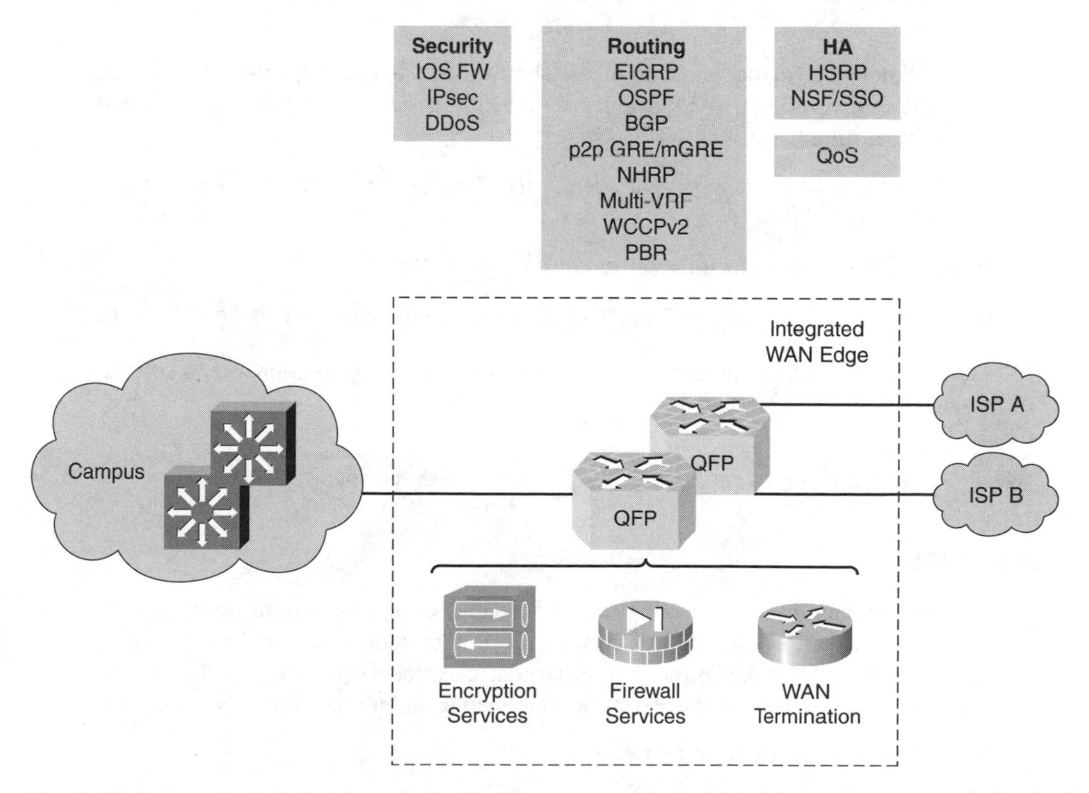

Figure 5-2 *Convergence of network elements.*

ASR 1000 Carrier-Class Attributes

Before delving into further detail about the platform itself, the sections that follow review the traits of carrier-class routing systems and how the ASR 1000 platform addresses them.

Availability

Networks are truly critical to businesses, and the need to minimize financial loss is a primary reason for nonstop network operations. Newer IP services are another big driver behind networks being highly available.

Cisco ASR 1000 series routers provide the following availability-related features:

- Five to six 9s, due to a full hardware and software redundancy system with sub-50-ms switchover for both control and data planes. 99.999% (five 9s) and 99.9999% (six 9s) correspond to 5.26 minutes and 31.5 seconds of downtime a year, respectively.
- Virtually zero scheduled downtime due to full control-plane (CP) and forwarding-plane (FP) redundancy.
- In-box stateful failover to virtually eliminate downtime during routing or data-plane switchover.
- IOS nonstop forwarding/stateful switchover (NSF/SSO), along with graceful restart and nonstop routing (NSR) wherever applicable to avoid a drop of Layer 3 neighborships during CP switchover.
- Capability to maintain system operation and quality of service (QoS) during oversubscription.
- QoS and ingress oversubscription buffering on SIPs.
- In-box monitoring options by way of platform-specific **show** and **debug** CLI commands.

Figure 5-3 shows the breakdown of total time until service restoration after a software or hardware failure has occurred.

Note NSR is slated for a future release of the Cisco IOS XE software.

Reliability

Reliability is simply a measure of being dependable. Compensation for poor router reliability usually comes at the cost of network-level router redundancy and interconnects, increasing network cost significantly. Enterprise customers often indicate that reliability is perhaps the single biggest criterion when selecting an Internet service provider (ISP).

Router reliability consists of two major factors:

- **Mission reliability:** The average time between hardware or software failures that impact the service (that is, the mission)

- **Maintenance reliabilities:** The mean time between failure (MTBF) or the average time between hardware failures that require corrective maintenance actions

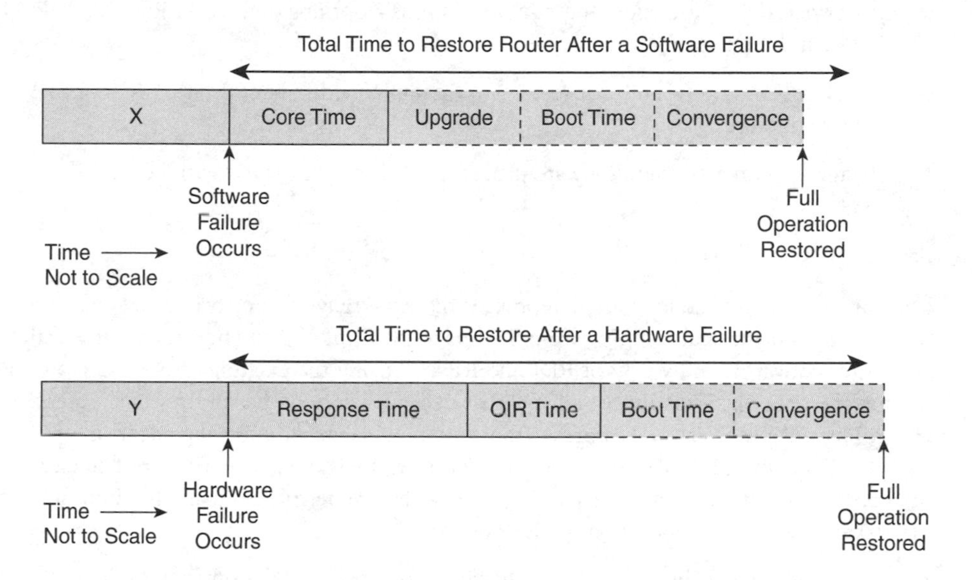

Figure 5-3 *Anatomy of a typical software or hardware failure to illustrate the importance of a carrier-class system.*

Cisco ASR 1000 series routers provide the following reliability-related features:

- Modern system design with local CPUs on all system boards (including the RP, ESP, and SIP).
- Capability to take corrective action for a failed component (for example, an enhanced Universal Serial Bus [eUSB] bad block, which, once found and marked, the system software does not write on, so it results in no immediate service impact).

Note An eUSB, located on the RP, is used as system flash media to store the system files and router configuration and is used as a boot device for the IOS consolidated package (that is, booting from a single binary).

- Presence of Inter-Integrated Circuit (I^2C) Bus for detecting failed components in the system. (This is in addition to the Ethernet Out of Band Channel [EOBC] bus, used for Inter-Process Communication [IPC].)
- All system memories are single- and multibit error-correcting code (ECC) protected.

- In-service SPA driver upgrade by way of modular SPA software, resulting in nonstop operation for all the other SPAs for the given SIP.
- In-service IOS upgrade/downgrade on all chassis options (that is, ASR 1002, ASR 1004, and ASR 1006).
- Quick restoration (via reboot/restart) upon unplanned failure of either IOS or SPA driver software.
- Restart of noncritical middleware processes without bringing down the RP.

Scalability

The Cisco ASR 1000 series routers represent the wide range of performance spectrum, with the data-plane scale ranging from 5 Gbps to 20 Gbps and an enormous route scale and faster convergence by way of RP1 and RP2, all using the existing chassis. Cisco QFP defines the data plane for almost all IOS features, such as zone-based firewalls, access control lists (ACL), Network Address Translation (NAT), generic routing encapsulation (GRE), Multi-Link PPP (MLPP), QoS, and NetFlow, IPv6, and so on. IPsec and Secure Sockets Layer virtual private networking (SSL VPN) are performed using the built-in crypto engine also integrated on the ESP board.

In a rather subtle way, because of the physical separation of the control and data planes, this platform also allows for the gradual upgrade of both control and data plane, as in RP and ESP.

Note A built-in crypto engine on the ESP is capable of performing SSL VPN in hardware, although as of this writing this is not yet available via IOS XE.

Quality of Service

Quality of service (QoS) is one of the fundamental design traits of this platform family. QoS is accelerated using the Cisco QFP (more specifically, with the chip known as the traffic manager doing all the buffering, queuing, and scheduling operations in the system without incurring any performance penalty or significant latency increase). QFP supports up to five levels of hierarchies, although currently IOS XE supports three levels (as in class, subinterfaces, and port).

The ASR 1000 can schedule the full system bandwidth (that is, 5, 10, or 20 Gbps) without causing any degradation in the system forwarding rate. Continuous Metro Ethernet penetration at the WAN aggregation and a need to do more granular and hierarchical QoS are the type of trends that make the ASR 1000 an ever better fit for WAN aggregation while being sensitive to application availability.

ROI and Investment Protection

Among many other things, a network's return on investment (ROI) is a function of various factors, including the following:

- **Operational savings:** The ASR 1000 preserves the existing investment in IOS scripts and monitoring tools because it uses the same IOS look and feel as Cisco 7600 series routers. Modular system design enables granular hardware upgrade and common sharing and sparing of all field-replaceable units (FRUs) across the chassis.
- **System life span:** The ASR 1000 has an extremely long life span because of system modularity and because of its brand new and modern silicon-based design based on multigenerational network processors (QFP).
- **Hidden costs:** The ASR 1000 is designed around a unified forwarding hardware (that is, ESP) that can accelerate almost all IOS basic and advanced services without requiring a new service acceleration module every time a new service is added (for example, IPsec, firewalls, NetFlow, Multilink PPP [MLP], compressed RTP [cRTP], and many others).

ASR 1000 Applications

The Cisco ASR 1000 addresses both enterprise and SP segments. The sections that follow discuss some of the prominent applications and required high-level feature sets.

ASR 1000 Enterprise WAN Aggregation

WAN aggregation typically means the router is positioned at the main or regional headquarters and is aggregating either legacy WAN (for example, ATM, MLP, or Frame Relay permanent virtual circuits [PVC] or Layer 3 Multiprotocol Label Switching [MPLS] VPNs). The capability to support various flavors of I/O interfaces, including low/high-speed serial, clear/multichannel DS3/DS1, ATM, and Ethernet, is extremely crucial.

The ASR 1000 has the features, performance, scale, and interface diversity to be an extremely good fit for this place in the network.

Figure 5-4 shows the traditional WAN aggregation or edge router role.

Enterprise Internet Gateway

The Internet gateway could be positioned in a large branch or data center, where secure, high-bandwidth access to the Internet is necessary. The typical feature set components required for this place are high-speed NAT, firewalls, NetFlow, the capability to secure the infrastructure itself, and the capability to hold multiple copies of the full Internet routing table.

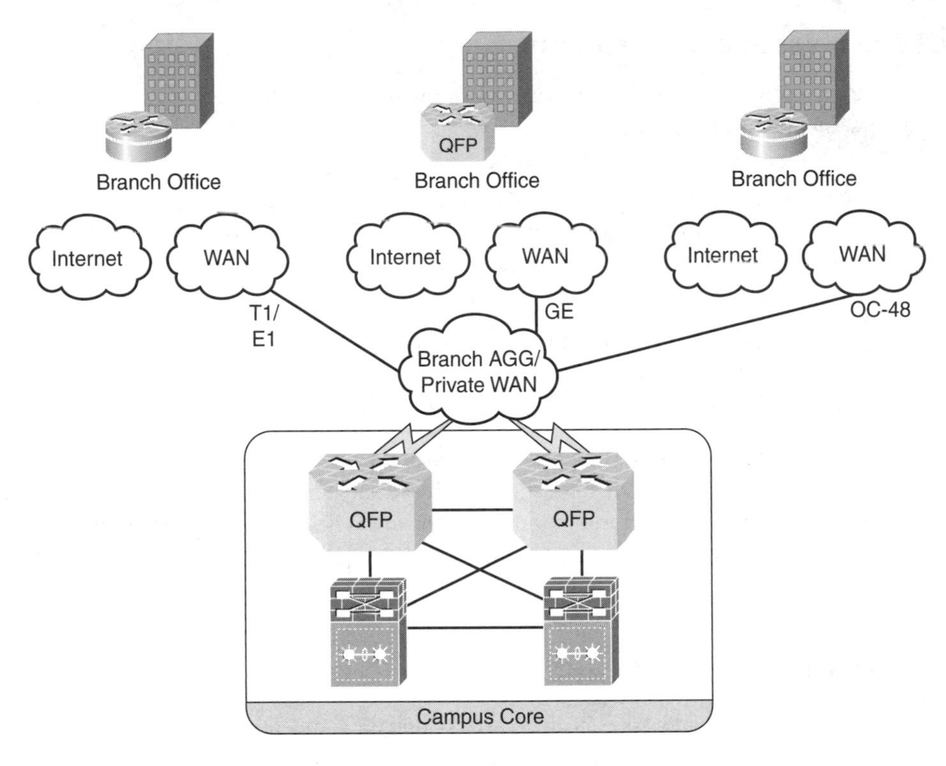

Figure 5-4 *Enterprise WAN aggregation.*

The ASR 1000 supports all of these features at 5- to 20-Gbps performance in a highly scalable manner, based on the modular RP and ESP in the system. None of these features requires a service module for acceleration.

Figure 5-5 shows the typical Internet gateway role in an enterprise.

Enterprise Security Headend (Branch and Remote User Aggregation)

Security for user traffic is needed when traffic is traversing an unsecure infrastructure (Internet or even private) and requires encryption. The driver behind this security could also be pure regulatory compliance (for example, HIPAA or SOX).

The ASR 1000 supports multigigabit encryption without requiring an encryption module. IOS Dynamic Multipoint VPN (DMVPN), EasyVPN, virtual tunnel interfaces (VTI), and GETVPN are all supported.

Note ESP-5G, ESP-10G, and ESP-20G support 1, 2.5, and 5.5 Gbps of IPsec encryption throughput, respectively, at an Internet MIX (IMIX). The built-in crypto engine supports GETVPN in hardware starting with IOS XE Release 2.3.0.

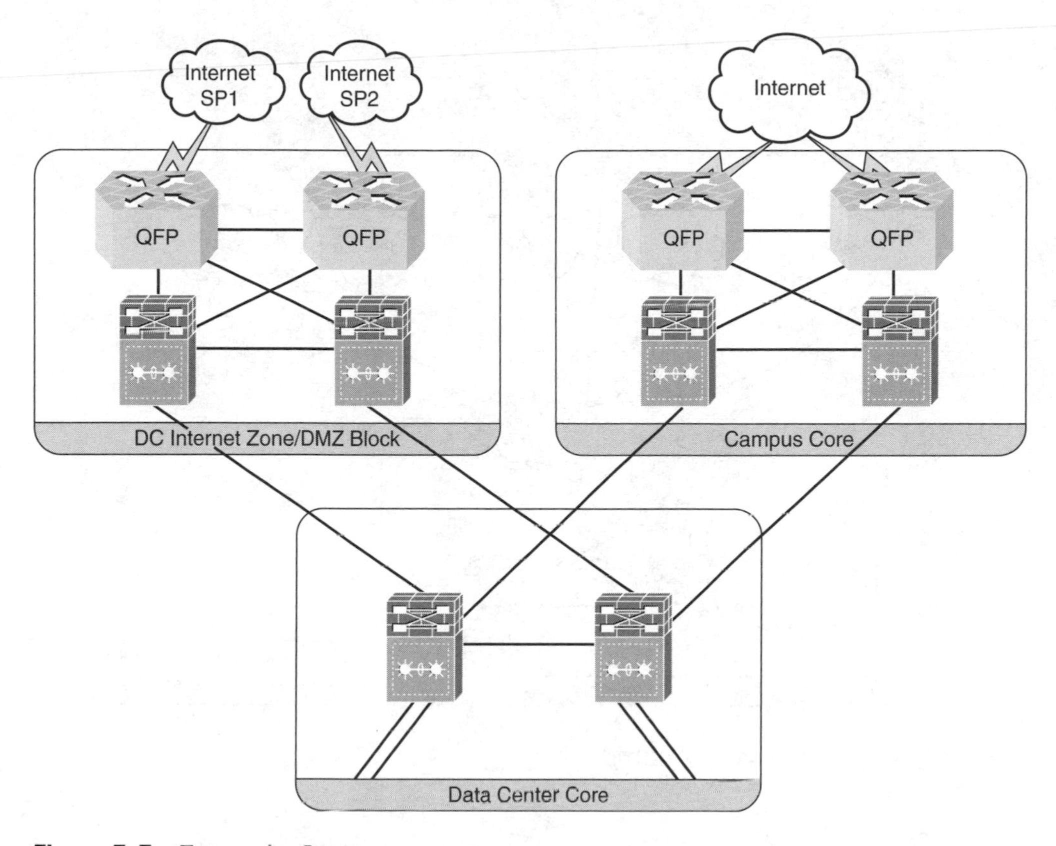

Figure 5-5 *Enterprise Internet gateway.*

Figure 5-6 shows the secure headend router role.

Service Provider Layer 3 VPN

The ASR 1000 platform provides an attractive platform option for SPs looking to provide managed Layer 3 IP VPN services to enterprise customers, including but not limited to intranet, extranet, and remote-access services. SPs can also sell add-on services such as encryption, firewalls, and multicast, to name a few.

Figure 5-7 shows the ASR 1000 platform as a Layer 3 VPN provider edge router.

Service Provider Layer 2 VPN

The ASR 1000 can also be used as a Layer 2 VPN provider edge platform, providing enterprise customers pseudowire services based on Layer Distribution Protocol (LDP) (using Ethernet over MPLS) along with integrated QoS and encryption.

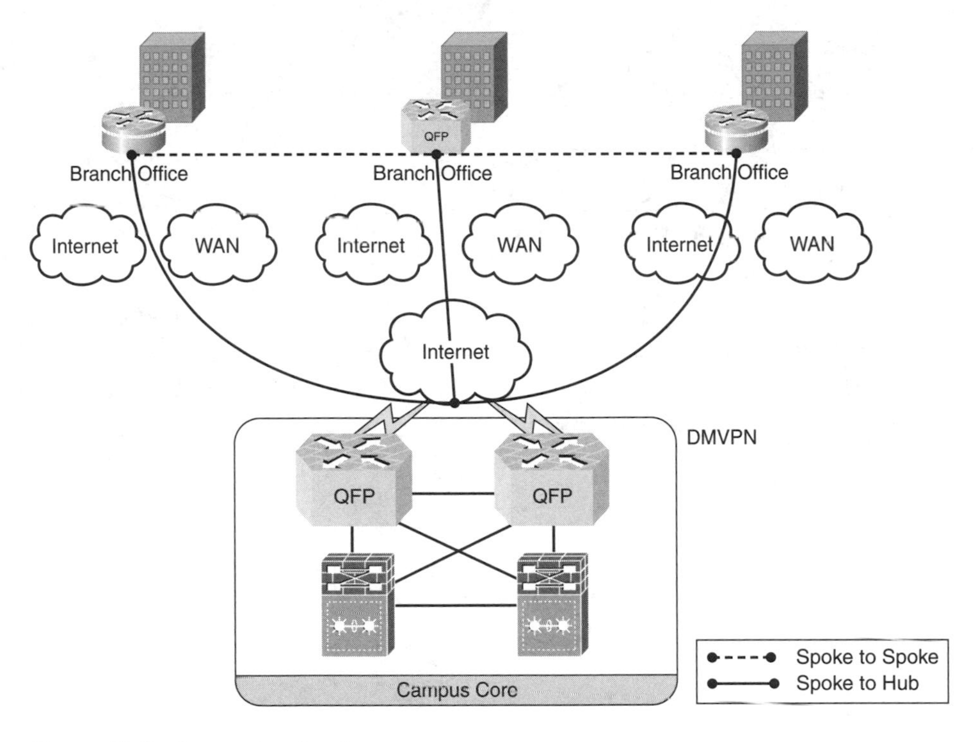

Figure 5-6 *Secure headend router.*

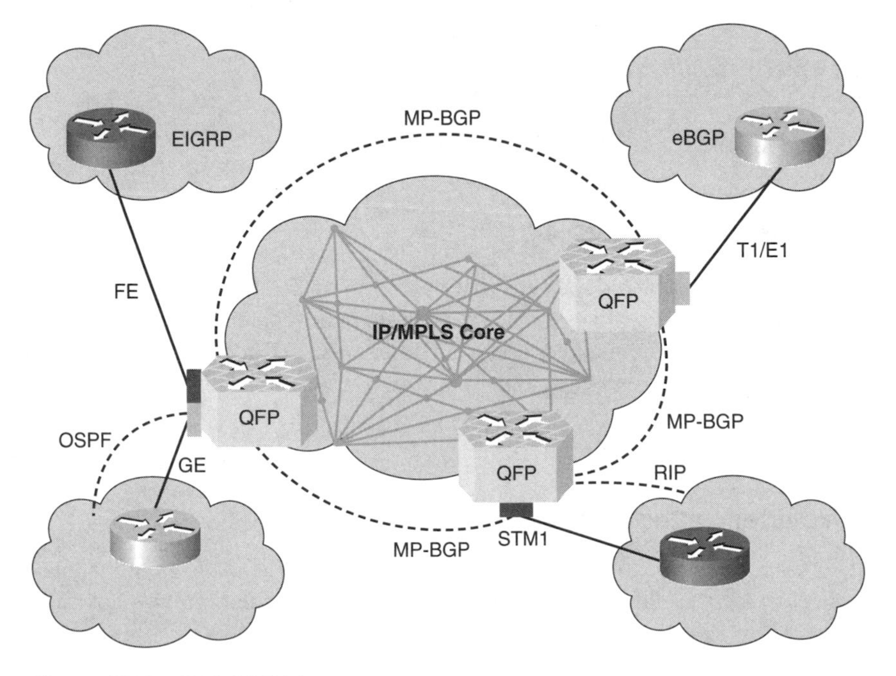

Figure 5-7 *SP L3 VPNs.*

Figure 5-8 shows the ASR 1000 platform as a Layer 2 VPN provider edge router.

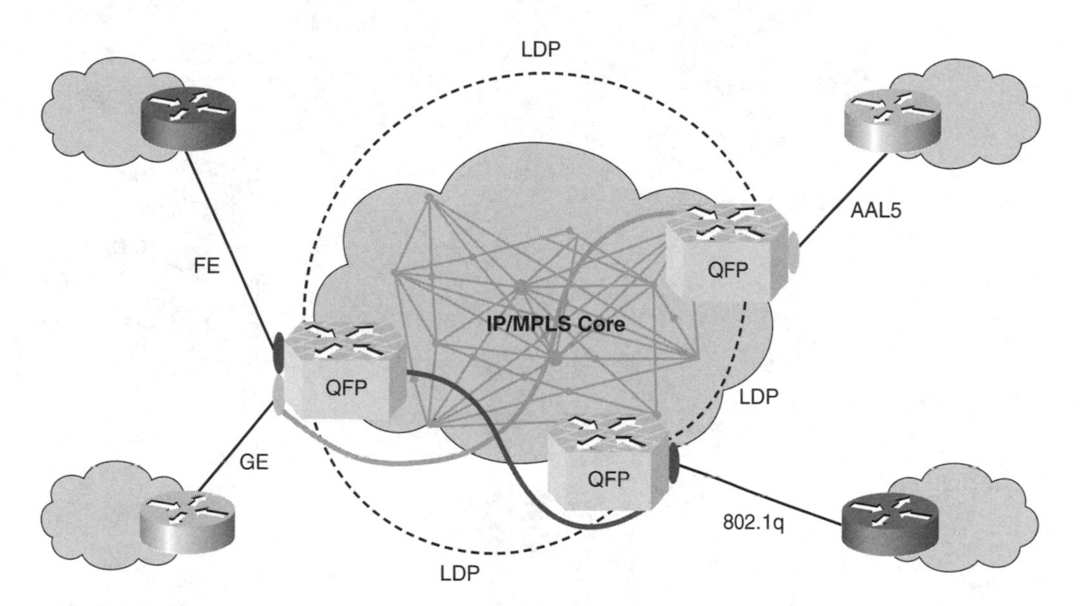

Figure 5-8 *SP L2 VPNs.*

Broadband Aggregation, Including FTTH and DSL LNS, LAC, and PTA

The ASR 1000, because of its flexible system architecture, can serve as a full featured integrated services edge distributed broadband aggregation system (BRAS), PPP Termination and Aggregation (PTA) router for Fiber To The Home (FTTH). SPs can thus offer high-speed Internet access to residential and business customers. As a BRAS router, the ASR 1000 can support up to 32K subscribers, even with QoS.

Figure 5-9 shows the ASR 1000 deployed as both LAC and LNS, offering wholesale Internet access to SPs supporting up to 16K Layer 2 Tunnel Protocol (L2TP) tunnels.

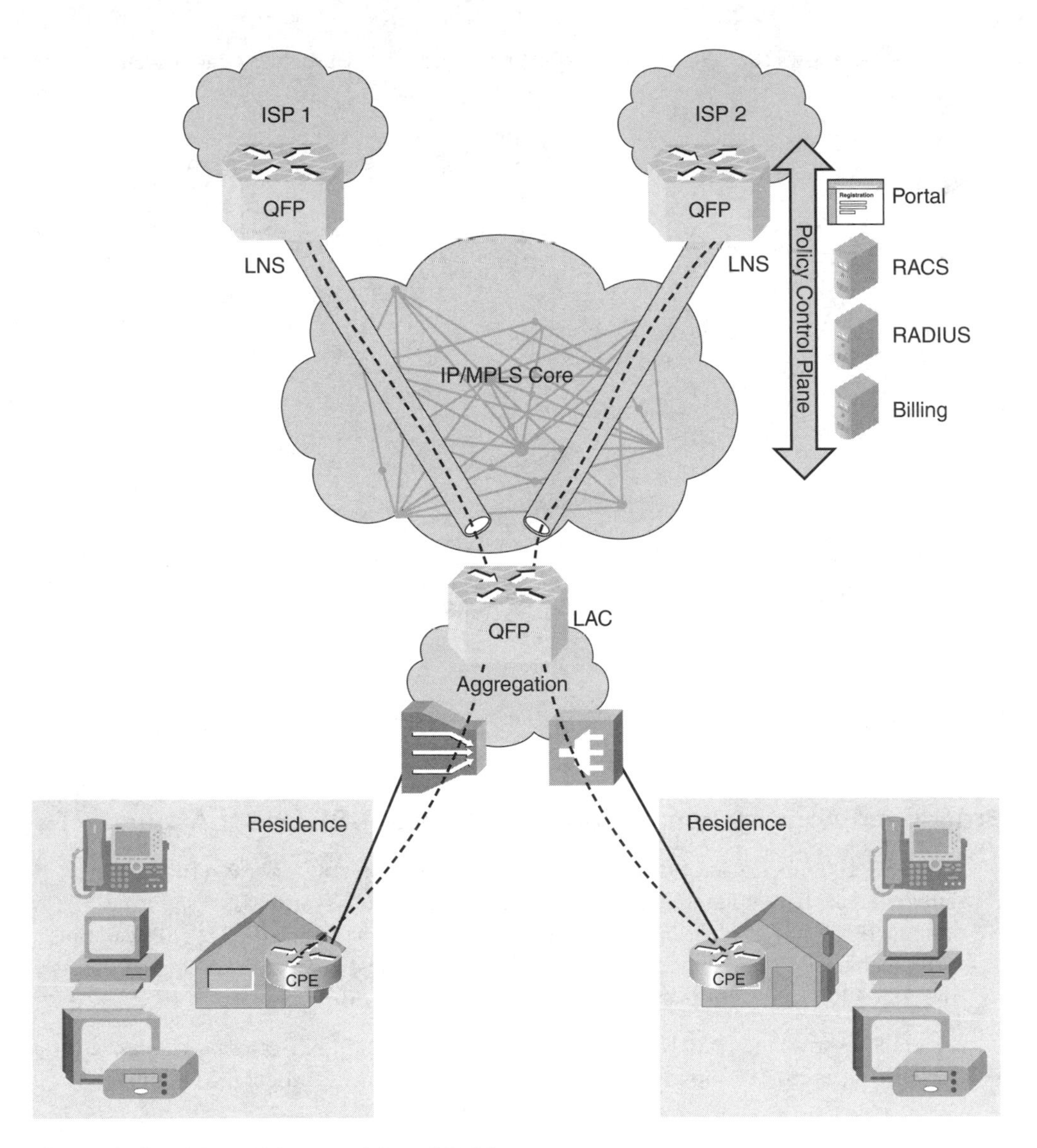

Figure 5-9 *ASR 1000 as a LAC and LNS.*

Figure 5-10 shows the ASR 1000 deployed as a BRAS providing high-speed Internet access to residential customers.

High-End Customer Premises Equipment

The ASR 1000 provides an attractive space and power footprint and can therefore facilitate a highly optimized customer premises equipment (CPE) platform. Services such as voice, firewall, encryption, and WAN optimization can be provided as a managed Layer 3 VPN offering by SPs.

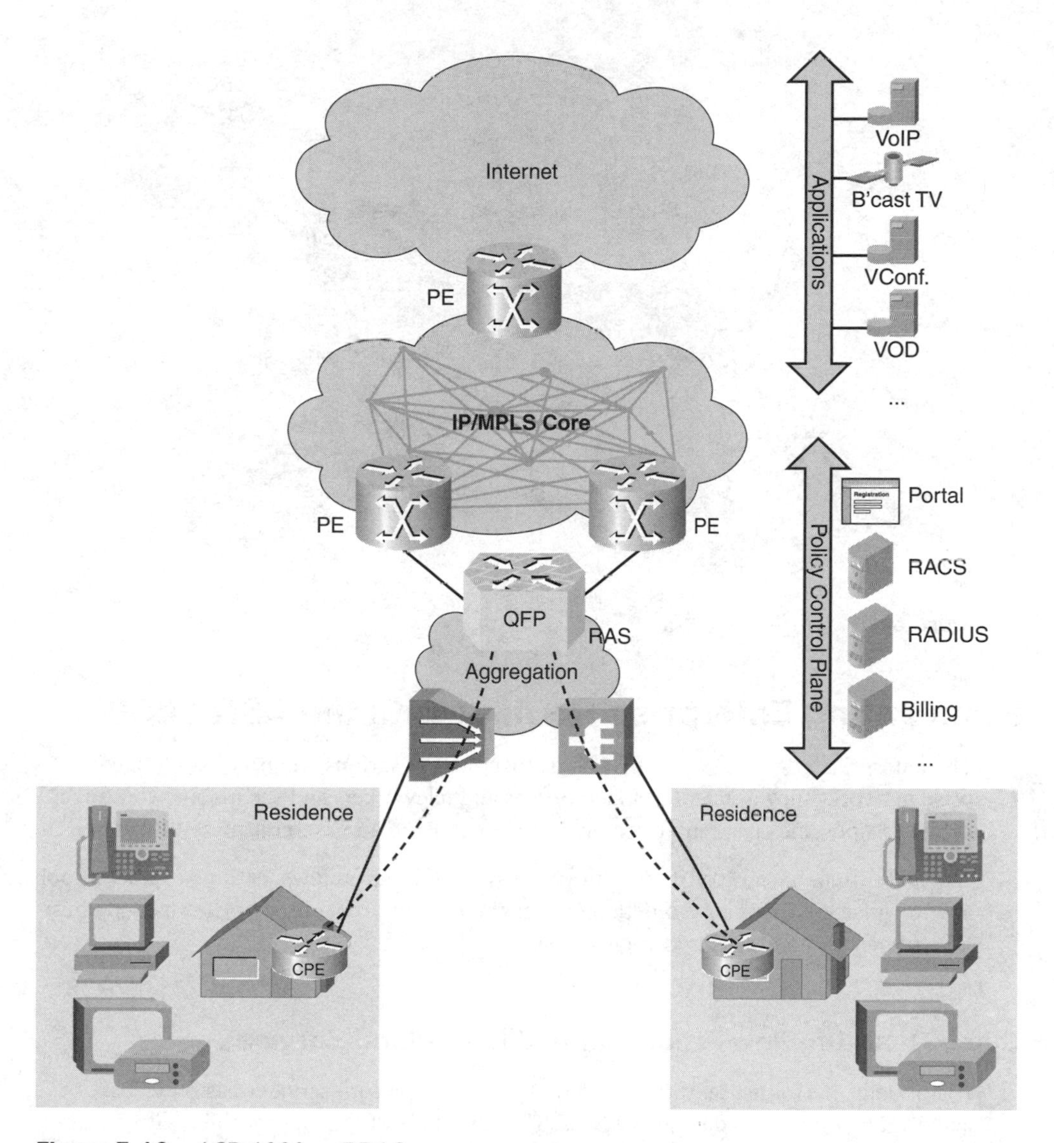

Figure 5-10 *ASR 1000 as BRAS.*

Note This book focuses on enterprise networks. Further discussion about SP broadband and edge specifics is beyond the scope of this text.

Figure 5-11 shows the ASR 1000 as a high-end CPE supporting up to 10-Gbps bandwidth in a 2-rack unit form factor.

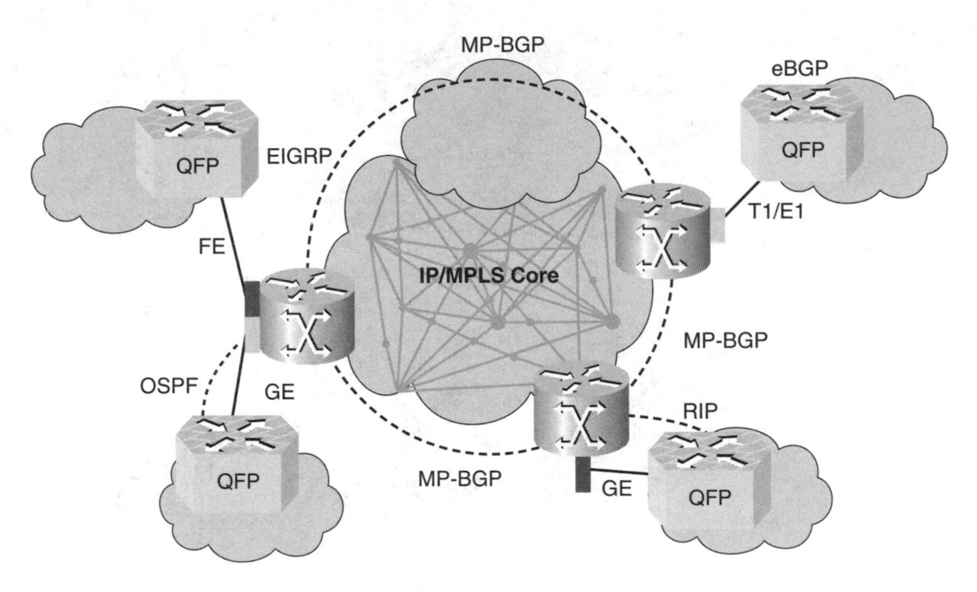

Figure 5-11 *High-end CPE.*

Reinventing Enterprise Routing with the ASR 1000

The enterprise edge is the glue that binds together the various components of an enterprise network, such as remote branch offices and teleworkers and the mobile workforce, to the campus and data center core and thus to nonstop access to business applications.

The ASR 1000, because of its revolutionary system design, allows us to take another look at enterprise edge routing (something we might want to do because of the changing business trends outlined in previous chapters).

Cisco QuantumFlow Processor and Embedded Services

Historically, performance in the range of 10 to 40 Gbps with services has only been achieved using custom-designed ASICs. The advantage of that approach is that you can realize high performance and scale for which the ASIC was designed, whereas the tradeoff is that any substantial changes or support for new features/protocols requires respinning the ASIC, which is a lengthy process. Network processors, by design, provide the flexibility to support newer features over time, but have always lacked the performance and scale to support the changing and growing needs of enterprise headend and SP applications. High-performance network processors usually require a fair bit of low-level (such as microcoding) programming language to introduce new features, which results in a slowdown of feature introduction over time.

Cisco QFP is the industry's most advanced and most flexible networking silicon chipset and features a 40-core chip, with each core running at 900 to 1200 MHz and able to perform almost all the IOS feature functionality, except for part of the QoS. QoS is offloaded to the other chip (the traffic manager) providing line-rate performance for functions such as shaping, queuing, and scheduling.

This custom-designed network processor runs four threads on each packet-processing core, with support for the full IOS feature set, including NAT, IOS zone-based firewall, GRE, MPLS L2/L3 VPNs, NetFlow, and Web Cache Communication Protocol Version 2 (WCCPv2), to name a few. A centralized data-plane platform with true services integration results in a lot fewer touches through the silicon, making troubleshooting rather straightforward.

Note ESP-10G and ESP-20G cores are clocked at 900 and 1200 MHz, respectively.

True Carrier-Class Routing

Carrier-class routing means that a routing system can deal with scheduled and unscheduled events in a manner that barely impacts service. Hence, carrier-class routing requires system hardware and software to be robust and redundant enough to continue operations when such events occur. In a sentence: How a system responds to failure events that are internal and external dictates the resiliency of the system.

Contrary to popular belief, carrier-class requirements are not limited to the SPs anymore. Because of heavy reliance on the networks for continuous business operations, enterprises want (and need) a true carrier-class system.

The sections that follow discuss how the ASR 1000 series measure against the carrier-class benchmark.

Chassis Design and Modularity

It all starts with the system design, right at the drawing board when architecting a brand new router. The ASR 1000 is designed to be fully modular; the chassis contains only the midplane, which connects the Power Entry Module (PEM) to the system RP, ESP, and SIP/SPAs. This design minimizes the chassis forklift often caused by chassis failure itself.

Operating System Modularity

It is important to understand why and how much software modularity is required. As to the why, the answer simply has to do with the compartmentalization and isolation of software failures that may occur (such as memory leaks or exceptions/crashes), along with an ability to upgrade/downgrade the software component without impacting the service. There is no simple answer to "how much"; that answer is relative to the specific network and what will actually be used in that environment. Modularity should not come at the cost of increased operational complexity.

The ASR 1000 uses Cisco IOS XE to bring modularity to this family of routers. IOS XE is just a hybrid approach: It is an IOS blob running monolithically on the given hardware, and it exposes the low-level implementation to the end user. IOS XE preserves the decades of IOS innovation, while providing the modularity for all practical purposes. IOS still runs as a blob on top of a Linux kernel, along with robust middleware processes that run as a go-between IOS and the underlying hardware.

In-Service Software Upgrade

In-service software upgrade (ISSU) is a must-have trait for all modern network operating systems. Simply put, ISSU is the capability to upgrade or downgrade software with no service impact.

The ASR 1000 supports ISSU for all middleware, IOS blob, and SIP mini-IOS SPA drivers. ISSU has been supported from day one, but it can also run the system in a nonmodular fashion if so desired for the sake of less operational complexity. For the first time, the ASR 1000 (specifically, the ASR 1002-F, ASR 1002, and ASR 1004) also allows ISSU on single-RP hardware packaging, by way of dual IOS instances.

Chapter 8, "Cisco ASR 1000 Initial Setup and Configuration," covers this feature in greater detail.

Separation of Planes

A network router or appliance is usually made up of several planes (namely, control, data, input/output, and service). Logical separation of the first three planes in a given device results in higher uptime in cases of planned or unplanned events.

The ASR 1000, by way of IOS XE and modular system design, separates the control, data, and I/O planes both logically and physically. This is a subtle aspect of the platform and a true innovation and result of a well-thought-out design. Modular RP, ESP, and SIP blades define the control, data, and I/O planes in the system. Logical isolation of these planes helps reduce the failure domains within the system, and loading of one does not cause loading of the other. (For example, heavy stress of the data plane has no bearing on the control plane, which runs on the RP in the system.)

Every SPA bay in the system runs its own SPA driver instance; therefore, failure of one SPA driver does not cause the failure of the overall SIP. All other SPA bays continue to forward traffic unaffected, except for the given SPA. SPA drivers can also be individually patched (via subpackages) to pick up a bug fix without bringing down the whole SIP.

Table 5-1 outlines the characteristics of the data, control, and management planes of the router.

Table 5-1 *Router Planes*

Plane	Characteristics
Data	Detects traffic anomalies and respond to attacks in real time Technologies: NetFlow, IP source tracker, ACLs, uRPF, RTBH, QoS tools
Control	Defense-in-depth protection for routing control plane Technologies: Receive ACLs, CP policing, iACLs, neighbor authentication, BGP best practices
Management	Secure and continuous management of Cisco IOS network infrastructure Technologies: Protected memory space, image verification, SSHv2, SNMPv3, security audit, CLI views

Dealing with Oversubscription

A modern network system must be capable of dealing with more network traffic than the system can theoretically pass without dropping any packets and impacting any of the existing users of system. This is known as *oversubscription*.

The ASR 1000 is built to deal with system oversubscription, and it all starts at the SIP, where traffic comes into or leaves the system. Imagine a 10-Gb SIP faced with 40 Gbps worth of traffic. For such scenarios, the user can use the IOS physical line interface module (PLIM) command-line interface (CLI) to define two classes of traffic (high and low), and can classify all the high-priority traffic into a strict priority queue right at the SIP level. Thus, so long as the priority traffic does not exceed the 10 Gbps (or the capacity of the given SIP and ESP), no packets will be dropped. In addition, SIP contains decent ingress oversubscription and microburst buffers that can absorb that extra traffic while ESP is busy servicing other traffic.

Note Two classes of traffic, high and low, are specific to SIP-10G, and later versions of this SIP might bring even more sophisticated hierarchies. PLIM, at the time of this writing, is supported only for Ethernet SPAs.

Integrated QoS

Any modern high-performance router design will not be complete without embedding high-performance and sophisticated QoS design.

The ASR 1000 dedicates half of QFP (that is, traffic manager) to this purpose, along with some off-chip storage for maintaining queues. This chip effectively does all the IOS Modular QoS CLI (MQC) buffering, queuing, and scheduling for the overall system without incurring any performance penalty. This is all done without ever requiring a separate acceleration module for such basic functions.

BITS Reference Clock

Building Integrated Timing Source (BITS) is a technology to distribute a precise clock in internetworking equipment via a physical T1/E1 (DS1) connection. Faster synchronous networks depend on an accurate timing source. With the increasing number of transmission rates, the time in which to look for any particular bit significantly decreases. In the world of synchronous networking, it is largely about distribution of accurate timing relationships. The network timing function allows the platform to receive a Stratum III reference from the RJ-45 BITS plug on either the RP card or any SPA in the system.

The RP in the ASR 1000 system has an integrated BITS reference clock RJ-45 input port to bring in the Stratum III clock from an outside source and distribute it down to SIPs/SPAs in the system. The RP in the system also hosts a Stratum III clock source.

BITS redundancy is achieved by providing a BITS RJ-45 plug on each RP card. Because the BITS plug is local to the RP, the BITS reference clocks are passed between the two RPs over the midplane; therefore, each RP receives both of the BITS references. Because the logic receiving the BITS clock on an RP is quite small, failure of the local BITS reference will not cause an RP switchover. The active RP can simply use the BITS reference from the standby RP. Therefore, the selection of the active BITS reference is independent of the RP on which the BITS plug is physically located.

Nonstop Router Management

In almost all modern (and even older) system design, management access to the chassis is provided via a management Ethernet port.

The RP on an ASR 1000 has a Gigabit Ethernet port dedicated to management purposes and completely isolated from the system data plane and residing in its own VPN Routing and Forwarding (VRF) instance. If configured so, the system also allows access to this Ethernet port even when IOS is down, by way of a feature known as persistent Telnet or Secure Shell (SSH). This feature provides integrated lights-out management or forensics even before you recover the system from an IOS failure.

Breadth and Diversity of LAN/WAN Interfaces

A true carrier-class system must support a large number of interfaces at varying speeds and density to accommodate changing network requirements. This support allows an even higher degree of consolidation of network infrastructure (for example, by eliminating the need for separate boxes for T1/E1 and OC-192).

The ASR 1000 supports a wide array of existing interfaces that are available in the form of Cisco SPA offerings already supported on 7600, 12000, and CRS-1 series routers.

The ASR 1000 supports most flavors of low- and high-speed serial interfaces, both clear and multiple channel, Packet over Synchronous Optical Network (SONET), ATM, and a wide variety of Ethernet (Fast [FE], Gigabit [GE], 10 Gigabit [TENGE]) with myriad fiber and copper options.

Note ASR 1000 routers support only the later versions of Gigabit Ethernet SPAs, also known as V2. An example is SPA-10x1GE-V2=, which is a 10-port full-height Gigabit Ethernet SPA.

Introducing ASR 1000 System Hardware Components

Currently, the ASR 1000 is available in three chassis packagings, optimized for various price/performance points. They are numbered in the order of rack units of space they occupy.

Chassis Options

Currently, the Cisco ASR 1002-F, ASR 1002, ASR 1004, and ASR 1006 are the four available chassis packaging options, as illustrated in Figure 5-12.

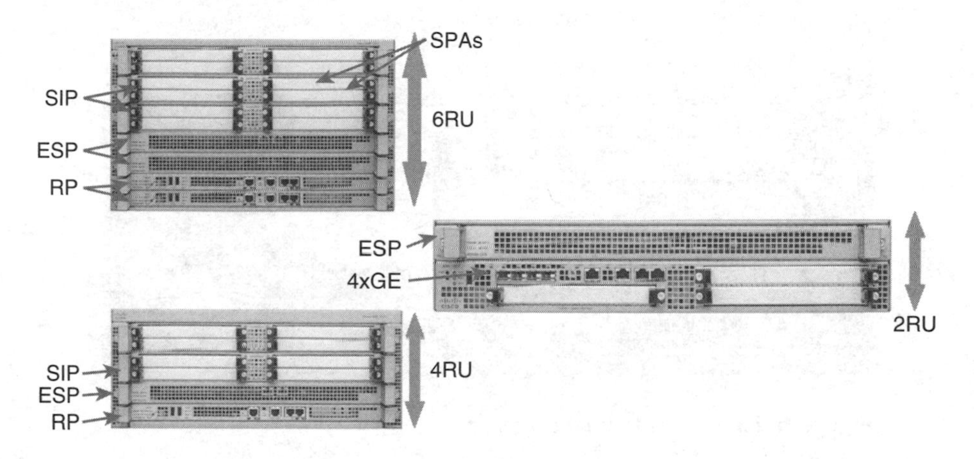

Figure 5-12 *Cisco ASR 1002, 1004, and 1006 chassis.*

These chassis packaging options are alike in some ways, different in others. They all contain a modular ESP slot, redundant power supplies (AC or DC), and a common set of software that runs of them.

The ASR 1002 is a 2-rack unit chassis and differs from all other chassis in the way it integrates the system RP and SIP on the motherboard and has four built-in routable Gigabit Ethernet ports that function just like ports in an SPA-nx1GE.

The ASR 1004 is a 4-rack unit design, containing modular RP and ESP in the system, with no built-in Gigabit Ethernet ports. The ASR 1002 and ASR 1004 have provisions for three and eight half-height (HH) SPAs, respectively. There is no hardware RP or ESP redundancy option available for these chassis packaging options (unlike the ASR 1006), although a CP redundancy option is available by way of dual IOS instances.

The ASR 1006 is a 6-rack unit design, fully hardware redundant, and modular chassis containing up to 2 RPs, 2 ESPs, and 12 HH SPAs for extremely higher I/O density. Note that the ASR 1006 can also be run with single RP and ESP, and this is a valid configuration for users who want more I/O density (without having to purchase a fully hardware-redundant system).

> **Note** RP1 and RP2 contain 40-GB and 80-GB rotary hard drives, respectively (applicable to both the ASR 1004 and ASR 1006), whereas the ASR 1002 contains an 8-GB solid-state hard disk, which is used for trace logs, core dumps (much like RP1), and system bootflash and NVRAM.

Chassis Slots Naming and Numbering

Chassis slots and numbering are pretty straightforward, as illustrated in Figure 5-13.

SIP# /Slot# /Sub-Slot#

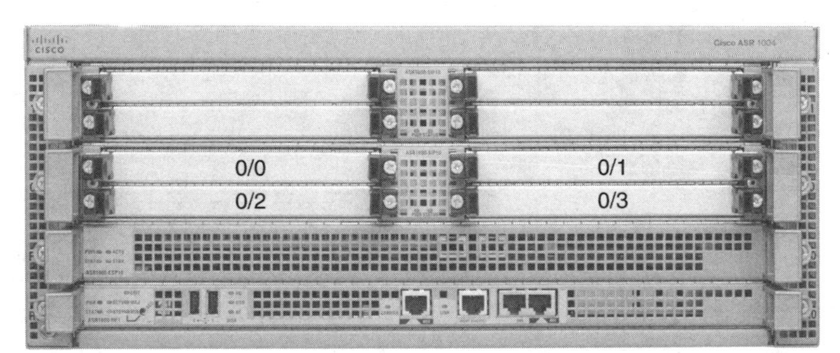

Figure 5-13 *SIP slot numbering.*

Route Processor

The Route Processor (RP) in the system defines the CP and runs routing protocols; manages traffic destined to the system's interfaces; and handles punt traffic (for example, traffic with IP option bits set), management traffic, platform-specific CLIs, and the IOS CLI.

In terms of software, the RP CPU runs the Linux kernel (also known as the base OS), middleware processes (also known as software managers), and the IOS process itself. In this software architecture, IOS does not control the system hardware; instead, it is controlled by the middleware managers. Two generations of RP hardware exist at this time, namely RP1 and RP2, differing in computing power, memory, and storage resources on them.

RP2 mostly doubles or quadruples the memory and compute cycles over RP1. RP2 uses a dual-core Intel processor, where each core is clocked at 2.66 GHz. RP2 also comes with default DRAM of 8 GB (4x of RP1 default) and can take up to 16 GB of DRAM for extreme route scale.

Embedded Service Processor

The forwarding processor, known as the Embedded Service Processor (or active ESP for the ASR 1006), in the system defines the centralized data plane, which processes all IOS features supported in the given software release. This is the most sophisticated piece of hardware in the system, and it hosts the Cisco QFP chipset and hardware assists that work with QFP, along with the encryption engine to accelerate IPsec and SSL VPN. All the ingress/egress feature processing and packet-forwarding decisions are made here. Three generations of ESP hardware exist today: ESP-5, ESP-10, and ESP-20 Gbps.

SPA Interface Processor

The ASR 1000 SPA Interface Processor (SIP), in concept, is much like the Cisco 7600 SIP, although there are some major differences between them, including the following:

- All SPAs are supported in all SIPs (as long as software running in the system supports them).
- All half height/full height (HH/FH) SPA bays run their own instance of the SPA driver, and thus limit the failure domain for an SPA driver exception to a single HH/FH SPA bay.
- SIP does not process any packets, because the ASR 1000 is a centralized data-plane system design.

Introducing ASR 1000 Software Components

The ASR 1000 system has local CPUs on all system boards, which thus run their own copy of the Linux kernel, middleware managers, and in the case of the RP, IOS.

IOS XE

IOS XE is the overall operating system, including the Linux kernel, middleware managers, and the IOS (of course, on the RP). Figure 5-14 shows RP, ESP, and SIP software architecture.

RP Software

RP software includes the Linux kernel (base OS), middleware processes (chassis, forwarding, and interface managers), and the IOS. Four flavors of IOS are supported:

- IP-BASE
- IP-BASE with SSH
- Advance IP Services (AIS)
- Advanced Enterprise Services (AES)

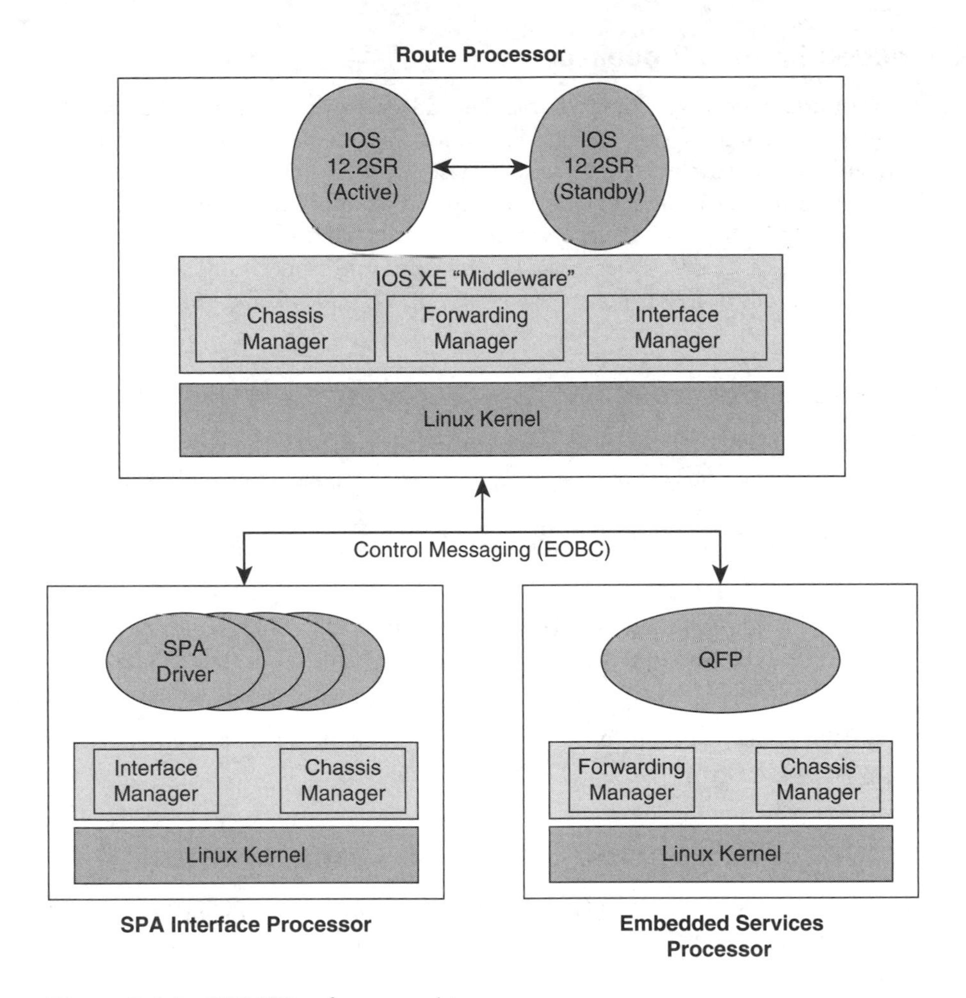

Figure 5-14 *IOS XE software architecture.*

Middleware processes communicate with their peer processes (where applicable) via Inter-Process Communication (IPC) across the Ethernet Out of Band Channel (EOBC) bus and maintain a database of objects that are needed for the features running on the ASR 1000. The chassis manager inventories the overall system, and you can use the **show inventory** command to display this information. The forwarding manager extracts the Routing Information Base/Forwarding Information Base (RIB/FIB) from the IOS and downloads the FIB in the QFP on the ESP board by communicating with its peer process on the ESP board. The RP interface manager handles associated IOS daemon (IOSD) events, communication with the appropriate SIP's Input/Output Control Processor (IOCP), and the ESPs. The RP interface manager also provides the path for collecting and returning statistics to the IOSD.

- **Chassis manager:** It is responsible for the initialization and booting of the various processes on the RP. In addition, it detects the online insertion and removal (OIR) of the other cards and coordinates their initialization and booting (including image download).

- **Forwarding manager:** The RP forwarding manager is responsible for propagating IOSD CP operations to the FP. It also provides the communication path for returning state, statistics, and so on back to the IOSD.
- **Interface manager:** The RP interface manager is responsible for communicating IOSD events associated with the creation and teardown of interfaces (physical and logical), tunnels, and so on to the appropriate SIP IOCP and the two ESPs, as needed.

Figure 5-15 illustrates the RP software architecture.

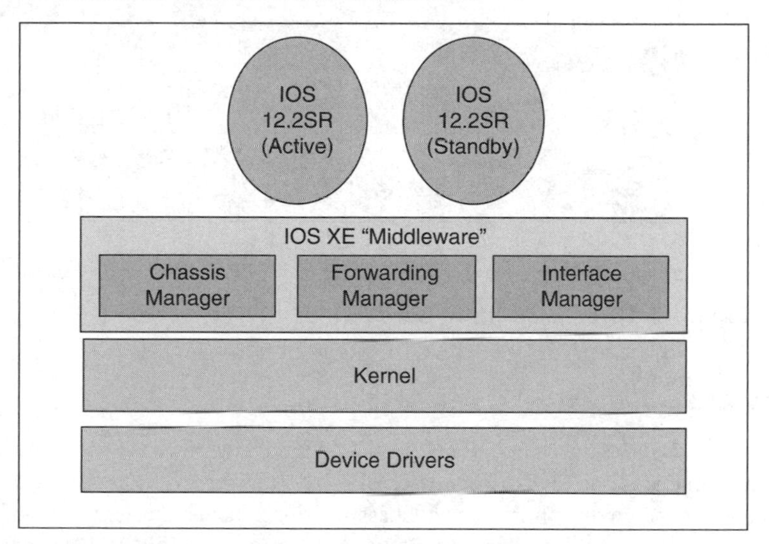

Figure 5-15 *RP software architecture.*

ESP Software

ESP software includes the Linux kernel (base OS) and middleware processes (forwarding and interface managers). The forwarding manager on the ESP communicates with its peer process on the system RP and downloads the FIB information to program the QFP. The forwarding manager also helps maintain the state in case of switchover of ESP and is responsible for downloading the statistics to the RP.

- **Chassis manager:** The chassis manager on the ESP CPU is responsible for managing the local resources of the ESP. It manages the Enhanced Serdes Interface (ESI) links to the RPs, SIPs, and the other ESPs. It communicates with the chassis manager on the RP to report the status/health (including detected hardware failures, ESI status, software process status, and the state of thermal sensors).

- **Forwarding manager:** The forwarding manager on the ESP CPU is responsible for interpreting requests and queries from the forwarding and interface managers on the active RP.

Figure 5-16 shows the ESP software architecture.

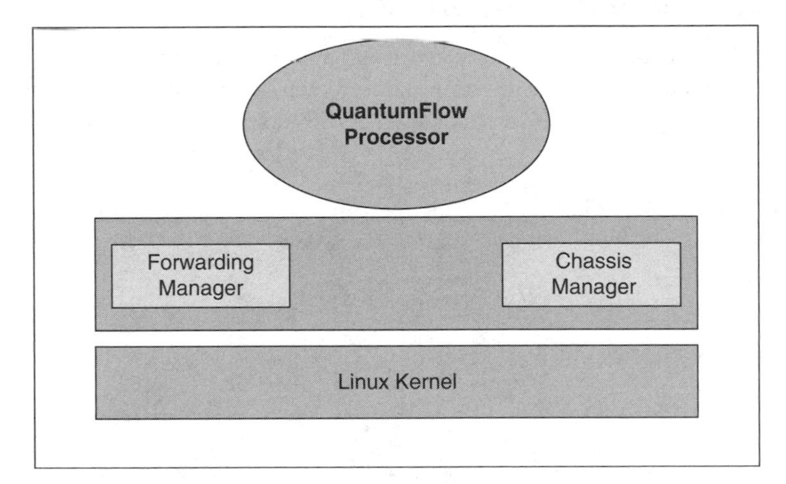

Figure 5-16 *ESP software architecture.*

SIP Software

SIP software includes the Linux kernel (base OS), middleware processes (chassis and interface managers), and SPA drivers. Each SPA bay runs its own copy of the SPA driver instance in a protected memory space. Chassis and interface managers communicate with their peer processes on the RP via the EOBC bus (what we call IPC), as discussed earlier. There is also a flow-control mechanism that runs between QFP and SIP to manage the oversubscription scenarios.

- **Chassis manager:** The chassis manager on the SIP CPU is responsible for managing the local resources of the SIP.
- **SPA driver:** SPA drivers run on the SIP CPU directly. They are loaded as new SPAs are inserted and enabled. For each SPA, its SPA driver and its own private copy of the IOS run as a separate process.
- **Interface manager:** The interface manager receives requests for the creation or takedown of network interfaces (physical and sometimes logical) from the RP interface manager via IPC over EOBC.

Figure 5-17 shows the SIP software architecture.

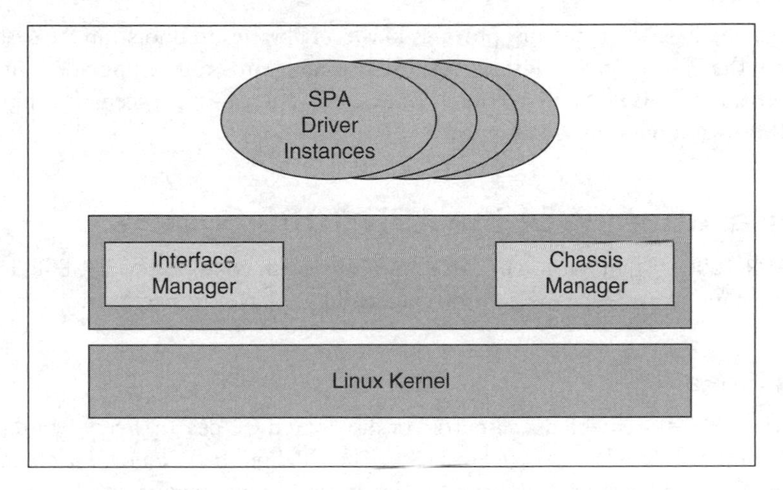

Figure 5-17 *SIP software architecture.*

IOSD and Linux Kernel

The IOS daemon (IOSD) or process is an application process that runs on top of the Linux kernel (2.6.x) stack. This is where the entire feature resides, although IOS does not control any hardware in the system. Middleware software essentially does that job by extracting from the IOS what it needs to program the QFP hardware underneath (for example, the FIB) and providing to the IOS what it requires (for example, various statistics via **show/debug** command output).

The ASR 1000 runs the same Linux kernel across all the system boards for the given software image, and no root access is available to this kernel. The Linux kernel uses both EXT2/3 and FAT16/32 file systems.

Example 5-1 shows the interface to the Linux kernel from Cisco IOS CLI enable mode.

Example 5-1 *Displaying the Linux Kernel Version via RP System Shell*

```
ASR1006# request platform software system shell r0
*********************************************************************
Activity within this shell can jeopardize the functioning of the system.
Session will be logged to:
harddisk:tracelogs/system_shell_R0.log.20080604141557
*********************************************************************
Terminal type 'network' unknown.  Assuming vt100
[ASR1006_RP_0:/]$
[ASR1006_RP_0:/]$
*Jun  4 14:15:57.998: %IOSXE-5-PLATFORM: R0/0: %SYSTEM-3-SYSTEM_SHELL_LOG: Shell
started: con 0
[ASR1006_RP_0:/]$ uname -a
Linux ASR1006_RP_0 2.6.18.8 #1 Thu May 22 21:48:46 EDT 2008 ppc ppc ppc GNU/Linux
```

System ROMMON

ROMMON, like other systems, provides low-level libraries to bootstrap the system and perform the Power On Self-Test (POST). All system boards can be upgraded simultaneously to a newer ROMMON version if so desired. In a real-world scenario, upgrading ROMMON is a one-time occurrence.

Basic Partitioning of the ASR 1000 System

The ASR 1000 system is made of three physical system components: RP, ESP, and SIP. These components define the control, data, and I/O planes, respectively.

Routing Plane

The ASR 1000 system is a decentralized or distributed CP design. Every board (RP, ESP, or SIP) in the system has its own local CPU. The CPU on the ESP board (also known as the FECP) is used to bootstrap the QFP chipset and crypto engine, in addition to many other tasks. However, the CPU on SIP (also known as IOCP) is used to run SPA drivers.

Data Plane

The ASR 1000 system is based on a centralized data-plane design; that is, only the active QFP/ESP is used to forward packets in the system. Active/active is not allowed for RP or ESP boards. This restriction is to avoid the possibility of packet reordering and other issues that may occur under such a scenario.

System bandwidth is a function of the ESP used in the system and is defined via the aggregate total traffic out of the system.

Figure 5-18 shows two ESP/system oversubscription scenarios: with and without ESP/system oversubscription.

Input/Output Plane

The I/O plane is defined in the form of SIP in the system, and there is no redundancy available for it (unlike for the RP or ESP). Although some network approaches such as distributing the SPA interfaces across SIPs, and then creating ether channel (in case of Ethernet) among them can help overcome this limitation. As discussed previously, all SPA bays run their own isolated driver instances to avoid the malfunctioning of SIP itself in case of a given SPA driver failure.

Introduction to ASR 1000 System Redundancy and Modularity

The ASR 1000 is built around various hardware and software redundancies. Various IOS features leverage these redundancies. For example, NAT and the firewall statefully replicate the state across the 11.5-Gbps link between the two QFPs. This is one of the first platforms to bring true in-box high availability for the firewall, and NAT for both RP and ESP failovers. IPsec redundancy is a little different; only ESP-to-ESP failover is stateful, whereas RP-to-RP failover is stateless.

- ESP bandwidth denotes the total aggregate bandwidth of the system, regardless of the direction.
- As long as high-priority traffic is not oversubscribed; that is, <=10Gb for ESP10, it will make it through the system at the expense of other nonpriority traffic.

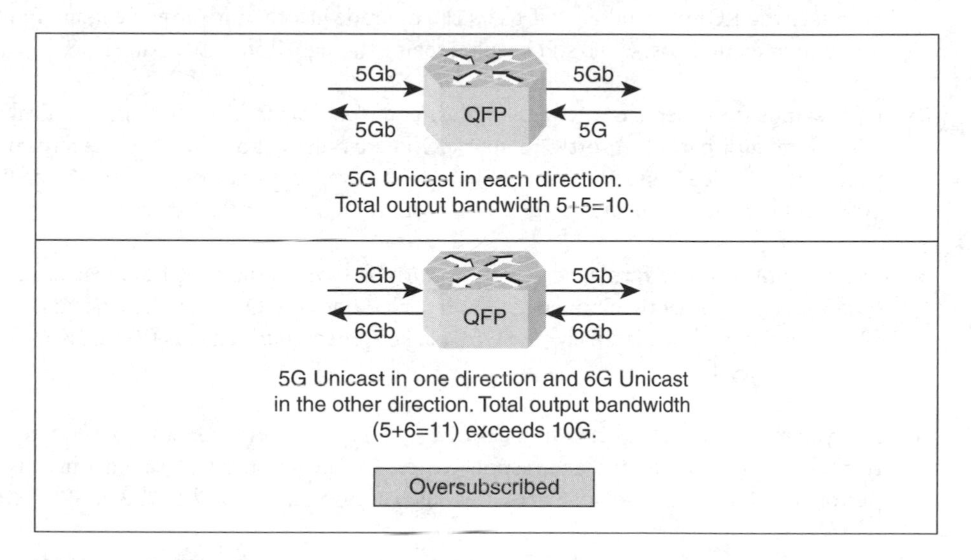

Figure 5-18 *ESP oversubscription.*

Summary

This chapter barely scratched the surface by providing an overview of the overall system hardware and software and how to help make a system highly available and reliable. The Cisco ASR 1000 essentially consists of three major components: the RP, ESP, and SIP. QFP is the foundational technology behind this platform. The next chapter discusses overall system hardware and software in more detail.

Chapter Review Questions

1. Why is logical and physical isolation of the router's planes so crucial?
2. What is ISSU, and how does it translate into higher network availability?
3. What is the penalty for turning on various QoS functions such as queuing, buffering, and shaping?

4. Why do all the system boards have their own local CPUs?
5. What are the top enterprise applications for ASR 1000 series routers?

Answers

1. Logical isolation of the routing, data, and input/output planes is a fundamental aspect of all modern routing and switching systems, to minimize the impact of one on the others. The Cisco ASR 1000 takes this to the next level by providing physical isolation so that they can be upgraded in a modular fashion and as desired. This isolation increases the ROI tremendously if users can upgrade just the forwarding engine (ESP) for an incremental cost while still keeping their existing RP and SIP boards.

2. ISSU stands for in-service software upgrade and is the capability of a system to deal with system (or part of it) software upgrade/downgrade without that causing any impact to the service being provided. ISSU has been available since day one on the ASR 1000 and is available on all chassis with or without redundant RP hardware.

3. There is almost no performance penalty to turn on QoS on the ASR 1000 platform. QoS functions (other than policing) are offloaded onto the QFP's traffic manager chip. Policing is offloaded using the QFP packet-processing elements (PPEs, also known as cores).

4. All system boards have their own local CPUs. This design principle was adopted to further boost system agility and responsiveness by having local CPUs on the boards perform various control-related activities, such as bootstrapping the QFP or SPA OIR.

5. Top enterprise applications (WAN aggregation with integrated services) include traditional or next-generation WAN aggregation, Internet gateways, secure headends for VPN termination, data center interconnect, and so on.

Further Reading

"The Cisco QuantumFlow Processor: Cisco's Next Generation Network Processor," white paper: http://tinyurl.com/264rb5

"Cisco ASR 1000 Series Aggregation Services Router High Availability: Delivering Carrier-Class Services to Midrange Router": http://tinyurl.com/co2uey

"Cisco ASR 1000 Series Aggregation Services Routers": http://tinyurl.com/cq678o

"Miercom ASR 1006 Performance Report": http://tinyurl.com/c2eoeh

"Cisco ASR1000—Aggregation Service Router Product Evaluation Report": http://tinyurl.com/65xtqh

Cisco ASR 1000 RP, ESP, SIP system detail: http://tinyurl.com/cu3og2

Chapter 6

Cisco ASR 1000 Series Router Hardware and Software Details

When trying to successfully implement, deploy, manage, and troubleshoot a routing device, the first step is to understand the underlying system architecture. This is indeed the focus of this chapter for the Cisco ASR 1000 series aggregation services routers.

This chapter covers in detail system hardware components, including the Route Processor (RP), Embedded Service Processor (ESP), Shared Interface Processor (SIP), and their associated functional elements. This chapter also discusses the software that runs on them. The chapter also highlights a packet path by walking through a day in the life of a packet through the platform.

Route Processor Overview

The RP is a separate board or module in the ASR 1000 series routers. It is a general-purpose CPU subsystem running the network operating system and platform-specific code. It is modular in all chassis except for the ASR 1002-F and ASR 1002, where it is integrated with the system board itself. No differences exist in terms of computational power and available CPU DRAM compared to the ASR 1004 and ASR 1006.

Route Processor Functional Elements

The RP can be divided into two major parts:

- The front panel, which contains the external interfaces and light-emitting diodes (LED)
- The circuitry contained on the RP's base board

At the time of this writing, the ASR 1000 has two RPs available: the ASR1000-RP1 (first generation) and the ASR1000-RP2 (second generation).

Front Panel

Figure 6-1 shows the ASR1000-RP1 front panel.

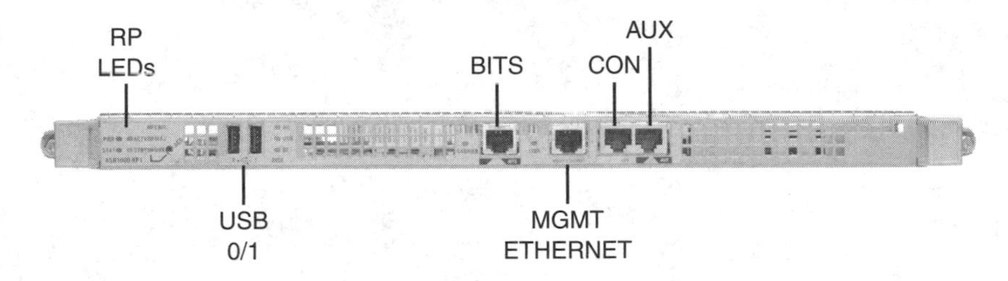

Figure 6-1 *The ASR1000-RP1 front panel.*

Table 6-1 lists the various items shown, from left to right, on the front panel of the RP board.

Table 6-1 *Interfaces Present on the RP1*

Item	Description	Additional Comments
USB 0/1	High-speed USB slots	To boot the IOS or store the configuration.
BITS	BITS input reference clock	For distributing Stratum III clock down to SIPs/SPAs.
MGMT ETHERNET	Ethernet port for management purposes only	Traffic to/from this port cannot traverse the SPA ports. Only a limited set of IOS features can be applied to it.
CON	RP console	
AUX	RP aux	

Table 6-2 shows various RP LEDs, their colors, and associated meanings.

Table 6-2 *RP LEDs and Their Description*

LED	Color	Meaning
PWR Power	Green	All power rails are within spec.
STAT Status	Green	IOS booted.
	Yellow	ROMMON loaded.
	Red	System failure.

Table 6-2 *RP LEDs and Their Description (continued)*

LED	Color	Meaning
ACTV	Active Green	Active RP.
STBY Standby	Yellow	Standby RP.
CRIT Critical	Red	On at power-up, turned off by IOS.
MAJ Major	Red	Major alarm indicator.
Min Minor	Amber	Minor alarm indicator.
ACO Alarm Cutoff	N/A	Recessed button to cut off the audible alarm. This will get triggered when CRIT/MAJ/MIN LED is set.
HD HDD	Flashing green	Activity indicator. Off = no activity.
USB	Flashing green	Activity indicator. Off = no activity.
BF Bootflash	Flashing green	Activity indicator. Off = no activity.
Link Management Ethernet	Flashing green	Activity indicator. Off = no activity.
Carrier BITS	Green	In frame / working. Off = no activity.
	Amber	Fault or loop condition.

CPU, DRAM, Bootflash, Hard Disk Drive, and Interconnect Application-Specific Integrated Circuits

In Figure 6-2, you can see that RP1 CPU is clocked at 1.5 GHz and has control links to other RPs, ESPs, and SIPs. DRAM is physically split into two dual in-line memory modules (DIMM), with two 1-GB DIMMs as the default and two 2-GB DIMMs as the maximum. The HDD on an ASR1000-RP1 is a 40-GB rotary drive. This is used to store core dumps from ESP and SIP, along with boot and trace logs. Core dumps and logs from the RP go to RP's bootflash on the ASR 1002 and to the hard disk of the modular RP on the ASR 1004 and ASR 1006.

As you might have noticed from Figure 6-1, there is no external bootflash slot or onboard Ethernet port. Bootflash (based on enhanced Universal Serial Bus [eUSB] flash media) is mounted on the RP board and is 1 GB in size on the ASR 1004 and ASR 1006 and 8 GB on the ASR 1002. NVRAM is basically a statically carved-out 32-MB portion on the bootflash media. This bootflash is a field-replaceable unit (FRU).

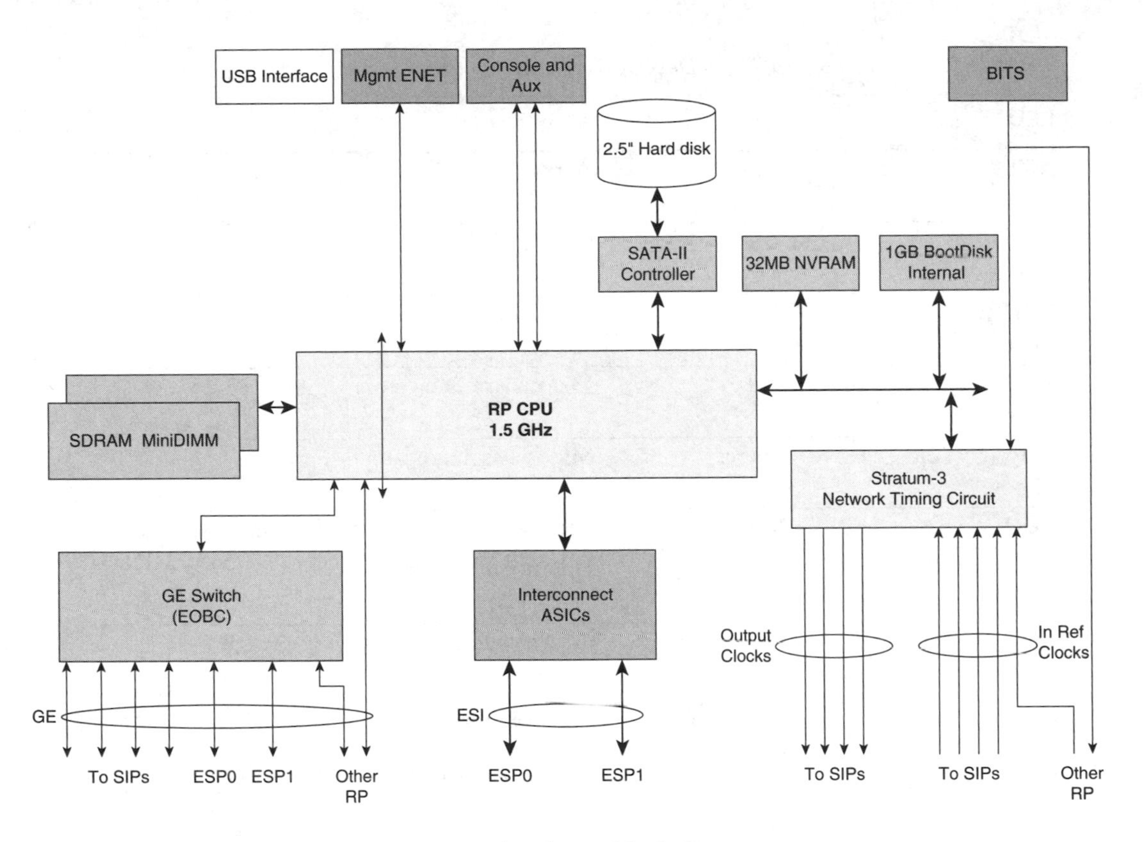

Figure 6-2 *High-level ASR1000-RP1 hardware block diagram.*

Note The hard disk drive (HDD) is a noncritical component in the system, and therefore its failure does not stop the RP from booting or cause a running RP to switch over in a fully functioning system. Booting the IOS from the HDD is possible but not recommended. The HDD is to be used exclusively for boot logging, system trace logs, and core dumps from ESP and SIP.

Interconnect application-specific integrated circuits (ASIC) provide RP1 connectivity to the data plane for punt and inject traffic. Ethernet Out of Band Channel (EOBC) is a Gigabit Ethernet (GE) switch that connects the control links from all system components, and this is how they communicate via Inter-Process Communication (IPC) over Ethernet.

Note Punt means all traffic sent from the ESP to the system RP, including IP unicast or multicast traffic with Type of Service (TOS) bits set. Inject, on the other hand, is the opposite of punt: Traffic is sent from the RP to the ESP. An example of inject is legacy protocol (such as IPX or DECnet) traffic that is handled at the system RP.

RP Initialization

The ASR 1000 design is based on a distributed control plane and centralized forwarding paradigm. A separate control processor is included on each major component of the ASR 1000 (RP, ESP, and SIP) and is responsible for managing the local resources, data structures, and so on, on that component. In addition, the RP controls other components of the system, such as power entry modules, midplane ID, and so on, via dedicated signals.

The ROM monitor (ROMMON) is responsible for board initialization and Power On Self-Test (POST). After completion of initialization, the monitor performs initial system software bootstrap from the media specified in the system configuration. As an ASR 1000 system boots, it completes the following sequence:

Step 1. Power is turned on.

Step 2. ROMMON executes POST and initializes memories.

Step 3. The ASR 1000 kernel is booted on the RP, followed by the spawning of various manager processes.

Step 4. The chassis manager process, once it receives the hello from the ESPs and SIPs, via Inter-Integrated Circuits (I^2C), starts booting up ESP and SIP. The chassis manager also collects the initial inventory of the system at this time.

Step 5. The IOS daemon (IOSD) process is spawned; IOS boots and parses the configuration from persistent storage (if there is one). At this time, the RP boot is considered complete.

RP Packet Handling

All transit traffic (coming via the shared port adapter [SPA] ports) is not seen by the active RP. The RP sees only traffic that is destined for the router interfaces (such as L2/L3 keepalives), punt traffic, and legacy protocol traffic.

All traffic that ends up going to an active RP comes from the active ESP. (The only exception to this is the traffic received on the Ethernet management port on the RP.) Let's take a detailed look at what is getting punted for Cisco IOS XE Software Release 2.1.0. These statistics are important because they affect the system RP performance. RP packet-forwarding and packet-processing potential is always limited (in contrast to the system data plane).

Example 6-1 shows the output of the **show platform hardware qfp active infrastructure punt statistics type per-cause** command.

Example 6-1 *Displaying Punted Traffic*

```
ASR1006# sh platform hardware qfp active infrastructure punt statistics type
  per-cause
Global Per Cause Statistics
  Number of punt causes =   35
  Per Punt Cause Statistics
                                                     Packets          Packets
 Counter ID  Punt Cause Name                         Received         Transmitted
 -----------------------------------------------------------------------------
  00           RESERVED                              0                0
  01           MPLS_FRAG_REQUIRE                     0                0
  02           IPV4_OPTIONS                          0                0
  03           L2 control/legacy                     0                0
  04           PPP_CONTROL                           0                0
  05           CLNS_CONTROL                          0                0
  06           HDLC_KEEPALIVE                        0                0
  07           ARP                                   1078             1078
  08           REVERSE_ARP                           0                0
  09           LMI_CONTROL                           0                0
  10           incomplete adjacency punt             8026             8026
  11           FOR_US                                0                0
  12           MCAST_DCS                             0                0
  13           MCAST_IPV4_OPTIONS                    0                0
  14           SKIP_PATH                             0                0
  15           MPLS_TTL                              0                0
  16           MPLS_RES_LABEL                        0                0
  17           IPV6_BADHOP                           0                0
  18           IPV6_HOP_OPTIONS                      0                0
  19           MCAS_SEND_INTERNAL_COPY               0                0
  20           CPP generated packets                 0                0
  21           CPP DIAG PUNT                         0                0
  22           CPP Fwall generated packet            0                0
  23           CPP MCAST IGMP UNROUTABLE             0                0
  24           glean adjacency punt                  0                0
  25           MCAST PIM signalling punt             0                0
  26           CPP ICMP generated packet             0                0
  27           ESS session control pkts              0                0
  28           ESS data switching back               0                0
  29           ICMP configured punt                  0                0
  30           RP injected FOR_US                    0                0
  31           punt adjacency                        0                0
  32           SBC DTMF                              0                0
  33           PW VCCV control channel               0                0
  34           ipwrite_keep_gpm                      0                0
```

Other than showing the several types of traffic that are being punted, this platform-specific command-line interface (CLI) command also comes in handy while troubleshooting RP CPU usage. As the counters show, punts can result when routing protocols (for example, OSPF/RIP/EIGRP) hellos are received by the router. The command output in Example 6-1 shows only punt traffic, but it is equally important to see the injected packets as captured in the output in Example 6-2.

Inject, the opposite of punt, takes place when traffic leaves the active RP and goes back into the active ESP. Examples of inject include packets sourced from the system RP, such as routing protocol hellos or Layer 2 keepalives, and going into the active ESP.

Example 6-2 shows the rest of the output of the **show platform hardware cpp active infrastructure punt statistics type per-cause** command.

Example 6-2 *Displaying the Types of Causes for Injected Packets and Associated Packet Counts*

```
Number of inject causes = 12
Per Inject Cause Statistics
                                            Packets         Packets
Counter ID  Inject Cause Name               Received        Transmitted
-------------------------------------------------------------------------
00          RESERVED                        0               0
01          L2 control/legacy               18924           18924
02          CPP destination lookup          0               0
03          CPP IPv4/v6 nexthop lookup      0               0
04          CPP generated packets           0               0
05          CPP diagnostic test packet      0               0
06          CPP Fwall generated packet      0               0
07          CPP adjacency-id lookup         0               0
08          mcast specific inject packet    0               0
09          CPP ICMP generated packet       0               0
10          CPP/RP->CPP, ESS data packet    0               0
11          SBC DTMF                        0               0
```

Note All traffic that gets punted is policed at the active ESP, and this policing nearly eliminates the possibility of the system RP CPU being saturated by punt traffic. The global value for policing is 150,000 packets per second (pps) for both ASR1000-RP1 and RP2 at the time of writing this book.

Hardware-Assisted Control-Plane Protection

Hardware-assisted control-plane protection refers to the system capability to police traffic destined for the system control plane (defined by the RP) in the ESP hardware.

As evident in Figure 6-3, all traffic coming to the control plane goes via the active ESP first, and therefore you can use the supported IOS control-plane policing (CoPP) feature to effectively deal with that traffic. A global policer is effective in addition to the IOS CoPP and is always turned on. Policing in the ASR 1000 system is offloaded using 40 cores or packet-processing elements (PPE).

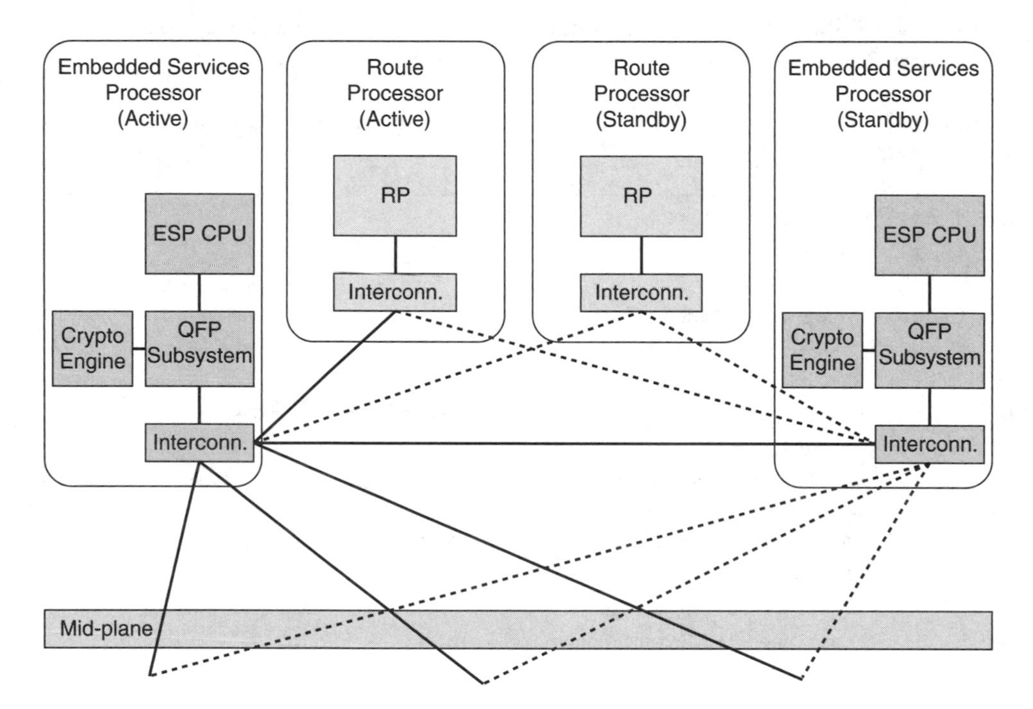

Figure 6-3 *Architecture of an ASR 1006 chassis with redundant RP, ESP, and various data-plane links.*

Legacy Protocol Traffic

The QuantumFlow Processor (QFP), the packet processor present on the system ESP, does not process legacy (IPX, DECnet, and so on) protocol traffic, and therefore the data plane for these protocols exists in the RP or IOS. Aggregate legacy traffic cannot exceed 150,000 pps for ASR1000-RP1.

Example 6-3 shows output from the **sh platform hardware qfp active statistics drop | i Global** command, which enables you to track the system-policed drops.

Example 6-3 *Displaying Packet-Drop Statistics for the Entire ASR 1000 System*

```
ASR1006# sh platform hardware qfp active statistics drop | i Global
Global Drop Stats                                   Octets       Packets
  PuntGlobalPolicerDrops                               0             0
```

Note A quick way to see the overall nonzero drop statistics is to execute the **sh platform hardware qfp active statistics drop** | e _0_ command. You can also clear statistics by using the **clear** switch at the end of this **show** command.

ESP Overview

Within the ASR 1000 system architecture, the forwarding processor (or ESP) is a separate board altogether that can be upgraded/downgraded without touching the control plane (RP) in the system. QFP is the custom piece of silicon that does all the data-plane packet processing, even including IP packet fragmentation and reassembly in hardware.

At this time, three ESPs are available: ESP-5G, ESP-10G, and ESP-20G. All ESPs are based on the QFP, so the same feature set is supported on all chassis using any of the ESPs.

This section covers the ESP functional elements, initialization, packet handling, and interaction with the crypto engine.

ESP Functional Elements

Table 6-3 shows various ESP LEDs, their colors, and meanings.

In Figure 6-4, you can see that the ESP CPU is clocked at 800 MHz and has control links to other RPs, ESPs, and SIPs. There are various types of memories on this board. All per-session databases are kept in QFP resource DRAM. Interconnect ASICs provide ESP connectivity to the other ESPs in the system for checkpointing the various states of IOS features such as Network Address Translation (NAT) or firewalls. EOBC is a GE switch that connects the control links from all system components; communication is through the EOBC via IPC over Ethernet.

Table 6-3 *ESP Front-Panel LEDs*

LED	Color	Meaning
PWR Power	Green	ESP is powered.
STAT Status	Green	ESP software is booted.
	Yellow	ROMMON is loaded.
	Red	System failure.
ACTV Active	Green	Active ESP.
STBY Standby	Yellow	Standby ESP.

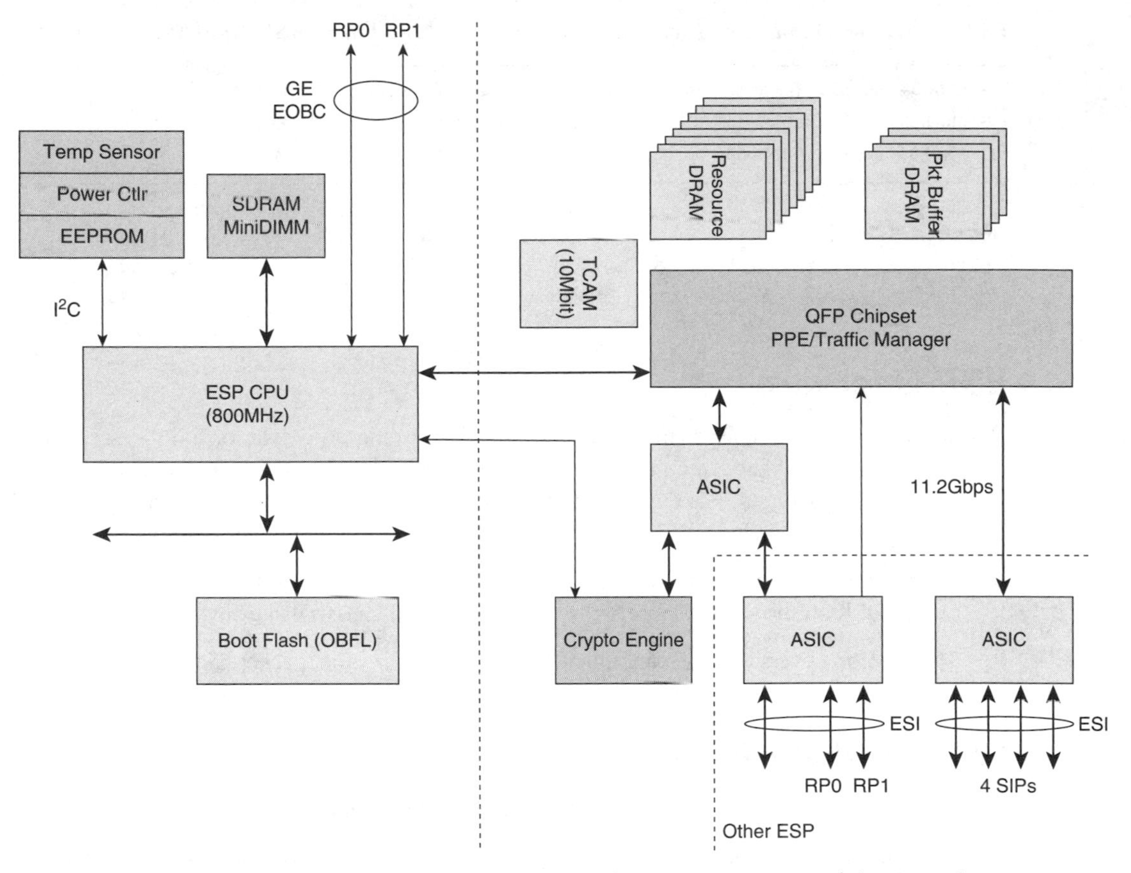

Figure 6-4 *High-level ESP block diagram showing the interconnection of the QFP chipset, ESP CPU, crypto engine, and various interconnect ASICs.*

Tertiary content-addressable memory (TCAM) on the ESP is used to store access control lists/entries (ACL/ACE), class maps, policy maps, and the IPsec Security Policy Database (SPD). The amount of available space in TCAM is what defines the upper limit on these IOS features, and there is no performance penalty for using them. Hence, an ACL of 10 ACEs or 10,000 ACEs will not cause any degradation in the forwarding performance. ESP-10 and ESP-20 have 10- and 40-Mb TCAMs, respectively.

Figure 6-5 shows an ESP system board with a QFP chipset, crypto engine, and local CPU, along with various types of memory and interconnect ASICs

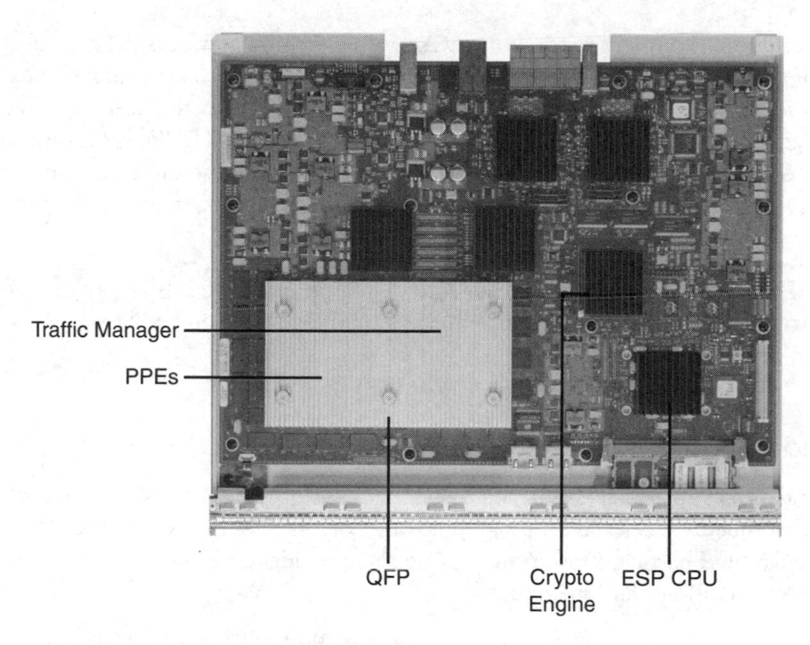

Figure 6-5 *ESP system board.*

ESP Initialization

The following events take place as ESP initializes from scratch:

Step 1. The ESP ROMMON boots from the ESP CPU's ROM and initializes memory, data buses, Ethernet controllers connecting to RPs, and the vty console.

Step 2. This ROMMON routine runs self-tests and optional diagnostics for the crypto engine, interconnect ASICs, ESP CPU, and the QFP chipset. The ESP ROMMON then connects with the active RP chassis manager for ESP CPU image download. After successful download of the image, ROMMON starts executing the downloaded image.

Step 3. The forwarding manager, chassis manager, and many other local processes are started.

Note If both ESPs try to come up at the same time (as in ASR 1006 chassis), ESP in slot 0 is always preferred as the active ESP, unless of course if it fails to fully come up for some reason. The I^2C bus detects which ESP comes up first.

ESP Packet Handling

The ESP provides the centralized forwarding engine responsible for most of the data-plane processing tasks. It performs all the traditional baseline router packet operations, including MAC classification, Layer 2 and the various Layer 3 forwarding, quality of service (QoS) classification, security ACLs, virtual private networks (VPN), policing, shaping, load balancing, NetFlow, and so on. It is also responsible for more complex features such as firewalls, Flexible Packet Matching (FPM), Network Based Application Recognition (NBAR), Web Cache Communication Protocol (WCCP), NAT, various tunneling protocols, compression (crypto, header, and RTP/IP), and so on. It also performs the egress packet buffering, queuing, and egress packet scheduling functions for the system.

Note Having two different ESPs is not recommended. However, it is fine to migrate and temporarily have this situation, because the system understands and will continue to function in this scenario.

ESP and Crypto Engine

ESP hosts a crypto engine chip and therefore does not require an external IPsec/SSL VPN module to accelerate cryptographic functions such as bulk encryption/decryption, antireplay, and hashing. This crypto engine also provides acceleration of Internet Key Exchange (IKE) module operations.

Figure 6-6 shows the performance details of ASR1000-ESP10. Performance with 1000 tunnels (left side) and 4000 tunnels (right side) is nearly identical. This is the result of a careful implementation approach taken that maintains the crypto throughput even at the highest end of the supported number of tunnels (that is, 4000).

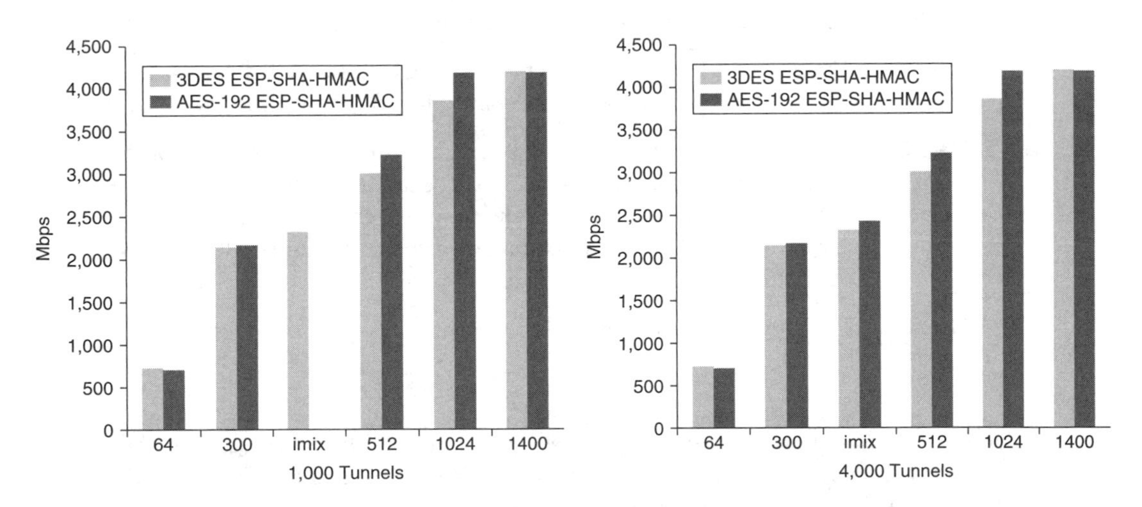

Figure 6-6 *IPsec performance and scale for ASR1000-ESP10 Gbps for various packet sizes and their respective throughput levels.*

When deploying the ASR 1000 as a secure headend, remember the following key points:

- With the crypto engine being maxed out, the system still has the headroom to push clear-text traffic through it up to the system bandwidth.

- The number of tunnels does not seem to have any significant impact on IPsec forwarding or throughput.
- There is no significant difference in performance with 1, 10, or 1000 tunnels.
- There is no significant difference in performance for various Advanced Encryption Standard (AES) key sizes (128 to 256 bits) or Triple Data Encryption Standard (3DES).
- There is no significant difference in performance for different Diffie-Hellman (DH) groups (that is, DH 1, 2, 14, 15, 16).
- Average latency in all testing scenarios for IPsec remains below 200 usec (micro seconds).
- The IPsec session setup rate is up to 130 tunnels per second (tps) with ASR1000-RP2.

The ASR 1000 has an interesting design for encryption handling, and it proves particularly useful for encrypting IP multicast traffic. The usual problem when encrypting multicast traffic is the quasi-instantaneous exhaustion of the Rx (receive) ring of the crypto engine due to oversubscription caused by the multicast packet burst. Any packet that needs to be encrypted is sent to the QFP's traffic manager and only forwarded to the crypto engine if it has the bandwidth to encrypt those packets. Otherwise, those packets remain inside the traffic manager. On the other hand, encrypted packets waiting inside the crypto engine remain inside until the traffic manager has bandwidth to deal with them that essentially creates a full circle-of-feedback (or back-pressure) mechanism for encryption and nearly eliminates the multicast encryption problem outlined previously.

Note Low-latency queuing (LLQ) before crypto is supported on the ASR 1000 starting with IOS XE Release 2.1. With LLQ before crypto, a priority queue and a best-effort queue are maintained before the encryption engine, making sure that priority traffic does not have to compete with best-effort traffic during times of congestion at the crypto engine. It is enabled as a result of a QoS service policy on a physical interface that has a crypto map applied to it.

SPA Interface Processor Overview

SIP provides the physical and electrical termination for up to four half-height SPAs (or two full-height SPAs or two half-height and one full-height SPAs).

SIP provides packet prioritization for ingress packets from the SPAs and a relatively large ingress burst absorption buffer for ingress packets awaiting transfer to the ESP for processing. SIP also provides just enough egress buffering to smooth the burstiness of the ESP scheduler and to ensure full link utilization on transmit. SIP also generates egress queue events to the ESP indicating whether there is room in each egress queue (both on the SIP and on the Ethernet SPAs) for additional packets. This is used by the ESP to qualify its packet-egress scheduling.

SIP also includes the circuitry for passing network timing references between RP cards and the SPAs. It provides a mux for selecting among a single reference clock from each of the four SPAs and for sending the selected reference clock to each RP.

Figure 6-7 shows the detailed block diagram for ASR1000-SIP10. SIP10 hardware has Input/Output Configuration Program (IOCP) and two types of ASICs for connecting it to SPAs and ESPs. It also has a connection to the system EOBC.

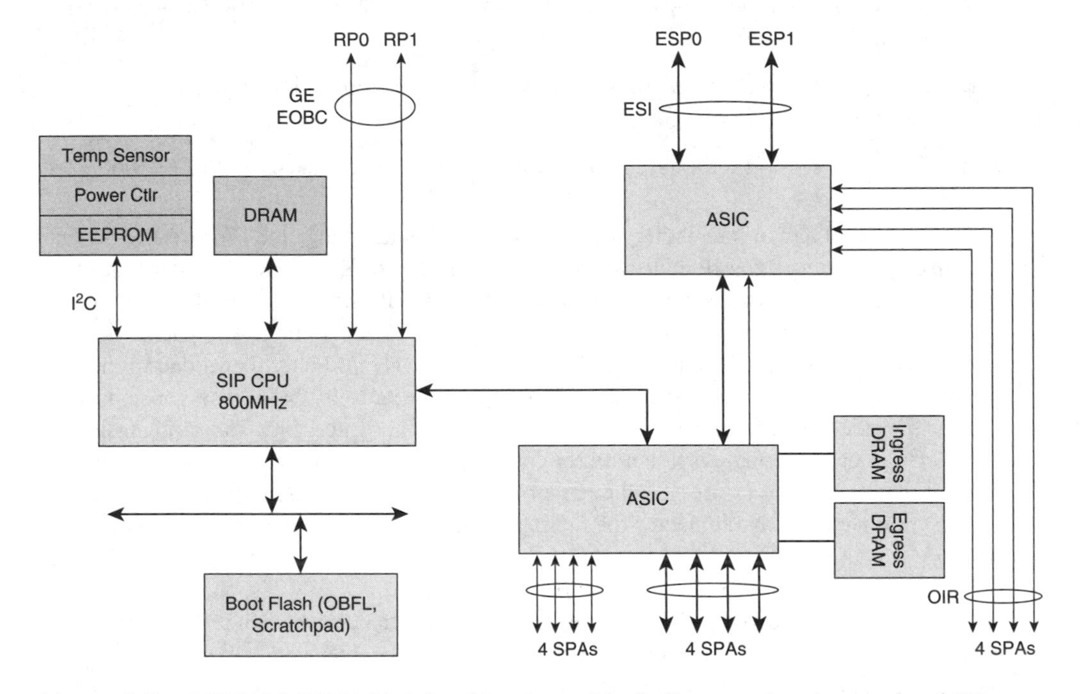

Figure 6-7 *ASR1000-SIP10 high-level hardware block diagram showing the local I/O control CPU, various ASICs, and DRAM.*

You can use the **sh plat hardware slot** command with various switches to display different statistics for the SIP.

Example 6-4 shows the complete list of options available for SIP hardware.

Example 6-4 *Displaying SIP Slot 0 Statistics*

```
ASR1006# show platform hardware slot 0 ?
  dram      MCP85xx DRAM commands
  eobc      Show EOBC
  fan       Fan commands
  io-port   IO Port information
  led       LED-related commands
  mcu       MCU related commands
  plim      PLIM information
```

```
sensor    Sensor information
serdes    Serdes information
spa       SPA related information
voltage   Voltage commands
```

High-Level System Software Architecture

This section discusses RP, ESP, and SIP software architecture details. System software plays a pivotal role in the functioning of a routing system. In the case of the ASR 1000, the system software maintains the data structures that are running on local CPUs on the respective system components. Therefore, it is necessary to understand the various tasks that are done by different middleware managers and how they communicate to each other across EOBC.

The ASR 1000 is a distributed control-plane architecture where each component has its own local CPU for control-related tasks. The tasks performed by the RP CPU are as follows:

- Runs the router control plane (IOSD), including processing of network control packets, computation of routes, connection setup, and processing of select legacy protocols not handled by ESP
- Hosts management ports, indicators, CLI, alarms, and network management (for example, Simple Network Management Protocol [SNMP])
- Code management and storage, including downloading to other components
- Active RP and ESP selection and standby synchronization
- Passing network and interface configuration and state to the other control processors
- Logging facilities, onboard failure logging, statistics aggregation, and so on
- Chassis management (environmental, power and fans, online insertion and removal [OIR] except for SPAs, and so on)
- EOBC switch management for IPC communication

RP Software Details

As you know, the RP runs three major processes (also known as daemons or managers). All of these are statefully restartable. For crashes, we allow a restartable process to fail once in 30 minutes. If it fails more than that, the process is considered to be in a state of persistent failure and is not restarted. This section discusses in more detail specific functions that chassis, forwarding, and interface managers perform.

RP Chassis Manager

The RP chassis manager is responsible for the basic operations of the platform. It is responsible for the initialization and booting of the various processes on the RP. In addition, it detects the OIR of the other cards and coordinates their initialization and booting (including image download). It also selects the active versus standby RP and ESP and coordinates their switchover based on failure of processes, card removal, other card failure, operator command, and so forth. The chassis manager monitors the environmental condition of the chassis, including the power supplies and fans, thermal sensors on the RP, and the status from the thermal sensors from the other cards (reported via IPC).

The chassis manager is also responsible for managing the alarms (including processing alarm requests from IOSD). It also controls the reset and power down of the other system FRUs. Like the other managers on the RP, it maintains its latest state in persistent storage in memory and shadows this to the other RP.

RP Forwarding Manager

The RP forwarding manager is responsible for propagating IOSD control-plane operations to the ESP. It also provides the communication path for returning state, statistics, and so on back to IOSD. The forwarding manager on the active RP also maintains the state for the standby ESP so that it is ready if a switchover occurs. If the forwarding manager fails or is upgraded, it resumes using the state from the persistent storage.

RP Interface Manager

The RP interface manager is responsible for communicating IOSD events associated with the creation and teardown of interfaces (physical and logical), tunnels, and so on to the appropriate SIP CPU and to the ESP as needed. It also provides the path for collecting and returning statistics to the IOSD. Similar to the forwarding manager, the interface manager holds the state from the IOSD, the ESPs, and the SIPs in a persistent storage in memory that is shadowed to the interface manager of the other RP. If the interface manager fails or is upgraded, it resumes using the state from the persistent storage without impacting established interfaces.

ESP Software Details

The ESP comprises several software components, including chassis, and a forwarding manager and the client and service process to interact with the QFP/PPE software.

QFP Software

The QFP subsystem hosts 40 packet-processing cores, and each runs 4 contexts. At any given time, therefore, QFP can process 160 packets. Each core, in this case, can process all IOS features supported in the given IOS XE release. QFP is programmable in C language, and therefore you can introduce new features quicker than you can in other network processors that require low-level microcode for the same purpose.

ESP Forwarding Manager

The forwarding manager on the ESP CPU is responsible for interpreting requests and queries from the forwarding and interface managers on the active RP.

ESP Chassis Manager

The chassis manager on the ESP CPU is responsible for managing the local resources of the ESP. It manages the ESI (Enhanced Serdes Interconnect, basically peer-to-peer [P2P] data-plane connection) links to RPs, SIPs, and the other ESP. It communicates with the chassis manager on the RP to report status/health (including detected hardware failures, ESI status, software process status, and the state of thermal sensors).

SIP Software Details

SIP software comprises three major processes: interface, chassis managers, and SPA drivers.

SIP Chassis Manager

The chassis manager on the SIP CPU is responsible for managing the local resources of the SIP. It manages and monitors the ESI links to the ESPs and handles the switchover to the standby ESP's ESI when an ESP switchover occurs. It communicates with the chassis manager on the RP to report status/health (including detection of hardware failures, ESI status, software process status, and the state of thermal sensors). In addition, the chassis manager detects the OIR of SPAs, queries SPA type, controls the SPA power up and initialization, and loads and starts the appropriate SPA driver.

SIP Interface Manager

The interface manager receives requests for the creation or takedown of network interfaces (physical and sometimes logical) from the RP interface manager via IPC over EOBC. The interface manager also collects status and statistics from the SPA drivers and reports them back to the RP.

SPA Drivers

SPA drivers run on the SIP CPU directly. They are loaded as new SPAs are inserted and enabled. For each SPA, its SPA driver, along with its own private copy of the IOS, runs as a separate process. Therefore, the failure or upgrade of an SPA driver for a particular SPA does not affect the other SPAs in the same SIP. The SPA drivers receive requests and reports status via the interface manager running on the SIP CPU. SPA subpackages can be upgraded/downgraded without affecting the given SIP.

Note ASR 1000 system supports running the overall system in a modular fashion by way of booting and running the system in subpackages mode. Although as an alternative to that, running the system in a nonmodular fashion is also available, and you can boot ASR 1000 system much like c7200VXR using one consolidated binary package (called a consolidated package). Chapter 7, "Cisco IOS XE Software Packaging, Releases, and Licensing," covers this in more detail.

Day in the Life of a Packet

Now that you understand the basics in terms of hardware and software architecture, this section explains the various steps a transit packet takes through the ASR 1000 system from the time it is received into the platform to the time it leaves it. This section covers the ingress process, the arrival process, and the egress process.

Ingress Processing

The ingress processing procedure is as follows:

Step 1. The SPA receives packet data from its network interfaces and transfers the packet to the SIP.

Step 2. The SPA aggregation ASIC classifies the packet into high or low priority. (If not configured, it will prioritize based on preconfigured criteria.)

Step 3. Ingress buffer memory is carved into 64 queues. Channels on "channelized" SPAs share the same queue.

Step 4. The SPA ASIC selects among ingress queues for the next packet to send to the active ESP over the ESI link. It prepares the packet for internal transmission.

Step 5. The interconnect transmits data of selected packet over ESI to the active ESP at up to 11.5 Gbps.

Step 6. The active ESP can back pressure SIP via ESI to slow packet transfer over the ESI if overloaded (provides separate back pressure for high- versus low-priority packet data).

Arrival Processing

The arrival processing procedure is as follows:

Step 1. Packets on the QFP are received in GPM (Global Packet Memory) from HyperTransport, the SPI, or the traffic manager (for recycled packets).

Step 2. The hardware moves packets from GPM and assigns them to one of many distribution FIFOs.

Step 3. The hardware distributor assigns packets to an available PPE thread. (Remember each PPE is running four threads.)

Step 4. The PPE thread processes the packet in a feature chain similar to Cisco IOS Software Release 12.2SR.

Example 6-5 shows a sample feature-invocation list and the order in which it is enforced. Highlighted rows show the details of the feature-invocation order.

Example 6-5 *IOS XE Feature-Invocation Order Related to a Given Interface*

```
ASR1006# show platform hardware qfp active int GigabitEthernet0/0/0
General interface information
  Interface Name: GigabitEthernet0/0/0
  Platform interface handle: 6
  CPP interface handle: 6
  Parent Name: (none)
  Rx uidb: 1023
  Tx uidb: 65529
SPA/plim interface information
  Remap table entry
    Marmot channel ID: 0
    Valid bit: 1
    SPA format: FORMAT D
    Indirect bit: 0
    UIDB index: 1023
  Tx subblock
    Tx SPA format: FORMAT D
    Tx Marmot channel: 0x03000000
    Tx SPA header length: 0
BGPPA/QPPB interface configuration information
  Ingress: BGPPA/QPPB not configured. flags: 0000
  Egress : BGPPA not configured. flags: 0000

ipv4_input enabled.
ipv4_output enabled.
layer2_input enabled.
layer2_output enabled.
ess_ac_input enabled.
Features Bound to Interface:
 1 GIC FIA state
22 PUNT INJECT DB
15 ethernet
 9 icmp_svr
11 ipfrag_svr
12 ipreass_svr
Protocol 0 - ipv4_input
FIA handle - CP:0x10427bb0  DP:0x802df000
```

```
        15. IPV4_INPUT_DST_LOOKUP_ISSUE*
        16. IPV4_INPUT_ARL_SANITY*
        18. IPV4_INPUT_DST_LOOKUP_CONSUME*
        22. IPV4_INPUT_FOR_US_MARTIAN*
        50. IPV4_INPUT_LOOKUP_PROCESS*
        52. IPV4_INPUT_IPOPTIONS_PROCESS*
        53. IPV4_INPUT_GOTO_OUTPUT_FEATURE*
Protocol 1 - ipv4_output
FIA handle - CP:0x10427bf0  DP:0x802fb400
        15. IPV4_OUTPUT_L2_REWRITE*
        32. IPV4_OUTPUT_FRAG*
        44. IPV4_OUTPUT_DROP_POLICY*
        58. MARMOT_SPA_D_TRANSMIT_PKT
        59. DEF_IF_DROP_FIA*
Protocol 8 - layer2_input
FIA handle - CP:0x10c1fae0  DP:0x803c1000
        10. LAYER2_INPUT_LOOKUP_PROCESS*
        11. LAYER2_INPUT_GOTO_OUTPUT_FEATURE*
Protocol 9 - layer2_output
FIA handle - CP:0x10c1fcd0  DP:0x803dd880
        14. LAYER2_OUTPUT_DROP_POLICY*
        26. MARMOT_SPA_D_TRANSMIT_PKT
        27. DEF_IF_DROP_FIA*
Protocol 14 - ess_ac_input
FIA handle - CP:0x10c311d0  DP:0x8046a800
        3. PPPOE_GET_SESSION
        4. ESS_ENTER_SWITCHING
        5. DEF_IF_DROP_FIA*
```

Step 5. The L2 header check is performed.

Step 6. A forwarding decision is made, and output features are applied.

Step 7. The packet is released from on-chip memory to the traffic manager (queued).

Step 8. The traffic manager schedules which traffic to send to which SIP interface (or RP or crypto chip) based on priority and what is configured in the Modular QoS CLI (MQC).

Step 9. The SIP can independently back pressure ESP via an ESI control message to pace the packet transfer if overloaded.

Egress Processing

The egress processing procedure is as follows:

Step 1. The interconnect receives packet data over the ESI from the active ESP at up to 11.5 Gbps.

Step 2. The SPA aggregation ASIC receives the packets and writes it to external egress buffer memory.

Step 3. Egress buffer memory is also carved into 64 queues. Channels on "channelized" SPAs share the same queue.

Step 4. The SPA aggregation ASIC selects and transfers packet data from eligible queues to an SPA-SPI (SPA stateful packet inspection) channel. (High-priority queues are selected before low-priority queues.)

Step 5. The SPA can back pressure transfer of packet data burst independently for each SPA-SPI channel using the SPI FIFO status.

Step 6. The SPA transmits the packet data on the network interface.

Note All components in the system (that is, ESP, RP, and SIP) can back pressure each other, both ways, to deal with oversubscription and still provide preferential treatment to priority traffic if so configured.

Use the **show plat hardware qfp active system state** command to see the active ESP status, including the high-availability client status.

Summary

This chapter discussed ESP, RP, and SIP hardware and software architectural details. It also covered some of the platform-specific CLI commands and how they enable you to both understand and troubleshoot the ASR 1000 platform. The next chapter discusses the various Cisco IOS XE Software packages, licensing, and release cycles.

Review Questions

1. What are the three major middleware processes running on the RP CPU?

2. What is the global policing value enforced for the RP1 punt path?

3. Does the ASR 1000 use the same crypto engine chip on all types of ESPs?

4. What function does the forwarding manager running on the ESP CPU perform?

5. How does the ASR 1000 encryption handling solve the multicast encryption issues with crypto engine Rx ring exhaustion?

Answers

1. The three major middleware processes running on the RP are the chassis manager, forwarding manager, interface manager (and the IOSD).

2. The global policing value for the punt path for ASR1000-RP1 is fixed at 150,000 packets per second and cannot be changed. All drops are accounted for and available via a platform-specific CLI command. At the time of this writing, 150,000 pps also applies to ASR1000-RP2, although this will likely change to a higher value because RP2 can take a lot more punted packets than RP1.

3. No, all ESPs use crypto engines of different scale. ESP-5 starts out with 1 Gbps at IMIX, whereas ESP-10 is nearly double for almost all packet sizes (in this case, 2.5 Gbps).

4. The forwarding manager on the ESP interacts with its peer process on the RP to download the FIB via IPC over EOBC to program QFP.

5. No packet that needs encryption/decryption is thrown at the crypto engine unless it is known that the crypto engine has the headroom to take this task. So, there is an in-built feedback mechanism between the crypto engine for both pre- and post-encryption.

Further Reading

"The Cisco QuantumFlow Processor: Cisco's Next Generation Network Processor," white paper: http://tinyurl.com/264rb5

"Cisco ASR 1000 IPsec," solution paper: http://tinyurl.com/cq678o

Miercom ASR1006 Performance Report: http://tinyurl.com/c2eoeh

Cisco ASR1000—Aggregation Service Router Product Evaluation Report: http://tinyurl.com/65xtqh

Chapter 7

Cisco IOS XE Software Packaging, Releases, and Licensing

The preceding two chapters covered the ASR 1000 system hardware and software architectures. This chapter covers Cisco IOS XE Software packages, release cycles, and licenses that are available on the ASR 1000 platform.

Cisco IOS XE Software Overview

Cisco IOS XE is the operating system that runs on all Cisco ASR 1000 series routers. It includes the IOS and various middleware processes (known as managers). Cisco IOS XE represents a hybrid approach that combines the feature richness coming from classical IOS and marries it with the software modularity inherent in IOS XE. Both feature richness and software modularity are critical to an enterprise network.

Cisco IOS XE Software represents the best of both worlds, with rich Cisco IOS Software features and software modularity. The Cisco IOS Software included with Cisco IOS XE Software packaging is 12.2SR based, and therefore all control-plane bounded features such as routing protocols, or platform-independent Simple Network Management Protocol Management Information Bases (SNMP MIB) are supported. Two types of features are present in any routing operating system from a system software architecture perspective: platform-independent and platform-dependent features. *Platform independent* refers to features that might not be written strictly for specific hardware, such as all routing protocols (Open Shortest Path First [OSPF], Enhanced Interior Gateway Routing Protocol [EIGRP], Border Gateway Protocol [BGP]). *Platform dependent* refers to features that are written specifically for a specific routing system.

In terms of modularity, Cisco IOS XE Software not only provides it in the form of subpackages but also supports backward compatibility for the sake of operational simplicity.

Cisco IOS XE Software comprises four major components:

- IOS daemon (IOSD), also referred as the Cisco IOS Software process running on top of the Linux kernel

- Middleware processes (or managers)
- QuantumFlow Processor (QFP) software (sometimes also referred to as microcode, although that is a misnomer, because most of it is C language code)
- Linux 2.6.x kernel

There is just one copy of the Cisco IOS Software, QFP software, and Linux kernel in a Cisco IOS XE Software release. Middleware managers are coded and named differently based on the system boards they are running on. For example, the forwarding manager works differently on the Route Processor (RP) and Embedded Service Processor (ESP), as discussed in the preceding chapter.

The various Cisco IOS XE Software benefits are as follows:

- **Modularity:** Fault isolation, package-level restartability, and package upgrade/downgrade support
- **Security:** Restricted system resource access by processes, protected memory allocation, and no root access to the Linux kernel
- **High availability:** In-service software upgrade (ISSU), nonstop routing (NSR), Hot Standby Routing Protocol (HSRP), and nonstop forwarding/stateful switchover (NSF/SSO), among others
- **Feature support:** Enterprise, service provider edge, and broadband (both broadband aggregation system [BRAS] and point-to-point termination and aggregation [PTA])
- **Unified management interface:** Familiar Cisco IOS Software command-line interface (CLI) experience and SNMP MIBs

Cisco IOS XE Software Packaging

Cisco IOS XE Software distribution (as downloadable from Cisco.com) is in the form of a single binary file (.bin) for the respective RPs (ASR1000-RP1 and ASR1000-RP2 at this time). This single binary file is also known as a *consolidated package*.

This consolidated package can also be expanded, and the resulting files coming out of consolidated packages are known as subpackages (with the extension of .pkg). Expansion details are provided later in this chapter.

Besides ROMMON, which is common across all system boards, Cisco IOS XE Software consists of seven subpackages. Cisco IOS XE Software can also be booted in a monolithic fashion by way of running the single consolidated package or binary, much like booting an IOS binary on c7200 or c7300 routers.

Table 7-1 describes the various Cisco IOS XE Software subpackages.

Note All process or subpackage types run only one instance, with the exception of SPA drivers. Up to four instances can exist, should there be four half-height SPAs in the given SIP.

Table 7-1 *Cisco IOS XE Software Subpackages*

System Component	Subpackage Name
RP	(i)IOSD (ii)RP Control (iii)RP Access (iv)RP Base and Linux Software
ESP	(v)ESP Base: ESP Managers, QFP, and Linux software
SPA Interface Processor (SIP)	(vi)SIP Base: SIP Managers and Linux software (vii)SIP SPA: SPA Drivers

The list that follows outlines the various packages and their subpackages in detail:

- **RP** contains the following subpackages:

  RP Base (asr1000rp1-rpbase): Contains the Linux kernel and some loadable libraries.

  RP Control (asr1000rp1-rpcontrol): Control-plane processes or managers that interface between the IOS and the rest of the platform.

  RP IOS (asr1000rp1-packages-adventerprisek9): Contains the given copy of the ASR 1000 IOS. This is modified to run on top of the Linux kernel. This process is named ppc_linux_iosd-.

  RP Access (asr1000rp1-rpaccess): Software required for router access; two versions are available. One version contains open Secure Shell (SSH) and Secure Sockets Layer (SSL); and one is without (RP Access and RP Access-K9), to go with non-K9 and K9 IOS software.

- **ESP** contains the following subpackage:

  ESP Base (asr1000rp1-espbase): ESP Linux kernel and control processes (or managers) and QFP software (or microcode)

- **SIP** contains the following subpackages:

  SIP Base (asr1000rp1-sipbase): Contains the Linux kernel and control processes (managers).

  SIP SPA (asr1000rp1-sipspa): SPA drivers and field-programmable device (FPD) (SPA field-programmable gate array [FPGA] image).

  ROM Monitor: One ROM Monitor package containing ROMMON for RP, ESP, SIP (released when needed). This is common across components.

Example 7-1 shows the file system structure on the RP's hard disk drive (HDD).

Example 7-1 *RP HDD File System Structure*

```
[ASR1006_RP_0:/]$ ls -la
total 40
drwxr-xr-x    19 18346    25      0 May 23 16:06 .
drwxr-xr-x    19 18346    25      0 May 23 16:06 ..
-rw-r--r--     1 root   root      0 May 23 16:05 .autofsck
-rw-r--r--     1 18346    25    486 Jan  1  1970 .pkgset
drwxr-xr-x     2 root   root      0 May 23 16:05 auto
drwxr-xr-x     2 18346    25      0 May 23 16:05 bin
drwxr-xr-x     7 root   root   4096 Jun  8 12:50 bootflash
-rwxrwxrwx     1 18346    25  21572 Jan  1  1970 common
lrwxrwxrwx     1 root   root     10 May 23 16:05 config -> /bootflash
drwxrwxrwt     6 root   root  14000 May 23 16:06 dev
lrwxrwxrwx     1 root   root     10 May 23 16:05 disk0 -> /vol/disk0
drwxr-xr-x    15 18346    25      0 May 23 16:05 etc
lrwxrwxrwx     1 root   root     13 May 23 16:05 harddisk -> /misc/scratch
lrwxrwxrwx     1 root   root     33 May 23 16:05 issu -> /tmp/sw/rp/0/0/rp_base/
   mount/issu
drwxr-xr-x     3 18346    25      0 May 23 16:05 lib
-rwxrwxrwx     1 18346    25   4071 Jan  1  1970 lkern_init
drwxr-xr-x     3 root   root      0 May 23 16:05 misc
drwxr-xr-x     3 root   root      0 May 23 16:05 mnt
dr-xr-xr-x   157 root   root      0 Jan  1  1970 proc
-rwxrwxrwx     1 18346    25   1077 Jan  1  1970 rommon_to_env
drwx------     2 root   root      0 Jun  5 15:43 root
drwxr-xr-x     2 18346    25      0 May 23 16:05 sbin
drwxr-xr-x    10 root   root      0 Jan  1  1970 sys
drwxr-xr-x     2 root   root      0 May 23 16:06 tftp
drwxr-xr-x    14 root   root      0 Jun  8 12:50 tmp
lrwxrwxrwx     1 root   root      9 May 23 16:05 usb0 -> /vol/usb0
lrwxrwxrwx     1 root   root      9 May 23 16:05 usb1 -> /vol/usb1
drwxr-xr-x     7 18346    25      0 May 23 16:05 usr
drwxr-xr-x    10 root   root      0 May 23 16:05 var
drwxr-xr-x     2 root   root      0 Jun  2 17:15 vol
[ASR1006_RP_0:/]$
```

Notice that bootflash and usb0/usb1 are all mounted volumes on the Linux file system. The file system used here is EXT2/EXT3. Recommended practice dictates shutting down the RP board before removal to avoid any possible file system corruption. Booting of IOS is recommended and supported via either bootflash or external USB slots.

Booting the system in a modular fashion is done via booting off of a file called packages.conf, which essentially describes and dictates the provisioning of subpackages for the RP. This file and other subpackages are extracted using the consolidated package or binary file. The consolidated package or binary file is the only method of publishing the released image. This file must be in the same directory as the other subpackages file.

Note The file packages.conf and other subpackages are extracted using the consolidated package or binary file. The consolidated package or binary file is the only method of publishing the released image for Cisco ASR 1000 series routers.

The following procedures will help solidify the concept. These are the steps involved in booting the system.

The nonmodular boot procedure is as follows:

Step 1. Download the Cisco IOS XE Software consolidated package file from Cisco.com (2.1.0 AdvEnterprise, asr1000rp1-adventerprisek9.02.01.00.122-33.XNA.bin).

Step 2. Create a boot system command and point it to the preceding file.

The modular boot procedure is as follows:

Step 1. Download the Cisco IOS XE Software consolidated package file from Cisco.com (2.1.0 AdvEnterprise, asr1000rp1-adventerprisek9.02.01.00.122-33.XNA.bin).

Step 2. Expand the downloaded file using the platform CLI:

```
ASR1006# request platform software package expand file harddisk:
  asr1000rp1-adventerprisek9.02.01.00.122-33.XNA.bin to bootflash:/
    modular

ASR1006# dir bootflash:/modular

Directory of bootflash:/

    12  -rw-  52064460 asr1000rp1-espbase. 02.01.00.122-33.XN.pkg

    13  -rw-    21833932  asr1000rp1-rpaccess-k9. 02.01.00.122-
                          33.XN.pkg

    14  -rw-    21516492  asr1000rp1-rpbase.02.01.00
                          .122-33.XN.pkg

    15  -rw-    24965324  asr1000rp1-rpcontrol. 02.01.00.122-33.XN.pkg

    16  -rw-    48451788  asr1000rp1-rpios-
                          advipservicesk9.02.01.00.122-33.XN.pkg

    17  -rw-    36954316  asr1000rp1-sipbase. 02.01.00.122-33.XN.pkg

    18  -rw-    14782668  asr1000rp1-sipspa.02.01.00
                          .122-33.XN.pkg

    19  -rw-        6225  packages.conf
```

Step 3. Create a boot system command and point it to the packages.conf file.

The next time ASR1000-RP boots, it will boot in a modular fashion, and you can perform an IOS ISSU (requires dual IOS) and ASR1000-SIP SPA drivers upgrade.

You can also take a snapshot of the running consolidated package on bootflash (as opposed to expanding it as shown before, where you actually need the file at the time of expanding it). Snapshotting can prove helpful if you did a network boot and want all your subsequent boots to be based on subpackages or modular.

You can take a snapshot of the consolidated package loaded in the RP0 (first RP in an ASR 1006 chassis) DRAM by entering the following command:

```
ASR1006# request platform softwar package install rp 0 snapshot to bootflash:
```

Note It is not allowed to boot the system in subpackages (or in a modular fashion) via removable media such as USB sticks, and therefore only consolidated packages are supported with removable media such as USB.

Four flavors of IOSD are packaged inside the various Cisco IOS XE Software sub or consolidated packages.

- **Cisco ASR 1000 Series RP1 ADV ENTERPRISE SERVICES** provides the following:

  All features, including legacy protocols

  Session Border Controller or CUBE

  Lawful intercept

  SNA switching not supported

- **Cisco ASR 1000 Series RP1 ADVANCED IP SERVICES** provides the following:

  All features, excluding legacy protocols

  Session Border Controller or CUBE

  Lawful intercept

  SNA switching not supported

- **Cisco ASR 1000 Series RP1 IP BASE** provides basic IP features with SSH support. It also includes features such as Border Gateway Protocol (BGP), Web Cache Communication Protocol Version 2 (WCCPv2), generic routing encapsulation (GRE), and multi-Virtual Routing and Forwarding (multi-VRF).
- **Cisco ASR 1000 Series RP1 IP BASE W/O CRYPTO** provides basic IP features without SSH support.

Software Redundancy

Cisco IOS XE Software also supports *software redundancy*, which is the capability to run NSF/SSO with single-RP systems (that is, ASR 1002 and ASR 1004). This is achieved by running two copies of the same or different versions of IOS (within the boundary of

ISSU) on a single-RP CPU. This also enables ISSU on these systems, and is particularly useful in shrinking down the time it takes to qualify new Cisco IOS Software. Chapter 9, "In-Service Software Upgrade and Software Modularity," covers ISSU in greater detail.

Cisco IOS XE Software Releases

To have a rapid acceleration in the availability of software and hardware features, the ASR 1000 is based on a time-based software release schedule where software is introduced frequently and made obsolete quickly.

The overall release plan is as follows:

- **Time-based releases:** Released three times per year (every 4 months). New software features and/or hardware support are introduced in each release.
- **Rebuilds scheduled at regular intervals:** There are only three planned rebuilds for every release. Rebuilds are only for bug fixes, and no new features are introduced in rebuilds. The three rebuilds are as follows:

  First rebuild: 2 months after first customer shipment (FCS)

  Second rebuild: 4 months after FCS

  Third rebuild: Only if needed, hence, no set time schedule

The first IOS XE release is named 2.1.0, and subsequent rebuilds will be called 2.1.1 and 2.1.2. The next major release version will be named 2.2.1, and rebuilds will be called 2.2.2 and 2.2.3. The Cisco IOS Software packaged inside the Cisco IOS XE Software release is based on 12.2SR.

The ASR 1000 release naming is as follows:

MajorRelease.ReleaseVersion.Rebuild

Where

- *MajorRelease* (2) is the first production release.
- *ReleaseVersion* starts with 1 for release 1 and increments for every release.
- *Rebuild* starts with a nonzero number for every first rebuild of a new release and increments thereafter.

For example:

- The general availability (GA) release is release 1.
- The name of the release is 2.1.
- Rebuilds will be 2.1.1, 2.1.2, and so on.

This release contains Cisco IOS Software based on 12.2SR.

Some of the releases are supported longer than 1 year. An example of that is IOS XE Software Release 2.4, which is supported for 2 years after FCS.

Cisco IOS XE Software Licensing

Because the ASR 1000 does not require acceleration modules for various Cisco IOS Software services (such as IPsec, firewalls, Network Based Application Recognition [NBAR], and high availability), it instead uses right to use (RTU) or licenses for them. These licenses are not enforced as of the writing of this book (so they are based on trust, much like c7200), although in the future they might be enforced via the Cisco IOS Software licensing model.

Table 7-2 summarizes the licenses available for Cisco ASR 1000 series routers, and what feature set they entitle the user to run.

Table 7-2 *Cisco IOS XE Software License Features*

Feature License	Software Features
IPsec, FLASR1-IPSEC-RTU	All IOS IPsec solutions, including but not limited to IPsec, IPsec/GRE, DMVPN, GETVPN, EasyVPN
Firewall, FLASR1-FW-RTU	IOS zone-based firewall
Packet Inspection, FLASR1-FPI-RTU	IOS NBAR, and FPM (Flexible Packet Matching)
High Availability (2/4RU), FLASR1-IOSRED-RTU	IOS-to-IOS high availability for ASR 1002 and ASR 1004 chassis
SBC (H248), FLASR1-H248-RTU	Session Border Controller base license

Note There are other licenses, such as broadband (both RTU and per session), but these are beyond the scope of this book.

Summary

This chapter discussed in detail the various Cisco IOS XE Software packages, Cisco IOS XE Software release cycles, and licensing. This material should help you understand the overall operating system (Cisco IOS XE Software) and the level of software modularity available. The next chapter covers in-service software upgrades (ISSU), their various caveats, the scope of the feature set, and how ISSU can solve operational headaches associated with such maintenance windows and other service-impacting events.

Review Questions

1. What is Cisco IOS XE Software, and what are several benefits of using it?
2. What are the possible booting methods that Cisco IOS XE Software can be used with?
3. What is a consolidated package and a subpackage?
4. How many subpackages does Cisco IOS XE Software contain?
5. What does running two instances of IOS mean, and why are they restricted to only ASR 1002 and ASR 1004?

Answers

1. Cisco IOS XE Software is the overall operating system for the Cisco ASR 1000 series routers. It basically consists of four major components: IOSD, various control processes or managers, QFP software, and the Linux kernel. The IOSD or IOS is one component of it and provides the feature set supported in the given Cisco IOS XE Software release. The real benefit of IOS XE is the combining of the decades-long IOS innovation with software modularity to help keep the system up and running in the face of various service-impacting hardware/software failures.

2. Cisco IOS XE Software can be booted in two fashions: modular or nonmodular. Modular booting requires booting via subpackages (done using the packages.conf file), whereas nonmodular booting is done in a similar fashion as c7200 or c7300 routers. Modular booting is mandatory to have IOS-to-IOS software redundancy in Cisco ASR 1002 and ASR 1004 chassis.

3. A consolidated package is one single consolidated binary that can be used to boot the system (2.1.0 is named as asr1000rp1-adventerprisek9.02.01.00.122-33.XNA.bin). Subpackages are smaller binaries that can be booted (so to speak) and updated in a modular fashion without updating the overall system software.

4. Besides ROMMON, Cisco IOS XE Software consists of seven subpackages. RP runs four, ESP runs one, and SIP runs two packages when booted in a modular fashion.

5. Dual IOS is a Cisco IOS XE Software innovation that enables you to run two copies of IOS (can be different versions) to have full NSF/SSO on a single-RP system: ASR 1002 and ASR 1004. ASR 1006 is a fully hardware redundant system with provision to have two RPs, and two ESPs, so it does not need dual IOS; instead, it runs RP-to-RP redundancy with one IOS instance running on each RP. This is the reason the ASR 1006 does not support running dual IOS, because the hardware packaging is designed to accommodate dual RPs instead.

Further Reading

Bulletins: Cisco ASR 1000 Series Aggregation Services Routers:
http://tinyurl.com/chyop4

Cisco ASR 1000 Cisco IOS XE Software download tool (requires a Cisco.com account):
http://tinyurl.com/cvzuyn

Chapter 8

Cisco ASR 1000 Initial Setup and Configuration

Now that you have a basic understanding of the ASR 1000 system hardware, software and IOS XE, this chapter covers the basics of platform boot and the initial configuration, and then delves deeper into other system aspects, such as in-service software upgrades (ISSU) and software modularity.

Booting the ASR 1000

One of the first things that you will notice as you rack the system is that every ASR 1000 chassis comes with dual power supplies, DC and AC. Keep in mind that these power supplies have different form-factor and power ratings; therefore, they are not interchangeable across chassis. Power connectors on all chassis use right-angle connectors to avoid accidental disconnect. The ASR 1002 and ASR 1004 use a 15A service connector, whereas the ASR 1006 uses a 20A service connector.

The ASR 1000 system can run off of a single power supply or Power Entry Module (PEM). Fans on each power supply are powered through the midplane so that even if power fails to one power supply, its fan will remain functional as long as the other PEM is still receiving power. The system will not shut down with one fan failure. If more than one fan fails or one of the PEMs is taken out, however, the system will shut down within 5 minutes to avoid overheating the system. The revolutions per minute (RPM) of the fans is controlled through software and can be raised as high as 7000. Upon system powerup, fans default to 100 percent duty cycle until the system can fully boot and the software can recognize the ambient temperature and take control of fan speed accordingly.

As established in previous chapters, an ASR 1000 system consists of three major components: the Route Processor (RP), Embedded Service Processor (ESP), and Shared Interface Processor (SIP). The ASR 1000 builds upon a flexible system architecture that allows various combination of those major components in a single system. However, you still need to understand the caveats involved. Table 8-1 uses all available systems as examples and identifies the valid (and supported) combinations.

Table 8-1 *ASR 1000 System Valid Configurations*

ASR 1000 System	RP/ESP/SIP	Valid
ASR 1002-F	Fixed, single, or dual IOSD daemon (IOSD)	N/A
ASR 1002	1 x ESP-5 or ESP-10 (1 RP1 and 1 SIP-10 are embedded), single or dual IOS daemon (IOSD)	Yes.
ASR 1004	1 x ESP-10 or higher 1 x RP1/RP2 or higher (single or dual IOSD) 1 or 2 x SIP-10 or higher	Yes.
ASR 1006	1 or 2 x ESP-10 or higher 1 or 2 x RP1/RP2 or higher 1-3 x SIP-10 or higher	Yes.
ASR 1006	1 or 2 RP1/RP2 or higher (with dual IOSD)	No, dual IOSD is supported only on ASR 1002/ASR 1004 systems.

eUSB (part number M-ASR1K-EUSB-1GB; that is, NVRAM and bootflash in the system are field replaceable), although no upgrade is available for RP1. The DRAM on RP, however, is upgradable from 2 to 4 GB with part number M-ASR1K-RP1-4GB. The default ASR 1002 setup has 4 GB of RP DRAM, and therefore no upgrade is required.

When the system is powered up for the first time, it boots with the default image (last release ASR 1000 image) that comes with the router. Using the command-line interface (CLI), you can set the confreg value to 0x0 to reload the router and go back to ROMMON to change some necessary ROMMON parameters as per the network requirements.

Example 8-1 illustrates the ROMMON options.

Example 8-1 *ROMMON Options*

```
System Bootstrap, Version 12.2(33r)XN1, RELEASE SOFTWARE (fc1)
Technical Support: http://www.cisco.com/techsupport
Copyright (c) 2007 by cisco Systems, Inc.
Compiled Tue 20-Nov-07 17:43 by cii
Current image running: Boot ROM0
Last reset cause: LocalSoft
ASR1000-RP1 platform with 4194303 Kbytes of main memory
rommon 1 > ?
alias                   set and display aliases command
boot                    boot up an external process
break                   set/show/clear the breakpoint
confreg                 configuration register utility
```

```
context             display the context of a loaded image
cookie              display contents of cookie PROM in hex
dev                 list the device table
dir                 list files in file system
dis                 display instruction stream
frame               print out a selected stack frame
help                monitor builtin command help
history             monitor command history
meminfo             main memory information
repeat              repeat a monitor command
reset               system reset
set                 display the monitor variables
showmon             display currently selected ROM monitor
stack               produce a stack trace
sync                write monitor environment to NVRAM
sysret              print out info from last system return
unalias             unset an alias
unset               unset a monitor variable
```

The ROMMON system variables most often used by router administrators are as follows:

- **boot:** To start booting of an IOS image from the ROMMON CLI
- **set:** To set the value of ROMMON variables
- **sync:** To save the ROMMON variables to NVRAM

Example 8-2 shows the ROMMON variable used to boot the system using TFTP.

Example 8-2 *ROMMON Variable to Boot the System Using TFTP*

```
rommon 2 > set
PS1=rommon ! >
IP_SUBNET_MASK=255.255.0.0
IP_ADDRESS=2.1.35.5
DEFAULT_GATEWAY=2.1.0.1
TFTP_SERVER=2.8.54.2
TFTP_FILE=asr1000rp1-advipservicesk9.02.00.00.122-33.XN.bin
```

The highlighted variables in Example 8-2 need to be set as per the given network, and management Ethernet (Gi0) on the RP needs to be connected:

- **IP_ADDRESS:** Valid IP address routable in the network.
- **IP_SUBNET_MASK:** Valid IP subnet mask for the IP address.
- **DEFAULT_GATEWAY:** Valid default gateway for the IP subnet.

- **TFTP_SERVER:** TFTP server IP address that is reachable via the previously mentioned IP address.
- **TFTP_FILE:** File that's available via the TFTP server (with directory structure). It is not mandatory to set this but is highly recommended to point to a specific directory/file.

Once set, all you need to do is issue a **boot** command from a ROMMON prompt pointing to **tftp:** to start the image download into RP DRAM and eventual execution.

> **Note** You can only boot the consolidated package via TFTP boot. Once booted, a snapshot can be taken, and the system subsequently can be booted in modular fashion.

The boot sequence is as follows:

Step 1. ROMMON does the Power On Self-Test (POST).

Step 2. The ASR 1000 image is located and system starts booting up (either manually by the administrator or based on the configuration register and boot system CLI.)

Step 3. The IOS XE kernel is among the first pieces of software that boots.

Step 4. Once IOS XE kernel is booted up, the IOS instance is started.

Step 5. Interface Ethernet Out of Band Channel0 (EOBC0) comes up, followed by Linux Shared Memory Punt Interface0 (lsmpi0), which are used for Inter-Process Communication (IPC) and punt traffic, respectively.

Example 8-3 shows the EOBC and lsmpi interfaces coming up.

Example 8-3 *EOBC/lsmpi Interface Initialization*

```
*Jun 16 14:39:45.388: %LINEPROTO-5-UPDOWN: Line protocol on Interface EOBC0,
  changed state to up
*Jun 16 14:39:45.388: %LINEPROTO-5-UPDOWN: Line protocol on Interface Lsmpi0,
  changed state to up
*Jun 16 14:56:17.884: %LINK-3-UPDOWN: SIP0/2: Interface EOBC0/1, changed state to
  up
*Jun 16 14:56:10.670: %LINK-3-UPDOWN: SIP0/0: Interface EOBC0/1, changed state to
  up
*Jun 16 14:56:14.483: %LINK-3-UPDOWN: SIP0/1: Interface EOBC0/1, changed state to
  up
```

At this time, ESP and SIP start downloading their software.

Example 8-4 shows that the QuantumFlow Processor (QFP)microcode is initialized and booted.

Example 8-4 *QFP Microcode Initialization/Boot*

```
Jun 16 14:39:21.185: %CPPHA-7-SYSREADY: F1: cpp_ha:  CPP client process FMAN-FP (5
  of 5) ready.
*Jun 16 14:39:21.466: %CPPHA-7-START: F1: cpp_ha:  CPP 0 preparing image
  /usr/cpp/bin/cpp-mcplo-ucode
*Jun 16 14:39:21.721: %CPPHA-7-START: F1: cpp_ha:  CPP 0 startup init image
  /usr/cpp/bin/cpp-mcplo-ucode
```

Initial Cisco ASR 1000 Configuration

The system comes up with a blank configuration the first time it boots, as shown in Example 8-5.

Example 8-5 *Gigabit Ethernet Management Interface Placement upon Initial Boot*

```
Router# show ip vrf interfaces Mgmt-intf
Interface              IP-Address      VRF                              Protocol
Gi0                    unassigned      Mgmt-intf                        up
```

The first thing that you will notice here is the definition of the "Mgmt-intf" VPN Routing and Forwarding (VRF) instance (as always, this is case sensitive), which includes the RP Mgmtport seen as GigabitEthernet0 (Gi0) in the CLI.

Note The management Ethernet interface is not a general interface that is routable and does not support transit packets. The management VRF needs to be explicitly specified in all commands that need to connect over the management Ethernet interface. Note that traffic cannot traverse between Gi0- and SPA-based interfaces.

Next, assign the Gi0 interface an IP address, and set the default route in the VRF, using the following command:

```
ip route vrf Mgmt-intf 0.0.0.0 0.0.0.0 gateway_ip_address
```

The default route or route to the Mgmt-intf gateway must be defined within the VRF.

Next, set the TFTP source interface to Gi0 for file transfers. Make sure that all TFTP traffic originating from the router is sourced from Gi0:

```
ip tftp source-interface gigabitEthernet 0
```

Note Make sure that config-register is set to 0x2102 if you would like subsequent boot off of bootflash (recommended) or USB without going back to ROMMON.

As noted in earlier chapters, the base operating system for all system boards is Linux. Therefore, it is possible in the system to connect to ESPs and SIPs via the RP console by using a platform-specific CLI command. This is basically done via in-band Ethernet Out of Band Channel (EOBC).

Example 8-6 shows the platform-specific command to attach to a shell on the ESP and SIP in the system.

Example 8-6 *Determining How to Shell into Linux for Respective Hardware Components*

```
Router# request platform software system shell ?
  0    SPA-Inter-Processor slot 0
  1    SPA-Inter-Processor slot 1
  2    SPA-Inter-Processor slot 2
  F0   Embedded-Service-Processor slot 0
  F1   Embedded-Service-Processor slot 1
  FP   Embedded-Service-Processor
  R0   Route-Processor slot 0
  R1   Route-Processor slot 1
  RP   Route-Processor
```

Example 8-7 shows the connection to the active RP's shell and displays the directory structure.

Example 8-7 *Screen Output as a User Shells into Linux*

```
ASR1006# request platform software system shell r0
ASR-3# request platform software system shell r0
Activity within this shell can jeopardize the functioning of the system.
Are you sure you want to continue? [y/n]y

2009/05/13 23:56:29 : Shell access was granted to user <anon>; Trace file: ,
  /harddisk/tracelogs/system_shell_R0.log.20090513235629
***********************************************************************
Activity within this shell can jeopardize the functioning
of the system.
Use this functionality only under supervision of Cisco Support.

Session will be logged to:
  harddisk:tracelogs/system_shell_R0.log.20090513235629
***********************************************************************
Terminal type 'network' unknown.  Assuming vt100
[Router_RP_0:/]$ [ASR1006_RP_0:/]$ ls -la
total 40
drwxr-xr-x    19 904735    25      0 Jun 16 14:55 .
drwxr-xr-x    19 904735    25      0 Jun 16 14:55 ..
-rw-r--r--     1 root    root      0 Jun 16 14:55 .autofsck
```

```
-rw-r--r--    1 904735    25    486 Jan  1  1970 .pkgset
drwxr-xr-x    2 root    root      0 Jun 16 14:54 auto
drwxr-xr-x    2 904735    25      0 Jun 16 14:55 bin
drwxr-xr-x    8 root    root   4096 Jun 16 16:36 bootflash
-rwxrwxrwx    1 904735    25  21572 Jan  1  1970 common
lrwxrwxrwx    1 root    root     10 Jun 16 14:54 config -> /bootflash
drwxrwxrwt    6 root    root  14000 Jun 16 14:56 dev
lrwxrwxrwx    1 root    root     10 Jun 16 14:54 disk0 -> /vol/disk0
drwxr-xr-x   15 904735    25      0 Jun 16 14:55 etc
lrwxrwxrwx    1 root    root     13 Jun 16 14:54 harddisk -> /misc/scratch
lrwxrwxrwx    1 root    root     33 Jun 16 14:55 issu -> /tmp/sw/rp/0/0/rp_base/
  munt/issu
drwxr-xr-x    3 904735    25      0 Jun 16 14:55 lib
-rwxrwxrwx    1 904735    25   4071 Jan  1  1970 lkern_init
drwxr-xr-x    2 root    root      0 Jun 16 14:54 misc
drwxr-xr-x    3 root    root      0 Jun 16 14:54 mnt
dr-xr-xr-x  140 root    root      0 Jan  1  1970 proc
-rwxrwxrwx    1 904735    25   1077 Jan  1  1970 rommon_to_env
drwx------    2 root    root      0 Jan  1  1970 root
drwxr-xr-x    2 904735    25      0 Jun 16 14:55 sbin
drwxr-xr-x   10 root    root      0 Jan  1  1970 sys
drwxr-xr-x    2 root    root      0 Jun 16 14:55 tftp
drwxr-xr-x   14 root    root      0 Jun 16 16:36 tmp
lrwxrwxrwx    1 root    root      9 Jun 16 14:54 usb0 -> /vol/usb0
lrwxrwxrwx    1 root    root      9 Jun 16 14:54 usb1 -> /vol/usb1
drwxr-xr-x    7 904735    25      0 Jun 16 14:55 usr
drwxr-xr-x   10 root    root      0 Jun 16 14:55 var
drwxr-xr-x    3 root    root      0 Jun 16 14:55 vol
```

Note The **system** option will become available for the **request platform software** command only after you enter the **service internal** command in releases earlier than 2.2.3 and configure **platform shell** in releases starting with 2.3.0. This is done to ensure that this action is being taken deliberately.

Understanding the Cisco ASR 1000 File System Structure

Refer to Example 8-7 for the following detailed look at the Linux directory structure. In IOS XE, the main system flash is divided into several partitions/regions:

- **/boot:** Contains bootable images and SW packages for RP, SIP, and ESP
- **/config:** Contains latest saved IOS configuration

- **/config-backup:** Contains backup copies of IOS configuration files
- **/crash:** Contains crashinfo files for RP

Via an optional rotating/solid-state media disk, additional partitions may be made available:

- **/swap:** One or more swap files
- **/harddisk:** Contains crashinfo files for SIP
- **/harddisk/tracelogs:** Contains system event log files (more storage available than logging on system flash)

The recommended way to shut down an RP (reload the RP for safe removal from chassis) is to gracefully shut down via the following platform-specific command:

```
ASR1006# hw-module slot r0 reload
```

Online insertion and removal is supported and doable even for RP. To avoid the file system corruption that might take place on the RP during that event, however, this is not recommended. The system can self-heal in those cases and will try to autocorrect.

Note You can also reload any system field-replacable unit (FRU) (that is, RP, ESP or SIP) using the **hw-module reload** command, but reload of the active RP using the **hw-module** command is not allowed.

Summary

This chapter discussed first-time boot and the initial configuration of the ASR 1000 to have a stable system started. This chapter identified valid hardware and software combinations and the Linux file system structure. The next chapter covers the system ISSU and walks through different real-world scenarios.

Chapter Review Questions

1. Do the fans in the given Power Entry Module (PEM) continue to function if power to it is cut off while other PEM is still connected to power source?
2. How long will the system stay up after more than one fan failure?
3. Is booting off of an HDD supported?
4. What is the **platform shell** command used for on the ASR 1000?
5. Is access to the system shell protected?

Answers

1. Yes, fans in the PEM continue to function in this scenario.
2. The system will shut down within 5 minutes (not configurable, to avoid permanent damage to the system) in this case.
3. Booting from the HDD is not supported (although this is not enforced, and so it still continues to work).
4. The **platform shell** command is required starting from IOS XE Software Release 2.3.0 before you can enter into the Linux shell on RP, ESP, or SIP. If you attempt to enter the shell without entering the command, the system will give you the following error message:

   % Error: Shell access is not available
5. Yes. System shell access is only available after entering **system internal** or **platform shell** where applicable, which can only be done from router global configuration mode.

Further Reading

Cisco ASR1000 Frequently Asked Questions: http://tinyurl.com/r46dyt

Cisco ASR 1000 Series Routers Power Up and Initial Configuration: http://tinyurl.com/r5dw9q

Troubleshooting Initial Startup Problems: http://tinyurl.com/o4hws7

Chapter 9

In-Service Software Upgrade and Software Modularity

No discussion of system high availability is complete without discussing in-service software upgrade (ISSU). One of the biggest challenges faced today in the WAN is availability in the face of vulnerabilities, bugs, outages, or the introduction of new services. All these events require upgrading at least a subset of system software (and at most the entire system software) without impacting the services.

The Cisco ASR 1000 supports IOS ISSU across all the systems, while maintaining the backward compatibility with the older uniprocessor systems booting off of IOS as one monolithic binary file. This chapter covers the need for ISSU and ISSU procedures for the ASR 1000.

Why ISSU Is Needed

It is almost a universal operational fact that software is more prone to failure than hardware. The sections that follow briefly explain the most common operational and business reasons for having ISSU support. ISSU is a user-controlled and -initiated process for upgrading or even downgrading system software.

Operational Benefits

ISSU brings nonstop network operations to unified WANs, where all your IP applications are converged and links are aggregated. Notable operational benefits include the following:

- Almost complete elimination of planned network downtime
- Easier adoption of newer hardware/software
- Flexible application of existing hardware/software bug fixes
- Flexible timing for the network maintenance window

- Easier fallback to last known good software image to minimize upgrade risk
- Reduction of operational costs

Business Benefits

Apart from most of the operational benefits that directly affect the operational expense (OPEX), there are many other obvious and subtle benefits of ISSU. Salient benefits include the following:

- Business continuity resulting in more productivity
- Easier adoption of newer IP services for continuous top-line growth
- Network security due to the timely application of vulnerability fixes
- Maintenance windows during regular business hours

ASR 1000 ISSU Details

This section examines ISSU in more detail, especially as it pertains to the ASR 1000 platform. This discussion follows a methodical fashion, dividing the overall ISSU information into two larger areas:

- ISSU on the ASR 1006 system (with dual Route Processor [RP] and Embedded Service Processor [ESP]) for using the consolidated package
- ISSU on the ASR 1002 or ASR 1004 system (with dual IOS daemon [IOSD]) and the ASR 1006 system for IOSD and subpackages

Table 9-1 provides a snapshot of the various subpackages and their expected outcome during ISSU across systems and configurations (redundant or nonredundant).

The following assumptions apply to our overall ISSU discussion in the rest of this chapter:

- The system is running image A, and going to image B in the case of IOSD ISSU.
- Both image A and image B are present on the active RP's and the standby RP's bootflash (where applicable).
- The system configuration register is set to 0x2 (that is, autoboot via the **boot system** command).
- In the case of the dual RP (ASR 1006) and the dual IOSD (ASR 1002/1004), the full SSO state is already reached (verifiable via **show redund state**); that is, the standby RP or standby IOSD is in the standby hot state.
- R0/F0 and R1/F1 are active and standby RPs/ESPs, respectively.
- No other ISSU is in progress.

Table 9-1 *ASR 1000 Subpackages and ISSU Impact Summary*

Subpackage	Cisco ASR 1002/1004	Cisco ASR 1006
RPBase (Linux OS, and a few loadable modules)	This contains the underlying Linux kernel, so it cannot be upgraded "in service." *Impact*: Requires reboot.	The standby RP in the Cisco ASR 1006 chassis can be upgraded and then switched over to active mode "in service." *Impact*: Requires RP switchover; no transit packet loss.
RPControl (RP IOS XE managers)	Can be upgraded "in service." *Impact*: No transit packet loss.	Can be upgraded "in service" on both the active and standby RP. *Impact*: No transit packet loss.
RPAccess (RP access software for SSH/Telnet in IOS XE)	Can be upgraded "in service." *Impact*: No transit packet loss.	Can be upgraded "in service" on both the active and standby RP. *Impact*: No transit packet loss.
RPIOS (actual IOS package)	Can be upgraded "in service" if the system is running in dual IOS mode. *Impact*: Requires IOS processes switchover; no transit packet loss.	Can be upgraded on the standby RP and switched over active "in service." Requires RP (IOS) switchover. *Impact*: No transit packet loss.
ESPBase (Linux OS, and complete software for ESP in one package)	Upgrade causes a complete loss of local state (that is, statistics, stateful FW/NAT) on the ESP "in service" affecting forwarding interruption until upgrade is completed. Router is still accessible. *Impact*: No reboot required.	Upgrade causes a complete loss of local state (that is, statistics, stateful FW/NAT) on the ESP being upgraded and will result in a small traffic interruption when switching to the standby ESP. *Impact*: Minimal transit packet interruption < 50 ms; no RP switchover required.

continues

Table 9-1 *ASR 1000 Subpackages and ISSU Impact Summary*

Subpackage	**Cisco ASR 1002/1004**	**Cisco ASR 1006**
SIPBase (Linux OS, and IOS XE software managers)	Upgrades cause a complete loss of local state on the affected SIP; however, the other SIP in the Cisco ASR 1004 router is unaffected by this activity. *Impact*: Hitless for the other SIP in the Cisco ASR 1004 router not being upgraded.	Upgrades cause a complete loss of local state on the affected SIP; however, other SIPs are unaffected by this activity. SIPBase upgrades take place only if initiated from the active RP. *Impact*: Hitless for other SIPs not being upgraded.
SIPSPA (SPA drivers)	Upgrades cause a specific SPA to completely reboot and affect service. SIPSPA can be upgraded on a per-SPA basis. *Impact*: Hitless for other SPAs not being upgraded.	Upgrades cause a specific SPA to completely reboot and affect service. SIPSPA can be upgraded on a per-SPA basis. SIPSPA upgrades take place only if initiated from the active RP. *Impact*: Hitless for other SPAs not being upgraded.

Note *Legacy* refers to **issu** commands throughout the text, while *native* refers to ASR 1000 platform-specific **request platform** commands. Neither is preferred over the other, but the legacy **issu** commands are used to maintain backward compatibility, because they are available across various Cisco IOS-based platforms, such as Cisco 7600 series routers. The examples in this chapter use the legacy **issu** commands.

Example 9-1 illustrates an ASR 1006 system with full SSO state reached between the two RPs. This will be the baseline state throughout the chapter before starting an ISSU process.

Example 9-1 *ASR 1006 System with RPs in Active and Hot Standby States*

```
ASR1006# show redundancy states
       my state = 13 -ACTIVE
     peer state = 8  -STANDBY HOT
           Mode = Duplex
        Unit ID = 48

Redundancy Mode (Operational) = sso
Redundancy Mode (Configured)  = sso
Redundancy State              = sso
     Maintenance Mode = Disabled
    Manual Swact = enabled
 Communications = Up
```

```
   client count = 65
 client_notification_TMR = 30000 milliseconds
           RF debug mask = 0x0
ASR1006# show platform
Chassis type: ASR1006

Slot      Type                State                 Insert time (ago)
--------- ------------------- --------------------- -----------------
0         ASR1000-SIP10       ok                    00:04:12
 0/1      SPA-5X1GE-V2        ok                    00:02:58
 0/3      SPA-8X1GE-V2        ok                    00:02:58
R0        ASR1000-RP1         ok, active            00:04:12
R1        ASR1000-RP1         ok, standby           00:04:12
```

Note As stated previously, the ASR 1006 system does not support dual IOSD configuration. Therefore, for doing IOSD ISSU, you must have a dual RP/ESP system.

A Consolidated Package ISSU on a Fully Redundant 6RU

The example in this section starts with a fully redundant ASR 1006 system, the one that has two RPs and ESPs in it, both up and running. In this example the system is booted using the consolidated package. Consolidated package booting is just about the same as booting a Cisco 7200VXR series router (that is, off of a single binary file). Begin by looking at both the active RP's and the standby RP's bootflash.

Example 9-2 shows the contents of bootflash before starting the ISSU.

Example 9-2 *Both Binary IOS Images Exist on the System Bootflash to Ensure That They Are Locally Available Throughout the ISSU Process*

```
ASR1006# dir bootflash:
Directory of bootflash:/
    12  -rw-   208208076  Jan 16 2001 11:00:12 +00:00  image-A.bin
    13  -rw-   206483660  Jan 16 2001 11:00:58 +00:00  image-B.bin

ASR1006# dir stby-bootflash:
Directory of stby-bootflash:/

    12  -rw-   208208076  Jan 16 2001 10:59:08 +00:00  image-A.bin
    13  -rw-   206483660  Jan 16 2001 11:00:38 +00:00  image-B.bin
ASR1006# show bootvar
BOOT variable = bootflash:image-A.bin,12;
CONFIG_FILE variable =
BOOTLDR variable does not exist
```

```
Configuration register is 0x2

ASR1006-stby# show bootvar
BOOT variable = bootflash:image-A.bin,12;
CONFIG_FILE variable =
BOOTLDR variable does not exist
Configuration register is 0x2

ASR1006# show issu state detail
--- Starting installation state synchronization ---
Finished installation state synchronization
No ISSU operation is in progress
```

ISSU on 6RU System (with Dual RP and ESP) for IOSD Using Legacy `issu` Commands

At a high level, the following are the steps that you need to take for ISSU using the legacy **issu** commands:

Step 1. Enter the **issu loadversion** command, which allows you to load the image B, update the boot variable, and reboot the standby RP with image B loaded. Remember that this doesn't result in any traffic disruption.

Step 2. Enter the **issu runversion** command, which allows you to actually reload the active RP; at this time, the standby RP will become active with image B while RP0 (the new standby) comes back up with image A. This command will also cause a rolling upgrade of the ESPs, where the first standby ESP will reboot and come back with the updated software, followed by a reboot of the active ESP (and hence the former standby takes over and becomes active). Issuing this command also causes a reload of all the SIPs/SPAs in the system (so a traffic disruption will occur).

Step 3. Enter the **issu acceptversion** command, which allows you to stop only the rollback timer. At this time, your active RP is running image B, while the standby RP is running image A.

Step 4. Enter the **issu commitversion** command, which allows you to set the boot variables on both the active and standby RP to image B in addition to adding the **boot system** command on both RPs. After issuing this command from the active RP, you can complete the ISSU by issuing the **hw-module slot** *standby RP*> **reload** command. Once completed, the standby RP will come up with the image B loaded, too.

Note Use the **issu set rollback-timer** command in config mode to change the rollback timer setting. For example, you might use this command if you want some extra time after the **issu loadversion** is executed. Extra time might be required in the cases of routers with large configurations. You can always view the amount of time left using the **show issu rollback-timer** command.

The examples that follow demonstrate the procedures outlined in the preceding list and show how the various commands are used during these steps.

Example 9-3 outlines the execution of the **issu loadversion** command, along with verification of the configuration by way of various **show** commands.

Example 9-3 *Loading the Target Consolidated Package (image-B.bin) onto the Standby RP*

```
ASR1006# issu loadversion rp 1 file stby-bootflash:image-B.bin
--- Starting installation state synchronization ---
Finished installation state synchronization
--- Starting file path checking ---
Finished file path checking
--- Starting system installation readiness checking ---
Finished system installation readiness checking
--- Starting installation changes ---
Setting up image to boot on next reset
Starting automatic rollback timer
Finished installation changes
SUCCESS: Software will now load.

ASR1006# show platform
Chassis type: ASR1006
Slot      Type                State                 Insert time (ago)
--------- ------------------- --------------------- -------------
0          ASR1000-SIP10       ok                    00:16:16
 0/1       SPA-5X1GE-V2        ok                    00:15:02
 0/3       SPA-8X1GE-V2        ok                    00:15:02
R0         ASR1000-RP1         ok, active            00:16:16
R1         ASR1000-RP1         init, standby         00:16:16

ASR1006# sh plat
Chassis type: MCP6RU

Slot      Type                State                 Insert time (ago)
--------- ------------------- --------------------- -------------
0          ASR1000-SIP10       ok                    00:18:46
 0/1       SPA-5X1GE-V2        ok                    00:17:32
 0/3       SPA-8X1GE-V2        ok                    00:17:32
R0         ASR1000-RP1         ok, active            00:18:46
```

```
R1        ASR1000-RP1          ok, standby           00:18:46

ASR1006# show bootvar
BOOT variable = bootflash:image-A.bin,12;
CONFIG_FILE variable =
BOOTLDR variable does not exist
Configuration register is 0x2

ASR1006# show issu state detail
--- Starting installation state synchronization ---
Finished installation state synchronization
Slot being modified: R1
  Loadversion time: 20010116 11:34:37 on con 0
  Last operation: loadversion
  Rollback: automatic, remaining time before rollback: 00:38:33
  Original (rollback) image: bootflash:image-A.bin
  Running image: bootflash:image-B.bin
  Operating mode: sso, terminal state reached

ASR1006-stby# show version
Cisco IOS Software, IOS-XE Software (PPC_LINUX_IOSD-ADVIPSERVICESK9-M),
  Experimental Version 12.2(20080327:084220) [BLD-
  v122_33_xna_asr_rls1_throttle.MCP_CRYPTO_RLS1_THROTTLE_BLD_20080327 104]
Copyright (c) 1986-2008 by Cisco Systems, Inc.
Compiled Thu 27-Mar-08 01:44 by mcpre
ROM: IOS-XE ROMMON
 ASR1006 uptime is 19 minutes
Uptime for this control processor is 5 minutes
System returned to ROM by reload
System image file is "bootflash:image-B.bin"
Last reload reason: EHSA standby down

ASR1006-stby# show bootvar
BOOT variable = bootflash:image-A.bin,12;
CONFIG_FILE variable =
BOOTLDR variable does not exist
Configuration register is 0x2

ASR1006-stby# show redundancy states
       my state = 8  -STANDBY HOT
     peer state = 13 -ACTIVE
           Mode = Duplex
        Unit ID = 49
Redundancy Mode (Operational) = sso
Redundancy Mode (Configured)  = sso
```

```
Redundancy State              = sso
     Maintenance Mode = Disabled
    Manual Swact = cannot be initiated from this the standby unit
 Communications = Up
   client count = 66
 client_notification_TMR = 30000 milliseconds
           RF debug mask = 0x0
```

Example 9-4 outlines the execution of the **issu runversion** command, along with verification of the configuration by way of various **show** commands.

Example 9-4 *Running the Consolidated Package That Was Loaded in the Previous Step*

```
ASR1006# issu runversion
--- Starting installation state synchronization ---
Finished installation state synchronization
Initiating active RP failover
SUCCESS: Standby RP will now become active
```

At the conclusion of the **issu runversion** command execution, the former standby becomes the active RP, with image B running on it, and the active RP will reboot into the newly standby state running image A.

Example 9-5 shows the set of commands that you can use to verify that the former standby RP is now running the target image (image-B.bin), whereas the boot system is still pointing to image-A.bin

Example 9-5 *Current System State of the System After Executing Commands in Examples 9-3 and 9-4*

```
ASR1006# show run | i boot
boot-start-marker
boot system bootflash:image-A.bin
boot-end-marker

ASR1006# show issu state detail
Slot being modified: R1
  Loadversion time: 20010116 11:34:37 on con 0
  Last operation: runversion
  Rollback: automatic, remaining time before rollback: 00:11:23
  Original (rollback) image: bootflash:image-A.bin
  Running image: bootflash:image-B.bin
  Operating mode: sso, terminal state reached
  Notes: runversion executed, active RP is being provisioned
```

Now, take a look at the new standby RP console shown in Example 9-6.

Example 9-6 *Verifying That the Active RP Still Has the Bootsystem Variable Pointing to Pld image-A, Although It Is Running image-B.bin*

```
ASR1006-stby# show version
Cisco IOS Software, IOS-XE Software (PPC_LINUX_IOSD-ADVENTERPRISEK9-M),
  Experimental Version 12.2(20080327:084220) [BLD-
  v122_33_xna_asr_rls1_throttle.MCP_CRYPTO_RLS1_THROTTLE_BLD_20080327 106]
Copyright (c) 1986-2008 by Cisco Systems, Inc.
Compiled Thu 27-Mar-08 01:44 by mcpre
ROM: IOS-XE ROMMON
 ASR1006 uptime is 50 minutes
Uptime for this control processor is 11 minutes
System returned to ROM by reload
System image file is "bootflash:image-A.bin"
Last reload reason: RF failure to send prog message
```

Note You can also use the **show version installed** command to get a detailed view of packages that the system is running. On a related note, if you are using the native platform CLI to perform ISSU, it doesn't start a rollback timer unless the **auto-rollback** option is used in the **request platform software package install** command line.

Example 9-7 outlines the results of the **issu acceptversion** command to cancel the rollback timer on the active RP. At this stage, the active RP is running image B, although the boot variable still points to image A. Because the output shows the desired result, you can cancel the rollback timer at this time by using the **issu acceptversion** command.

Example 9-7 *Stopping the Rollback Timer*

```
ASR1006# issu acceptversion
Cancelling rollback timer
SUCCESS: Rollback timer cancelled

ASR1006# show issu state detail
Slot being modified: R1
  Loadversion time: 20010116 11:34:37 on con 0
  Last operation: acceptversion
  Rollback: inactive, timer canceled by acceptversion
  Original (rollback) image: bootflash:image-A.bin
  Running image: bootflash:image-B.bin
  Operating mode: sso, terminal state reached
  Notes: runversion executed, active RP is being provisioned
```

Example 9-8 shows the final step, executing the **issu commitversion** command on the active RP, which clears the ISSU state on the active RP and sets the boot variables on both RPs to image B.

Example 9-8 *Stopping the Rollback Timer (Which Can Also Be Done via the* **issu acceptversion** *Command), and Committing the ISSU Upgrade Process*

```
ASR1006# issu commit
--- Starting installation changes ---
Cancelling rollback timer
Saving image changes
Finished installation changes
Building configuration...
[OK]
SUCCESS: version committed: bootflash:image-B.bin

ASR1006# show bootvar
BOOT variable = bootflash:image-B.bin,12;bootflash:image-A.bin,12;
CONFIG_FILE variable =
BOOTLDR variable does not exist
Configuration register is 0x2
Standby BOOT variable = bootflash:image-B.bin,12;bootflash:image-A.bin,12
Standby CONFIG_FILE variable =
Standby BOOTLDR variable does not exist
Standby Configuration register is 0x2

ASR1006# show run ¦ i boot
boot-start-marker
boot system bootflash:image-B.bin
boot system bootflash:image-A.bin
boot-end-marker
```

Finally, you need to reload the standby RP to boot into image B, as demonstrated in Example 9-9.

Example 9-9 *Reloading RP0 (New Standby RP)*

```
! ON ACTIVE RP:

ASR1006# show platform
Chassis type: ASR1006

Slot      Type                State                 Insert time (ago)
--------- ------------------- --------------------- -----------------
0         ASR1000-SIP10       ok                    01:05:57
```

```
 0/1        SPA-5X1GE-V2        ok                        00:42:28
 0/3        SPA-8X1GE-V2        ok                        00:42:25
R0          ASR1000-RP1         ok, standby               01:05:57
R1          ASR1000-RP1         ok, active                01:05:57

ASR1006# hw-module slot r0 reload
```

Subpackage ISSU on a Fully Redundant 6RU

At a high level, the following are the steps that you need to complete to enable subpackage ISSU using the legacy **issu** commands. The assumption is that the existing IOS XE (image A) is loaded in the subpackages fashion (that is, booted off of the *packages.conf* file):

Step 1. Expand image B on both the active and RP standby media (bootflash).

Step 2. Enter the **issu loadversion** command, which allows you to load the IOS subpackage inside image B on the standby RP.

Step 3. Enter the **hw-module slot r1 reload** command to reload the standby RP.

Step 4. Upgrade SIP/SPA subpackages on the active and standby RPs (if so desired). This will result in traffic disruption.

Step 5. Upgrade the RP-specific subpackages on the active RP.

Step 6. Upgrade the ESP-specific package on the active ESP.

Step 7. Perform the redundancy switchover, and fail over to the former standby.

Note No traffic disruption occurs in this process except when you want to upgrade the entire SIP or the SPA driver packages. Note that you can upgrade a single Half Height (HH) SPA, too, if necessary (for example, a bug fix affecting only one type of SPA).

Example 9-10 shows a snapshot of a system that has booted in a modular fashion.

Note You can use the **show version installed** command to display installed packages.

Example 9-10 *Confirming That Subpackages Are Running Properly*

```
ASR1006# show version running
  Package: Provisioning File, version: n/a, status: active
  File: bootflash:packages_1.conf, on: RP0
  Built: n/a, by: n/a
  File SHA1 checksum: c4fb69dea72370c25f9e41a58f91481a94423474
```

```
Package: rpbase, version: 02.02.00.122-33.XNB-20080415_010002-mcp_dev_2, status:
  active
  File: bootflash:asr1000rp1-rpbase.02.02.00.122-33.XNB-20080415_010002-
    mcp_dev_2.pkg, on: RP0
  Built: 2008-04-15_10.54, by: mcpre
  File SHA1 checksum: 3c0c2a37b4652dc935a7fb14a093f4b0dea5672a

Package: rpaccess-k9, version: 02.02.00.122-33.XNB-20080415_010002-mcp_dev_2,
  status: active
  File: bootflash:asr1000rp1-rpaccess-k9.02.02.00.122-33.XNB-20080415_010002-
    mcp_dev_2.pkg, on: RP0
  Built: 2008-04-15_10.54, by: mcpre
  File SHA1 checksum: 5e66c1ea0ffdc839800ca0f120051fcd5e1fe288

Package: rpcontrol, version: 02.02.00.122-33.XNB-20080415_010002-mcp_dev_2,
  status: active
  File: bootflash:asr1000rp1-rpcontrol.02.02.00.122-33.XNB-20080415_010002-
    mcp_dev_2.pkg, on: RP0/0
  Built: 2008-04-15_10.54, by: mcpre
  File SHA1 checksum: e244c412bfd3fd8a7dc1e12c6d71e3b88ddaeb02

Package: rpios-advipservicesk9, version: 02.02.00.122-33.XNB-20080415_010002-
  mcp_dev_2, status: active
  File: harddisk:asr1000rp1-rpios-advipservicesk9.02.02.00.122-33.XNB-
    20080415_010002-mcp_dev_2.pkg, on: RP0/0
  Built: 2008-04-15_10.54, by: mcpre
  File SHA1 checksum: 3dbbce130cb34e9d3998d771b70df54037aa1f07

Package: rpbase, version: 02.02.00.122-33.XNB-20080415_010002-mcp_dev_2, status:
  active
  File: harddisk:asr1000rp1-rpbase.02.02.00.122-33.XNB-20080415_010002-
    mcp_dev_2.pkg, on: RP1
  Built: 2008-04-15_10.54, by: mcpre
  File SHA1 checksum: 3c0c2a37b4652dc935a7fb14a093f4b0dea5672a
```

Example 9-11 shows the contents of the *packages.conf* file on the active RP. This file contains NFS, mount, and ISO directives. Note that this file is modified by the system itself, and there is no reason for the user to modify it.

Example 9-11 *Contents of the IOS XE Software Provisioning File, Also Known as* packages.conf

```
ASR1006# more bootflash:packages.conf
#! /usr/binos/bin/packages_conf.sh

sha1sum: c0d4d3566e5bcce8105be6f110bb1c02af403d06
```

```
# sha1sum above - used to verify that this file is not corrupted.

#
# package.conf: provisioned software file for build 2007-12-09_22.38
#
# NOTE: Editing this file by hand is not recommended. It is generated
#       as part of the build process, and is subject to boot-time
#       consistency checks. Automatically-produced package files are
#       guaranteed to pass those checks. Manually-maintained ones are
#       not. Because "nfs" and "mount" directives are processed first,
#       regardless of their position in the file, the recommended
#       approach is to keep a separate file containing JUST your
#       personal "nfs" and "mount" directives, and to append it to the
#       automatically-generated file.
#
#       Note further that when SHA-1 checksum verification is enabled,
#       you will NOT be able to alter this file without updating the
#       SHA-1 sum.

#
# This file can contain three types of entries:
#

# NFS directives (optional)
#     notes:    NFS directives are processed before all others (mount, iso).
#               Multiple NFS directives may appear so long as they do not
#               conflict — that is, specify the same source or mountpoint.
#     syntax:   nfs <IP ADDRESS>:<REMOTE_PATH> <LOCAL_MOUNTPOINT>
#     example:  nfs 127.0.0.1:/auto/some/nfs/path /auto/some/nfs/path
#

#
# mount directives (optional)
#     notes:    mount directives are processed after 'nfs' and before 'iso'.
#               One mount directive may appear for each F/S/B/P tuple
#     syntax:   mount FRU SLOT BAY    PACKAGE_NAME    LINUX_PATH
#     example:  mount rp 0 0 rp_base /auto/some/nfs/path/abs_soft/rp_base.ppc
#
#               The specified LINUX_PATH may be local [sata disk] or
#               reference the NFS mounts since they are processed first.
#
#               Mount directives cause the package-specific mount link to
#               be set to the specified path instead of to the mountpoint
#               in sw for the corresponding ISO.
```

```
#
# iso directives (mandatory)
#     notes:    iso directives are processed last: any package for which
#                a 'mount' directive does not appear will be mounted.
#                One iso directive may appear for each F/S/B/P tuple.
#     syntax:   iso FRU SLOT BAY   PACKAGE_NAME  PACKAGE_FILE.bin
#     example:  iso rp 0 0 rp_base rp_base.ppc.bin
#
#                PACKAGE_FILE.bin is a path relative to the packages.conf
#                file.  Although it supports sub-directories for development
#                purposes, in deployment the files will always be managed
#                as in the same directory as packages.conf so as to
#                guarantee that name collisions cannot occur.
#
# Note that the RP 0/1 distinction is a convenience for development
# and testing as it allows us to have a packages.conf describe a
# SW load that varies depending on whether the RP finds itself in
# slot 0 or 1.
#
# The ISSU process *must* update *both* RP slots simultaneously so that
# the RP will behave predictably whichever slot it finds itself on [e.g.,
# if package X is upgraded, and the RP is ejected and put into either
# slot of a new chassis, we expect to see the upgraded X without regard
# to slot].
#

iso    rp 0 0   rp_base       asr1000rp1-rpbase.02.00.00.122-33.XN.pkg
iso    rp 0 1   rp_base       asr1000rp1-rpbase.02.00.00.122-33.XN.pkg
iso    rp 0 0   rp_daemons    asr1000rp1-rpcontrol.02.00.00.122-33.XN.pkg
iso    rp 0 1   rp_daemons    asr1000rp1-rpcontrol.02.00.00.122-33.XN.pkg
iso    rp 0 0   rp_iosd       asr1000rp1-rpios-advipservicesk9.02.00.00.122-33.XN
  .pkg
iso    rp 0 1   rp_iosd       asr1000rp1-rpios-advipservicesk9.02.00.00.122-33.XN
  .pkg
iso    rp 0 0   rp_security   asr1000rp1-rpaccess-k9.02.00.00.122-33.XN.pkg
iso    rp 0 1   rp_security   asr1000rp1-rpaccess-k9.02.00.00.122-33.XN.pkg

iso    rp 1 0   rp_base       asr1000rp1-rpbase.02.00.00.122-33.XN.pkg
iso    rp 1 1   rp_base       asr1000rp1-rpbase.02.00.00.122-33.XN.pkg
iso    rp 1 0   rp_daemons    asr1000rp1-rpcontrol.02.00.00.122-33.XN.pkg
iso    rp 1 1   rp_daemons    asr1000rp1-rpcontrol.02.00.00.122-33.XN.pkg
iso    rp 1 0   rp_iosd       asr1000rp1-rpios-advipservicesk9.02.00.00.122-33.XN
  .pkg
iso    rp 1 1   rp_iosd       asr1000rp1-rpios-advipservicesk9.02.00.00.122-33.XN
  .pkg
```

```
iso    rp 1 0    rp_security    asr1000rp1-rpaccess-k9.02.00.00.122-33.XN.pkg
iso    rp 1 1    rp_security    asr1000rp1-rpaccess-k9.02.00.00.122-33.XN.pkg

iso    fp 0 0    fp              asr1000rp1-espbase.02.00.00.122-33.XN.pkg
iso    fp 1 0    fp              asr1000rp1-espbase.02.00.00.122-33.XN.pkg

iso    cc 0 0    cc              asr1000rp1-sipbase.02.00.00.122-33.XN.pkg
iso    cc 1 0    cc              asr1000rp1-sipbase.02.00.00.122-33.XN.pkg
iso    cc 2 0    cc              asr1000rp1-sipbase.02.00.00.122-33.XN.pkg

iso    cc 0 0    cc_spa         asr1000rp1-sipspa.02.00.00.122-33.XN.pkg
iso    cc 0 1    cc_spa         asr1000rp1-sipspa.02.00.00.122-33.XN.pkg
iso    cc 0 2    cc_spa         asr1000rp1-sipspa.02.00.00.122-33.XN.pkg
iso    cc 0 3    cc_spa         asr1000rp1-sipspa.02.00.00.122-33.XN.pkg

iso    cc 1 0    cc_spa         asr1000rp1-sipspa.02.00.00.122-33.XN.pkg
iso    cc 1 1    cc_spa         asr1000rp1-sipspa.02.00.00.122-33.XN.pkg
iso    cc 1 2    cc_spa         asr1000rp1-sipspa.02.00.00.122-33.XN.pkg
iso    cc 1 3    cc_spa         asr1000rp1-sipspa.02.00.00.122-33.XN.pkg

iso    cc 2 0    cc_spa         asr1000rp1-sipspa.02.00.00.122-33.XN.pkg
iso    cc 2 1    cc_spa         asr1000rp1-sipspa.02.00.00.122-33.XN.pkg
iso    cc 2 2    cc_spa         asr1000rp1-sipspa.02.00.00.122-33.XN.pkg
iso    cc 2 3    cc_spa         asr1000rp1-sipspa.02.00.00.122-33.XN.pkg
#
# -start- superpackage .pkginfo
#
# pkginfo: Name: rp_super
# pkginfo: BuildTime: 2007-12-09_22.38
# pkginfo: ReleaseDate: Sun 09-Dec-07 22:30
# pkginfo: .BuildArch: ppc
# pkginfo: RouteProcessor: rp1
# pkginfo: Platform: ASR1000
# pkginfo: User: klash
# pkginfo: PackageName: advipservicesk9
# pkginfo: Build: 02.00.00.122-33.XN
# pkginfo: .SupportedBoards: rp1
# pkginfo: .BuildPath: /auto/mcpbuilds/release/BLD-02.00.00/linkfarm/stage/hard/
  rp_super.ppc
# pkginfo:
#
# -end- superpackage .pkginfo
```

Note In Example 9-11, fp and cc simply refer to ESP and SIP components, respectively. It has a bit of history to it, where FP (forwarding processor) and CC (carrier card) are Cisco internal software lingo used to refer to ESP and SIP components.

Example 9-12 shows the expansion of the consolidated package downloaded from Cisco.com via the native **request platform** command.

Example 9-12 *The Consolidated Package, Once Downloaded onto Bootflash, Can Be Expanded via the Native* **request platform** *Command into Subpackages*

```
ASR1006# request platform software package expand file bootflash:image-B.bin to
  bootflash:temp verbose
Verifying parameters
... parameters verified
Validating package type
... package type validated
Copying package files
... package files copied
SUCCESS: Finished expanding all-in-one software package.
```

Repeat the preceding steps for the standby RP, so that you have all the subpackages expanded on the bootflash for both RPs and, alternatively, the hard disk drive (HDD).

Example 9-13 shows the expanded contents of image B onto the active RP's bootflash.

Example 9-13 *Viewing the Subpackages After Extraction into the bootflash:/temp Folder. Using a Folder Such as temp Is Recommended to Avoid Putting Many Files in the Root*

```
ASR1006# show bootflash:/temp
-#- --length-- ---------date/time--------- path
  1       4096 Jul 13 2008 12:46:43 +00:00 /bootflash/
  2      16384 Dec 10 2004 05:28:11 +00:00 /bootflash/lost+found
  3       4096 Dec 10 2004 05:29:10 +00:00 /bootflash/.rollback_timer
  4       4096 Dec 10 2004 05:29:42 +00:00 /bootflash/.installer
5   52064460 Feb 17 2005 03:10:37 +00:00 /bootflash/asr1000rp1-espbase.02.00.
 6   21833932 Feb 17 2005 03:11:01 +00:00 /bootflash/asr1000rp1-rpaccess-k9.02
 7   21516492 Feb 17 2005 03:11:37 +00:00 /bootflash/asr1000rp1-rpbase.02.00.0
 8   24965324 Feb 17 2005 03:12:01 +00:00 /bootflash/asr1000rp1-rpcontrol.02.0
 9   48451788 Feb 17 2005 03:12:44 +00:00 /bootflash/asr1000rp1-rpios-advipser
 10   36954316 Feb 17 2005 03:13:02 +00:00 /bootflash/asr1000rp1-sipbase.02.00.
 11   14782668 Feb 17 2005 03:13:34 +00:00 /bootflash/asr1000rp1-sipspa.02.00.0
 12       6225 Feb 17 2005 03:23:46 +00:00 /bootflash/packages.conf
```

Example 9-14 shows the results of executing the **issu loadversion** command on the active RP to upgrade the subpackages on the standby RP first, followed by a reload.

Example 9-14 *Upgrading All RP-Related Packages on the Standby RP*

```
ASR1006# issu loadversion rp 1 file stby-bootflash:temp/asr*rp*02.00.0.pkg
--- Starting installation state synchronization ---
Finished installation state synchronization
--- Starting file path checking ---
Finished file path checking
--- Starting image file verification ---
Checking image file names
Verifying image file locations
Locating image files and validating name syntax
Inspecting image file types
    WARNING: In-service installation of IOSD package
    WARNING: requires software redundancy on target RP
    WARNING: or on-reboot parameter
    WARNING: Automatically setting the on-reboot flag
    WARNING: In-service installation of RP Base package
    WARNING: requires software reboot of target RP
Processing image file constraints
Creating candidate provisioning file
Finished image file verification

--- Starting candidate package set construction ---
Verifying existing software set
Processing candidate provisioning file
Constructing working set for candidate package set
Constructing working set for running package set
Checking command output
Constructing merge of running and candidate packages
Finished candidate package set construction

--- Starting compatibility testing ---
Determining whether candidate package set is compatible
Determining whether installation is valid
Determining whether installation is valid ... skipped
Checking IPC compatibility for candidate software
Checking candidate package set infrastructure compatibility
Checking infrastructure compatibility with running software
Checking infrastructure compatibility with running software ... skipped
Checking package specific compatibility
Finished compatibility testing

--- Starting commit of software changes ---
Updating provisioning rollback files
Creating pending provisioning file
```

```
Committing provisioning file
Finished commit of software changes
SUCCESS: Software provisioned.  New software will load on reboot.
ASR1006# hw-module slot
ASR1006# hw-module slot r1 reload << reloading standby RP slot
```

Now if you execute **more stby-bootflash:packages_1.conf**, you should be able to note packages.conf, the BOOT variable, and **show version**, all showing the updated software subpackages.

Note Note the use of wildcard (*) in the **issu loadversion** command in Example 9-14 to simplify the upgrade process on the standby RP so that the user does not have to enter **issu loadversion** for each RP package separately. The subpackage upgrade of SIP and SPA on the active RP will cause packet drop.

Upgrading SIP/SPA Subpackages

Because upgrading SIP/SPA subpackages results in traffic disruption, you will want to use a few techniques to minimize that disruption. One prime example of such a technique for Ethernet SPAs is Gigabit Ethernet Channel (GEC).

For example, if a GEC is configured across SIPs, that will help in this case when upgrading the SIPBase package because that causes SIP to reload. When using GEC across SIPs, the traffic will still continue using the other SIP and SPA.

Refer to the "Further Reading" section at the end of the chapter, and read the ISSU deployment guide and case study for more information about creating the GEC.

The following steps outline how to upgrade the SIP/SPA subpackages:

Step 1. The subpackages for SIP and SPA will start with asr1000rp*-sip. You will use this and the wildcard character to upgrade the SIP and all the SPAs in it at the same time.

Step 2. The SIP and SPAs will be reloaded to perform the upgrade.

Step 3. Execute the **show issue state details** command. The ISSU state should say that you have completed the load version after the upgrade.

Step 4. Execute the **issu commit version** command after the load version to finalize the upgrade.

Step 5. The packages_1.conf file (in this example) should be updated with the new subpackages for the SIP and SPA.

Upgrading the RP-Specific Subpackages on the Active RP

At this point, you have upgraded all the subpackages on the standby RP, along with the SIPs and SPAs. In this step, you upgrade the following four RP-related subpackages on the active RP:

- RPBase
- RPAccess
- RPControl
- RPIOS

Example 9-15 shows the upgrade steps on the active RP.

Example 9-15 *ASR1000-RP1-Related RP Packages Being Loaded onto the Standby RP. For ASR1000-RP2, "rp1" will be replaced by "rp2" Because RP2 Uses Separate Binaries from RP1*

```
ASR1006# issu loadversion rp 0 file bootlfash:temp/asr1000rp1-rp*02.00.0.pkg
--- Starting installation state synchronization ---
Finished installation state synchronization

--- Starting file path checking ---
Finished file path checking

--- Starting image file verification ---
Checking image file names
Verifying image file locations
Locating image files and validating name syntax
Inspecting image file types
    WARNING: In-service installation of IOSD package
    WARNING: requires software redundancy on target RP
    WARNING: or on-reboot parameter
    WARNING: Automatically setting the on-reboot flag
    WARNING: In-service installation of RP Base package
    WARNING: requires software reboot of target RP
Processing image file constraints
Creating candidate provisioning file
Finished image file verification

--- Starting candidate package set construction ---
Verifying existing software set
Processing candidate provisioning file
```

```
Constructing working set for candidate package set
Constructing working set for running package set
Checking command output
Constructing merge of running and candidate packages
Finished candidate package set construction

--- Starting compatibility testing ---
Determining whether candidate package set is compatible

WARNING:
WARNING: Candidate software combination not found in compatibility database
WARNING:

Determining whether installation is valid
Determining whether installation is valid ... skipped
Checking IPC compatibility for candidate software
Checking candidate package set infrastructure compatibility
Checking infrastructure compatibility with running software
Checking infrastructure compatibility with running software ... skipped
Checking package specific compatibility
Finished compatibility testing

--- Starting commit of software changes ---
Updating provisioning rollback files
Creating pending provisioning file
Committing provisioning file
Finished commit of software changes

SUCCESS: Software provisioned.  New software will load on reboot.

ASR1006#

ASR1006# sh issu st detail
--- Starting installation state synchronization ---
Finished installation state synchronization

Previous provisioning action is pending reboot
```

You will perform ESPBase subpackage upgrades for both active and standby ESPs in the system on the active RP. You must enter the following two commands followed by the **issu commitversion** command:

```
issu loadversion rp active-RP file bootflash:asr1000rp1-esp*version*.pkg slot 1
issu loadversion rp active-RP file bootflash:asr1000rp1-esp*version*.pkg slot 0
```

This operation should cause minimal traffic disruption; basically, this will be the same as an ESP switchover time.

Now, before taking the final step (SSO switchover from the active to standby RP), take a quick look at what is to follow (that is, after the standby RP becomes the newly active RP):

Step 1. The SIPs and SPAs are already running the new subpackages, so they will not go through any change (and therefore, no traffic disruption).

Step 2. The RP that went down will boot back up with the new subpackages (except the ESP).

Step 3. The RP will come back up as the standby RP and will reach the standby hot state.

Step 4. The *packages_1.conf* file on the standby (former active) hard disk will be updated with the new subpackages (except the ESP).

Step 5. At this stage, the system is running image B.

> **Note** ESP switchover times are less than 50 ms, as shown by various lab tests.

At this point, you've upgraded the standby RP and all the subpackages on the active RP (except the ESP package on the active RP). Next, you perform a redundancy force-switchover. Redundancy switchover will cause the standby RP to become the active RP, and the former active RP will go into standby mode.

Example 9-16 shows how to perform the force SSO switchover from the active RP to the standby RP.

Example 9-16 *Redundancy Switchover Causes the Active RP to Switch Over to Standby State After It Comes Back Up*

```
ASR1006# redundancy for
ASR1006# redundancy force-switchover
Proceed with switchover to standby RP? [confirm]

>>> standby RP takes over as active at this time
ASR1006-stby#
ASR1006#
ASR1006# show platform
Chassis type: ASR1006
Slot       Type                 State                    Insert time (ago)
--------- ------------------- --------------------- -----------------
0          ASR1006-SIP10        ok                       02:16:17
 0/1       SPA-5X1GE-V2         ok                       01:36:51
 0/3       SPA-8X1GE-V2         ok                       01:36:46
R0         ASR1000-RP1          booting                  02:16:17
```

```
R1          ASR1000-RP1          ok, active             02:16:17
F0          ASR1000-ESP10        ok, active             02:16:17
F1          ASR1000-ESP10        init, standby          02:16:17
```

Upgrading the ESP Subpackage on the Standby RP (Formerly Active)

At this point, the *packages.conf* file on the formerly active RP is still pointing to the old ESP package, and therefore needs to be upgraded.

No traffic disruption occurs during this step. You execute the **issu loadversion** command followed by a **issu commitversion** command.

Example 9-17 shows the ESP package upgrade on the standby RP.

Example 9-17 *Loading the ESPBase Package*

```
ASR1006# issu loadversion rp 0 file stby-bootflash:temp/asr1000rp1-esp
  base.02.00.0.pkg

--- Starting installation state synchronization ---
Finished installation state synchronization

--- Starting file path checking ---
Finished file path checking

--- Starting image file verification ---
Checking image file names
Verifying image file locations
Locating image files and validating name syntax
Inspecting image file types
Processing image file constraints
Creating candidate provisioning file
Finished image file verification

--- Starting candidate package set construction ---
Verifying existing software set
Processing candidate provisioning file
Constructing working set for candidate package set
Constructing working set for running package set
Checking command output
Constructing merge of running and candidate packages
Finished candidate package set construction

--- Starting compatibility testing ---
```

```
Determining whether candidate package set is compatible
Determining whether installation is valid

WARNING:
WARNING: Candidate software combination not found in compatibility database
WARNING:

Software sets are identified as compatible
Checking IPC compatibility with running software
Checking candidate package set infrastructure compatibility
Checking infrastructure compatibility with running software
Checking package specific compatibility
Finished compatibility testing

--- Starting commit of software changes ---
Updating provisioning rollback files
Creating pending provisioning file
Committing provisioning file
Finished commit of software changes

--- Starting analysis of software changes ---
Finished analysis of software changes

--- Starting update running software ---
Blocking peer synchronization of operating information
Creating the command set placeholder directory
  Finding latest command set
  Finding latest command shortlist lookup file
  Finding latest command shortlist file
  Assembling CLI output libraries
  Assembling CLI input libraries
  Applying interim IPC and database definitions
  Replacing running software
  Replacing CLI software
  Skip Restarting software, target frus filtered out
    Applying final IPC and database definitions
    Generating software version information
    Notifying running software of updates
    Unblocking peer synchronization of operating information
  Unmounting old packages
  Cleaning temporary installation files
    Finished update running software

SUCCESS: Finished installing software.
```

```
ASR1006# sh issu state detail
--- Starting installation state synchronization ---
Finished installation state synchronization

Slot being modified: R0
  Install time: 20010201 06:51:08 on con 0
  Last operation: loadversion
  Rollback: automatic, remaining time before rollback: 00:44:16
  Running image: harddisk:packages_1.conf
  Operating mode: sso, terminal state reached
```

Running Dual IOSD on a 2 or 4RU System

To start a second IOSD instance (same or different version), you need to boot IOS XE in a modular fashion (as opposed to monolithic mode when the system is booted off of a consolidated package). When IOS XE is booted into the modular fashion, you need to enter the commands shown in Example 9-18 to spawn the new IOSD process.

Example 9-18 *Turning on SSO and Instantiating the Dual IOS Instances on the ASR 1002 or ASR 1004 System. This Is a Prerequisite to Software Redundancy or ISSU on These Systems*

```
ASR1004(config)# redundancy
ASR1004(config-red)# mode sso ?

ASR1004(config-red)# mode sso

ASR1004# show platform
Chassis type: ASR1004

Slot      Type                State                 Insert time (ago)
--------- ------------------- --------------------- ------------
0         ASR1000-SIP10       ok                    04:56:39
 0/0      SPA-4XOC3-POS       ok                    04:54:16
 0/1      SPA-4XCT3/DS0       ok                    04:54:10
 0/2      SPA-8X1GE-V2        ok                    04:54:19
 0/3      SPA-1X10GE-L-V2     ok                    04:54:18
1         ASR1000-SIP10       ok                    04:56:39
 1/1      SPA-8X1GE-V2        ok                    04:54:19
 1/2      SPA-8X1GE-V2        ok                    04:54:18
 1/3      SPA-1X10GE-L-V2     ok                    04:54:16
R0        ASR1000-RP1         ok                    04:56:39
 R0/0                         ok, active            04:56:39
```

```
 R0/1                           ok, standby          04:53:52
F0         ASR1000-ESP10       ok, active           04:56:39
P0         ASR1004-PWR-AC      ok                   04:55:47
P1         ASR1004-FAN         ok                   04:55:47
```

Note After you complete the configuration steps in Example 9-18, a ROMMON variable, called IOSXE_DUAL_IOS, is added with the value set to 1. Furthermore, you can use the **show platform** command to ensure that both R0/0 and R0/1 are in ok/active and ok/standby states, respectively. A router reload is required for this to take effect.

Summary

This chapter reviewed the overall operational and business benefits of having a fully ISSU-capable routing system. The chapter also used detailed examples and command snapshots to explain the intricacies of ISSU for a 6RU system running either a consolidated package or subpackages, the latter of which essentially results in a more controlled upgrade in a granular fashion.

The next few chapters look at ASR 1000 system management and troubleshooting.

Chapter Review Questions

1. Is ISSU possible when running a fully redundant 6RU system in consolidated mode without any traffic disruption?
2. Is IOSD ISSU possible when running a 6RU system in consolidated mode?
3. What platform-specific (native) command do you use to expand a consolidated package into seven subpackages?
4. Is ISSU possible on a 2 or 4RU system not running in dual IOSD mode?

Answers

1. No, in this scenario there will be some traffic disruption when the SIP/SPA goes through the upgrade process along with the rolling ESP upgrades.
2. No, the system must be running in subpackages mode for an IOSD subpackage upgrade.
3. Use the **request platform software package expand** command to extract subpackages from a consolidated package, downloadable from Cisco.com.
4. No, for a 2 or 4RU system to be ISSU capable, they must be running in dual IOS or what is known as software redundancy. This requires procuring the IOSRED-RTU= license for these systems.

Further Reading

Cisco IOS XE Software Packaging Architecture, document: http://tinyurl.com/qrsjt3

Cisco IOS XE Consolidated And Sub-Packages Management, document: http://tinyurl.com/rdp9ec

Cisco IOS XE ISSU Configuration Guide, document: http://tinyurl.com/5mdou5

Cisco IOS XE Software Package Compatibility for ISSU, document: http://tinyurl.com/ob8ns6

Cisco IOS XE ISSU Deployment Guide and Case Study, document: http://tinyurl.com/oru32e

Chapter 10

Using the ASR 1000 Embedded Graphical User Interface

The purpose of this chapter is to introduce the unique graphical interface that the ASR 1000 provides in addition to the plain old HTTP/HTTPS access to the router. This chapter examines how you can use this tool to aid in device operations.

Introduction to the ASR 1000 Web GUI

The ASR 1000 has a built-in web interface in addition to the regular HTTP interface that becomes available when the router is configured as the HTTP or HTTPS server. The ASR 1000–specific built-in web interface is a more improved and detailed version of the default HTTP/HTTPS interface. When accessed for the first time, it launches a dashboard that contains information such as system environmental, available memories, alarm states, and so on for both active and standby components in the system.

Table 10-1 outlines the broad categories of information made available via the built-in GUI.

Table 10-1 *ASR 1000 GUI Views*

Category	Description
System	Shows IOS version, running configuration, and dashboard status information.
Chassis	Shows environmental readings, fans status, file system, and I/O port information.
Memory Resource	Shows memory summary and system mounts.
Process Resource	Shows memory, CPU, CPU history, process list, sensors.
Alarms	Shows both audible and visual alarm status.
CEF	Shows Cisco Express Forwarding (CEF) (all), and Virtual Routing and Forwarding (VRF) summary (both system and user configured VRFs).

Table 10-1 *ASR 1000 GUI Views*

Category	Description
Diagnostics	Shows chassis manager (for all system field-replaceable units [FRU]), and slot status.
Interfaces	Shows Forwarding Manager (both on Route Processor [RP] and Embedded Service Processor [ESP]).
Modules	Shows FPD-related information.
Peers	Shows information regarding the peer processes on all FRUs. This also includes shell manager process details.
Web CLI	Shows web interface access to IOS for remote **show** command-line interface (CLI) execution.

The following section describes how to configure this GUI from scratch.

Configuring the ASR 1000 GUI

Example 10-1 shows the complete steps followed to turn the ASR 1000 GUI on.

Example 10-1 *Enabling the ASR 1000 Web GUI*

```
ASR10006(Config)# ip http server
 ASR10006(Config)# transport type persistent webui input http-ui
 ASR10006(Config)# transport-map type persistent webui http-ui
 ASR10006(Config-tmap)# server
 ASR10006(Config)# username cisco priv 15 password 0 cisco
```

After you complete the configuration in Example 10-1, you should be able to access the router via http://router-ip-address (or https://router-ip-address if you used Secure Sockets Layer [SSL]). When prompted for a user ID and password, enter **cisco/cisco**.

Figure 10-1 illustrates the dashboard status screen.

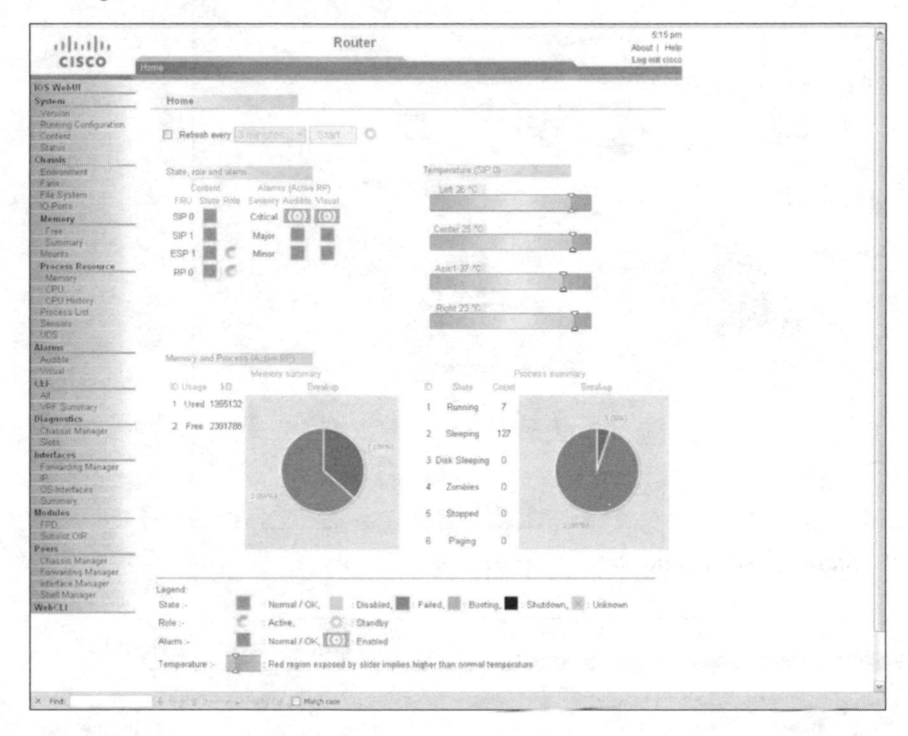

Figure 10-1 *ASR 1000 GUI dashboard Status screen.*

Common Usage Examples

This web interface is not for configuring the ASR 1000, but rather to graphically view the status of various resources in the system.

Some of the most useful and practical examples for this tool are as follows:

- **High-level system status overview:** This is available as part of the System category and is presented to a user as the home page. A refresh time interval can be selected (down to 1 minute), and this page can infinitely update itself. You can also look at the environmental status under **Chassis > Environment** and tune the refresh time interval to 5 seconds. Figure 10-2 shows the status window with refresh interval turned on.
- **Viewing the list of user VRFs at both the RP and ESP level:** This view can be used to confirm that the user VRFs are not only created on RP/IOS, but also successfully downloaded into ESP (data plane). Figure 10-3 shows the list of both system and user configured VRFs. You need to click **CEF > VRF Summary** to get to the output shown.

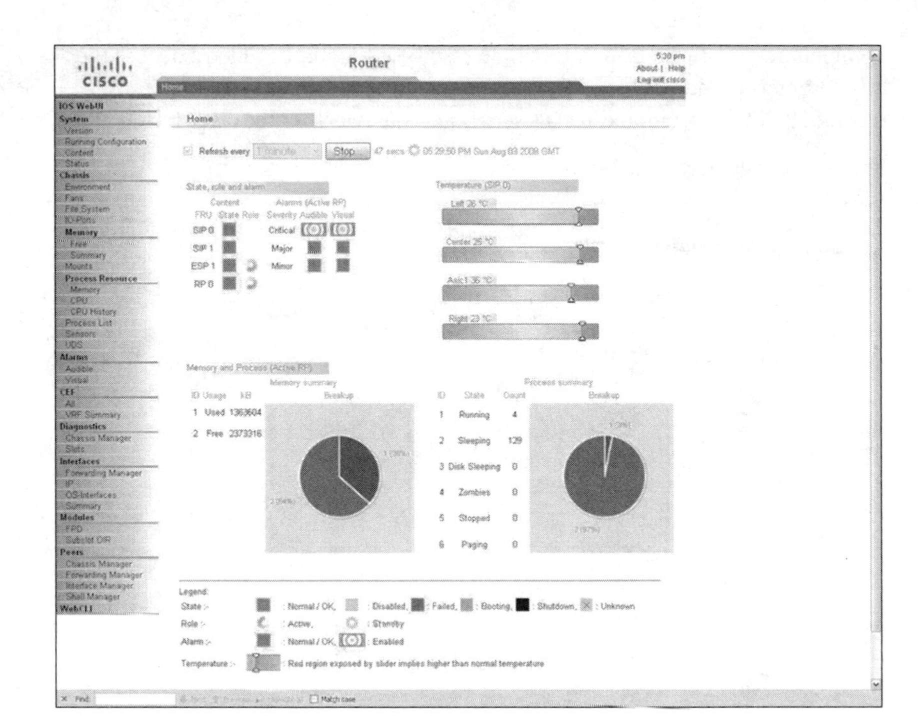

Figure 10-2 *Status window with Refresh Interval enabled.*

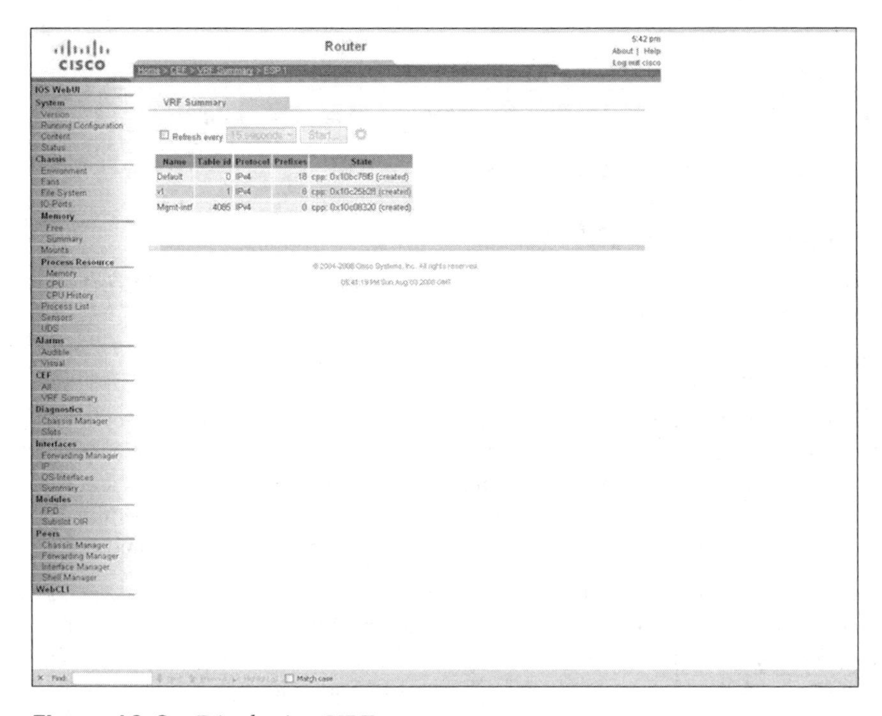

Figure 10-3 *Displaying VRF summary.*

- **Viewing the list of interfaces at both the RP and ESP level:** This view can be used to confirm both system- and user-configured interfaces at the RP (control plane, IOS) and ESP (data plane) levels. Figure 10-4 shows the list of both system- and user-configured interfaces. Click **Interfaces > Forwarding Manager** to get to the output shown.

- **Viewing the list of show platform CLIs without having to log in to the router via the console:** This view can be used to execute most of the platform-specific CLI **show** commands and collect information graphically. Figure 10-5 shows the list of all the possible **show** commands in IOS XE RLS 2.1.1. Click WebCLI at the bottom of the left pane to get to the output shown.

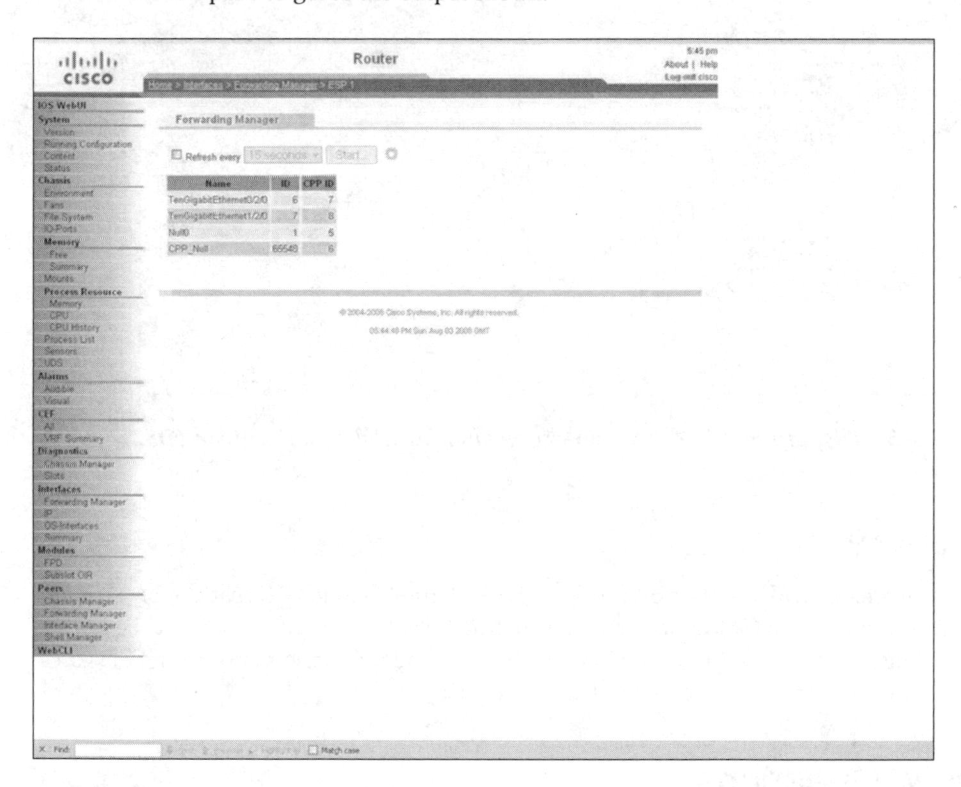

Figure 10-4 *Displaying interfaces from the data-plane perspective, TenGigabit Ethernet 0/2/0 and 1/2/0.*

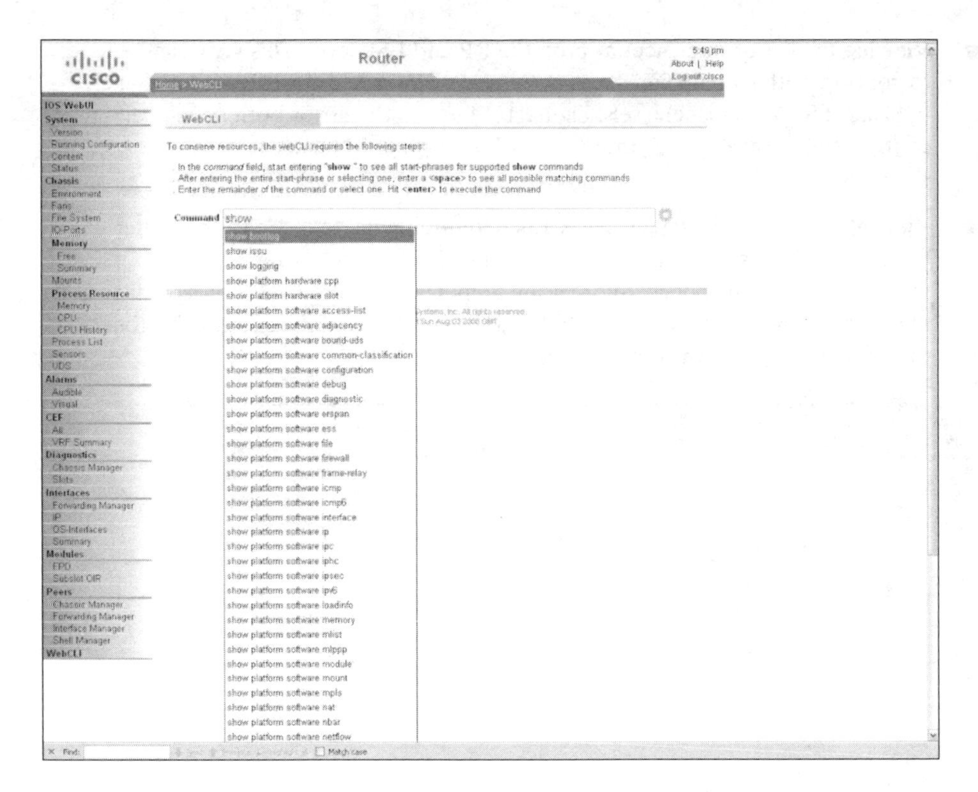

Figure 10-5 *Displaying Cisco IOS* **show** *commands available in the given IOS XE release.*

Summary

This chapter provided a brief overview of the ASR 1000 unique GUI that can be extremely handy and useful for looking at various IOS and platform-specific details of the system. This interface is only for monitoring purposes, and for configuration either the CLI or a Cisco Security Manager 3.3 or later can be used.

Review Questions

1. Is this ASR 1000–specific web interface turned on by default?
2. Can this ASR 1000–specific web interface be used over SSL?
3. Is the legacy HTTP/HTTPS interface still available along with enhanced ASR 1000 web GUI?
4. What are the benefits offered by the enhanced web GUI?

Answers

1. No, it must be turned on explicitly as outlined in Example 10-1.
2. Yes, it's possible to use either HTTP or HTTPS on both standard and nonstandard ports.
3. Yes, the legacy web interface is still available by clicking the IOS WebUI at the top of the left pane of the menu, as shown in Figure 10-1.
4. Enhanced web interface offers several benefits, including the following:
   - An interface that presents information in an easy-to-read graphical format
   - An interface that enables users to monitor most software processes, including processes related to the IOS and non-IOS subpackages within the Cisco IOS XE consolidated package
   - An interface that allows users to monitor most hardware components, including all RPs, ESPs, SPA Interface Processors (SIP), and shared port adapter (SPA) installed in the router
   - Access to the legacy web user interface in addition to the enhanced web user interface
   - The ability to gather output from **show** commands from the web user interface

Further Reading

Cisco IOS XE, Troubleshooting Initial Start-up Problems, document: http://tinyurl.com/o4hws7

Cisco IOS XE Configuration Guide, document: http://tinyurl.com/pt6yjx

Cisco IOS XE Command Reference, document: http://tinyurl.com/phuxsc

Cisco IOS XE Error and System Messages for IOS XE, document: http://tinyurl.com/qhgwyk

Cisco IOS XE New Features List, document: http://tinyurl.com/qrf7en

Cisco IOS XE SIP and SPA Hardware Installation Guide, document: http://tinyurl.com/qhxxmf

Chapter 11

Understanding ASR 1000 System Troubleshooting and Error Messages

The purpose of this chapter is to help isolate, understand, and rectify the issues that you might encounter when deploying and using the ASR 1000 system. This chapter focuses on the common problems found, and the steps needed to resolve them either by the user or by Cisco TAC (Technical Assistance Center). The chapter covers both platform-specific resolutions and IOS command-line interface (CLI) commands for this purpose. The chapter concludes with a comprehensive discussion of the common system error messages that will definitely aid in troubleshooting.

Troubleshooting Methodology

Troubleshooting without a solid methodology is like searching for a needle in a haystack. It just adds to the frustration. A formal methodology gives you a place to start. In a general sense, there can be two approaches:

- **Top-down:** You start troubleshooting at the application layer and work your way down to the physical layer.
- **Bottom-up:** You start at the physical layer and traverse the upper layer only if needed.

You can also throw your intuition and experience in the mix and start where it makes more sense.

Regardless of your approach, the overall troubleshooting flow should be similar to the following:

Step 1. **Problem appraisal:** Define the problem statement and problem description, and try to identify what has changed.

Step 2. **Problem analysis:** Look for possible causes and come up with a list of probable causes based on the previous step. This also includes testing various causes starting with the most probable one. If any of the these tests are disruptive, you need to schedule a network maintenance window.

Step 3. **Problem solution:** Implement the fixes, and verify whether the problem is resolved. If not, go back and check your analysis. Also, make sure that the fix didn't introduce a new problem.

Step 4. **Documentation:** After the problem has been resolved, document the fix. Over time, the repository of fixes can become a valuable knowledgebase and can be used to quickly resolve any recurrence of the past problems.

ASR 1000–Specific Troubleshooting Commands

In addition to the generic IOS commands, the ASR 1000 has many platform-specific **show** and **debug** commands for both understanding the platform architecture and troubleshooting purposes. These commands are divided into software and hardware categories, as demonstrated in Example 11-1.

Example 11-1 *Starting Point for Platform-Specific* **show** *and* **debug** *Commands on Cisco ASR1000 Series Routers*

```
ASR1006# show platform ?
  hardware   Show platform hardware information
  software   Show platform software information
ASR1006# debug platform ?
  all        Enable/disable all platform debugging
  hardware   Debug platform hardware information
  software   Debug platform software information
```

Note Usual **debug** commands, unlike software-based routers (such as the c7200), do not show transit traffic on ASR 1000 routers. An example of that is **debug ip packet**, the output of which shows only the traffic destined for the system itself or that ends up getting punted over to the Route Processor (RP).

As with all other platforms, use of the **debug platform all** command is not a recommended **debug** option, and debugging should be used under the supervision of an expert.

The examples that follow take a closer look at some of the most useful platform software and hardware command-line interface (CLI) commands available in IOS XE 2.1.1. Example 11-2 shows the platform-specific software and hardware commands.

Example 11-2 *Platform-Specific Software- and Hardware-Related* **show** *and* **debug** *Commands*

```
ASR1006# show platform software ?
  access-list              Access control list information
  adjacency                Adjacency platform commands
```

```
bound-uds               Show bound Unix-Domain-Sockets information
cce                     CCE platform commands
cef                     CEF platform commands
cman                    Chassis manager client
common-classification   Common classification
configuration           Show configuration commands
debug                   Debug information
diagnostic              Show diagnostic information
dpidb                   Datapath Interface Descriptor Block information
erspan                  Encapsulated Remote Switch Port Analyzer
ess                     Edge Switch Services
file                    Show file
filesystem              File system information
firewall                Firewall information
flow-control            Flow control Ids
fpm                     FPM information
frame-relay             Frame Relay
icmp                    ICMP platform commands
icmp6                   Show ICMP6 information
infrastructure          Platform infrastructure
inspect                 Inspect platform commands
interface               Interface information
ip                      IPv4 information
ipc                     Show ipc information
iphc                    Show IP Header Compression information
ipsec                   IPSec component information
ipv6                    IPv6 information
loadinfo                Loadbalance objects information
memory                  Show memory related information
mlist                   Multicast list information
mlp                     MLP platform commands
mlppp                   MLPPP information
module                  PSD modules
mount                   System mount information
mpls                    MPLS platform commands
multicast               MULTICAST platform commands
nat                     NAT platform commands
nbar                    NBAR platform commands
netflow                 NetFlow platform commands
object-manager          Object Manager information
os-interface            Show os-interface information
peer                    Show peer information
process                 Process information
punt                    Show punt/inject information
```

```
  push-counter            Push Counter OCE
  qos                     QoS platform commands
  route-map               Route-map platform commands
  sbc                     Session Border Controller
  shell                   Shell infrastructure
  slot                    Slot information
  spi4                    Mapping Ids of Spi4 to Marmot Buffers
  status                  Show system status
  tech-support            Show system information for Tech-Support
  trace                   Trace information
  urpf                    Unicast reverse path forwarding information
  vlans                   Vlan information
  vty                     Platform vty management
  zone                    Zone platform commands

ASR1006# debug platform software ?
  FPM               FPM platform commands
  acl               ACL platform commands
  adjacency         Adjacency platform message debug
  cce               CCE platform commands
  cef               CEF platform commands
  cman              Chassis manager client
  configuration     Configuration infrastructure
  dpidb             DPIDB commands
  entity            Platform entity MIBs
  ess               ESS platform commands
  icmp              ICMP platform commands
  infrastructure    ASR1000 infrastructure debug commands
  inspect           Inspect platform commands
  iphc              IPHC platform commands
  ipsec             IPSec platform commands
  issu              Platform ISSU debug
  kernel            Kernel debug
  liin              LIIN interface
  marmot            Marmot Ids
  mlp               MLP platform message debug
  mpls              MPLS platform message debug
  multicast         Multicast platform commands
  nat               NAT platform commands
  nbar              NBAR platform commands
  netflow           NF platform commands
  qos               QoS platform commands
  route-map         Route-ap platform commands
  shell             Shell infrastructure
```

```
  urpf              URPF platform commands
  vty               Platform vty management requests
  wccp              WCCP platform commands
  zone              Zone platform commands
ASR1006# show platform hardware ?
  qfp          Cisco packet processor
  interface    Interface information
  port         port information
  slot         Slot information
  subslot      Subslot information
ASR1006# debug platform hardware ?
  qfp  Cisco packet processor
```

As you can note, there is almost one command for each IOS feature set from the software perspective, in addition to platform hardware commands specific to ASR 1000 system components, namely QuantumFlow Processor/control-plane process (QFP/CPP), RP, Embedded Service Processor (ESP), and SPA Interface Processor/shared port adapter (SIP/SPA). Example 11-3 shows system software-related commands.

Example 11-3 *ASR 1000 System Software-Related Commands*

```
ASR1006# show version ?
  R0            <route-processor>slot 0
  R1            Route-Processor slot 1
  RP            Route-Processor
  installed     Show all installed platform software versions
  provisioned   Show all provisioned platform software versions
  running       Show all running platform software versions
ASR1006# show redundancy ?
  clients            Redundancy Facility (RF) client list
  config-sync        Show Redundancy Config Sync status
  counters           Redundancy Facility (RF) operational counters
  history            Redundancy Facility (RF) history
  idb-sync-history   Redundancy Facility (RF) IDB sync history
  linecard-group     Line card redundancy group information
  states             Redundancy Facility (RF) states
  switchover         Redundancy Facility (RF) switchover
```

The preceding examples show just the top-level view of these commands. A large number of options are available that help narrow down the information to a specific IOS feature or system aspect.

The sections that follow look at some of the common ones that you're likely to use for troubleshooting purposes.

Troubleshooting System Hardware and Software

This section looks at the commands relevant to identifying the system hardware- and software-related issues, specifically the following:

- Displaying the overall processor and memory utilization on an ASR 1000 system
- Displaying IPv4-related drops for the active QFP
- Displaying overall QFP memory statistics for Instruction RAM (i-RAM), dynamic RAM (DRAM), and static RAM (SRAM) usage
- Displaying IPv4-related drops for the active QFP
- Displaying QuantumFlow Processor (QFP) memory statistics on per IOS feature and internal usage basis
- Tracking control CPU usage from the Linux shell
- Tracking command output repeatedly using the **monitor** command
- Displaying the status of front panel LEDs using platform-specific commands
- Displaying status of SPAs in a SIP
- Displaying statistics for a slot or SIP
- Displaying drop statistics for all interfaces in the system
- Displaying interface-level feature invocation array for both ingress and egress feature set
- Displaying system components such as RP, ESP, and SIP insertion and uptime
- Displaying QFP Packet Processing Element (PPE) utilization information
- **debug platform** commands

Displaying the Overall Processor and Memory Utilization on an ASR 1000 System

Example 11-4 shows how the **show platform** command enables you to take a snapshot of all the control CPUs in the system and their associated memory utilization.

Example 11-4 *Determining Control CPU Memory Utilization*

```
ASR1002# show platform software status control-processor
RP0: online, statistics updated 2 seconds ago
Load Average: healthy
  1-Min: 0.16, status: healthy, under 5.00
  5-Min: 0.22, status: healthy, under 5.00
  15-Min: 0.19, status: healthy, under 5.00
Memory (kb): healthy
```

```
  Total: 3708928
  Used: 1680976 (40%), status: healthy, under 90%
  Free: 2027952 (49%), status: healthy, over 10%
  Committed: 2440576 (59%), status: healthy, under 90%
Per-core Statistics
CPU0: CPU Utilization (percentage of time spent)
  User:  1.01, System:  1.14, Nice:  0.00, Idle: 97.73
  IRQ:  0.00, SIRQ:  0.02, IOwait:  0.07

ESP0: online, statistics updated 9 seconds ago
Load Average: healthy
  1-Min: 0.00, status: healthy, under 5.00
  5-Min: 0.00, status: healthy, under 5.00
  15-Min: 0.00, status: healthy, under 5.00
Memory (kb): healthy
  Total: 983912
  Used: 512892 (48%), status: healthy, under 90%
  Free: 471020 (44%), status: healthy, over 10%
  Committed: 2784508 (265%), status: healthy, under 300%
Per-core Statistics
CPU0: CPU Utilization (percentage of time spent)
  User:  0.50, System:  0.58, Nice:  0.00, Idle: 98.89
  IRQ:  0.00, SIRQ:  0.00, IOwait:  0.00

SIP0: online, statistics updated 10 seconds ago
Load Average: healthy
  1-Min: 0.00, status: healthy, under 5.00
  5-Min: 0.00, status: healthy, under 5.00
  15-Min: 0.00, status: healthy, under 5.00
Memory (kb): healthy
  Total: 479924
  Used: 288568 (55%), status: healthy, under 90%
  Free: 191356 (36%), status: healthy, over 10%
  Committed: 199952 (38%), status: healthy, under 90%
Per-core Statistics
CPU0: CPU Utilization (percentage of time spent)
  User:  0.32, System:  0.41, Nice:  0.00, Idle: 99.23
  IRQ:  0.01, SIRQ:  0.01, IOwait:  0.00
```

Displaying IPv4-Related Drops for the Active QFP

Example 11-5 illustrates a way to see various drops on a systemwide basis. The resulting output proves useful in determining whether there are any drops in the system, usually due to a lack of compute or memory resources.

Example 11-5 *Displaying Systemwide Drops*

```
ASR1006# show platform hardware qfp active statistics drop | i Ipv4
  Ipv4Acl                              0                0
  Ipv4AclLookupMiss                    0                0
  Ipv4Fpm                              0                0
  Ipv4Martian                          0                0
  Ipv4Mtr                              0                0
  Ipv4NoAdj                            0                0
  Ipv4NoRoute                          0                0
  Ipv4Null0                            0                0
  Ipv4Pbr                              0                0
  Ipv4PopPipePhpTtlExpire              0                0
  Ipv4PopPipeUhpTtlExpire              0                0
  Ipv4PopUnfPhpTtlExpire               0                0
  Ipv4PopUnfUhpTtlExpire               0                0
  Ipv4RoutingErr                       0                0
  Ipv4Unclassified                     0                0
  Ipv4mcExtraReplicae                  0                0
  Ipv4mcInvalidReplicaRecord           0                0
  Ipv4mcNoRoute                        0                0
  Ipv4mcRpfFailed                      0                0
  Ipv4mcTtlThresholdChkFailed          0                0
  Ipv4UrpfNullPathList                 0                0
```

Note The **show platform hardware qfp active statistics drop** can quickly pinpoint the cause of any drops for various features, including IPv4, IPv6, Multiprotocol Label Switching (MPLS), Network Address Translation (NAT), firewall (FW), and Cisco Unified Border Element/Session Border Controller (CUBE/SBC), for example.

Displaying Overall QFP Memory Statistics for IRAM, DRAM, and SRAM Usage

Example 11-6 shows active QFP memory usage, which is very helpful to troubleshoot QFP memory-related issues.

Example 11-6 *Displaying QFP Memory Utilization*

```
ASR1006# show platform hardware qfp active infrastructure exmem statistics
CPP exmem statistics
Type: Name: IRAM, CPP: 0
  Total: 134217728
  InUse: 5191680
  Free: 128974848
```

```
  Free protected: 51200
  Free unprotected: 0
  Lowest free water mark: 129026048
  Largest free block: 129026048
Type: Name: DRAM, CPP: 0
  Total: 402653184
  InUse: 139530240
  Free: 260046848
  Free protected: 1313792
  Free unprotected: 1762304
  Lowest free water mark: 167115776
  Largest free block: 197131264
Type: Name: SRAM, CPP: 0
  Total: 32768
  InUse: 18176
  Free: 14336
  Free protected: 0
```

Displaying QFP Memory Statistics on a Per-IOS Feature and Internal-Usage Basis

Example 11-7 illustrates the QFP memory on a per-user basis, again very useful to troubleshoot any memory-consumption issues.

Example 11-7 *Displaying QFP Memory Statistics*

```
ASR1006# show platform hardware qfp active infrastructure exmem statistics user
CPP exmem user statistics

Type: Name: IRAM, CPP: 0
  Allocations Bytes-Allocated Bytes-Total User-Name
  2           126720          128000      CPP_FIA_PROT_00
  2           126720          128000      CPP_FIA_PROT_01
  2           126720          128000      CPP_FIA_PROT_02
  2           126720          128000      CPP_FIA_PROT_03
  2           126720          128000      CPP_FIA_PROT_04
  2           126720          128000      CPP_FIA_PROT_05
  2           126720          128000      CPP_FIA_PROT_06
  2           126720          128000      CPP_FIA_PROT_07
  2           126720          128000      CPP_FIA_PROT_08
  2           126720          128000      CPP_FIA_PROT_09
  2           126720          128000      CPP_FIA_PROT_10
  2           126720          128000      CPP_FIA_PROT_11
  2           126720          128000      CPP_FIA_PROT_12
```

```
  2           126720          128000       CPP_FIA_PROT_13
  2           126720          128000       CPP_FIA_PROT_14
  2           126720          128000       CPP_FIA_PROT_15
  2           126720          128000       CPP_FIA_PROT_16
Type: Name: DRAM, CPP: 0
  Allocations Bytes-Allocated Bytes-Total User-Name
  4           1004            4096         P/I
  9           270576          276480       CEF
  1           569328          569344       QM RM
  1           65536           65536        Qm 16
  3           16392           18432        ING_EGR_UIDB
  1           786432          786432       ING EGR INPUT CHUNK_Config_0
  1           16384           16384        ING EGR INPUT CHUNK_Sm_Name_0
  1           32768           32768        ING EGR INPUT CHUNK_Lg_Name_0
  1           688128          688128       ING EGR OUTPUT CHUNK_Config_0
  1           16384           16384        ING EGR OUTPUT CHUNK_Sm_Name_0
  1           32768           32768        ING EGR OUTPUT CHUNK_Lg_Name_0
  1           16384           16384        ING EGR OUTPUT CHUNK_Queue_0
  1           16384           16384        ING-EGR_IfMap_0
  13          9131392         9139200      ALG
  6           37376           40960        GIC
  2           8480            9216         ERSPAN
  2           1136            2048         cpp_erspan_sbs_client
  2           16000           16384        TUNNEL
  1           32000           32768        cpp_tunnel_hash_elem
  1           16000           16384        cpp_subblock_hash_elem
  1           4096            4096         Stile EA PD
  21          21027696        21036032     NAT
  1           10240           10240        DEBUGCOND BLOCK CHUNK
  2           2080            4096         cpp_tfc_sbs_client
  6           542768          544768       ESS
  1           262144          262144       L2TP HASH ELEM
  1           131072          131072       L2TP CXT SB
  1           131072          131072       L2TP TX SEQ ELEM
  1           262144          262144       PPPOE HASH ELEM
  1           131072          131072       ESS ppp cxt info
  1           2048            2048         IPSUB L2 HASH ELEM
  1           1024            1024         IPSUB DOWNSTREAM SESSION
  1           32768           32768        ESS switch encap info
  1           49152           49152        ESS switch encaps chunk
  1           131072          131072       ESS drop config block
  1           2097152         2097152      Qm 2048
  12          7085344         7090176      FW
  2           688             2048         cpp_icmp_sbs_client
```

```
2        32          2048        ICMP
1        24000       24576       cpp_icmp_sb_chunk
1        24000       24576       cpp_icmp6_sb_chunk
1        4096        4096        SPAMARMOT
2        181248      181248      PALCI CLIENT
1        2097152     2097152     PLU Mgr_0_0
1        2097152     2097152     PLU Mgr_0_1
1        1572864     1572864     PLU Mgr_0_2
1        2097152     2097152     PLU Mgr_0_3
1        2621440     2621440     PLU Mgr_0_4
1        1572864     1572864     PLU Mgr_0_5
1        1835008     1835008     PLU Mgr_0_6
1        2883584     2883584     PLU Mgr_0_7
1        3932160     3932160     PLU Mgr_0_8
1        2490368     2490368     PLU Mgr_0_9
1        3014656     3014656     PLU Mgr_0_10
1        3538944     3538944     PLU Mgr_0_11
1        4063232     4063232     PLU Mgr_0_12
1        2555904     2555904     PLU Mgr_0_13
1        3080192     3080192     PLU Mgr_0_14
1        3604480     3604480     PLU Mgr_0_15
1        2064384     2064384     PLU Mgr_0_16
1        2326528     2326528     PLU Mgr_0_17
1        2359296     2359296     PLU Mgr_0_18
6        18472       21504       cpp_punt_sbs_client
1        320         1024        punt path chunk 0
1        32000       32768       punt subblock chunk
1        384         1024        punt policer chunk
1        16          1024        CPP IPHC
1        512         1024        queue info chunk 0
8        175432      182272      PKTLOG
1        144000      144384      cpp_mlp_rxbundle_sb
1        32000       32768       cpp_mlp_rxlink_sb
1        224000      224256      cpp_mlp_txbundle_sb
1        112000      112640      cpp_mlp_txlink_sb
1        16000       16384       cpp_mlp_txbundle_queue
1        16384       16384       fr_relay subblock t
1        2304        3072        fr_relay subblock c
1        1024        1024        fr_frag_rx_sb_st su
1        4096        4096        frag_tx_sequence_nu
7        1081392     1083392     IPFRAG
1        16000       16384       cpp_ipfrag_sb_chunk
6        640         6144        cpp_ipfrag_sbs_client
1        32000       32768       cpp_ipreass_sb_chunk
```

```
  1          16000          16384        cpp_ipreass_cur_dgram_cnt_chunk
  1          64000          64512        cpp_ipvfr_sb_chunk
  1          64000          64512        cpp_ipv6reass_sb_chunk
  11         71808          78848        sbs_cef
  18         1475584        1475584      IPMC memory Mgr_0
  1          4096           4096         ERSPAN PORT UIDB SB
  1          2048           2048         ERSPAN TERM SESS DECAP INFO
  1          16384          16384        ERSPAN TERM SESS HASH ELM
  1          3072           3072         ERSPAN ENCAPS STR
  1          1024           1024         ERSPAN ENCAPS INFO
  1          8192           8192         ERSPAN REPLICA LIST ELM
  6          30208          32768        cpp_ess_sbs_client
  1          2097152        2097152      ESF PBHK CXT SB
  1          2097152        2097152      ESF PBHK PORT POOL
  2          16400          17408        IPSEC
  1          48000          48128        IPSec UIdb_0
  4          13336          16384        CPP IPSec Client
  1          1600           2048         PP_IPSEC_SPI_HASH_CHUNK
  1          65536          65536        IPSec InSA_0
  1          16384          16384        IPSec SP_0
  1          65536          65536        IPSec OutSA_0
  1          14336          14336        CPP FW ZONE TABLE CHUNK
  1          8192           8192         CPP FW FILLER BLOCK CHUNK
  1          262144         262144       CPP FW STATS TABLE CHUNK
  1          180224         180224       CPP FW ACTION BLOCK CHUNK
  1          131072         131072       CPP FW STATS BLOCK CHUNK
  1          12288          12288        CPP FW CLASS NAME TABLE CHUNK
  1          4096           4096         NAT SB
Type: Name: BQS_PQS, CPP: 0
  Allocations Bytes-Allocated Bytes-Total User-Name
  1          16384          16384        queue chunk
Type: Name: BQS_SCH_HANDLE, CPP: 0
  Allocations Bytes-Allocated Bytes-Total User-Name
  1          64             64           schedule handle chunk
Type: Name: BQS_MINP, CPP: 0
  Allocations Bytes-Allocated Bytes-Total User-Name
  1          4096           4096         min prof
Type: Name: BQS_MAXP, CPP: 0
  Allocations Bytes-Allocated Bytes-Total User-Name
  1          1024           1024         max prof
Type: Name: BQS_EXSP, CPP: 0
  Allocations Bytes-Allocated Bytes-Total User-Name
  1          1024           1024         excess prof
```

Here FIA refers to feature innovation array, which is how the IOS features are ordered for execution on ingress and egress interfaces. BQS refers to buffering, queuing, and scheduling chip (known as the traffic manager) of the QFP chipset. As discussed in previous chapters, the BFQ chip is used to offload various functions, such as shaping, queuing, and scheduling.

Note You can also use **show platform software memory qfp-control-process qfp active brief** and **show platform software memory qfp-driver qfp active brief** commands for QFP software memory-usage tracking. These are low-level hardware-related commands.

Tracking Control CPU Usage from the Linux Shell

Example 11-8 shows usage of the **top** command inside the Linux shell.

Example 11-8 *Tracking Control CPU Usage from Within Linux*

```
ASR1002# request platform software system shell f0
Activity within this shell can jeopardize the functioning of the system.
Are you sure you want to continue? [y/n] y
2009/05/19 23:55:41 : Shell access was granted to user <anon>; Trace file: ,
  /harddisk/tracelogs/system_shell_F0.log.20090519235541
**********************************************************************
Activity within this shell can jeopardize the functioning
of the system.
Use this functionality only under supervision of Cisco Support.

Session will be logged to:
  harddisk:tracelogs/system_shell_F0.log.20090519235541
**********************************************************************
Terminal type 'network' unknown.  Assuming vt100
[asr1002_ESP_0:/]$
[ASR1002_ESP_0:/]$top
top - 23:56:58 up 1 day,  7:54,  0 users,  load average: 0.00, 0.00, 0.00
Tasks:  83 total,   3 running,  80 sleeping,   0 stopped,   0 zombie
Cpu(s):  0.3% us,  0.0% sy,  0.0% ni, 99.7% id,  0.0% wa,  0.0% hi,  0.0% si
Mem:    982172k total,   527696k used,   454476k free,    24700k buffers
Swap:         0k total,         0k used,         0k free,   209256k cached

  PID USER       PR  NI  VIRT  RES  SHR S %CPU %MEM    TIME+  COMMAND
 5168 root       20   0  529m  65m  22m S  0.3  6.9   2:23.48 cpp_cp_svr
10976 root       20   0  2496 1208  972 R  0.3  0.1   0:00.05 top
    1 root       20   0  2132  632  544 S  0.0  0.1   0:09.51 init
    2 root       39  19     0    0    0 S  0.0  0.0   0:00.00 ksoftirqd/0
    3 root       15  -5     0    0    0 S  0.0  0.0   0:00.00 events/0
```

```
    4 root      15  -5     0    0     0 S  0.0  0.0   0:00.01 khelper
    5 root      15  -5     0    0     0 S  0.0  0.0   0:00.00 kthread
   21 root      15  -5     0    0     0 S  0.0  0.0   0:00.00 kblockd/0
   25 root      15  -5     0    0     0 S  0.0  0.0   0:00.00 pdflush
   61 root      20   0     0    0     0 S  0.0  0.0   0:00.00 pdflush
   62 root      15  -5     0    0     0 S  0.0  0.0   0:00.00 kswapd0
   63 root      15  -5     0    0     0 S  0.0  0.0   0:00.00 aio/0
  626 root      20   0     0    0     0 S  0.0  0.0   0:00.01 mtdblockd
 1358 root       0 -20     0    0     0 S  0.0  0.0   0:00.00 loop0
 1392 bin       20   0  2220  676   552 S  0.0  0.1   0:00.00 portmap
 1431 root       0 -20     0    0     0 S  0.0  0.0   0:00.13 loop1
 2123 root      16  -4  2112  496   376 S  0.0  0.1   0:00.32 udevd
```

This can be done for all the boards (RP, ESP, and SIP) in the system.

Tracking a Command Output Repeatedly Using the monitor Command

Example 11-9 shows a useful CLI method of tracking output of a command, and you can even pipe it to a file on attached storage media, such as a hard disk or bootflash.

Example 11-9 *Tracking Repeated Command Output*

```
ASR1006# monitor platform ?
  command    Monitor a command
  software   Monitor platform software information

! Monitoring a command:
ASR1006# monitor platform command show ?
  bootlog       Show bootlog contents
  issu          Show ISSU Information
  logging       Show logging
  platform      Show platform information
  rom-monitor   Show ROMMON version information
  version       Show version information
! Monitoring a file:
ASR1006# monitor platform software file contents
! Monitoring a standby RP:
ASR1006# request platform software console attach rp standby
```

Monitoring the standby RP console from the active RP can be very useful during troubleshooting high-availability (HA) issues.

Displaying the Status of Front-Panel LEDs Using the show platform hardware Command

Example 11-10 shows the status of front-panel LEDs for the RP, ESP, and SIP. This proves useful in case the system is at a remote location.

Example 11-10 *Determining RP, ESP, and SIP LED Status*

```
ASR1006# show platform hardware slot r0 led status
Current LED States
LED                 State
---------------
Front               Green
Active              On
Standby             Off
BITS                Off

ASR1006# show platform hardware slot f1 led status
Current LED States
LED                 State
---------------
Power               On
Front               Green
Active              On
Standby             Off
ASR1006# show platform hardware slot 0 led status
Current LED States
LED                 State
---------------
Power               On
Front               Green
```

Displaying the Status of SPAs in a SIP

Example 11-11 demonstrates how to display SPA status for a given SIP. The output here indicates that only one 10 Gigabit Ethernet SPA is in slot 0/2/0.

Example 11-11 *Displaying SIP SPA Status*

```
ASR1006# show platform hardware slot 0 spa status
Bay  SPA Type       State              PST   POK   SOK   PENB  RST   DENB  HSS
---------------------------------------------------------------------------------
0    Empty          Detection          1     0     0     0     1     1     0
1    Empty          Detection          1     0     0     0     1     1     0
```

```
2     1XTENGE-X...  Online          0    1    1    1    0    0    1
3     Empty          Detection      1    0    0    0    1    1    0
```

Displaying Statistics for a Slot or SIP

Example 11-12 demonstrates how to show SPA-level statistics.

Example 11-12 *TENGE SPA-Level Packet Statistics*

```
ASR1006# show platform hardware subslot 0/2 plim statistics
0/2, 1XTENGE-XFP-V2, Online
  RX Pkts 288697415   Bytes 20041034709
  TX Pkts 324140689   Bytes 109813068615
  RX IPC Pkts 0            Bytes 0
  TX IPC Pkts 0            Bytes 0
```

Displaying Drop Statistics for All Interfaces in the System

Use the **show platform hardware cpp active interface all statistics drop_summary** command to display overall statistics for all interfaces, as demonstrated in Example 11-13.

Example 11-13 *Displaying Overall Drop Statistics for All System Interfaces*

```
ASR1006# show platform hardware qfp active interface all statistics drop_summary
--------------------------------
Drop Stats Summary:
note: 1) these drop stats are only updated when PAL
         reads the interface stats.
      2) the interface stats include the subinterface
Interface                                      Rx Pkts              Tx Pkts
-------------------------------------------------------------------------.
TenGigabitEthernet0/2/0                         25307                    0
TenGigabitEthernet1/2/0                          7221                    0
```

To collect statistics for debugging purposes, you can track the packet path through the system starting with the SPA in question where the packet entered the system. The overall flow is as follows:

Step 1. Make sure traffic is being received on the SPA interface using the **show interface gi0/1/0** command. This output comes from the SPA interface. To troubleshoot an issue where the packet might have been dropped between the SPA and QFP path, you can use the **show platform...plim stat** command.

Step 2. Check whether the ESP is seeing the packets and doing feature processing by using the **show inter a/b/c statistics** command. The resulting output comes from the ESP hardware itself.

Step 3. Now focus on the individual feature status using the **show platform** command.

Displaying the Interface-Level FIA for Both the Ingress and Egress Feature Set

You can look at the feature binding on a per-interface basis with the **show hardwa qfp active interfac if-name** command, as demonstrated in Example 11-14.

Example 11-14 *Displaying Interface-Level Feature Binding*

```
ASR1002# show hardwa qfp active interfac if-name GigabitEthernet0/0/0
General interface information
  Interface Name: GigabitEthernet0/0/0
  Platform interface handle: 7
  QFP interface handle: 7
  Parent Name: (none)
  Rx uidb: 1023
  Tx uidb: 65529

SPA/plim interface information
  Remap table entry
    Marmot channel ID: 0
    Valid bit: 1
    SPA format: FORMAT D
    Indirect bit: 0
    UIDB index: 1023
  Tx subblock
    Tx SPA format: FORMAT D
    Tx Marmot channel: 0x03000000
    SPA header length: 0

BGPPA/QPPB interface configuration information
  Ingress: BGPPA/QPPB not configured. flags: 0000
  Egress : BGPPA not configured. flags: 0000

layer2_input enabled.
layer2_output enabled.
ess_ac_input enabled.

Features Bound to Interface:
 1 GIC FIA state
30 PUNT INJECT DB
23 ethernet
Protocol 8 - layer2_input
```

```
FIA handle - CP:0x0x10427630  DP:0x80393c00
  LAYER2_INPUT_LOOKUP_PROCESS (M)
  LAYER2_INPUT_GOTO_OUTPUT_FEATURE (M)
Protocol 9 - layer2_output
FIA handle - CP:0x0x10426e78  DP:0x8039e700
  LAYER2_OUTPUT_DROP_POLICY (M)
  MARMOT_SPA_D_TRANSMIT_PKT
  DEF_IF_DROP_FIA (M)
Protocol 14 - ess_ac_input
FIA handle - CP:0x0x10426e44  DP:0x8039eb80
  PPPOE_GET_SESSION
  ESS_ENTER_SWITCHING
  PPPOE_UNCLASSIFY_PUNT_PPP_CNTL
  DEF_IF_DROP_FIA (M)
CppEth Physical Information
  DPS Addr: 0x10dc7778
  Submap Table Addr: 0x00000000
  VLAN Ethertype: 0x8100
```

Displaying System Components Such as RP, ESP, and SIP Insertion and Uptime

You can display RP, ESP, SIP, and Power Entry Module (PEM) insertion and uptime as per software using the **show platform diag** command, as demonstrated in Example 11-15.

Example 11-15 *Displaying ASR 1002 System Component Such as ESP, RP, and SIP Insertion, Status, and Uptimes, Which Are Useful for Troubleshooting*

```
ASR1002# show platform diag
Chassis type: ASR1002
Slot: 0, ASR1002-SIP10
  Running state                : ok
  Internal state               : online
  Internal operational state  : ok
  Physical insert detect time : 00:01:02 (1d08h ago)
  Software declared up time   : 00:04:50 (1d08h ago)
  CPLD version                 : 07120202
  Firmware version             : 12.2(33r)XN2

Sub-slot: 0/0, 4XGE-BUILT-IN
  Operational status           : ok
  Internal state               : inserted
  Physical insert detect time : 00:03:29 (1d08h ago)
  Logical insert detect time  : 00:05:27 (1d08h ago)
```

```
Sub-slot: 0/1, SPA-4X1FE-TX-V2
  Operational status         : ok
  Internal state             : inserted
  Physical insert detect time : 00:03:29 (1d08h ago)
  Logical insert detect time  : 00:05:27 (1d08h ago)

Slot: R0, ASR1002-RP1
  Running state              : ok, active
  Internal state             : online
  Internal operational state  : ok
  Physical insert detect time : 00:01:02 (1d08h ago)
  Software declared up time   : 00:01:02 (1d08h ago)
  CPLD version               : 08011017
  Firmware version           : 12.2(33r)XN2

Slot: F0, ASR1000-ESP5
  Running state              : ok, active
  Internal state             : online
  Internal operational state  : ok
  Physical insert detect time : 00:01:02 (1d08h ago)
  Software declared up time   : 00:04:50 (1d08h ago)
  Hardware ready signal time  : 00:01:03 (1d08h ago)
  Packet ready signal time    : 00:04:56 (1d08h ago)
  CPLD version               : 07091401
  Firmware version           : 12.2(33r)XN2

Slot: P0, ASR1002-PWR-AC
  State                      : ps, fail
  Physical insert detect time : 00:04:49 (1d08h ago)

Slot: P1, ASR1002-PWR-AC
  State                      : ok
  Physical insert detect time : 00:04:50 (1d08h ago)
```

Displaying QFP PPE Utilization Information

The ASR 1000 provides detailed QFP data-path utilization statistics to gauge how busy the packet processing cores are while executing software features and packet forwarding.

Example 11-16 shows one of the most useful commands to gauge the overall data-path utilization.

Example 11-16 *Displaying Data-Path Utilization on the ASR 1000*

```
ASR1000# show platform hardware qfp active datapath utilization
  CPP 0                          5 secs       1 min       5 min      60 min
Input:   Priority (pps)               0           0           0           0
                  (bps)               0           0           0           0
     Non-Priority (pps)               2           1           1           1
                  (bps)             134          89          89          89
            Total (pps)               2           1           1           1
                  (bps)             134          89          89          89
Output:  Priority (pps)               0           0           0           0
                  (bps)               0           0           0           0
     Non-Priority (pps)               2           1           1           1
                  (bps)             115         230         230         230
            Total (pps)               2           1           1           1
                  (bps)             115         230         230         230
Processing: Load (pct)                0           0           0           0
```

Useful debug Commands

This section covers a few of the **debug** commands that are useful in debugging system or IOS features. As with other **debug** commands, they are meant to be run only during a scheduled maintenance window or in a very controlled manner on a production system.

Example 11-17 shows the most useful **debug platform** command options.

Example 11-17 **debug platform** *Options Available on the ASR 1000*

```
ASR1006# debug platform hardware qfp active ?
  classification        Debug classification
  datapath              Debug datapath
  feature               Debug features
  ignore-fault          Ignore CPP faults
  ignore-stuck-thread   Ignore stuck PPE threads
  infrastructure        Debug infrastructure
  interface             Debug interface
  system                Debug CPP system
```

Table 11-1 outlines the description of the various **debug** parameters shown in the output of Example 11-17.

Note In IOS XE 2.1.x, if you turn on any of the preceding platform-specific debugs, you need to repeat the command with a **no** in front of it to turn it off. Using the usual IOS **undebug all** command will not disable these platform-related debugs.

Table 11-1 debug *Command Parameters*

Parameter	Description
classification	Classification refers to a low-level database used for classifying various data structures used by QFP.
datapath	This allows you to debug packets, traces, and QFP instruction for a data path. You can also use an access control list (ACL) to narrow down the packets that you're trying to debug here.
feature	Refers to IOS features such as an access control list (ACL), Network Address Translation (NAT), Flexible Packet Matching (FPM), and quality of service (QoS). Like **datapath**, you can also use an ACL to narrow down the results here.
ignore-fault	Displays the faults that are being ignored by QFP software. This would disable reboot of ESP in the case of software/hardware error.
ignore-stuck-thread	Displays the faults that are being thrown by a stuck Packet Processing Element (PPE) thread.
infrastructure	Allows BQS-, punt-, or FIA-level debugging.
interface	Displays per-interface-level statistics that are attached to the system (by way of SPAs) or internal system only (for example, between an ESP and RP and QFP and crypto processor) interface.
system	Provides QFP HA-level debugging.

Troubleshooting IOS Features via Platform-Specific Commands

This section reviews some of the common IOS features and their associated platform hardware and software commands that you can use to troubleshoot the given feature.

Table 11-2 captures the IOS features and their respective ASR 1000 platform-related **show** and **debug** commands.

> **Tip** cpp_cp* and cpp_sp* logs can be very helpful to troubleshoot packets destined for the system or in some cases even through the system. For example, during IPsec troubleshooting, if your traffic is not passing and IOS commands are not revealing any useful information, you can turn on **debug platform hardware qfp active feature ipsec datapath info**. Doing so will start adding debug logs into /tmp/scratch/ in the ESP Linux folder. Actual files could be cpp_cp_f0-0.log or cpp_sp_f0-0.log. The CP and SP convention stand for ESP control and data plane, respectively. You can use the **more** command option when viewing these files in the platform shell on ESP. This allows you to look at the actual contents to serve as an aid in troubleshooting.

Table 11-2 *ASR 1000 Platform Software-Related* **show** *and* **debug** *Commands*

IOS Feature	Platform Software-Related Commands	Description
Access lists	**show platform software access-list** *route-processor* {**bind** | **information** | **name** | **statistics**}	Displays the RP forwarding manager access list interface binding, general information, name, and messaging statistics
	debug platform acl {**config** | **interface** | **statistics** | **template**}	Displays debugging information on access list configuration, interface configuration, statistics update, and template information for platform error, events, or trace
ERSPAN	**show platform software erspan** *route-processor* **session** {**session #** | **summary**}	Displays RP-related information for a particular ERSPAN session #, or summary
Fragmentation and VFR	**show platform software interface** [**route-processor**] [**active** | **standby**] **name** *GigabitEthernet2/2/0*	Displays RP-related statistics for the interface
	debug ip virtual-reassembly	Displays debugging information on virtual fragmentation and reassembly (VFR)
IPv4/6 CEF	**show platform software ip** *route-processor* **cef internal**	Displays RP forwarding manager Cisco Express Forwarding (CEF) v4 information
	show platform software ipv6 *route-processor* **cef detail**	Displays RP forwarding manager CEF v6 information
MLPPP	**show platform software mlppp** {**counter** | **index**}	Displays RP forwarding manager Multilink PPP (MLPPP)-related counter and index statistics
	debug platform software mlp {**bundle** | **link**}	Displays debugging information on (Multilink PPP) MLP bundle and member links

Table 11-2 *ASR 1000 Platform Software-Related* **show** *and* **debug** *Commands*

IOS Feature	Platform Software-Related Commands	Description
NetFlow	**show platform software netflow** *route-processor* **cache** **show platform software netflow** *route-processor* **exp-cfg** **show platform software netflow** *route-processor* **interface** **show platform software netflow** *route-processor* **a sampler** **show platform software netflow** *route-processor* **active stats** **show platform software netflow** *route-processor* **standby cache** **show platform software netflow** *route-processor* **standby exp-cfg** **show platform software netflow** *route-processor* **standby interface** **show platform software netflow** *route-processor* **standby sampler** **show platform software netflow** *route-processor* **standby stats**	Displays RP-related NetFlow statistics on exporter config, interface, sampler config, and messaging statistics
	debug platform software netflow **debug platform software netflow all** **debug platform software netflow cache** **debug platform software netflow export** **debug platform software netflow interface** **debug platform software netflow sampling** **debug platform software forwarding-manager** *route-processor* **active netflow** [*level*] **debug platform software forwarding-manager** *route-processor* **standby netflow** [*level*]	Displays debugging information for NetFlow on cache, export, interface, sampling, and so on

continues

Table 11-2 *ASR 1000 Platform Software-Related* **show** *and* **debug** *Commands*

IOS Feature	Platform Software-Related Commands	Description
QoS	**show platform software qos {class | statistics}**	Displays QoS-related class and general statistics
	debug platform software qos {actions | class | initialization | interface | messaging}	Displays debugging information for QoS actions (set/police/queue), class events, initialization events, interface specific events, and messaging events
SBC	**show platform software sbc** *route-processor* **tables**	Displays a platform SBC table summary that includes SBC's media pools and call events
	show sbc {signaling-flow-stats | addresses | controllers | flow-pair | flow-stats | forwarder-stats | signaling-flow-stats | version | version information}	Displays platform SBC's various control and messaging information
VRF-aware features	**show running vrf**	Displays the VRF present in the running configuration
	show ip vrf	Displays the VRF and their associated interface associations

Table 11-3 captures the IOS features and their respective ASR 1000 platform hardware-related **show** and **debug** commands.

Table 11-3 *ASR 1000 Platform Hardware-Related* **show** *and* **debug** *Commands*

IOS Feature	Platform Hardware-Related Commands	Description
Access lists	**show platform hardware qfp active classification class-group-manager class-group acl** *number*	Displays ESP-related information for ACL configuration in Class Group Manager (CGM)
	debug platform hardware qfp feature acl [info | error | warn | trace]	Displays debugging information on access lists based on information or error related

Table 11-3 *ASR 1000 Platform Hardware-Related* **show** *and* **debug** *Commands*

IOS Feature	Platform Hardware-Related Commands	Description
ERSPAN	**show platform hardware qfp active feature erspan** {**state** | **session**}	Displays ESP-related Encapsulated Remote Switched Port Analyzer (ERSPAN) state and session information
	debug platform hardware qfp active feature erspan {**client** | **datapath**} {**data** | **detail** | **error** | **feature** | **session**}	Displays debugging hardware information for ERSPAN
IPv4/6 CEF	**debug platform hardware qfp active cef-mpls** {**client** | **datapath**} {**ip** | **ipv6** | **v4mcast** | **v6mcast**}	Displays debugging hardware information for CEF, IPv4/IPv6 multicast, and so on
IPv4 tunneling	**show platform hardware qfp active interface tunnel_name** **show platform hardware qfp active infrastructure uidb tunnel_name input config**	Displays hardware information for interface tunnels
	debug platform ha qfp active feature tunnel datapath qfp {*qfp-id#* | **level**}	Displays debugging hardware information for tunnel interfaces
MLPPP	**show platform hardware qfp active feature mlppp datapath bundle** *intf-name* **detail**	Displays hardware information for MLPPP link and bundle in the data path (QFP)
	debug platform hardware qfp feature mlppp client **debug platform hardware qfp feature mlppp datapath**	Displays debugging hardware information for MLPPP client and data path, respectively
Multicast	**show platform hardware qfp active feature cef-mpls prefix** {**ip** | **ipv6** | **mpls** | **v4mcast** | **v6mcast**}	Displays hardware information for v4/v6 multicast information
	debug platform hardware qfp active feature multicast datapath {**v4mcast** | **v6mcast**}	Displays debugging hardware information for IPv4 and v6 multicast

continues

Table 11-3 *ASR 1000 Platform Hardware-Related* **show** *and* **debug** *Commands*

IOS Feature	Platform Hardware-Related Commands	Description
QoS	**show platform hardware slot f0 serdes statistics** **show platform hardware port** *interface* **plim statistics**	Displays platform slot/port-level Serdes and physical line interface module (PLIM) statistics
	show platform hardware qfp active infrastructure bqs {queue | schedule} out default interface *name* [**detail**]	Displays platform hardware-related queues/schedules
	show platform hardware port *slot/subslot/interface* **plim buffer settings**	Displays platform hardware-related interface buffer-level statistics
	show platform hardware qfp active statistics drop | incl Bqs	Displays platform hardware-related drops, possibly due to out of resource (OOR) in Buffering, Queuing, and Schedule BQS chipset, and so on
	debug platform hardware qfp active feature qos {client | datapath}	Displays debugging hardware information for both the client and data path on the ESP for QoS
SBC	show platform hardware qfp feature sbc {flow | global | logging | pfilter | sfx}	Shows platform hardware information on SBC flow, logging, packet filtering, and SIP Faster Register (SFX)
	debug sbc SBCname mps all debug sbc SBCname {filter | high-availability all | log-level | mpf}	Debugging information on SBC filter, HA, logging level, and Media Packet Forwarder (MPF)

Common System Error Messages

In this section, you will learn some of the most common error/log messages on an ASR 1000 system. Advanced knowledge of these messages can help lessen your confusion and speed up eventual problem resolution.

Message: "Warning: Filesystem Is Not Clean" During RP Boot

Cause: This message appears during RP boot. It mentions that since the last RP boot, the file system was not gracefully shut down and therefore is not clean. During RP boot, the

ASR 1000 system will also give the following message as it autocorrects and cleans up the file system:

```
%IOSXEBOOT-4-FILESYS_ERRORS_CORRECTED: (rp/1): bootflash contained errors which
  were auto-corrected.
```

Resolution: The system knows how to take care of this error, as outlined in the autocorrection message shown. To avoid this error message, bring down the RP using the **reload** command before yanking it out. The file system can also be cleaned manually using **fsck** from the Linux shell.

Message: "%IOSXE-7-PLATFORM: F0: sntp: Resetting on Error x > y"

Cause: This message can appear for either the Flow Processor (FP) (or Embedded Service Processor [ESP]) or for the SPA Interface Processor (SIP). This is a cosmetic error message that may appear with or without traffic passing through the system.

Resolution: This is just an informational message. Basically, the Simple Network Time Protocol (SNTP) on SIP and FP/ESP does small time adjustments, but when the drift is larger than a certain amount (for example, if you change the time manually on any of these components), it will treat it as "error" and reset the clock as per drift from RP. Functionally, it is not a problem. This should not appear on consoles starting from IOS XE Release 2.3.0.

Message: "%ASR1000_PEM-3-PEMFAIL: The PEM in Slot 0 Is Switched Off or Encountering a Failure Condition"

Cause: This message indicates that the Power Entry Module (PEM) in slot 0 is either switched off or disconnected.

Resolution: The ASR 1000 system can run on one PEM as long as the other PEM still remains inside the chassis with no more than one fan failure. This error message is not cosmetic; instead, it points to a failure. Be sure to visually inspect the system to carry out further troubleshooting.

Summary

In this chapter, you learned that troubleshooting requires a systematic approach, with a logical flow of steps for successful results. The chapter then discussed various useful ASR 1000-specific **show** and **debug** commands that enable you to carry out this task.

Furthermore, the chapter also reviewed the common system error messages, their meaning, and how they can be resolved.

The next five chapters look at real-world use cases and the value-add that ASR 1000 brings to them, to reinforce all the concepts that you've learned in the previous chapters. Along the way, you'll learn some more platform-related commands and the context where they are useful.

Review Questions

1. Is it possible to look at the status of LEDs on an RP, ESP, and SIP without any physical access?
2. Can you look at the cumulative RX/TX statistics for the whole SIP?
3. What is the best way to know that an ASR 1000 system is dropping packets and to determine the reasons for those drops?
4. What command enables you to look at all the control CPUs in the system and their associated memory utilization?

Answers

1. Yes, it's possible. You can use the **show platform hardware slot r0 led status** command to watch LEDs on RP0.
2. Yes, it's possible via the **show platform hardware subslot 0/2 plim statistics** command.
3. You can use the **show platform hardware qfp active statistics drop | e _0_** command to achieve this purpose.
4. You can use either the **top** command within the respective Linux shells for RP, ESP, or SIP. Alternatively, the **show platform software status control-processor** command can achieve that purpose.

Further Reading

Cisco IOS XE, Troubleshooting Initial Start-Up Problems, document: http://tinyurl.com/o4hws7

Cisco IOS XE Configuration Guide, document: http://tinyurl.com/pt6yjx

Cisco IOS XE Command Reference, document: http://tinyurl.com/phuxsc

Cisco IOS XE Error and System Messages for IOS XE, document: http://tinyurl.com/qhgwyk

Cisco IOS XE New Features List, document: http://tinyurl.com/qrf7en

Cisco IOS XE SIP and SPA Hardware Installation Guide, document: http://tinyurl.com/pw4fue

Chapter 12

IP Routing Use Cases

This chapter focuses on routing and switching with ASR 1000 series routers. The chapter starts with a brief discussion of the capabilities of the router family, and then reviews how those strengths can be used to address relevant problems.

This approach, with detailed configuration examples where applicable, will allow you to understand the problems, the challenges they represent, and how you can use the ASR 1000 to address them.

Introduction to the Scalable and Modular Control Plane on the ASR 1000

The control plane is a logical concept that defines the part of the router architecture responsible for building and drawing the network topology map (also known as the routing table) and manifesting it to the forwarding plane (where actual packet forwarding takes place) in the form of the Forwarding Information Base (FIB).

While the forwarding capacity of the routers has continuously scaled throughout the years (the Cisco CRS-1, for example; the forwarding capacity for which boosted up to 92 terabits per second [Tbps]), the control-plane scale is given less attention. When routing products are compared, the focus is usually on the forwarding capacity (packets per second or bits per second).

Contrary to this popular notion, the control-plane scale is equally critical to ensure that the platform has the compute cycles in the form of Route Processor (RP) CPU to perform the following (among other things):

- CLI, and similar external management functions performed via Simple Network Management Protocol (SNMP) or Extensible Markup Language (XML)
- Routing protocols and their associated keepalives (including crypto functions in the control plane)
- Link-layer protocols and their associated keepalives
- Services such as RADIUS, TACACS+, DHCP, Session Border Controller (SBC), and Performance-based Routing (PfR) Master Controller function
- All other traffic that cannot be handled at the data plane (for example, legacy protocols such as IPX), including punt traffic

The Cisco ASR 1000 router series delivers complete separation of the control and data plane, which enables the infrastructure's control plane to scale independently of the data plane. The ASR 1000 has two RPs on the market today: ASR1000-RP1 (first generation) and ASR1000-RP2 (second generation). ASR1000-RP1 is based on a 1.5-GHz RP CPU, whereas ASR1000-RP2 hosts a dual-core Intel 2.66-GHz processor, literally increasing the scale many times over the ASR1000-RP1.

The central benefit of physically separating the forwarding and control planes is that if the traffic load becomes very heavy (the forwarding plane gets overwhelmed), it simply doesn't affect the control plane's capability to process new routing information.

Another way of looking at it is if the routing plane gets very busy because of any of the relevant tasks, causing the control plane to be busy, perhaps because of a flood of new route information (even worse, peer or prefix flaps), busy-ness doesn't adversely affect the capability of the forwarding plane to continue forwarding packets. This is a common problem that plagues all software-based routers (due to a single general-purpose CPU running both control and data planes).

Note ASR1000-RP1 and ASR1000-RP2 use different binaries (RP packages), because of the different processor architectures, where ASR1000-RP1 uses PowerPC and ASR1000-RP2 uses an Intel-based architecture. Hence, in-service software upgrades (ISSU) between those two images is not possible without the RP reboot (for a single-RP platform). However, there is no difference in IOS feature content present in either of them.

Key applications that benefit the most, from a big picture perspective, are network virtualization, infrastructure consolidation, and rapid rollout of various network-based services.

Before delving further and discussing the actual use cases from real-world networks, a quick refresher is in order on some commonly used terms.

NSF/SSO, NSR, Graceful Restart to Ensure Robust Routing

Nonstop forwarding (NSF) refers to the capability of the data plane to continue to function hitless when the routing plane disappears (momentarily, that is) and most likely fails over to a standby RP. Of course, the routing information and topology might change during this time and result in an invalid FIB, and therefore the switchover times should be as small as possible. The Cisco ASR 1000 provides switchover times of less than 50 ms RP to RP (or IOS daemon [IOSD] to IOSD for the ASR 1002-F/ASR 1002/ASR 1004).

Stateful switchover (SSO) refers to the capability of the control plane to hold configuration and various states during this switchover, and to thus effectively reduce the time to utilize the newly failed-over control plane. This is also handy when doing scheduled hitless upgrades within the ISSU execution path. The time to reach SSO for the newly active RP may vary depending on the type and scale of the configuration.

Graceful restart (GR) refers to the capability of the control plane to delay advertising the absence of a peer (going through control-plane switchover) for a "grace period," and thus help minimize disruption during that time (assuming the standby control plane comes up). GR is based on extensions per routing protocol, which are interoperable across vendors. The downside of the grace period is huge when the peer completely fails and never comes up, because that slows down the overall network convergence, which brings us to the final concept: nonstop routing (NSR).

NSR is an internal (vendor-specific) mechanism to extend the awareness of routing to the standby routing plane so that in case of failover, the newly active routing plane can take charge of the already established sessions.

Table 12-1 shows the compatibility and support matrix for ASR 1000 IOS XE software 2.2, and outlines the various states that are preserved during FP/ESP failover.

See the "Further Reading" section at the end of this chapter to find out where to look for complete route scale testing details.

Use Case: Achieving High Availability Using NSF/SSO

To command higher revenues and consistent profitability, service providers and enterprises are increasingly putting more mission-critical, time-sensitive services on their IP infrastructure. One of the key challenges to this is achieving and delivering high network availability with strict service level agreement (SLA) requirements. It is universally understood that availability of the network is directly linked with the overall total cost of ownership (TCO).

An enterprise has an ASR 1006 / ASR1000-ESP10 router used in the core of the network running OSPF as the routing protocol used to connect to multiple distribution hub routers, where distribution hub routers might not all be Cisco.

The goal is to reduce the route/prefix recomputation churn caused by RP switchover and reestablishment of OSPF peers.

Table 12-1 *Protocols and Their State Preservation via NSF/SSO*

Technology Focus	NSF	SSO
Routing protocols	Enhanced Interior Gateway Routing Protocol (EIGRP), Open Shortest Path First Version 2 (OSPFv2), OSPFv3, Intermediate System-to-Intermediate System (IS-IS), and Border Gateway Protocol Version 4 (BGPv4)	
IPv4 services	—	Address Resolution Protocol (ARP), Hot Standby Routing Protocol (HSRP), IPsec, Network Address Translation (NAT), IPv6 Neighbor Discovery Protocol (NDP), Unicast Reverse Path Forwarding (uRPF), Simple Network Management Protocol (SNMP), Gateway Load Balancing Protocol (GLBP), Virtual Router Redundancy Protocol (VRRP), Multicast (Internet Group Management Protocol [IGMP])
IPv6 services	—	IPv6 Multicast (Multicast Listener Discovery [MLD], Protocol Independent Multicast-Source Specific Multicast [PIM-SSM], MLD Access group)
L2/L3 protocols	—	Frame Relay, PPP, Multilink PPP (MLPPP), High-Level Data Link Control (HDLC), 802.1Q, bidirectional forwarding detection (BFD)
Multiprotocol Label Switching (MPLS)	—	MPLS Layer 3 VPN (L3 VPN), MPLS Label Distribution Protocol (LDP)
SBC	—	SBC Data Border Element (DBE)

To address the requirements, you need to implement Internet Engineering Task Force (IETF) NSF for OSPF because that is interoperable with all vendors that are NSF-aware (a term used for a neighboring router that understands the GR protocol extensions). In this case, when NSF-capable ASR 1000 switches over from active RP to standby RP, there will be no packet loss at all, and downstream neighbors will not restart adjacencies.

Figure 12-1 shows the ASR 1000 core router and its neighbors, which are all NSF-aware and can act as helpers during RP SSO.

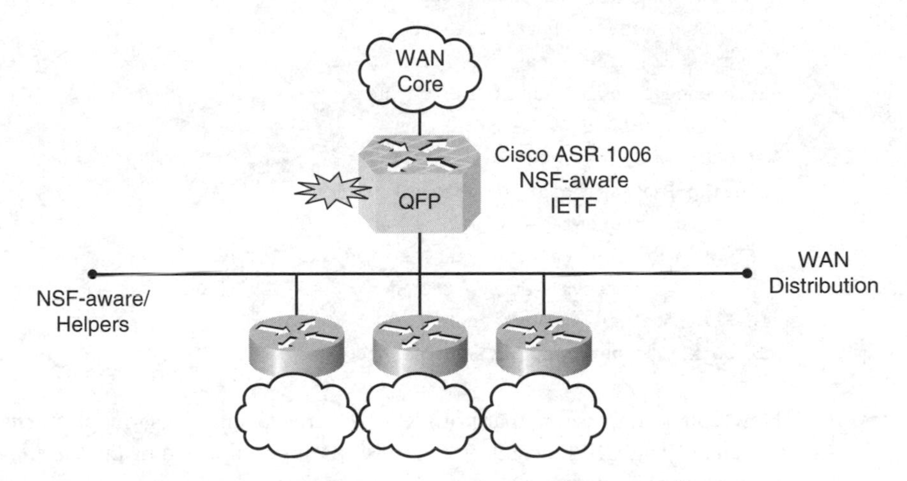

Figure 12-1 *Logical view of many regional WAN aggregation routers coming into a consolidated WAN campus edge router.*

To turn on IETF helper mode on all the distribution hub routers, including the Cisco ASR 1000, you need to execute the following configuration steps:

Step 1. Configure NSF within the given OSPF process ID:

```
ASR1006# configure terminal
ASR1006(config)# router ospf 100
ASR1006(config-router)# nsf ietf restart-interval 300
```

Note By default, both IETF and Cisco NSF helper modes are turned on.

Step 2. Check that the NSF is turned on, for sure, on the helper router:

```
Router-helper# show ip ospf 100


 Routing Process "ospf 100" with ID 172.16.1.2
 --output truncated--
 IETF Non-Stop Forwarding enabled
    restart-interval limit: 300 sec
 IETF NSF helper support enabled
 Cisco NSF helper support enabled
 Reference bandwidth unit is 100 mbps
    Area BACKBONE(0)
ASR1006# sh ip ospf 100
 Routing Process "ospf 1" with ID 10.1.1.1
 --output truncated--
 IETF Non-Stop Forwarding enabled
    restart-interval limit: 300 sec
 IETF NSF helper support enabled
 Cisco NSF helper support enabled
```

Step 3. Now you need to verify that both RPs are active (using the **show platform** command) and OSPF neighbor relationships are established (using the **show ip ospf neighbors** command):

```
! active ESP:
ASR1006# show platform software ip fp active cef summary
Forwarding Table Summary
Name        VRF id   Table id    Protocol       Prefixes     State
----------------------------------------------------------------
Default      0        0            IPv4           10000        cpp:
                                                               0x10e265d8
                                                               (created)
! standby ESP:
ASR1006# show platform software ip fp standby cef summary
Forwarding Table Summary
Name        VRF id   Table id    Protocol     Prefixes  State
----------------------------------------------------------------.
Default      0        0           IPv4         10000     cpp: 0x10e265d8
                                                         (created)
```

You can also view the prefixes downloaded into both the active and standby Embedded Service Processor (ESP) before failing over the router.

The preceding output shows that about 10K routes are created and exist in both ESPs before the failover.

Step 4. Now you'll induce the RP SSO failover (using **redundancy force-switchover**) from the active RP enable mode CLI. The following output shows the effects from the newly active RP:

```
ASR1006# show ip ospf 100
 ——output truncated——
 IETF Non-Stop Forwarding enabled
    restart-interval limit: 300 sec, last IETF NSF restart 00:00:10 ago
IETF NSF helper support enabled
 Cisco NSF helper support enabled
```

Note The FIB remains detached from the Routing Information Base (RIB) until the routing protocol reconverges; therefore, both ESPs retain the pre-failover FIB copies until that time. Packet forwarding continues based on the last-known FIB and adjacency entries. The newly active RP sends GR link-state advertisements (LSAs, grace LSAs) to the NSF-aware/helper routers (again, distribution hub routers in this case). With ASR1000-RP1 and ASR1000-ESP10/ESP20, FIB download times are in the neighborhood of 5 k prefixes/sec. It is also worth noting that large number of peers will cause RIB/FIB calculation to put more stress on RP CPU, and similarly large number of prefixes (with or without large number of peers) will cause longer FIB download times. You can tune BGP timers and GR timers for scenarios where you have a large number of prefixes as default values, which might not be the most optimal.

Step 5. RP SSO will not result in any packet loss, because forwarding continues during this entire process. During this switchover process, you can execute the **show platform** command to verify that the former active RP is booting ("booting" state).

In case of ASR1000-ESP10 failover, some small packet loss will occur (packets that are being processed inside the QuantumFlow Processor [QFP]), although that would account for much less than 1-ms worth of transit traffic loss.

NSF/SSO allows RPs to fail over without any packet loss, and ESPs can fail over with extremely small packet loss. The Cisco ASR 1000 shows core benefits of a carrier-class router where failover times beat even the Automatic Protection Switching (APS) gold standard of 50 ms.

In today's networks, where SLAs are enforced and networks are participating in life- and mission-critical scenarios, a robust infrastructure with faster failover based on modern architectures is a must.

Packet Capture Using Encapsulated Remote SPAN

For various reasons, including compliance, enterprises are looking for ways to capture data for further analysis (using an intrusion detection/prevention system [IDS/IPS] or some other advanced analysis system). NetFlow proves handy for this purpose, where you can get detailed IP flow accounting information for the given network.

NetFlow, however useful, still does not provide full packet capture capability from Layer 2 to 7. This is where the Switch Port Analyzer (SPAN) function steps in, although as the name says, this is limited to switches only. SPAN or Remote SPAN (RSPAN), where monitored traffic can traverse a Layer 2 cloud or network, essentially creates an opportunity to capture and analyze traffic on two different switches that are part of a single Layer 2 domain (as opposed to a Layer 3 routing domain). Encapsulated Remote SPAN (ERSPAN), as the name says, brings generic routing encapsulation (GRE) for all captured traffic and allows it to be extended across Layer 3 domains. Until recently, ERSPAN has been available only on Catalyst 6500 and 7600 platforms.

The Cisco ASR 1000 originated with ERSPAN support and can operate in two ways:

- As source or destination for ERSPAN sessions
- As source and destination for ERSPAN sessions at the same time

Note, as well, that this implementation is interoperable with Catalyst 6500 and 7600, and so traffic captured on a port/interface attached to an ASR 1000 can be sent to a destination monitoring station over to a 6500/7600 across a Layer 3 domain as a GRE packet.

Use Case: Ethernet Frame Capture and Transport Across a Layer 3 Cloud

An enterprise has an ASR 1000 being used at one of the regional HQs in San Francisco, and needs to capture traffic from an interface on an on-demand basis and bring it to the centralized data center location in Austin, terminating it on a Catalyst 6500 switch in the core. The San Francisco and Austin locations are connected via a shared MPLS IP VPN cloud.

Note ERSPAN is a Cisco proprietary feature and is available only to Catalyst 6500, 7600, Nexus, and ASR 1000 platforms to date. The ASR 1000 supports ERSPAN source (monitoring) only on Fast Ethernet, Gigabit Ethernet, and port-channel interfaces. The ASR 1000, being a router, does not support regular SPAN or RSPAN functions. For source interface and source VLAN configuration, the default SPAN direction is "both."

To meet the requirement needed for this enterprise, you need to implement ERSPAN on the ASR 1000 in the SF HQ location as a source session and terminate it at the Catalyst 6500 switch in the core.

Figure 12-2 shows the ERSPAN source (monitored) and destination (monitoring) ports on the ASR 1000 and Catalyst 6500, respectively.

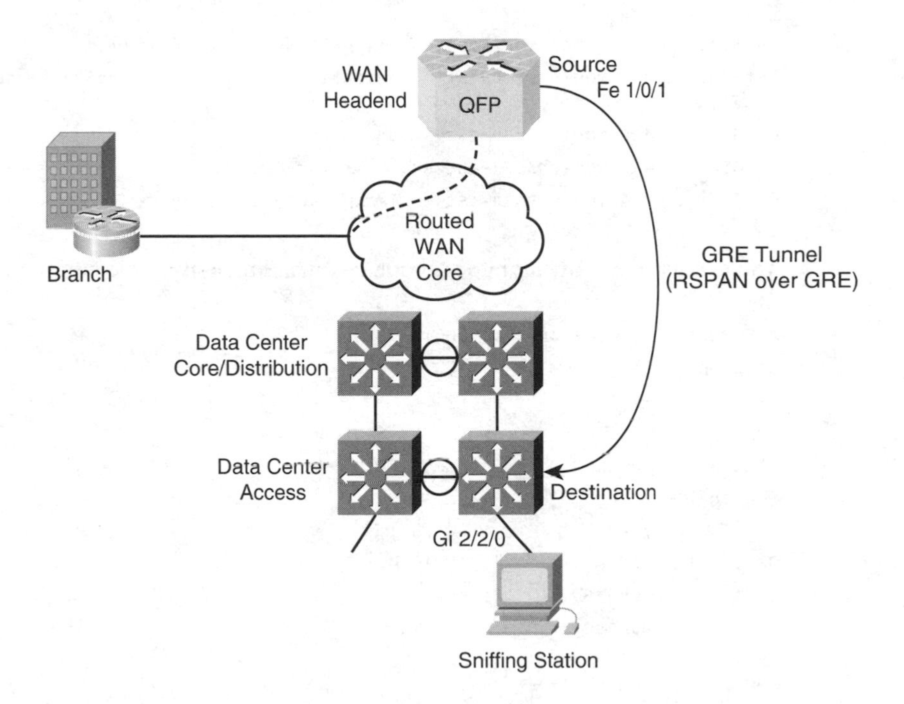

Figure 12-2 *Ethernet frame capture at the WAN headend and transporting them to data center via a Layer 3 cloud.*

Begin with the configuration on the ASR 1000. Here we'll configure source interface, direction of traffic, and ERSPAN session ID.

Step 1. Identify the ports/interfaces that need to be monitored, and the direction of traffic that needs to be captured, (for example, Rx) by entering the following commands:

```
ASR1006(config)# monitor session 1 type erspan-source
ASR1006(config-mon-erspan-src)# source interface Fe1/0/1 rx
ASR1006(config-mon-erspan-src)# destination
ASR1006(config-mon-erspan-src-dst)# erspan-id 100
ASR1006(config-mon-erspan-src-dst)# ip address 10.10.0.1
ASR1006(config-mon-erspan-src-dst)# ip ttl 32
ASR1006(config-mon-erspan-src-dst)# origin ip address 172.16.0.1
```

Note The ASR 1000 supports up to 1024 sessions that can be source, destination, or a combination per system. This provides tremendous flexibility in data capturing and monitoring to a routing platform.

Step 2. Configure the Catalyst 6500 to receive traffic from the source session on the ASR 1000 from Step 1:

```
Cat6500(config)# monitor session 2 type erspan-destination
Cat6500(config-mon-erspan-dst)# destination interface gigabitEthernet
  2/2/0
Cat6500(config-mon-erspan-dst)# source
Cat6500(config-mon-erspan-dst-src)# erspan-id 100
Cat6500(config-mon-erspan-dst-src)# ip address 172.16.0.1
```

You can use the **show monitor session** command to verify the configuration:

```
ASR1006# show monitor session 1
Session 1
----.
Type                       : ERSPAN Source Session
Status                     : Admin Enabled
Source Ports               :
    RX Only                : Fe1/0/1
Destination IP Address     : 10.10.0.1
Destination ERSPAN ID      : 100
Origin IP Address          : 172.16.0.1
IP TTL                     : 32
```

Step 3. To be able to monitor the statistics of monitored traffic, you need to use **show platform hardware qfp active feature erspan state** command:

```
ASR1006# show platform hardware qfp active feature erspan state
ERSPAN State:
  Status    : Active
--output truncated--
System Statistics:
  DROP src session replica  :        0 /        0
  DROP term session replica :        0 /        0
  DROP receive malformed    :        0 /        0
  DROP receive invalid ID   :        0 /        0
  DROP recycle queue full   :        0 /        0
  DROP no GPM memory        :        0 /        0
  DROP no channel memory    :        0 /        0
```

This will achieve the purpose of capturing received traffic on the ASR 1000 (FE1/0/1) to Catalyst 6500 GE2/2/0. This traffic will simply be captured, encapsulated in GRE by ASR 1000 natively by the QFP chipset and routed over to the Catalyst 6500. A sniffing station on the 6500 attached to GE2/2/0 will see the complete Ethernet frame (L2 to L7) up to jumbo size (assuming the routed WAN infrastructure can carry jumbo frames end to end).

The ASR 1000, being the first midrange routing platform to support ERSPAN, adds tremendous value to data capturing and data visibility end to end from a branch, or from HQ to data center, a common requirement in medium to large enterprise networks. ERSPAN packet replication is natively done by the QFP chipset, and therefore no external modules are required. ERSPAN, when combined with NetFlow, can result in detailed end-to-end network visibility.

Achieving Segmentation Using MPLS over GRE and MPLS VPNs over GRE Solutions

In today's world, an enterprise campus is home to many different and often competing users. Multitenant environments such as universities, airports, and some public-sector networks (including educational networks) fall under this category.

Such enterprises leverage their high-touch intelligent networking infrastructure to provide connectivity and network services for all stakeholders. For instance, different airlines could share one physical airport network and get billed for this connectivity. This setup accelerates the return on network infrastructure investment, and it optimizes network operations and operational expenses through virtualization. Regulatory compliance, mergers and acquisitions (M&A), and network infrastructure consolidation are among the many drivers. For the users of this single physical network, it results in seamless and instant-on delivery of services, which in turn results in increased revenue streams.

MPLS (or MPLs-based applications) has gained a lot of ground because of its capability to provide this virtualization within a large enterprise network and still provide the much-needed segmentation. The relevant technologies that you hear about are usually MPLS/LDP over GRE, and MPLS VPNs (2547) over GRE, in addition to a host of other MPLS-based technologies.

Use Case: Self-Managed MPLS and Enterprise Private WAN Segmentation

An enterprise is running a "self-managed" or "self-deployed MPLS" core to achieve this network segmentation. Deploying MPLS (or RFC 2547) over a mesh of GRE tunnels (enterprise provider edge [PE] to enterprise PE) allows the enterprise to extend their MPLS network over almost any IP network. Additional benefits include flexibility of edge router roles (provider [P] or PE), independence from the service provider (SP) cloud (which sees those packets as IP packets), and an easier add-on encryption capability, something you can call MPLS over GRE over IPsec. Several large enterprises today are running this environment in their production network.

Configurations of such deployments are fairly straightforward, where WAN edge routers (or customer edges [CE]) basically serve as enterprise Ps or PEs (also referred to as E-Ps or E-PEs), as documented in the text that follows.

Figure 12-3 shows the isolated self-deployed enterprise MPLS clouds that are connected together via an SP MPLS core using LDP over GRE.

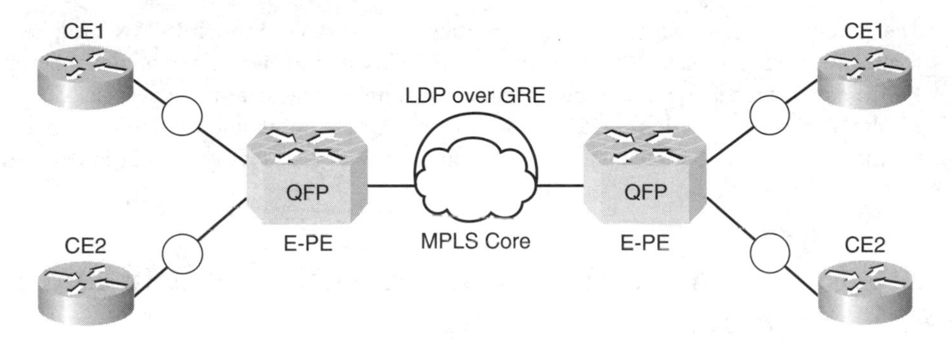

Figure 12-3 *Enterprise PEs (E-PE) are connected across the enterprise-owned/managed MPLS cloud.*

A point-to-point GRE tunnel is set up between each WAN edge router pair if a full mesh is desired. From a control-plane perspective, the following protocols are to be run within the GRE tunnels:

- An IGP such as EIGRP or OSPF for MPLS device reachability. (This makes the E-PE, E-P, and route reflectors [RRs], if configured, reachable to each other.)
- LDP, to allow the formation of LSPs over which traffic is forwarded.
- MP-iBGP for VPN route and label distribution between the E-PE devices.

You will need to configure MPLS labeling, using the **mpls ip** command, on the tunnel interfaces rather than on the WAN edge router physical interfaces. You can verify this configuration with the **show platform software interface** command:

```
E-PE-SF(config)# interface Tunnel10
 description GRE tunnel to E-P-NY
 bandwidth 10000
 ip address 172.16.10.5 255.255.255.0
 ip mtu 1400
 mpls ip
 tunnel source Loopback10
 tunnel destination 10.10.10.1

E-PE-SF# sh platform software interface fp active name Tunnel10
Name: Tunnel10, ID: 24, CPP ID: 25, Schedules: 0
——output truncated——
Flags: ipv4, mpls
ICMP Flags: unreachables, redirects, no-info-reply, no-mask-reply
ICMP6 Flags: unreachables, redirects
Dirty: unknown
AOM dependency sanity check: PASS
AOM Obj ID: 1081
```

Figure 12-4 shows the end-to-end protocol stacks for an MPLS/LDP over GRE scenario.

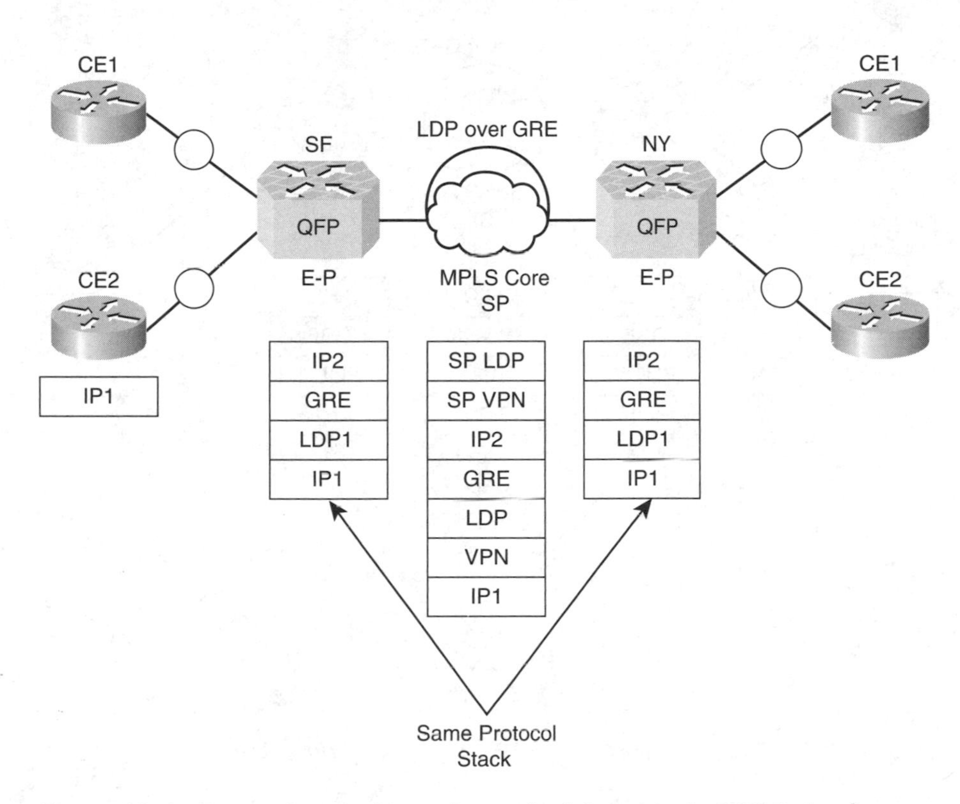

Figure 12-4 *Protocol stacks for packets at both P and in the MPLS cloud.*

This will effectively create an LSP from E-P-SF to E-P-NY, and the intermediary SP cloud does not have to be an MPLS-based service.

Note There is a subtle but critical difference between the enterprise WAN edge routers being configured as P or PE. In the former case, there will be an additional label and LSP, whereas in the latter case there will be no LSP and no additional label because of penultimate hop pop (PHP) behavior. The only use of the labeling in case of E-PE enterprise segmentation is to map Virtual Routing and Forwarding (VRF) instances (as in per customer or network) within the same GRE tunnel and still be able to multiplex and demultiplex them to correct customer VRF instances.

Cisco ASR 1000, starting from IOS XE 2.2, supports both MPLS/LDP over GRE and MPLS VPNs (2547) over GRE with and without encryption.

Figure 12-5 shows the end-to-end protocol stacks for an MPLS VPNs over GRE scenario, or something also known as 2547 VPNs over GRE.

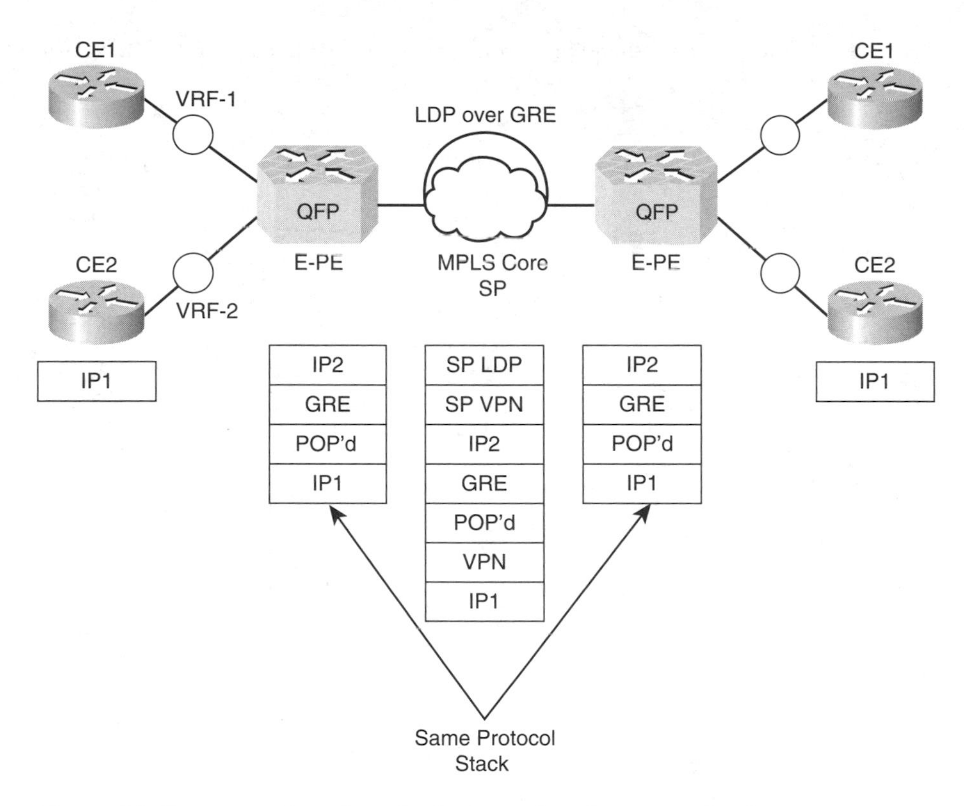

Figure 12-5 *Protocol stacks at both PEs and in the MPLS cloud.*

Full-mesh peer-to-peer (p2p) GRE tunnels can easily become an administrative hassle in a network with large number of WAN edge routers. In those cases, enterprises can also consider 2547 over Dynamic Multipoint VPN (DM VPN), or 2547 over mGRE over IPsec, to ease the burden of tunnel administration. These solutions will be supported on ASR 1000 in the future IOS XE versions.

The Cisco ASR 1000 provides the extreme flexibility necessary to meet the changing business environments that need virtualization in today's multitenant enterprise networks by supporting MPLS/2547 over GRE solutions at serial interface, Fast Ethernet, Gigabit Ethernet, or even 10 Gigabit Ethernet speeds natively or higher with the unique capability to perform all these encapsulations inside the single QFP chipset.

Scalable v4/VPNv4 Route Reflector

With the growing adoption of MPLS in the enterprises to achieve large-scale virtualization and segmentation, there is also a need for enterprises to have their own route reflector (RR) for VPNv4 routes, deployed separately or combined in a PE router. An RR simplifies the iBGP full-mesh restriction where all PEs don't have to mesh with all other PEs, rather just with the RR.

Use Case: Route Reflection

Figure 12-6 shows the RR used by the enterprise in the self-managed MPLS clouds.

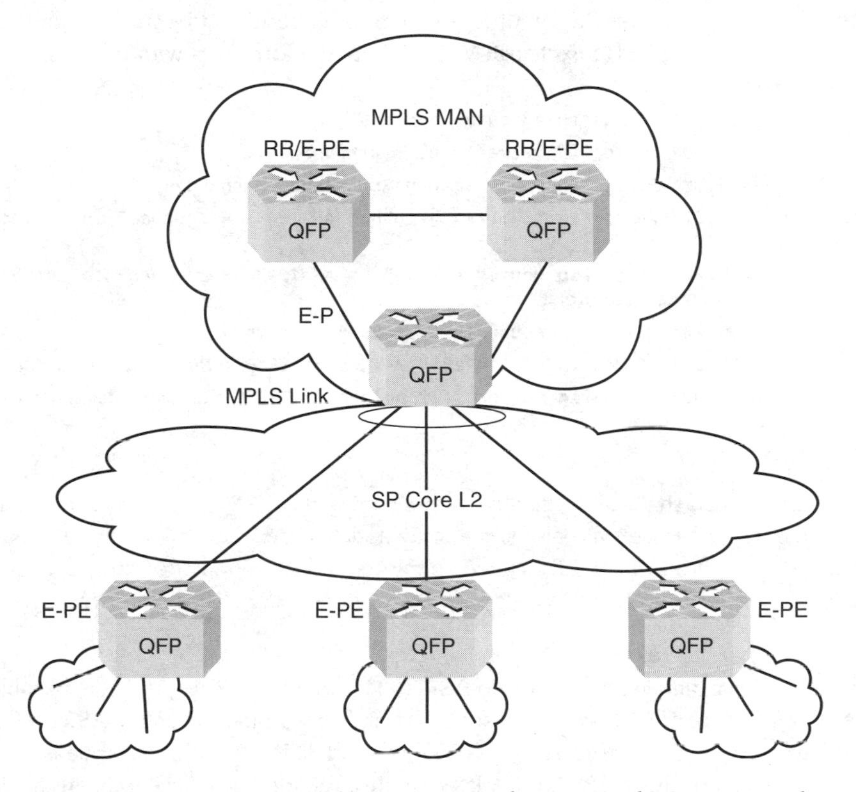

Figure 12-6 *MAN using the same router for E-PE and VPNv4 RR roles.*

To meet this requirement of avoiding the full mesh of iBGP, you need to configure the Cisco ASR 1000 as the RR for VPNv4 routes using the following steps:

Step 1. Configure RRs to peer with PEs to reflect VPNv4 routing information learned from other PEs:

```
ASR1004-RR(config)# router bgp 100
ASR1004-RR(config-router)# neighbor A-PE peer-group
ASR1004-RR(config)# neighbor A-PE remote-as 100
ASR1004-RR(config)# neighbor A-PE update-source Loopback100
ASR1004-RR(config)# neighbor PE loopback# peer-group A-PE
```

Step 2. Configure RRs for VPNv4 BGP peering between PEs and RRs:

```
ASR1004-RR(config-router)# address-family vpnv4
ASR1004-RR(config-router-af)# neighbor A-PE activate
ASR1004-RR(config-router-af)# neighbor A-PE route-reflector-client
```

```
ASR1004-RR(config-router-af)# neighbor A-PE send-community extended
ASR1004-RR(config-router-af)# neighbor PE loopback# peer-group A-PE
```

Step 3. Configure the PE for VPNv4 BGP peering between PEs and RRs (thus enabling PEs to exchange VPNv4 routing information with the RRs):

```
ASR1004-PE(config)# router bgp 100
ASR1004-PE(config-router)# no synchronization
ASR1004-PE(config-router)# bgp log-neighbor-changes
ASR1004-PE(config-router)# neighbor ASR1004-RR loopback ip# remote-as
  100
ASR1004-PE(config-router)# neighbor ASR1004-RR loopback ip# update-
  source Loopback0
ASR1004-PE(config-router)# address-family vpnv4
ASR1004-PE(config-router-af)# neighbor ASR1004-RR loopback ip# activate
ASR1004-PE(config-router-af)# neighbor 172.16.1.1 send-community
  extended
```

Note It is assumed that LDP is enabled on the core routers, RR, and PE core-facing interfaces. When RRs are in use, and all the outgoing updates have the same policy, it makes sense to use peer groups on the RRs because this reduces the number of outgoing updates (per client) that an RR router has to generate.

Although this example uses the Cisco ASR 1004 as the VPNv4 RR, this is applicable to the IPv4 RR, too. The VPNv4 route scale is completely a function of the ASR1000-RP you have in the system. With the ASR1000-RP1 and ASR1000-RP2, the scale is up to 1M and 4M, respectively, for IPv4. For VPNv4 routes, ESP does not have to be in the data path, and therefore any ESP can be used. Currently for IPv4, FIB entries are still populated, hence limiting the RR scale. This will change in a future IOS XE version.

The Cisco ASR 1000, by virtue of the ASR1000-RP1 and ASR1000-RP2, provides the largest scale for Route Reflector deployments in the Cisco midrange routing portfolio. The ASR1000-RP2, with 16-GB DRAM, truly raises the bar, with 64-bit IOS XE that allows the routes to scale up to 20M, which essentially rivals even the largest core routers available today.

In general, the ASR1000-RP2 (16-GB DRAM) provides four times the route scale over RP1 (4-GB DRAM), three times the number of peers/sessions (with the given convergence time) and is at least twice as fast in terms of route convergence (for the given set of routes and peers).

Scalable and Flexible Internet Edge

When we talk about a router to be placed at the edge of the network facing the public Internet, a few things come to mind. An ideal router needs to be flexible and scalable with regard to features and variety of interfaces, without requiring service modules for every basic service, such as Network Based Application Recognition (NBAR), Flexible Packet Matching (FPM), firewalls, and IPsec. Other critical attributes include high availability, deep packet inspection, and near-line-rate quality of service (QoS).

High availability enables applications to remain available in case of software or hardware failure that causes a data- or control-plane problem. Deep packet inspection helps classify the data based on application header or payload; it also addresses zero-day attacks.

Use Case: Internet Gateway/Edge Router

An enterprise is looking for, in a smaller-compact factor, an Internet edge that can natively accelerate NAT, firewall, NetFlow, and access control lists (ACL), along with ISSU and RP SSO. This device should also be able to scale up to 10 Gbps if needed in the future.

To meet these requirements, you could use the ASR 1002 with ASR1000-ESP5, which provides 5-Gbps system bandwidth with four built-in Gigabit Ethernet ports ready to be used as fiber or copper and facing either the inside LAN or Internet (usually provisioned via an Ethernet link).

The ASR 1002 can also take the ASR1000-ESP10, which satisfies the requirements of 10 Gbps, essentially doubling the bandwidth from initial deployment.

Figure 12-7 shows the ASR 1002/ASR1000-ESP5 deployed at the Internet edge.

There are no configurations to be shared in this use case, but note the performance and scale numbers for the ASR 1000 series routers relevant to the previously mentioned features.

Table 12-2 shows the various features and their respective performance and scale relevant to Internet edge.

> **Note** IOSD failover, IOS Firewall, and IPsec require their respective right to use (RTU) licenses. (At the time of this writing, however, these are only honor-based paper licenses and, as such, not enforced via the CLI.)
>
> Tunnels per second (TPS), as mentioned in Table 12-2, is basically a function of RP compute cycles, because all Internet Key Exchange (IKE) packets are sent to the RP. In some environments, such as remote-access VPN aggregation/head-end where tunnel churn is expected, the ASR1000-RP2 is an option to get higher scalability.

The Cisco ASR 1000 not only meets the typical Internet gateway router requirements here, but also exceeds them from both control- and data-plane perspectives. The capability to have two IOS daemons running at the same time, and providing IOSD-based SSO, is second to none!

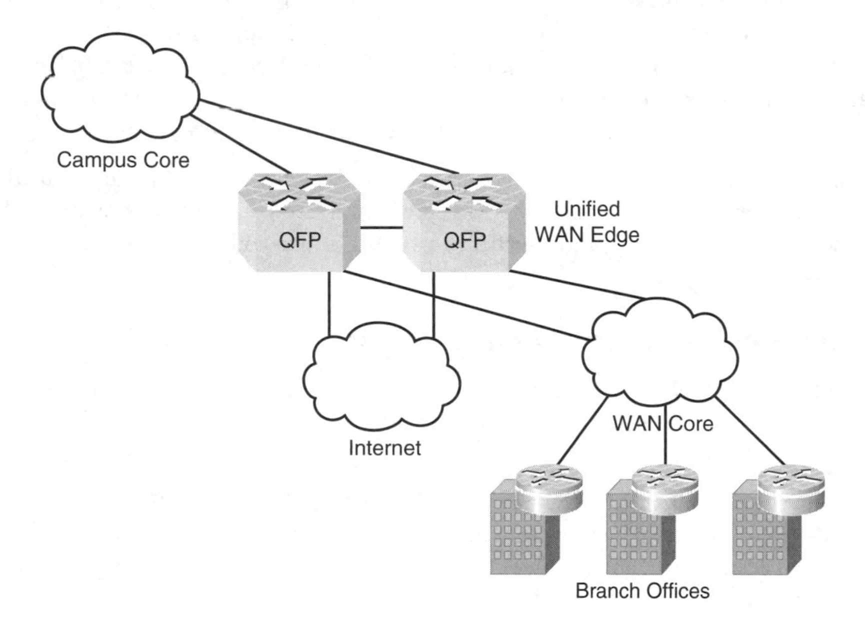

Figure 12-7 *Single router used for both the WAN edge and Internet gateway router.*

Table 12-2 *Various ESPs and Their Scale and Performance for IOS Zone-Based Firewall, NetFlow, and IPsec*

Feature	ASR1000-ESP5	ASR1000-ESP10	ASR1000-ESP20
IOS zone-based firewall (L4 inspection)	5 Gbps	10 Gbps	20 Gbps
NetFlow (v5, v8, v9)	500K flow cache entries	1M flow cache entries	2M flow cache entries
IPsec	1 Gbps at IMIX 4000 tunnels 90 tunnels/sec with ASR1000-RP1	2.5 Gbps at IMIX 4000 tunnels 90 tunnels/sec with ASR1000-RP1	5.2 Gbps at IMIX 4000 tunnels 90 tunnels/sec with ASR1000-RP1
Dual IOSD failover	< 50 ms	< 50 ms for ASR 1002-F/ASR 1002/ASR 1004 chassis	< 50 ms for ASR 1002-F/ASR 1002/ASR 1004 chassis

Scalable Data Center Interconnect

Today's businesses are seeing more and more consolidation for both file and application servers into a small number of data centers. Major drivers for this trend include cost savings, regulatory compliance, and ease of backup and administration.

At the heart of this, there is also a virtualization trend, where compute cycles are being isolated or abstracted from storage. This has created newer technologies for virtual machine high availability, and migration such as VMotion, clustering, or even geo-clustering of servers, which require extending Layer 2 VLANs across the WAN (data center interconnect).

Now, when looking at the data center connection and trying to tie it up with the application vendor requirements, almost all suggest using Layer 2 adjacent servers. To satisfy or emulate the requirement of L2 adjacencies across the WAN, various requirements emerge from these trends:

- **Loop prevention:** This refers to isolation of Spanning Tree Protocol (STP) to each data center itself, and not extended across the data center interconnect (DCI).
- **Redundancy:** This refers to the DCI solution itself not being prone to node or link failures. That, of course, requires redundancy.
- **Convergence times:** Apparently, there is no set standard for this requirement for DCI. It really depends on what applications are being run (for example, a requirement driven by VMotion stipulates no more than a couple of seconds for convergence).
- **Usage of multiple paths:** This is where technologies such as Virtual Switching Systems (VSS) and Multichassis EtherChannel (MEC) come into play. There is another similar solution known as virtual port channel (vPC), which essentially allows creating an EtherChannel where member links are across two different physical systems.

Note The Nexus 7000 supports vPC today. VSS/MEC are supported in the 6500 beginning with 12.2(33)SH1 code. Both technologies are slightly different but are beyond the scope of this book. TrustSec (802.1AE) is done using the port ASICs, and hence there is no degradation to the forwarding while encryption is added to the mix on Nexus 7K.

Interested readers should point to the links provided in the "Further Reading" section at the end of the chapter for more information.

Three types of transport are common for DCI:

- **Dark fiber:** Fiber that is not lit yet is called dark fiber. Not very many organizations have access to dark fiber, but the ones who have see it as the most preferred way of doing DCI. This is usually limited in distance.
- **IP:** This is a rather common medium and usually consists of some kind of private IP services that most SPs offer across geographies.
- **MPLS:** This is one of the more common ways to connect data centers.

The ASR 1000 supports almost all forms of Gigabit Ethernet coarse/dense wavelength-division multiplexing (CWDM/DWDM) optics, although the Catalyst 6500 with VSS/MEC has a solution that meets all the requirements in this arena, including multisite DC connectivity.

For IP and MPLS, the ASR 1000 offers (complementing the Cisco 6500 solution) Ethernet over MPLS and Ethernet over MPLS over GRE, starting from IOS XE 2.4 for dual-site DCI.

Figure 12-8 shows the MPLS transport and active/active EoMPLS pseudowires across DCI routers.

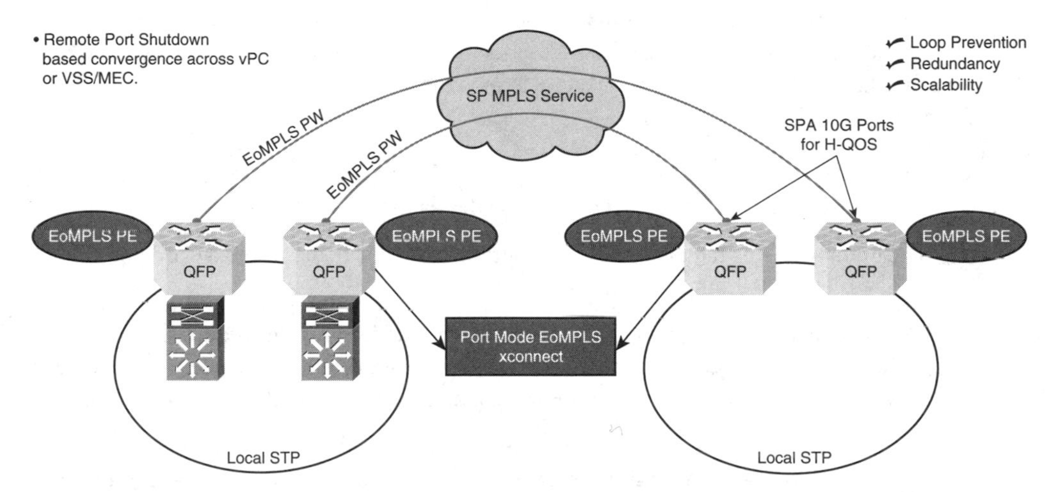

Figure 12-8 *Encrypting Ethernet frames at Layer 2 using TrustSec and avoiding the use Layer 3 encryption such as IPsec.*

Figure 12-9 shows the MPLS transport and active/active EoMPLS pseudowires across DCI routers. Here the DC core switches are Nexus 7Ks running TrustSec to encrypt packets at Layer 2 hop by hop.

The solution in Figure 12-9 shows a unique advantage where any traffic leaving the premise is required to be encrypted, as this provides a native way to encrypt all traffic. This requirement is common in government and state agencies.

Note The Nexus 7000 switch has always supported TrustSec. Interested readers should point to links in the "Further Reading" section at the end of the chapter for more information.

Figure 12-10 shows the IP transport and active/active EoMPLSoGRE tunnels across DCI routers.

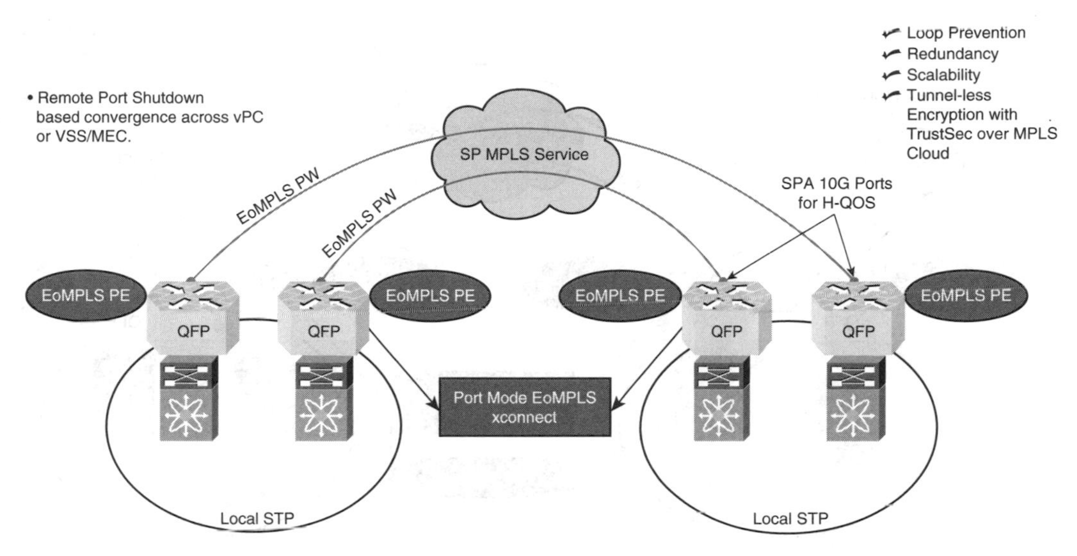

Figure 12-9 *EoMPLS scenario where the transport cloud is MPLS.*

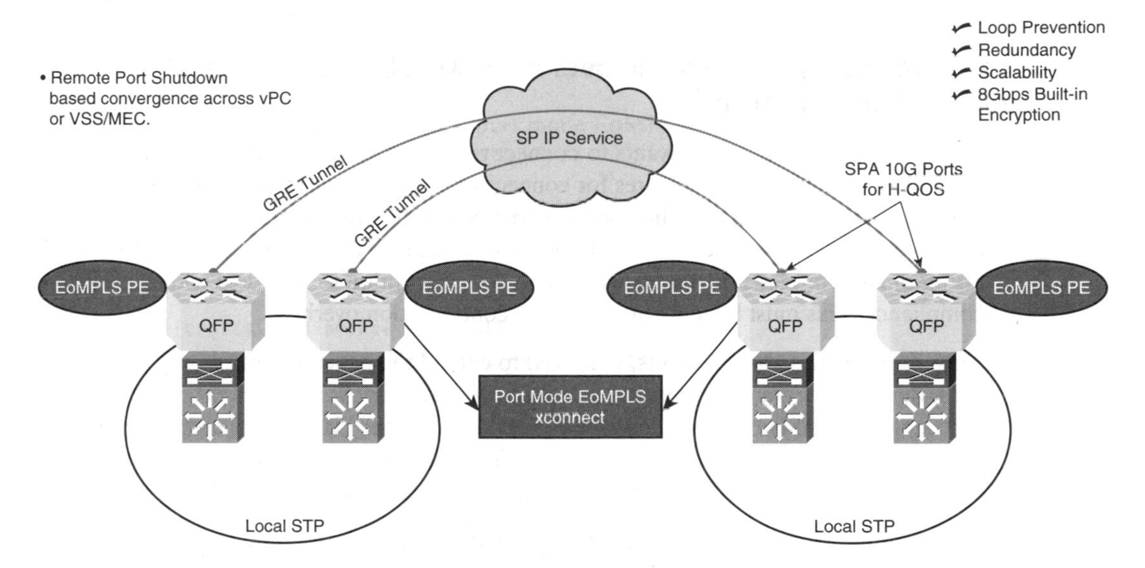

Figure 12-10 *EoMPLSoGRE scenario where the transport cloud is IP.*

This can also be seen as a consolidation strategy, especially for green-field deployments, where ASR 1000 working as a DCI LAN extension router can also serve as a consolidated unified WAN services router. This brings down the TCO much lower and at the same time allows for faster qualification, where the ASR 1000 functions as a private WAN aggregation, and even perhaps the Internet edge can be collapsed at the consolidated WAN edge.

Figure 12-11 shows the unified WAN edge, which consolidates the DCI with multiple other functions.

```
ASR1000-1(config-if)# negotiation auto
ASR1000-1(config-if)# mpls label protocol ldp
ASR1000-1(config-if)# mpls ip
!
!
ASR1000-1(config)# interface GigabitEthernet0/0/3
ASR1000-1(config-if)# description to ASR-2
ASR1000-1(config-if)# mtu 9216
ASR1000-1(config-if)# ip address 10.1.1.1 255.255.255.0
ASR1000-1(config-if)# load-interval 30
ASR1000-1(config-if)# negotiation auto
ASR1000-1(config-if)# mpls label protocol ldp
ASR1000-1(config-if)# mpls ip
```

```
ASR1000-2:
ASR1000-2(config)# interface Loopback0
ASR1000-2(config-if)# ip address 192.168.100.2 255.255.255.255
!
ASR1000-2(config)# interface GigabitEthernet0/0/0
ASR1000-2(config-if)# mtu 9216
ASR1000-2(config-if)# no ip address
ASR1000-2(config-if)# negotiation auto
ASR1000-2(config-if)# xconnect 192.168.100.1 100 encapsulation mpls
!
ASR1000-2(config)# interface GigabitEthernet0/0/1
ASR1000-2(config-if)# description to ASR-1
ASR1000-2(config-if)# mtu 9216
ASR1000-2(config-if)# ip address 10.1.2.2 255.255.255.0
ASR1000-2(config-if)# load-interval 30
ASR1000-2(config-if)# mpls label protocol ldp
ASR1000-2(config-if)# mpls ip
!
!
ASR1000-2(config)# interface GigabitEthernet0/0/3
ASR1000-2(config-if)# description to ASR-1
ASR1000-2(config-if)# mtu 9216
ASR1000-2(config-if)# ip address 10.1.1.2 255.255.255.0
ASR1000-2(config-if)# mpls label protocol ldp
ASR1000-2(config-if)# mpls ip
```

Example 12-2 shows the Nexus 7000 configuration to use TrustSec for all traffic going outbound on to the EoMPLS pseudowires (over an MPLS cloud).

Example 12-2 *Nexus 7K TrustSec Configuration*

```
Nexus-7K-1# sh run cts
version 4.1(2)
feature dot1x
feature cts
cts device-id Nexus-7K-1 password 7 qxz12345

interface Ethernet1/12
  switchport
  switchport access vlan 666
  cts manual
    sap pmk abcdef1234000000000000000000000000000000000000000000000000000000
  mtu 9216
  no shutdown

interface Vlan666
  no shutdown
  ip address 155.5.5.1/24
```

```
Nexus-7K-2# sh run cts
version 4.1(2)
feature dot1x
feature cts
cts device-id Nexus-7K-2 password 7 qxz12345
interface Ethernet1/12
  switchport
  switchport access vlan 666
  cts manual
    sap pmk abcdef1234000000000000000000000000000000000000000000000000000000
  mtu 9216
  no shutdown
interface Vlan666
  no shutdown
  mtu 9216
  ip address 155.5.5.2/24
```

Example 12-3 shows that the TrustSec session is established.

Example 12-3 *Confirmation That TrustSec Is Negotiated and Is Up*

```
Operational Status (TrustSec 802.1AE SAP negotiation successful):
Nexus-7K-1# show cts interface e 1/12
CTS Information for Interface Ethernet1/12:
    CTS is enabled, mode:   CTS_MODE_MANUAL
    IFC state:               CTS_IFC_ST_CTS_OPEN_STATE
    Authentication Status:  CTS_AUTHC_SKIPPED_CONFIG
```

```
      Peer Identity:
      Peer is:                  Not CTS Capable
      802.1X role:              CTS_ROLE_UNKNOWN
      Last Re-Authentication:
    Authorization Status:     CTS_AUTHZ_SKIPPED_CONFIG
      PEER SGT:                 0
      Peer SGT assignment:   Not Trusted
      Global policy fallback access list:
    SAP Status:               CTS_SAP_SUCCESS
      Configured pairwise ciphers: GCM_ENCRYPT
      Replay protection: Disabled
      Replay protection mode: Strict
      Selected cipher: GCM_ENCRYPT
      Current receive SPI: sci:1b54c148d80000 an:2
      Current transmit SPI: sci:225577968c0000 an:2
Operational Status (TrustSec 802.1AE SAP negotiation successful):
```

```
Nexus-7K-2# show cts interface e 1/12
CTS Information for Interface Ethernet1/12:
    CTS is enabled, mode:    CTS_MODE_MANUAL
    IFC state:                CTS_IFC_ST_CTS_OPEN_STATE
    Authentication Status:   CTS_AUTHC_SKIPPED_CONFIG
      Peer Identity:
      Peer is:                  Not CTS Capable
      802.1X role:              CTS_ROLE_UNKNOWN
      Last Re-Authentication:
    Authorization Status:     CTS_AUTHZ_SKIPPED_CONFIG
      PEER SGT:                 0
      Peer SGT assignment:   Not Trusted
      Global policy fallback access list:
    SAP Status:               CTS_SAP_SUCCESS
      Configured pairwise ciphers: GCM_ENCRYPT
      Replay protection: Disabled
      Replay protection mode: Strict
      Selected cipher: GCM_ENCRYPT
      Current receive SPI: sci:225577968c0000 an:2
      Current transmit SPI: sci:1b54c148d80000 an:2
```

As shown in Figure 12-12, the two ASR 1000s are connected via two active/active EoMPLS pseudowires. To deal with a failure scenario, the ASR 1000 uses a feature called Remote Pseudo Wire Shutdown. The behavior on the ASR 1000 is a bit different than on the Catalyst 6500/7600, where the feature does not depend on interworking with the Ethernet LMIs.

On the ASR 1000, this feature, upon pseudowire down state, shuts down the local laser on the port with "**xconnect**", **gi0/0/0**, as shown in the use case. This is seen by the peer

Ethernet port as the interface going down, and it will go to down/down. This allows the downstream devices to stop sending traffic to the port and results in almost instant convergence EoMPLS remote port shutdown provides faster failover times for both local/remote node or link failure scenarios.

This behavior is very helpful in the vPC scenario, because it will trigger the LACP (Link Aggregation Control Protocol) to converge instantly and will remove the member link from the virtual port channel.

Summary

This chapter discussed six use cases for Cisco ASR 1000 to provide the following variety of solutions:

- High availability using NSF/SSO in an enterprise
- Data capture using ERSPAN in a router
- MPLS over *x* solutions in a large enterprise that needs virtualization/segmentation at 10 Gbps or higher speeds
- VPNv4 RR in a self-deployed MPLS enterprise
- Highly available Internet gateway router
- DCI WAN router

The goal was really to go over a diverse set of technology problem statements and solutions that are common in an enterprise and to cover how the ASR 1000 addresses them.

Chapter Review Questions

1. Is NSF for IGPs enabled by default?
2. What is the difference between an NSF-aware and NSF-capable router?
3. What is ERSPAN, and which Cisco platforms support ERSPAN today?
4. How does IOS, being a 32-bit OS, address 16-GB DRAM in ASR1000-RP2 to achieve such a high route scale?
5. Does the ASR 1000 require a feature license to turn on and use MPLS, BGP, NAT, GRE, or NetFlow?
6. What is DCI, and how does the pseudowire failover work for remote node/link failure?

Answers

1. No, it is not turned on by default. You need to turn it on by entering the **nsf** command within IGP configuration mode.
2. NSF-aware means that the device can participate in an NSF restart by virtue of understanding the GR LSA, but might not undertake the restart itself. NSF-capable

routers, on the other hand, can both understand GR LSA and can also undergo an NSF restart. Cisco ASR 1000 is an NSF-aware and -capable device.

3. ERSPAN stands for Encapsulated Remote SPAN, which essentially encapsulates the SPAN-ed traffic inside a GRE header so that it can be routed across a Layer 3 domain. This enables data capturing on one device on a given set of interfaces and direction, whereas monitoring station could be placed several L3 hops away on another device (such as Cisco ASR 1000). Cisco Catalyst 6500, 7600, Nexus, and ASR 1000 are the only platforms that support ERSPAN.

4. The RP IOS package for ASR1000-RP2 and most of the underlying software infrastructure has been extended to 64 bits, hence it can therefore address beyond 4 GB DRAM.

5. No, the Cisco ASR 1000 does not require any software RTU licenses for these basic features. Hence, they can be used as long as they are available in the given IOS image.

6. DCI stands for data center interconnect, which is a common way to extend Layer 2 or Layer 3 connectivity across the data centers. The ASR 1000 can be used at this time for p2p connectivity across two data centers for IP and MPLS transport types. EoMPLS can be used to extend the L2 connectivity and VLANs across the DCI WAN link. The ASR 1000 has a unique feature known as Remote Port Shutdown, which functions similar to GSR. So, to avoid traffic blackholing and to allow faster convergence, as soon as a pseudowire goes down, the router switches off the port laser to let the peer port (customer edge [CE]) know that the link has gone down, which immediately goes to down/down. This proves handy to achieve extremely fast convergence end to end. As soon as the pseudowire comes back up, it turns the laser on, signaling the CE port that it can resume traffic via the given EoMPLS PE. This feature is enabled by default and does not require any additional configuration.

Further Reading

Graceful OSPF Restart, document: http://tools.ietf.org/html/rfc3623

Configuring ERSPAN on Catalyst 6500 Switches, document: http://www.cisco.com/en/US/docs/switches/lan/catalyst6500/ios/12.2SX/configuration/guide/span.html#wp1063324

Internet Gateway Router Design Using Cisco ASR 1000 Series Routers, document: http://tinyurl.com/l6nbcp

Cisco 6500 Virtual Switching Systems (VSS), document: http://tinyurl.com/5zph8e

Configuring vPC (Virtual Port Channel), document: http://tinyurl.com/l37wqp

Cisco Nexus 7000 Security Features, document: http://tinyurl.com/n2nx99

Data Center Interconnect, document: http://tinyurl.com/rclv2f

"Route Reflector Scale," report: http://tinyurl.com/kmc89b

Chapter 13

IP Services Use Cases

This chapter extends upon what you have learned in the previous chapters with discussion on topics such as quality of service (QoS), Network Address Translation (NAT), Network Based Application Recognition (NBAR), Flexible Packet Matching (FPM), NetFlow event logging, and IP multicast.

The format will continue by outlining the problems, challenges they represent, and how (with detailed configuration examples) you can use the ASR 1000 to address them.

Introduction to IOS IP Services on the ASR 1000

Today's networks must provide a robust, flexible, scalable, reliable, and adaptable network fabric where new services and solutions can be deployed quickly and without causing a service hit to the existing infrastructure. IT managers are facing various issues, including the need for rapid deployment, cost containment, potential interop issues, and a way to achieve the faster return on investment (ROI) to justify the network total cost of ownership (TCO) to CxOs.

Cisco IOS Software contains more than two decades' worth of innovation in its core IP routing/switching and services. Single-CPU routers (also known as software-based routers) have been successful in bringing those features to market as quickly as possible. Although you get extremely fast feature velocity because of common data-plane software, it unfortunately comes at the price of limited performance. The Cisco ASR 1000 leverages the existing IOS investment in IP services and adds the performance component lacking in software-based routers, without severely degrading the router's forwarding potential.

Much of that has been possible because of custom built, in-house Cisco QuantumFlow Processor (QFP). This network processor truly enables a way to accelerate almost all the IOS services natively (that is, without requiring the added cost, configuration, and management of IP service acceleration modules).

Note Turning on some of the ASR 1000 services does require licenses; for example, the Flexible Packet Inspection (FPI) license for FPM or NBAR.

Scalable In-Built QoS Using QFP's Traffic Manager

As indicted in Chapter 6, "Cisco ASR 1000 Series Router Hardware and Software Details," the overall QFP is divided into two chips:

- One dedicated to processing packets and services application
- One dedicated to buffering, queuing, and scheduling (BQS)

The BQS chip is also known as the *traffic manager*. The ASR 1000 implements a centralized packet buffering model with the following key attributes:

- Oversubscription handling, which protects high-priority packets and controls traffic going through and for the router, respectively
- Multiple types of buffering at different points in the system (ASR 1000 SPA Interface Processor [SIP] and traffic manager)
- Capability to customize packet classification and tune queue depths to optimize use of buffer memory
- Simple, efficient, and scalable packet-buffering model to support existing and future features
- ASR 1000 Embedded Service Processors (ESP) (where the QFP chipset resides), based on the Hierarchical Queuing Framework (HQF), support the following:

  Total of 64K and 128K bandwidth queues in hardware for the ASR1000-ESP5 and ASR1000-ESP10/ASR1000-ESP20, respectively, for network interfaces (with some additional system queues for features such as crypto)

  Two-level priority queuing

  Three-parameter scheduling: max rate, min rate, excess weight available in QFP

  Multiple levels of hierarchies for egress hierarchical queuing (Modular QoS CLI [MQC], Enhanced Serdes Interface [ESI], Shared Port Adapter [SPA], SPA Interface Processor [SIP]) for some interface types

  Support for excess bandwidth allocation ("bandwidth remaining" command line)

  Support for maximum bandwidth ("shaping" command line)

Note ASR 1000 quality of service (QoS) is based on the Hierarchical Queuing Framework (HQF), which allows greater control and consistent queue definition (among other infrastructure changes). This is not to be confused with Hierarchical QoS (H-QoS), which is a way to do multiple levels of nesting of QoS policies. HQF support came in Cisco IOS Software Release 12.4(20)T for software-based routers such as 7200VXR. Some of the notable benefits of HQF-based QoS implementation are as follows:

- Capability to provide multiple levels of packet scheduling
- Capability to support integrated class-based shaping and queuing
- Capability to apply fair queuing and drop policy on a per-class basis
- Fair queuing can be set for class default

Active ASR1000-ESP performs the overall packet forwarding, buffering, and output queuing/scheduling for all packets going through the QFP. Key aspects of this implementation include the following:

- ASR 1000 SIPs and SPAs do not require any packet-forwarding logic because this is done only on the active QFP in a centralized manner.
- Buffering on the SIP in an egress direction is rather shallow because the ESP scheduler will not send more traffic than the given SIP can handle.
- Ingress buffering and scheduling (to ensure that high-priority traffic does not get dropped during times of oversubscription) on SIP. Note that every SIP has four half-height SPA bays and has the potential to exceed the SIP-to-ESP link oversubscription. This is a full-duplex 11.2-Gbps link. As an example, a 10-Gb SPA has a half-height form factor; hence you can practically have up to 4 x 10-Gbps SPAs, and thus apply up to 40-Gbps worth of traffic even to a single ASR1000-SIP10. This will be a case of oversubscription by a factor of 4x.

Ingress SIP Buffering

Each ingress SIP card has 128 MB of packet buffer memory to deal with oversubscription, and is equally divided into 32-MB chunks for each SPA (4 * 32 MB = 128 MB). Consider an example of 5x1Gb SPA, where this 32 MB is further divided equally into these five ports. This per-port amount of memory is shared among both high- and low-priority traffic queues.

In cases of low-speed interfaces such as Fast Ethernet (100 Mbps), 4-MB memory for each port (32 MB / 8 = 4 MB) is further divided into high and low, hence yielding 2 MB for each. This will result in around 160-ms worth of buffering for each queue, which is undesirable because of latency reasons, and therefore only a portion of this memory will actually be used, and latency will be limited to about 16 ms.

> **Note** You can see the amount of ingress buffer using the **show platform hardware subslot** *x/y* **plim buffer** command. This also includes the Fill Status and Drop Threshold counters for each port.

Example 13-1 shows the details for subslot 1/0, which has a 10x1Gb SPA.

Example 13-1 *PLIM Buffers and the Respective Drop Threshold*

```
ASR1006-1# show platform hardware subslot 1/0  plim buffer
Interface 1/0/0
  RX Low
    Buffer Size 2064384 Bytes
    Drop Threshold 1020864 Bytes
    Fill Status Curr/Max 0 Bytes / 0 Bytes
  TX Low
    Interim FIFO Size 48 Cache line
    Drop Threshold 35136 Bytes
    Fill Status Curr/Max 0 Bytes / 0 Bytes
  RX High
    Buffer Size 2064384 Bytes
    Drop Threshold 402624 Bytes
    Fill Status Curr/Max 0 Bytes / 0 Bytes
  TX High
    Interim FIFO Size 48 Cache line
    Drop Threshold 35136 Bytes
    Fill Status Curr/Max 0 Bytes / 0 Bytes
... output truncated beyond this point ...
```

Table 13-1 shows the latency values used by the system for various speeds, density, and types of SPAs for an ASR1000-SIP10.

Now, moving on to the centralized QFP based buffering, there are two main points of buffering when the packet is already inside the QFP.

- **Global packet memory (GPM):** This is a small size on-chip SRAM, where the packet will remain stored during the entire processing by the packet-processing element (PPE) and will only be transferred to the traffic manager when the processing is complete. GPM can receive packets from all the SIPs and RPs in the system.
- **Packet buffer DRAM in the traffic manager:** This is an off-chip packet buffer to which packets will be transferred after the PPE has finished processing. Its size varies depending on the type of ESP (64 MB for ESP-5, 128 MB for ESP-10, and 256 MB for ESP-20). Reasons why a packet could be transferred to this buffer include the following:

Table 13-1 *GE SPA Interfaces and Their Respective Hi/Lo Buffering; This Is Where PLIM Is Currently Supported*

Example SPA Types	Low-Priority Buffering (ms)	High-Priority Buffering (ms)
4-Port 10BASE-T/100BASE FE 8-Port 10BASE-T/100BASE FE	16	6
2-Port OC3c/STM-1c POS 4-Port OC3c/STM-1c POS	20	1
1-Port OC12c/STM-4c POS	20	1
2-Port Gigabit Ethernet 5-Port Gigabit Ethernet 8-Port Gigabit Ethernet 10-Port Gigabit Ethernet	16	3
1-Port 10 Gigabit Ethernet	23	3

The packet needs to be scheduled by the traffic manager for output (likely scenario most of the time).

The packet needs to be punted to the RP (only in cases where the packet is destined for the router or needs the RP's attention).

The packet needs to be recycled through the PPEs again for further processing (applies to a few features, such as encryption, fragmentation, multicast, and so on).

Traffic Manager Packet Buffering

This is the main buffering and scheduling point for the ASR 1000 system. The following all take up space in this buffer:

- Packets coming from PPEs on their way out
- Packets needing to recycle through the PPE for further feature processing
- Punts to the RP

This packet buffer memory is treated as one large pool to be shared among all configured queues, and it handles all packet sizes.

To understand the overall system buffering mechanism, consider the examples discussed in the following sections that deal with unicast packets, multicast packets, and punt packets.

Unicast Packets

This example covers any IPv4 or IPv6 packets and the steps that they go through while being processes by QFP:

Step 1. Ingress packet is received and stored in the GPM.

Step 2. The packet is assigned to a PPE, and input/output feature processing is performed. The processing order of features is similar to any other IOS platform.

Step 3. The PPE fixes up the outgoing Layer 2 encapsulation of the packet within the GPM.

Step 4. The PPE completes processing, and the packet moves from GPM to traffic manager packet buffer DRAM where it is enqueued to be transmitted.

Multicast Packets

The traffic manager's buffering architecture helps with implementing features such as multicast, essentially requiring a packet to be replicated *n* times to reach the desired number. The steps that follow capture that details in the order the process takes place:

Step 1. The ingress multicast packet is received and stored in the GPM.

Step 2. The packet is assigned to a PPE, and input feature processing is performed.

Step 3. Up to seven copies are made, and each is enqueued on the recycle queue. Each enqueued packet has a unique copy in packet buffer DRAM. At this point, the original packet is moved out of the GPM.

Step 4. Each copy goes back into the GPM and is assigned to a PPE for egress feature processing (or to make up to another seven copies) and to fix up the outgoing Layer 2 encapsulation. When the copy moves back into the GPM, the associated packet buffer space in DRAM is released.

Step 5. Each unique copy of the output packet is sent to the traffic manager packet buffer DRAM and is enqueued to be transmitted.

Punt Packet

The steps that follow are those taken by a packet that ends up getting punted over to the active RP. Note that even all punt packets, even those eventually destined for the RP, still go through the system data plane (by way of the QFP):

Step 1. The ingress packet is assigned to a PPE, and feature processing is performed.

Step 2. During this processing, it's discovered that this packet is destined for the RP.

Step 3. Packets then move from GPM to traffic manager queues, which are specific for RP punting.

Egress SIP Buffering

The SIP10 has about 72 MB of memory for egress buffers; however, egress buffering is kept very small to avoid head-of-line blocking issues (because the QFP is always aware of the queue status on the egress SIP by way of queue status updates that get sent from the SIP to the QFP flow control mechanism).

The Cisco ASR 1000 has a robust and unique buffering architecture throughout the packet-forwarding path, starting from the SIP to the QFP. This allows protection of priority traffic across the entire packet lifetime through the system and oversubscription buffering.

Example 13-2 shows the default configuration for the Gigabit Ethernet interface for strict-queue treatment.

Example 13-2 *Default PLIM Packet Treatments for Packets Coming into the System via Gi1/0/0*

```
ASR1006-1# show platform hardware interface gigabitEthernet 1/0/0 plim qos input
  map
Interface GigabitEthernet1/0/0
    Low Latency Queue(High Priority):
        IP PREC, 6, 7
        IPv6 TC, 46
        MPLS EXP, 6, 7
ASR1006# show platform hardware interface gigabitEthernet 1/1/1.1 plim qos input
  map
Interface GigabitEthernet1/1/1.1
    Low Latency Queue(High  Priority):
        COS, 6, 7
```

To customize the treatment and coordinate that with MQC-based QoS on the QFP, you can configure the **plim qos map** command for G1/0/0 as demonstrated in Example 13-3.

Example 13-3 *Customizing the PLIM Parameters*

```
ASR1006-1(config-if)# plim qos input map ?
  ip     IP packets
  ipv6   IPv6 packets
  mpls   MPLS packets

ASR1006-1(config-if)# plim qos input map ip ?
  all                 All IP packets
  dscp                IP DSCP
  dscp-based          IP DSCP based configuration
  precedence          IP Precedence
  precedence-based    IP Precedence based configuration
```

As outlined in Example 13-3, ingress SIP QoS is configurable on either port or VLAN. This classification can be based on 802.1P, IPv4 TOS, IPv6 TC, or MPLS EXP. Default ingress scheduling is based on weighted fair queuing (WFQ), and you can define a minimum per port, along with weight for excess bandwidth sharing during congestion.

Note Ingress SIP QoS handling is currently available only for Ethernet (10 Gigabit Ethernet, Gigabit Ethernet, or Fast Ethernet) interfaces. However, in the future it might be expanded to all other interface types.

The following are examples of SIP10 classification:

- Map a range of values to an ingress queue:

  ```
  plim qos input map ip dscp af11-af31 queue strict-priority
  ```

- Map all values to an ingress queue:

  ```
  plim qos input map ip all queue 0
  ```

- Map a list of values to an ingress queue:

  ```
  plim qos input map ipv6 tc cs3 cs4 queue strict-priority
  ```

- Map 802.1P value 5 to high priority (802.1Q VLANs only):

  ```
  plim qos input map cos 3 queue strict-priority
  ```

Example 13-4 shows the 10x1 Gbps SPA and the default behavior of the ingress scheduler at SIP10.

Example 13-4 *Default Bandwidth Value for Min and Excess*

```
ASR1006-1# show platform hardware subslot 1/0 plim qos input bandwidth
Interface 1/0/0
  BW : 1015424  Kbps, Min BW: 0        Kbps, Applied On Low-latency, Excessive
    Weight: 1015000  Kbps
... output truncated ...
```

Note No minimum bandwidth is assigned by default (configurable using **plim qos input bandwidth**); this might require customization.

Each port has an excessive weight proportional to its bandwidth (configurable using **plim qos input weight**).

ESP Interconnect Scheduler Default Behavior (Aggregating All SIP Traffic)

The scheduler applies to all ESPs (ESP5, ESP10, ESP20, and so on). QFP uses this scheduler to backpressure the SIPs, and separate schedulers are used for high- and low-priority queues.

With the ingress interconnect scheduler algorithm

- Selection is done among SIPs based on their minimum bandwidth and weight.
- Within each SIP, the scheduling is strict priority (high versus low), as discussed previously.
- Configurable parameters are minimum bandwidth and excess weight.

Example 13-5 demonstrates output from the **show platform** command that you can use to view the ESP scheduler details.

Example 13-5 *Min and Excess Bandwidth Distribution at the ESP Scheduler*

```
ASR1006-1# show platform hardware slot f0 serdes qos
Qos Settings on FP:
slot #     Min BW (Kbps)  Min BW Mode    Slot Weight
   RP1          99975          HILO            256
   RP0          99975          HILO            256
  ESP1          99975          HILO            256
  SIP2          49987            HI             50
  SIP1          49987            HI             50
  SIP0          49987            HI             50
```

Note Each SIP has roughly around 49.98 Mbps of minimum bandwidth for the HI priority queue (configurable via the **hw-module slot** *y* **qos input bandwidth** command).

Each SIP has the same weight (50), so the excess bandwidth is, by default, distributed equally among SIPs during congestion (configurable via **hw-module slot <#> qos input weight**).

ASR 1000 Traffic Manager Priority Queues

The ASR 1000 provides two levels of priority queues (P1 and P2), which can be used for voice (P1) and video (P2) traffic, for example.

The caveats regarding how the two priority queues get serviced by QFP are as follows:

- Priority level 1 traffic is served before priority level 2 traffic.
- Priority level 2 traffic is served before nonpriority traffic.

- Priority is propagated through the hierarchy, which means that the priority defined at the IOS MQC class layer in the hierarchy propagates to both logical and physical layers.
- Priority queuing and propagation work together to ensure low latency.
- Explicit policer or conditional policer can be used to limit priority traffic in a class.
- QFP listens to queue status updates from both SIP and SPA high- and low-priority queues to ensure that priority traffic is protected.

Note You need to pay careful attention to **tune queue-limit** to get the optimal latency for the rest of the traffic going into class default. Usual latency through a strict priority class should be well below 100 microseconds.

Table 13-2 compares the conditional and unconditional policing behavior within the PQ (priority queuing) on the ASR 1000.

Similarly, Table 13-3 demonstrates minimum and excess bandwidth usage and associated meaning.

Priority is served first, followed by minimum bandwidth classes.

Excess bandwidth is shared by all classes as per their remaining ratios.

Table 13-2 *CLI Differences for Conditional and Unconditional Policing*

Conditional Policing Example	Unconditional or Explicit Policing Example

`Policy-map Cond`
`class Voice`
`priority Y bps`
`class 5_pct`
`bandwidth percent 5`
	`Policy-map U-Cond`
	`class Voice`
	`priority`
	`police Y bps`
	`class 15_pct`
	`bandwidth percent 15`

Under congestion, the Voice class is policed to Y bps rate. However, in the absence of congestion, the Cond class is allowed to exceed its configured bits per second rate.	The Voice class is policed to *x* bps rate regardless of congestion. This is the preferred method for policing, especially when dealing with voice in low-latency queuing (LLQ).

Table 13-3 *Examples of Minimum and Excess Bandwidth Distribution*

Minimum Bandwidth Example	Excess Bandwidth Example
`Policy child`	`Policy child`
`  class Voice`	`  Class Voice`
`     priority 20`	`     priority 20`
`  class Data-1`	`class Data-1`
`     bandwidth 30`	`     bandwidth  remaining ratio 30`
`  class  class-default`	`  class  class-default`
`     bandwidth 50`	`     bandwidth  remaining ratio 50`
`Policy parent`	`Policy parent`
`  class  class-default`	`  class  class-default`
`    shape average  100`	`    shape average  100`
`    service-policy  child`	`    service-policy  child`

Note Both "bandwidth remaining" ratios and percent are supported. The former is recommended for dynamic environments or for a large number of interfaces, whereas the latter is better suited to usual enterprise environments with static class queues. If no excess bandwidth is configured, the excess bandwidth is shared equally across classes during congestion.

Another QoS concept unique to the ASR 1000 is called *policy aggregation*. To better understand the concept, consider an example of a Fast Ethernet interface (100 Mbps). Assume that you have 100 subscribers or network users, and each is sending voice, video, and data traffic on their respective VLANs.

In terms of real-world requirements or usage for this, assume that you need to cap/shape the quota for each user for data traffic only. Two-level hierarchies will not make the cut because doing shaping at the interface level will shape all traffic at the interface level, whereas doing per-VLAN shaping will shape all subscriber/user's voice, video, and data traffic. Both outcomes are undesirable as per the requirement we have.

But, what if you have the capability to shape at a "logical" interface that aggregates all the data traffic from all subscribers/users to satisfy the requirement. This will not only achieve the objective, but also will not affect voice/video traffic coming from the same subscriber/user. This concept is called *policy aggregation* because it allows selecting an arbitrary set of classes and defining the maximum bandwidth behavior for them. This is done within IOS MQC using the **service-fragment** command. The section "Scalable Hierarchical QoS and Metro-E Use Case," later in this chapter, delves into this shaping technique.

Note This concept is also sometimes called *economy-class treatment* because economy-class passengers in an airplane are limited to their assigned seat quota, and that is done without putting any limit on the first/business-class passengers.

Before wrapping up the QoS discussion, review the QoS scaling guidelines for ASR 1000 (up to and including IOS XE 2.3). Table 13-4 shows the QoS scaling guidelines for the Cisco ASR 1000 and 7200VXR in a side-by-side comparison.

Note Starting with IOS XE 2.3.0, two-level H-QoS with user-defined class (as opposed to only class default) is also supported.

Now, let's go over a few use cases to solidify the concepts you've learned thus far.

Table 13-4 *ASR 1000 and 7200VXR QoS Scaling Guidelines*

QoS Feature and Scale	ASR 1000	7200 (12.4T)
Total global policy maps	4K	4K
Total global class maps	4K	1K
Total class maps per policy map	256	256
Hardware queues	64K (ESP-5), 128K (ESP-10/20)	Not applicable
Policer shaper accuracy	99%	~99%, except during CPU saturation
Policer/shaper granularity	8 Kbps	8 Kbps

Scalable Hierarchical QoS and Metro-E Use Case

An enterprise is connected to a service provider (SP) using Metro Ethernet service, where the handoff is a Gigabit Ethernet link, although the committed rate is 80 Mbps. Any data exceeding that will be dropped by the SP. In addition, the enterprise has three tenants connected to the ASR 1000 via their respective VLANs, one for voice and one for data traffic. All voice traffic from all VLANs/tenants must get low-latency treatment. All data traffic further needs to be divided, where tenant one, two, and three get guaranteed data throughput of 8, 32, and 40 Mbps, even during congestion.

To meet these requirements, use the **fragment** command available within the IOS MQC on the ASR 1000. Table 13-5 shows the "bandwidth remaining" ratio distribution across tenants.

Table 13-5 *Bandwidth Remaining Ratio Distribution Across Tenants*

Tenant ID	Bandwidth (Mbps)	Bandwidth Ratio	BRR value
1	8	8/80 = 0.10	10
2	32	32/80 = 0.40	40
3	40	40/80 = 0.50	50

Figure 13-1 shows the problem and requirements description pictorially.

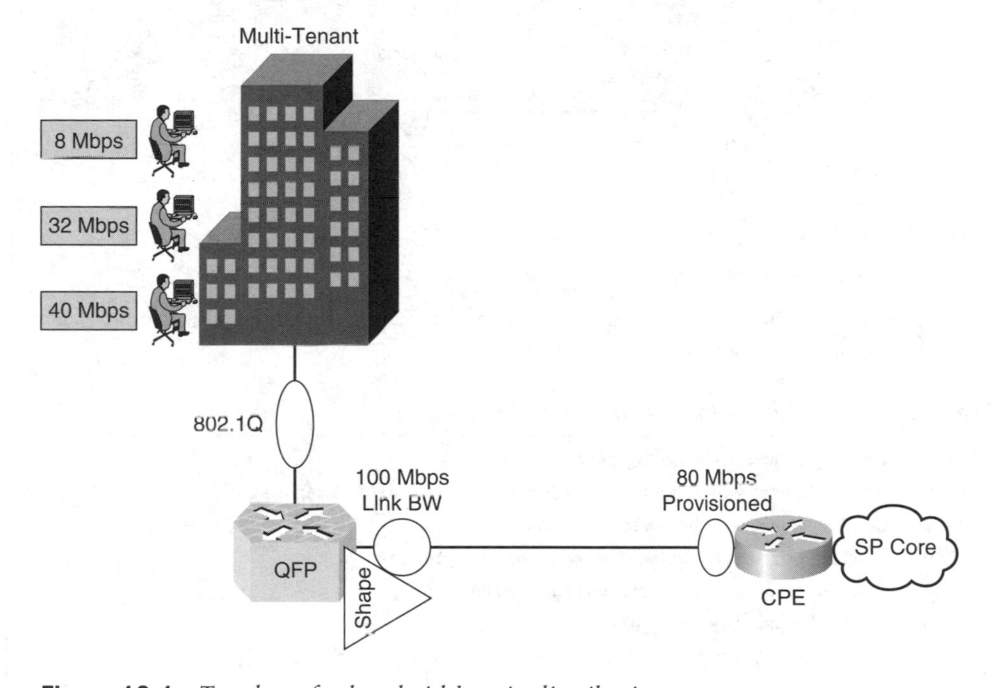

Figure 13-1 *Topology for bandwidth ratio distribution across tenants.*

Figure 13-2 shows the solution description pictorially.

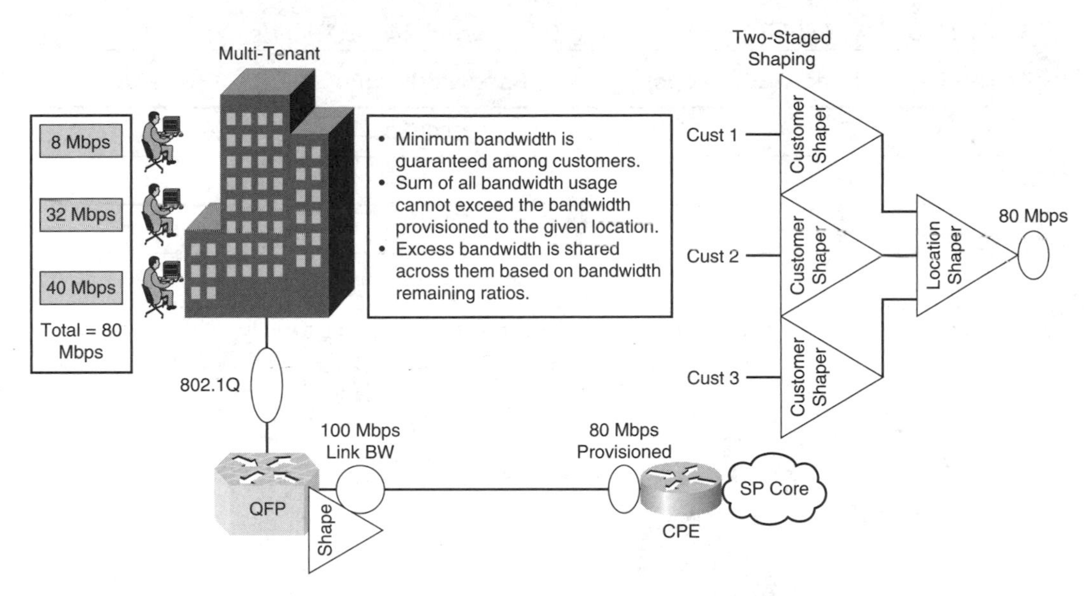

Figure 13-2 *Topology and overall solution details.*

Example 13-6 shows a snippet of how the **service-fragment** command is used to achieve the previously mentioned requirements.

Example 13-6 *Detailed QoS Configuration Solution*

```
ASR1000(config)# policy-map Tenant1
ASR1000(config-pmap-c)# class class-default fragment Common-Data
ASR1000(config-pmap-c)# bandwidth 8 Mbps
ASR1000(config-pmap-c)# bandwidth remaining ratio 10
ASR1000(config-pmap-c)# service-policy CHILD
ASR1000(config)# policy-map CHILD
     ASR1000(config-pmap-c)# class Voice
     ASR1000(config-pmap-c)# priority
ASR1000(config)# policy-map Tenant2
 ASR1000(config-pmap-c)# class class-default fragment Common-Data
      ASR1000(config-pmap-c)# bandwidth remaining ratio 40
      ASR1000(config-pmap-c)# bandwidth 32 Mbps
      ASR1000(config-pmap-c)# service-policy CHILD
ASR1000(config)# policy-map Tenant3
 ASR1000(config-pmap-c)# class class-default fragment Common-Data
      ASR1000(config-pmap-c)# bandwidth remaining ratio 50
      ASR1000(config-pmap-c)# bandwidth 40 Mbps
```

```
     ASR1000(config-pmap-c)# service-policy CHILD

ASR1000(config)# policy-map interface
 ASR1000(config-pmap-c)# class data service-fragment Common-Data
 ASR1000(config-pmap-c)# shape average  80 Mbps
```

This configuration achieves the purpose of protecting the low-latency traffic (voice in this case) and minimum bandwidth during times of congestion. At the same time, the entire data bandwidth from all data VLANs is capped at 80 Mbps for the GE interface.

Scalable IPv4 and IPv6 Multicast Acceleration Using Cisco QuantumFlow Processor

For years now, both enterprise and SP customers have benefited from bandwidth-conserving attributes of IP multicast. As a result, more and more applications are using multicast for data transport, requiring and depending more on the network infrastructure. IPTV for video and financial applications that deliver ticker-related information are two common examples.

Cisco ASR 1000 series routers bring the highest performance, reliability, security, scalability, and control for multicast applications, all without comprising the command-line interface (CLI) experience common in software-based routers. The feature set support is extensive and includes PIMv2 and Multicast Listener Discovery (MLD, v1 and v2) for IPv6.

The three main components involved in the implementation of the multicast feature on the ASR 1000 are as follows:

- The IOS daemon (IOSD), which implements the multicast protocols, features, Multicast Routing Information Base (MRIB), and Multicast Forwarding Information Base (MFIB) code in the control plane
- The platform component, which implements the infrastructure to propagate the MFIB to the data plane
- The QuantumFlow Processor (QFP) data plane, which performs the multicast packet replication and forwarding in the data plane

Table 13-6 shows the breakdown of multicast functions and where they are performed in ASR 1000 hardware.

Note The MRIB stores the multicast routing table in a "protocol-independent" form. The MFIB process creates its own copy of the forwarding table. The MFIB is used

- To inform the platform code about changes to the MFIB table
- To generate notifications about QFP-level changes

Table 13-6 *IP Multicast Features and Their Associations with Different Hardware Components*

Hardware Component	Multicast Functions
RP	IP PIM, IGMP/MLD packets are processed here, including the computation of the MFIB.
ESP	Multicast forwarding is handled using MFIB, which is platform and routing protocol independent. Therefore, ESP needs only a minimal knowledge of the multicast routing protocols.
SIP	Just like unicast, SIPs do not participate in packet/protocol processing, except providing Physical Line Interface Module (PLIM) QoS (buffering and scheduling).

Multicast High Availability on the ASR 1000

The overall ASR 1000 high-availability (HA) goals translate into the fact that the multicast data path must be able to seamlessly handle the failure of a number of components, both hardware and software, in the system. These components include the Route Processor (RP), the Forwarding Processor (ESP), QFP, and the IOSD. RP and IOSD failure HA relies on support from the IOSD MFIB component.

Table 13-7 outlines the RP and ESP failover scenarios and how the platform responds to them (assume a fully populated ASR 1006 system).

Table 13-7 *IP Multicast HA Aspects with Regard to System RP and ESP*

Failing Component	Multicast HA Implications
Active RP	On the active RP failure, the standby takes over, and the newly active RP rebuilds the PIM state. The MFIB proceeds to incorporate refreshed PIM state and the active ESP continues to forward multicast traffic based on its version of the MFIB. Forwarding of IP multicast packets is *not* disrupted.
Active ESP	On the active ESP failure, the standby ESP takes over, and forwarding is disrupted by a *momentary packet loss* (similar to unicast). This loss can be reduced by prioritizing multicast traffic over other types of traffic. After restart, the ESP receives state information from the active RP via reliable IPC communication over the EOBC.

Note The IP multicast packet/byte statistics get lost during the ESP switchover.

Multicast Replication on the ESP

Multicast packets handling is just about the same as they enter the system on the given SIP; however, once they are inside the ESP, the packet processing is a bit different because they need to be replicated, which is done using an efficient in-built algorithm on the QFP:

- As soon as a multicast packet is assigned to a PPE, the PPE does not by itself try to create the final number of replications required for the all the outbound interfaces joined to that group.
- Instead, the receiving PPE performs a set number of replications and then recycles the packet to be processed by many PPEs, each of which performs the same replication until the required number of replications is attained in a few passes (depending on the number of replications required) through the Cisco QFP.
- This efficient replication algorithm helps ensure that latency and jitter are kept to a minimum for IP multicast traffic.

The native abilities to perform multicast replications without burdening the rest of the system, to provide high availability, and to provide close interaction with the encryptor when multicast traffic requires encryption are a few distinguishing capabilities of the Cisco ASR 1000.

Scalable In-Built Multigigabit NAT

Enterprises commonly deploy Network Address Translation (NAT) when connecting their private networks to the public Internet. A few other features also usually get deployed at the Internet edge, such as firewalls, NetFlow, and so on. Besides protecting the user traffic, the router at the Internet edge should protect itself and the entire infrastructure behind it from distributed denial-of-service (DDoS) attacks. The ASR 1000 combines the feature richness of Cisco IOS and extends the performance and scale for functions such as NAT to up to multi–10 Gigabit Ethernet levels.

NAT configurations are received and processed by the IOS NAT subsystem (as entered by the router administration via the Cisco IOS CLI) and are downloaded to the QFP via the forwarding manager (FMAN) process. One key attribute is that NAT session creation, teardown, and management are done on the QFP only, as are any header and payload translations, and therefore there is no impact to the system RP. There are no punt packets for the NAT translations on the ASR 1000 platform, even including application layer gateway (ALG) processing such as H.323, SIP, and FTP. NAT statistics are passed up to IOS from QFP, and so the user can use the existing IOS commands to manage the system.

Two tables are involved during NAT processing:

- Translation table
- Session/flow table

Example 13-7 shows a sample NAT configuration.

Example 13-7 *Dynamic NAT Configuration*

```
ASR1000(config)# ip nat pool mypoo 10.0.0.1 10.0.255.254 netmask 255.0.0.0 type
  match-host
ASR1000(config)# ip nat inside source list 101 pool mypool
ASR1000(config)# access-list 101 permit ip 172.16.10.0 0.0.0.255 any
```

As packets traverse the router, for each unique source IP address within the 172.16.10.0 network it matches, the ASR 1000 creates a translation entry in the translation table that contains the mapping information for the inside private addresses to the corresponding public IP addresses.

The user from the same source IP address could generate traffic to different destinations, protocols, and port numbers. For each different combination of protocol/SRC/DST/port, the ASR 1000 creates a session entry in the session table. Each session represents the entire Layer 4 information.

Example 13-8 shows the translation and session entries.

Example 13-8 *NAT Translation and Session Entries*

```
ASR1000# show ip nat translation

Pro  Inside global   Inside local      Outside local  Outside global
---  10.0.0.1        172.16.10.1       ---            ---          < Translation entry
---  10.0.0.2        172.16.10.2       ---            ---          < Translation entry
tcp  10.0.0.1:4242   172.16.10.1:5000 161.0.0.10:80  161.0.0.10:80  < Session entry
tcp  10.0.0.1:6262   172.16.10.1:6000 161.0.0.9:80   161.0.0.9:80   < Session entry
```

The purpose of creating the session table is that it improves the overall NAT performance (albeit at the cost of consuming more QFP memory).

Also note that this is same for both IOS XE on the ASR 1000 and platforms supported in IOS 12.4T.

Note On c800 to c7200, the network administrator can, to consider memory utilization, disable creating the session table by adding the **no ip nat create flow-entries** command. However, on the ASR 1000 platform, better and higher performance for NAT is the goal and therefore this command is not supported.

NAT testing has shown the following concurrent connections depending on the ESP type:

- **ASR1000-ESP5:** 250,000
- **ASR1000-ESP10:** 500,000
- **ASR1000-ESP20:** 1,000,000

High-Speed Logging Using NetFlow v9 Format for NAT and Firewall

Various platforms can deliver firewall and NAT performance that are in multi-Gigabit Ethernet or even multi–10 Gigabit Ethernet rates, although when it comes to system logging at those rates, you can hardly find a system that can generate logging at rates of up to hundreds of thousands of connections/sec. In the world of IOS firewalls and NAT, these will be audit trails and translation records. There is absolutely nothing wrong with the syslogging requirement; it is an essential part of network behavior analysis (correlation among various sources of information).

The text-based syslog is commonly used for this. However, that results in limited capacity and essentially turns into a performance hog at those rates and ends up consuming significant RP compute cycles because of high rates of Inter-Process Communication (IPC) messages that it has to deal with, followed by string formatting task.

The Cisco ASR 1000 platform innovatively addresses this age-old issue with NetFlow event logging (NEL). NEL uses NetFlow v9 templates and allows exporting of firewall and NAT session creation/deletion records in binary format directly from the data plane (that is, QFP).

This has various benefits apart from the obvious benefit that it allows you to log data at those rates. These benefits include

- NetFlow v9 uses standard templates that can be used to export NetFlow data to any collector as long as it knows how to interpret various fields inside the template.
- NetFlow data is exported out of data plane, and therefore there is no impact on RP processing, which allows it to be used for other critical functions such as routing and CLI.
- Binary-based (NetFlow) syslog data can also be converted back into textual syslog and then eventually sent to age-old syslog or network behavior system without requiring any modifications.
- Allows syslog to scale beyond 40K events per second. (To give you an idea, at this rate, the total logging traffic is going to be more than 30 Mbps!)

Note Currently, only User Datagram Protocol (UDP) is supported as transport for NEL, and it remains in clear text.

Example 13-9 shows the NEL configuration that is needed on the ASR 1000 platform for IOS firewalls.

Example 13-9 *NetFlow Event Logging Configuration*

```
ASRS1000(config)# parameter-map type inspect global
log dropped-packets
log flow-export v9 udp destination 172.16.1.1 2055
log flow-export template timeout-rate 30

class-map type inspect match-any fw-class
 match protocol udp
 match protocol icmp
 match protocol tcp
!
policy-map type inspect fw-policy
class type inspect fw-class
 drop log
class class-default
!
zone security pvt
zone security pub
zone-pair security pvt-to-pub source pvt destination pub
service-policy type inspect fw-policy

int gi 0/0/0
 zone-member security pvt
int gi 0/0/1
 zone-member security pub
```

Note To enable NAT logging, you can add the **ip nat log translations flow-export v9 udp destination** *ip-address port-no* command. In the case of firewalls, all you need is the **log flow-export v9 udp** command.

The NAT and firewall events that are sent via NEL are as follows:

- NAT:
  - Add event
  - Delete event
- Firewall:
  - Start audit record
  - Stop audit record
  - Flow denied event

  Alert events:
  - IPv4 TCP half-open alert
  - IPv4 half-open alert
  - IPV4 max session alert
  - IPv4 flow pass event
  - IPv4 flow summary record

Scalable In-Built Multigigabit NBAR and FPM

The level of service an application requires in today's network varies based on the part of business to which it applies. Once the requirements are understood, they can be translated into network policies and enforced within the network. NBAR does the job of application recognition and discovery and allows you to classify and identify different applications. After the applications have been identified, they can be given preferential or differential treatment over the network.

Cisco IOS FPM, on the other hand, is a feature that enables you to identify known patterns inside L2 to L7 packet headers or payload. It is an extremely powerful tool at the network entry points (Internet edge), where you can potentially receive some malicious worm or virus traffic. FPM enables you to create a packet filter to indentify all that traffic in a stateless manner using the Cisco IOS CLI. However, doing so requires knowing the attack vector beforehand.

NBAR and FPM are extremely powerful tools, although they come with a price: CPU cycles! These features are CPU intense, just like any other features that happen to go deep inside the packet header/payload. This problem becomes quite noticeable on software-based routers (those based on general-purpose CPUs running Cisco IOS Software).

Table 13-8 *IOS XE Versions and the Supported NBAR Protocol*

IOS XE Release	NBAR Protocol
2.1/2.2	CUseeME DHCP DNS POP3 Telnet HTTPS (Security HTTP) RTSP SIP Skype (TCP only) HTTP (no options, including URL and host) FTP H.323
2.3	PCAnywhere Novadigm Routing protocols (BGP, EIGRP, OSPF, RIP) ICMP SNMP Syslog NFS SQL-Exec Tunneling protocols (GRE, IPinIP, IPsec, L2TP, LDAP, PPTP, SFTP, SIRC, SIMAP, SNNTP, SPOP3, STELNET, SOCKS, SSH) IMAP/SMTP Finger/Kerberos RSVP Gopher IRC NetBIOS Notes NNTP NTP

The Cisco ASR 1000 solves this problem by providing the necessary acceleration natively within the QFP chipset, resulting in multi-Gigabit Ethernet NBAR and FPM performance.

Table 13-8 lists the protocols supported on Cisco ASR 1000 within NBAR in IOS XE 2.3.

Note At the time of writing this book, custom Packet Description Language Modules (PDLM) are not yet supported.

To understand FPM, consider the example of an enterprise that wants to block Skype usage based on TCP as transport.

The key here is to first locate the pattern that you want to filter. In the case of Skype, it is data pattern 0x17030100 at TCP payload start. Based on this knowledge, you can define a filter and apply it to the interface.

Example 13-10 shows the FPM configuration to prohibit Skype from using TCP transport.

Example 13-10 *Configuration Required to Match the Skype TCP Payload and Serve as a Filter*

```
ASR1000(config)# class-map type stack match-all ip_tcp
 ASR1000 (config-cmap)# match field IP protocol eq 6 next TCP
ASR1000 (config-cmap)# class-map type access-control match-all skype
  ASR1000 (config-cmap)# match start TCP payload-start offset 0 size 4 eq
    0x17030100
!
ASR1000 (config)# policy-map type access-control child
ASR1000 (config-pmap)# class skype
   ASR1000 (config-cmap)# drop
ASR1000 (config-pmap)# policy-map type access-control parent
 ASR1000 (config-cmap)# class ip_tcp
   ASR1000 (config-cmap)# service-policy child
!
ASR1000 (config)# interface ten1/1/0
 ASR1000 (config-if)# service-policy type access-control parent

! Verify that there were no QFP global drops

ASR1006# show plat hardware cpp active statistics drop ¦ e _0_
------------------------------------------------------------
Global Drop Stats                               Octets          Packets
------------------------------------------------------------
```

There are no drops here until the match happens (highlighted in the first few lines). Once the router starts matching on the pattern, you're going to see drops.

Example 13-11 shows the FPM-related drops that result because of a matching pattern.

Example 13-11 *Verification That Drops Are Happening In-Line with the FPM Packet Drops and the Drop Reason Is "IPv4FPM"*

```
ASR1006# sh plat hard cpp active statistics drop ¦ e _0_
------------------------------------------------------------
Global Drop Stats                               Octets          Packets
------------------------------------------------------------
  Ipv4Fpm                                  2327875500      38797925
```

There are really no limits as to how you can use FPM. The best example of its use is to deal with day-zero attacks with known attack vectors. The ASR 1000 bridges the performance gap and enables you configure and deploy FPM along with various other features at multigigabit rates.

Summary

This chapter examined various Cisco IOS and ASR 1000 solutions via use cases, specifically examining the following:

- H-QoS policy aggregation via MQC
- NetFlow binary-based event Logging for NAT and firewalls
- Using FPM to block out Skype connections that use TCP as transport

Chapter Review Questions

1. What are the uses for QoS policy aggregation?
2. Is there any punt involved when doing NAT or firewall processing on the ASR 1000?
3. Is there a way to convert the NetFlow binary-based data to textual syslog?
4. Is there any concept of bandwidth points in ASR 1000 like 7200VXR?

Answers

1. Policy aggregation can have a lot of creative uses within the enterprise and SP network. The most obvious ones are Metro Ethernet and per-user based QoS in a multi-subscriber scenario (for example, broadband with each subscriber coming with voice, video, and data traffic).
2. No packets are punted during the entire NAT or firewall processing to the RP. All L3 to L7 processing is done inside the QFP chipset, and therefore you save precious RP compute cycles. However, if you're doing auth-proxy or reaching out to a RADIUS/TACACS server, packets will need to be generated for the authentication to take place. Once done, all packets related to that session will pass through QFP only.
3. There is no automated way to do it at this time. However, you can use the Cisco NetFlow Collector (NFC) to log that data, which allows you to save the files in CSV format, which can be in turn imported into a syslog server that understands that format or into a network behavior analysis engine.

4. None. Oversubscription is valid in the ASR 1000 architecture, and therefore you can apply more traffic to the platform than it can pass without dropping through it. To deal with this scenario, the ASR 1000 has basic two-level QoS scheduling at the SIP10 level and centralized QoS at the QFP. There is a complete circle of backpressure between SIPs and QFP.

Further Reading

IP Multicast on ASR 1000 Series Aggregation Services Routers, document: http://tinyurl.com/lwyhfs

Cisco ASR 1000 Series Aggregation Services Routers: QoS Architecture and Solutions, document: http://tinyurl.com/nj6skz

The Cisco QuantumFlow Processor: Cisco's Next Generation Network Processor, document: http://tinyurl.com/264rb5

Cisco IOS Software Release 12.4T Features and Hardware Support, Cisco Hierarchical Queuing Framework, document: http://tinyurl.com/mts6r2

Chapter 14

Security Services Use Cases

This chapter covers two broad categories of network security: secure WANs and integrated threat control. The chapter covers the security-related services available in Cisco IOS such as Dynamic Multipoint VPN (DMVPN), EasyVPN, Group Encrypted Transport VPN (GETVPN), firewalls, NetFlow, and others. The focus will remain on how these solutions can be deployed on the Cisco ASR 1000, rather than on the individual technologies.

The format of this chapter will continue with what you saw in the last two chapters, outlining the problems, challenges they represent, and how you can use the ASR 1000 to address these problems and challenges, with detailed configuration examples where applicable.

Introduction to IOS Security Services on the Cisco ASR 1000

Network security used to be seen as an add-on bolted to an existing network. This is no longer the case. Because an increasing number of transactions involve networks, either within or outside an organization, policies/guidelines are used to help ensure network integrity and that data remains uncompromised. An effective network security strategy encompasses activities that identify the possible threats and allow the organization to respond (rather than react) to them with the best tools possible. From day one, network security is an essential element of good network design. Driving guidelines for such may originate from the organization itself and from standards bodies (such as the Payment Card Industry [PCI] Data Security Standard or the Health Insurance Portability and Accountability Act [HIPAA]).

Network security tools include both hardware and software. The Cisco Self-Defending Network builds upon a defined set of best practices and guidelines. These include endpoint defenses to incorporate innovative application security, content security, policy enforcement, identity management, security monitoring technologies, and security services.

Figure 14-1 shows the overall Cisco Self-Defending Network schema.

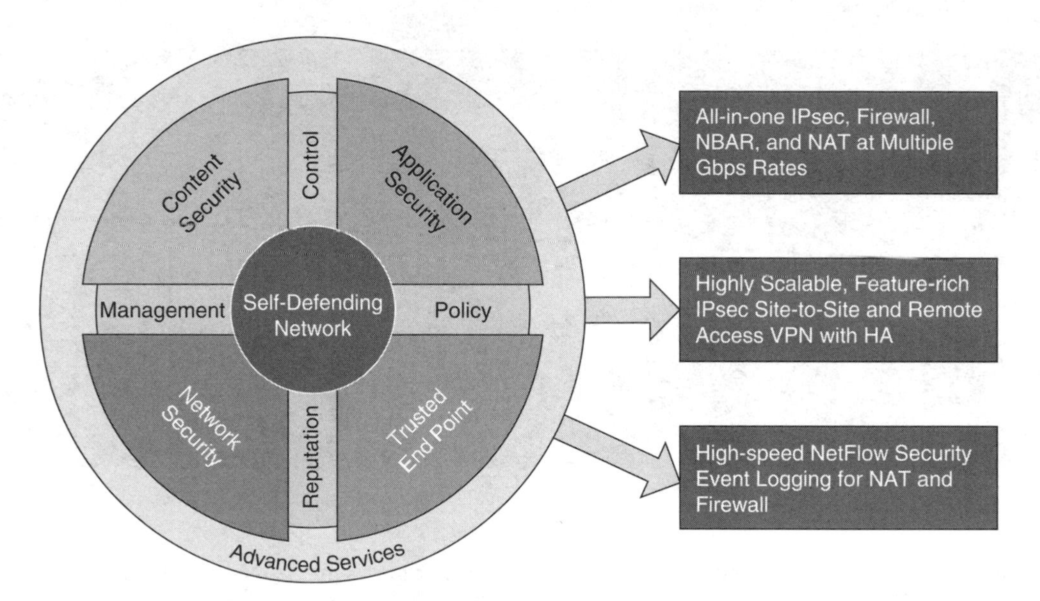

Figure 14-1 *Cisco Self-Defending Network schema and Cisco ASR 1000 service awareness.*

Secure Connectivity Solutions

Cisco IOS includes a wide variety of secure WAN connectivity solutions for all WAN transports, as illustrated in Figure 14-2.

The Cisco ASR 1000 leverages Cisco IOS strength in virtual private network (VPN)-based solutions, and takes them to an entirely new level of scale and performance with its unique system architecture. Every ASR 1000 Embedded Service Processor (ESP) includes a crypto engine chip that offloads the bulk encryption and Internet Key Exchange (IKE) acceleration functions, whereas the host network processor (that is, QuantumFlow Processor [QFP]) continues to perform routing and switching functions, including acceleration for all other IOS services.

Introduction to IPsec Solutions on the Cisco ASR 1000

The Cisco ASR 1000 is pretty much in parity with Cisco IOS Software Release 12.4T for most of the IPsec solutions, as outlined in Table 14-1.

Before looking at some use cases, you need to understand the IPsec implementation on the Cisco ASR 1000 from an architecture perspective and how it solves some of the problems that have plagued these solutions.

In the ASR 1000, the IPsec infrastructure spans both the Route Processor (RP) and Embedded Service Processor (ESP). Whereas the RP performs the control-plane tasks such as dealing with IKE packets, the ESP offloads the crypto data plane. This clear demarcation allows the IPsec control and data plane to scale independently.

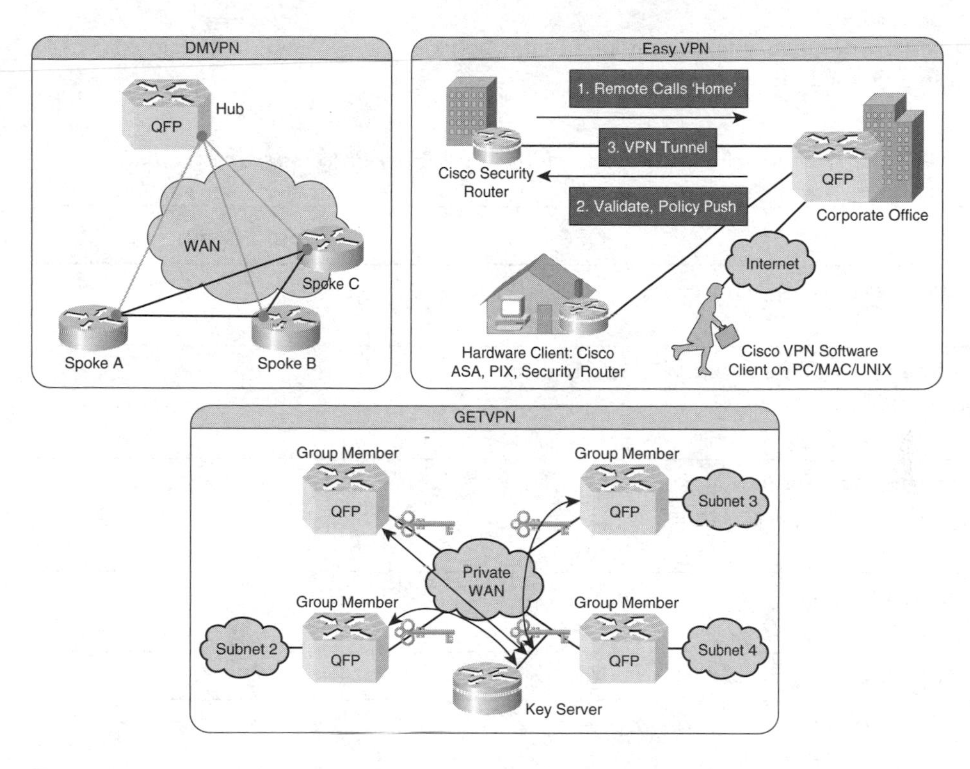

Figure 14-2 *DMVPN, EasyVPN, and GETVPN as secure WAN options.*

Table 14-1 *IPsec-Based VPN Solutions Supported on Cisco ASR 1000 Series Routers*

Feature Set	Cisco ASR 1000 Series /IOS XE
Site-to-site IPsec with static virtual tunnel interface (VTI)	Supported
Site-to-Site IPsec with generic routing encapsulation (GRE) and tunnel protection	Supported
DMVPNs	Phase 2.0 (Hub to Spoke and Spoke to Spoke)
Dynamic VTI	Supported
GETVPN v1.2	Supported
Inside VPN Routing and Forwarding (iVRF) GRE over IPsec	Supported
i-VRF/f-VRF for IPsec	Not supported; future IOS XE will support it.

Table 14-2 describes the distribution of tasks between the QFP and the crypto engine present on the ESP.

Table 14-2 *Distribution of Work Between the QFP (Host Processor) and the Built-In Crypto Engine*

Task	QFP	Crypto Engine
Outbound packet classification	Yes	—
Ingress lookup based on Security Parameter Index (SPI) value	Yes	—
Formatting packets for transmission (Tx) to and receiving packets from crypto Engine	Yes	—
Reassembly of fragmented IPsec packets	Yes	—
Antireplay check	Yes	—
Encryption/decryption, Diffie-Hellman (DH)	—	Yes
Network Address Translation (NAT) traversal (UDP port 4500)	—	Yes
Traffic-based lifetime expiry	—	Yes

As you can clearly note, the QFP uses the crypto engine when needed and remains in the driving seat for all other functions, thus keeping the overall architecture clean and minimizing the latency involved.

The sections that follow discuss two cases:

- The ASR 1000 is receiving the Internet Key Exchange (IKE) initiation request.
- ASR 1000 is initiating one itself based on some interesting traffic matching the security policy.

IPsec Packet Flow (Ingress)

The list that follows takes a close look at packet processing details related to IPsec encryption and how that is done on ASR 1000. This is to show how an ASR 1000 deals with IKE initiation requests received from the remote IPsec peer.

Step 1. Packets enter the QFP.

Step 2. For "us" check is performed, and if necessary, packets are sent for reassembly. "For us" means if the packet is destined for the router itself.

Step 3. The security association (SA) contains all the necessary information to encrypt or decrypt a packet, whereas a security policy database (SPD) is used for outbound packets to find out what SA database is to be used. SA lookup is performed for IPsec packets, and SPD lookup is performed for clear-text packets.

Step 4. For IPsec packets for which an IPsec SA is found, the packet is recycled to the crypto engine via the traffic manager.

Step 5. Packets come back from the crypto engine.

Step 6. IPsec post-processes the packet.

Step 7. IPsec invokes the next feature in the feature invocation array (FIA).

Step 8. For IPsec packets for which an IPsec SA is not found, an error is logged.

Step 9. For clear-text packets for which no SPD is found, the next IOS feature is invoked in the FIA.

Step 10. For clear-text packets for which a security policy is found, the packet is dropped.

IPsec Packet Flow (Egress)

The steps that follow explain what happens when IKE is initiated by the ASR 1000:

Step 1. On a crypto-enabled interface, all packets go via IPsec check.

Step 2. IPsec performs a packet classification to determine whether an SA or SPD is present.

Step 3. If SA, the packet is sent to the crypto engine via the traffic manager.

Step 4. If matches security policy, initiate IKE.

Step 5. If nothing is found, the packet is sent to the next IOS feature within the FIA for the associated interface.

Note *SPD* stands for security policy database, where *security policy* simply refers to what should be encrypted based on the crypto access control list (ACL).

IPsec High-Availability Considerations

High availability (HA) is an essential element of a carrier-class system. In case of IPsec, without HA, a failure will force tunnels to get reestablished from scratch. This will result in applications running over tunnels to time out because of both the time it takes to detect that the tunnel has gone down and the time it takes to reestablish it.

The Cisco ASR 1000 brings stateful in-box HA for IPsec, where in an ASR 1006 system with two ESPs, even in case of an ESP failure, you will not lose IPsec SAs and traffic will continue once the former hot standby becomes the active (< 50 ms). This is enabled by default and does not require any explicit IOS configuration from the router administrator. RP to RP, or IOSD to IOSD, HA is not supported, and therefore that will cause the tunnels to go down and require reestablishment.

IPsec and Interaction with IP Multicast

Because of its job, to encrypt and obfuscate packets, IPsec encryption has the potential to complicate things in the feature path. This is the reason why the only feature that happens post-encryption is queuing. IP multicast replication is done pre-encryption.

IPsec, per se, can support multicast encryption, but IKEv1 does not support multipoint key exchange (something that has been augmented in the form of RFC 3547 or Group Domain of Interpretation [GDOI]). Still, today, when you need to run routing protocols (which are frequently using multicast addresses to send routing updates), GRE over IPsec is required to encapsulate them into the generic routing encapsulation (GRE) tunnel and then encrypt the GRE tunnel.

This method works fine for control-plane multicasts (again, such as Interior Gateway Protocols [IGP]; for example, Open Shortest Path First [OSPF] or Enhanced Interior Gateway Routing Protocol [EIGRP]). However, when you try to encrypt multicast data traffic at higher rates, you might start to notice that some packets drop at the crypto engine Rx (receive) ring. This happens because of the nature of multicast replication. Imagine a single-packet payload being replicated into thousands of packets, all of which need to be encrypted and hence get sent into the crypto engine Rx ring (input queue). This causes a quasi-instantaneous oversubscription scenario where you see packet drops at the Rx ring; however, the crypto engine is not truly oversubscribed in a steady state fashion. The end result of this is manifested in the degraded application experience, depending on the data type being encrypted.

The Cisco ASR 1000 addresses this issue in an interesting and unique manner. The following steps are taken to avoid this situation:

Step 1. Packets are sent to the crypto engine via the traffic manager, which allows you to know what and how many packets are being sent to the crypto engine, and there is an in-built mechanism that enables the crypto engine to backpressure (a request to the traffic manager for slowdown) if it is unable to take more packets. The crypto engine also has an ingress buffer to deal with the instantaneous oversubscription scenario.

Step 2. Now how about when encrypted packets are coming back from the crypto engine, and the traffic manager is perhaps working at the limit with the packets it can contain? In this scenario, the traffic manager can also backpressure the crypto engine. This allows both components to work together and form a full-circle backpressure mechanism to deal with this situation. This results in a more predictable response within those multicast applications.

Scalable Encryption with QoS Before/After Crypto Engine

When quality of service (QoS) and crypto are discussed, the first thing that might come to mind is the impact of doing both of them together. Both are CPU-intense when it comes to software-based platforms, such as the Cisco 7200VXR, where a single CPU is doing both control- and data-plane processing. The nature of the QoS-related CPU burden varies with what you are doing within QoS. For example, policing is a relatively lot less CPU intense than shaping for the given rate of traffic. This applies to all midrange routers that are software-based; it also applies to using add-on modules to offload crypto or QoS.

The Cisco ASR 1000 tackles this issue by simple virtue of its system architecture, where QoS is done inside the QFP and therefore does not result in any severe degradation to traffic rate (packets per second [pps]) or increase in latency through the router. All IPsec-related acceleration happens without the user configuring it explicitly, because there is no need to invoke crypto engine or QoS functions. You just deal with the Cisco IOS command-line interface (CLI) as usual.

QoS interworks with IPsec in two ways:

- **QoS before the crypto engine:** This requires QoS to be applied on the actual egress interface, and the ASR 1000 abstracts that policy and applies it in a rather simplified manner in front of the crypto engine. Two queues are created: One accumulates low-latency traffic, and the other takes the rest of the traffic (think class-based weighted fair queues, for example).

  Figure 14-3 shows the interaction of IP multicast and encryption processing.

- **QoS post-encryption:** The dilemma here is once encryption has happened all packet payload and headers, which are used to classify traffic for QoS application, are obfuscated. Cisco IOS solved this problem years ago by introducing *QoS preclassify*, which basically means that IOS classifies packets that are getting encrypted before and saves a copy of all Layer 3 / Layer 4 headers for all of them for post-encryption QoS to take place, where classification can be based on anything inside those headers. This makes post-encryption QoS a lot more flexible and effective. In case of the ASR 1000, all of this is accelerated within the QFP.

Figure 14-4 shows the interaction of QoS and encryption processing.

Before wrapping up this section on secure solutions, consider the following key points:

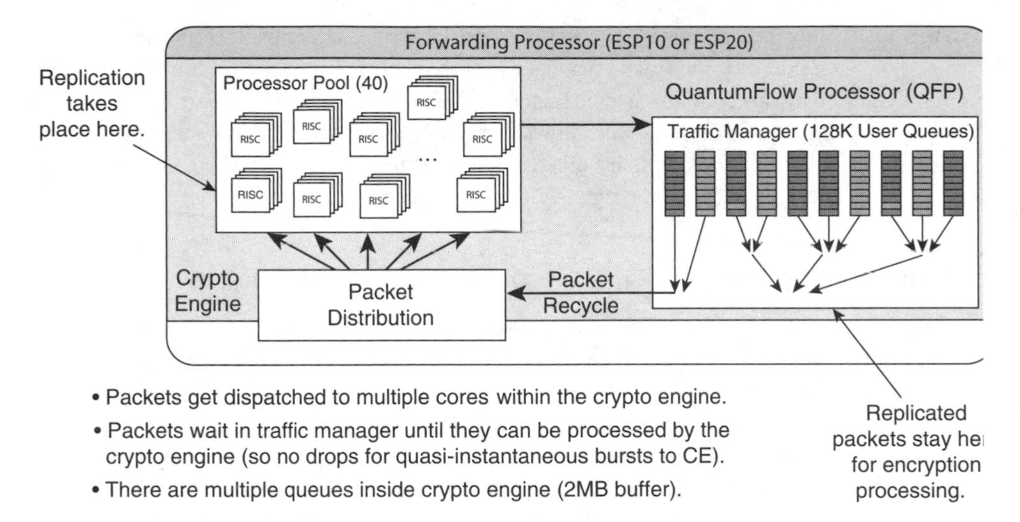
Forwarding Processor (ESP10 or ESP20)
Replication takes place here.
Processor Pool (40)
RISC
QuantumFlow Processor (QFP)
Traffic Manager (128K User Queues)
Crypto Engine
Packet Distribution
Packet Recycle
• Packets get dispatched to multiple cores within the crypto engine.
• Packets wait in traffic manager until they can be processed by the crypto engine (so no drops for quasi-instantaneous bursts to CE).
• There are multiple queues inside crypto engine (2MB buffer).
Replicated packets stay he
for encryption processing.

Figure 14-3 *Sophisticated IP multicast and encryption.*

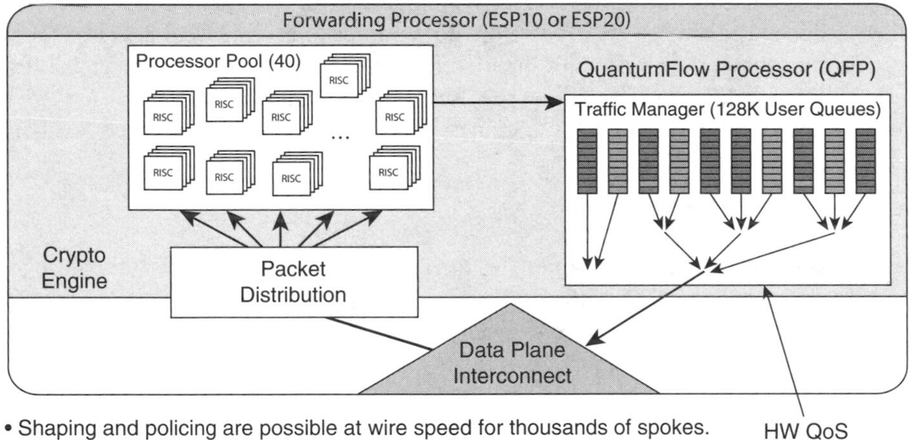
Forwarding Processor (ESP10 or ESP20)
Processor Pool (40)
RISC
QuantumFlow Processor (QFP)
Traffic Manager (128K User Queues)
Crypto Engine
Packet Distribution
Data Plane Interconnect
• Shaping and policing are possible at wire speed for thousands of spokes.
• Both pre-encryption (LLQ before crypto engine) and post-encryption QoS are supported.
HW QoS

Figure 14-4 *True encryption and QoS integration.*

- With the crypto engine being maxed out, the ASR 1000 system still has headroom to push clear-text traffic through up to the system bandwidth limit as per the given ESP.
- The number of tunnels does not have any impact on IPsec forwarding or throughput, and therefore there is no significant difference in performance with 1 or 10 or 1000 tunnels.
- There is no significant difference in performance for various Advanced Encryption Standard (AES) key sizes (128 to 256 bits) or Triple Data Encryption Standard (3DES).
- Latency in all testing scenarios for IPsec remains below 300 microseconds.

- The IKE session setup rate is up to 90 tps (IOS XE 2.2 and later) and around 130 (IOS XE 2.3 and later) with ASR1000-RP1 and ASR1000-RP2, respectively.
- With GRE over IPsec, or DMVPN (mGREoIPsec), the net throughput is limited by the crypto engine, which in turn is a function of ESP being used and not the GRE throughput. The ASR1000-ESP10 can provide almost 10 Gigabit Ethernet line rate for GRE encap/decap at 128 bytes or larger packets (which is more than the crypto throughput).

Now that the basics of IPsec implementation and the relevant issues have been covered, the sections that follow cover some of the use cases.

Scalable DMVPN Hub and Spoke

DMVPN is a Cisco IOS VPN solution that allows you to deploy encrypted VPNs in a point-to-point and point-to-multipoint (p2mp) fashion in almost an automated fashion after initial configuration is done. The secret sauce to the overall deployment is the following:

- **Next-Hop Resolution Protocol (NHRP):** NHRP enables you to maintain a "table of spokes" tunnel to public (nonbroadcast multiaccess [NBMA]) IP address mappings.
- **Multipoint GRE tunnel:** This simplifies the configuration by having one single GRE tunnel at the DMVPN hub router for all the spokes that are part of that DMVPN cloud.

The Cisco ASR 1000 can be an ideal choice for the DMVPN hub design because it

- Enables you to combine QoS and encryption in the same platform without any significant degradation or penalty for QoS (queuing, shaping).
- Enables you to deal with both unicast and multicast without requiring any special tweaks (because of the architectural benefits outlined previously).
- Enables you to just have single tier, and have all control (NHRP and IGP) and data plane (IPsec, mGRE encapsulations) in the same chassis or system. This simplifies the design and management of overall deployment.
- Enables you to combine IOS firewall and NAT within the same platform, as both are accelerated using QFP processor and cause no hit to system RP.
- Provides faster convergence for the IGP because of a large control-plane scale with the ASR1000-RP1 or ASR1000-RP2.
- Enables you to deploy a single platform family both at the headend (usually ASR 1004/1006) and branch office (usually ASR 1002).
- Enables you to scale both crypto and IGP control and data planes independently and transparently by upgrading the system RP or ESP. This does not require any IOS configuration changes whatsoever.

Example 14-1 provides a detailed configuration example where ASR 1000 is deployed as a DMVPN hub with QoS in a per-spoke fashion.

Example 14-1 *ASR 1000 QoS Configuration as a Hub*

```
ASR1000(config)# ip access-list extended Spoke1
      ASR1000(config-ext-nacl)# permit ip host 65.1.1.1 host 60.1.1.1
! per tunnel destination match
ASR1000(config)# ip access-list extended Spoke2
      ASR1000(config-ext-nacl)# permit ip host 65.1.1.1 host 61.1.1.1
ASR1000(config)# ip access-list extended Spoke3
      ASR1000(config-ext-nacl)# permit ip host 65.1.1.1 host 62.1.1.1
... and more...

ASR1000(config)# class-map spoke-1
 ASR1000(config-cmap)# match access-group Spoke1
ASR1000(config)# class-map spoke-2
 ASR1000(config-cmap)# match access-group Spoke2
ASR1000(config)# class-map spoke-3
 ASR1000(config-cmap)# match access-group Spoke3
... and more...

ASR1000(config)# class VoIP
 ASR1000(config-cmap)# match ip dscp 46
ASR1000(config-cmap)# class Video
 ASR1000(config-cmap)# match ip dscp 34
ASR1000(config-cmap)# class APPL-1
ASR1000(config-cmap)# match access-group 101
ASR1000(config-cmap)# class APPL-2
 ASR1000(config-cmap)# match access-group 102
ASR1000(config-cmap)# class APPL-3
 ASR1000(config-cmap)# match access-group 103


ASR1000(config)# policy-map Spoke1-policy
 ASR1000(config-pmap)# class VoIP
  ASR1000(config-pmap-c)# priority level 1
 ASR1000(config-pmap-c)# class Video
  ASR1000(config-pmap-c)# priority level 2
 ASR1000(config-pmap-c)# class APPL-1
  ASR1000(config-pmap-c)# bandwidth remaining ratio 5
 ASR1000(config-pmap-c)# class APPL-2
  ASR1000(config-pmap-c)# bandwidth remaining ratio 3
 ASR1000(config-pmap-c)# class APPL-3
  ASR1000(config-pmap-c)# bandwidth remaining ratio 1
 ASR1000(config-pmap-c)# class class-default
  ASR1000(config-pmap-c)# random-detect
```

```
ASR1000(config)# policy-map Spoke2-policy
 ASR1000(config-pmap)# class VoIP
  ASR1000(config-pmap-c)# priority level 1
 ASR1000(config-pmap-c)# class Video
  ASR1000(config-pmap-c)# priority level 2
 ASR1000(config-pmap-c)# class APPL-1
  ASR1000(config-pmap-c)# bandwidth remaining ratio 5
 ASR1000(config-pmap-c)# class APPL-2
  ASR1000(config-pmap-c)# bandwidth remaining ratio 3
 ASR1000(config-pmap-c)# class APPL-3
  ASR1000(config-pmap-c)# bandwidth remaining ratio 1
 ASR1000(config-pmap-c)# class class-default
  ASR1000(config-pmap-c)# random-detect
 ...more...


ASR1000(config)# policy-map Per-Spoke-QoS
! "one parent policy-map for each DMVPN spoke"
ASR1000(config-pmap)# class spoke1
  ASR1000(config-pmap-c)# shape average 2000000
  ASR1000(config-pmap-c)# service-policy Spoke1-policy
ASR1000(config-pmap-c)# class spoke2
  ASR1000(config-pmap-c)# shape average 2500000
  ASR1000(config-pmap-c)# service-policy Spoke2-policy
...more...
ASR1000(config)# interface <Outbound-Hub-WAN-link>
ASR1000(config-if)# description Outside interface
ASR1000(config-if)# service-policy output Per-Spoke-QoS
! applies the policy on the DMVPN hub interface"
```

Note The configuration in Example 14-1 requires IOS XE 2.3 as the number of supported class maps was changed to per policy-map.

Example 14-1 shows the flexibility and scale of the QFP QoS design with two-level hierarchy-QoS (H-QoS), where minimum, maximum, and excess bandwidth limits are provisioned along with the priority propagation across the hierarchy levels.

Scalable GETVPN Group Member for Data Center and Large Branch Solutions

Cisco IOS has multiple VPN solutions to address p2p and p2mp scenarios, although all of them require some sort of overlay tunneling and routing. To get a full mesh of connectivity over an encrypted tunnel requires a lot of configuration overhead, and at the end of the day still uses overlay tunnel routing, which may lead to suboptimal routing decisions.

To address the inherent limitation of tunnel-based VPNs, Cisco IOS introduced a new solution called Group Encrypted Transport VPN (GETVPN). At the core of this solution is the functionality called GDOI Group Domain of Interpretation (GDOI), which the Internet Engineering Task Force (IETF) introduced within RFC 3547 and which provides a mechanism to do multipoint key exchange. A platform can play two roles in that solution:

- **Group member (GM):** In a real network scenario, that will be your customer edge (CE) router, which could possibly have a large GM sitting at the data center or a small GM at one of the branch offices. There is really no sense of hub and spoke (as opposed to DMVPN) in this setup; instead, all GMs work as peers and use a group security association (SA) to encrypt/decrypt traffic. All routers can be GMs, from the c800 to the C7200, to the ASR 1000.
- **Key server:** This is a platform acting as a central policy server to disseminate the SA information and what should or should not be encrypted by GMs, on a GDOI group basis. All c2800 to c7200 routers can be very viable key servers (even up to 2000 GMs) because this function is mostly control plane (CPU) bounded.

Note At the time of this writing, the ASR 1000 does not support the key server function.

Cisco ASR 1000 GETVPN Solution Benefits

Table 14-3 outlines the major benefits of using GETVPN in Cisco ASR 1000 series routers.

Cisco ASR 1000 GETVPN Solution Architecture Overview

The GETVPN solution is based on the IETF group key management protocol GDOI and the Cisco innovation of "IPsec tunnel mode with IP header preservation" technique. With GDOI, a network device acts as a GDOI key server or a GDOI group member. A GDOI key server maintains group security policy and keys for group members. The group security policy and keys are pulled from a key server by group members when group members register to a key server or are pushed to group members by a key server when a key server performs rekey. Group members use the same group policy and keys to establish full-mesh IPsec connectivity among them without establishing pair-wise IPsec connections.

Figure 14-5 depicts the basic system architecture of GETVPN.

There are three typical steps for group members to get the group security policy and establish secure connectivity among the group members:

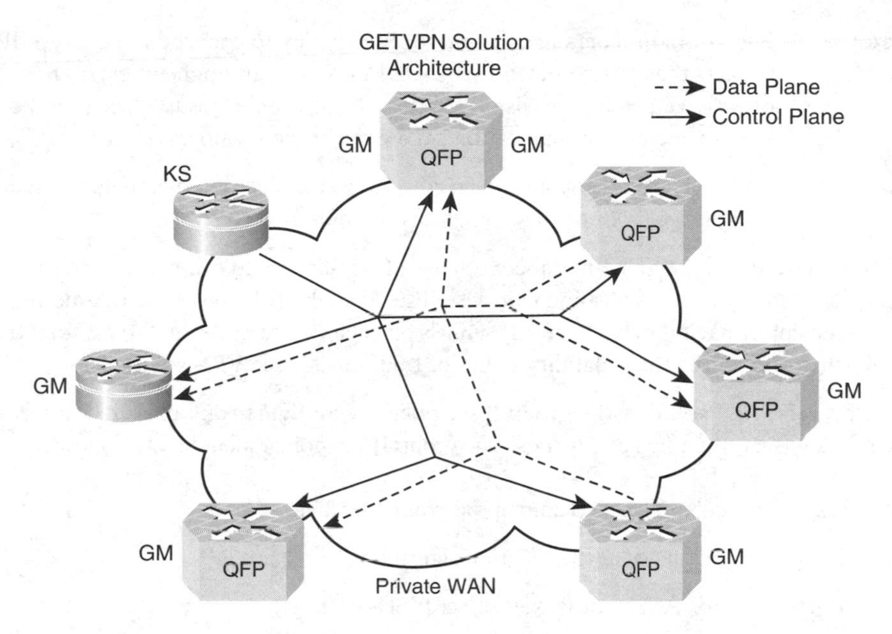

Figure 14-5 *GETVPN solution architecture.*

Step 1. Group members register with the key server via the GDOI protocol. The key server authenticates and authorizes the group members and downloads the group IPsec policy and keys to the group members.

Table 14-3 *The Benefits of Both GETVPN Solutions and ASR 1000 Platform Specifics*

Cisco ASR 1000 Platform Benefits	Cisco IOS GETVPN Benefits
Multigigabit and multimillion packets per second throughput and forwarding for encryption	Tunnel-less encryption solution
Support for up to GDOI Groups per GM	End-to-end security for voice, video, and data traffic
Support for up to 100 access control entries (ACEs) per GM for traffic exclusion (ACLs are done in hardware)	Capability to provide multicast encryption natively, and replication in the core
Combines the crypto acceleration with QoS, IP multicast in ASR1000-ESP	Optimal routing by preserving the source and the destination IP addresses
Time-based antireplay support in hardware for robust security	Centralized policy control and management for keys
Embedded encryption module enabling instant turn-on via IPsec “right to use” license	Zero-touch provisioning on key server for adding new group members

Step 2. The group members use the group IPsec policy to encrypt and decrypt IP packets that are protected by the GETVPN. The group members do not directly establish pair-wise IPsec tunnel, but use the group IPsec policy and keys to secure communication among the group members.

Step 3. The key server distributes new group keys to the group members as needed using the GDOI protocol via unicast or multicast.

Using these steps, the group members can have IPsec-protected full-mesh connectivity among them without establishing pair-wise IPsec tunnels. This solves the full-mesh requirement of having to build (n – 1) tunnels on each device or n * (n – 1) / 2 total tunnels (that is, it solves the scalability issues of traditional IPsec VPN solutions).

With a GETVPN solution, the group IPsec policy is configured and managed in the group key server via IOS commands. The group IPsec policy includes the following:

- IPsec protocols to be used among the group members
- IPsec encryption and authentication algorithms
- Traffic selector ACL (that is, key server [KS] access list)
- Group SA mode (for example, receive only, passive)
- Group SA lifetime
- Group SA level (for example, per host)
- Group SA antireplay type and window size
- KS pseudo time for time-based antireplay support

For each permit access control element (ACE) in the group KS access control list (ACL), the KS will construct an inbound SA and an outbound SA. These group SAs, along with the IPsec keys and the group IPsec policy, will be downloaded to a group member by the KS when a group member registers to the KS. The KS also pushes the policy, SAs, and keys down to registered group members when a rekey is needed because of SA expiration or any policy change that results from configuration.

With the group policy management, all group members use the same policy and SAs and are not aware what the policy is before registering to a KS. The number of SAs, which is the key scaling factor for IPsec VPN, is determined by the group policy (that is, the number of permit ACEs in the KS ACL), not by the number of group members. So adding or removing a node (a GM) for a GETVPN will not affect the group IPsec policy and SAs.

A GDOI group member starts its registration process when a crypto map set with a GDOI type crypto map is attached to an interface. As part of the registration process, a group member receives group policy, IPsec SAs, and IPsec encryption/authentication keys from the KS. After a group member finishes the registration process, the group member is ready to communicate with other registered group members via IPsec-protected, secure connectivity using the group IPsec SA and the group keys.

GDOI group member registration consists of two phases:

- The first phase is run by IKE main mode to establish the IKE SA between the KS and the group member.
- The second phase, protected by the IKE SA established in the first phase, is run by GDOI to download group policy, IPsec SAs, and IPsec keys from the KS to the group member.

For both the IKE phase and the GDOI phase, the GM registration is done using UDP at port 848, which is different from the IPsec IKE port. Cisco IOS uses IKE port number 500 for the GDOI phase 1 exchanges. The GDOI port number 848 is used in GDOI phase 2 exchanges for the inner IP.

In the ASR 1000, the IPsec data path functionality is implemented jointly by the crypto engine and QFP. QFP is responsible for packet classification and decides whether a packet needs to be sent to the crypto engine for IPsec processing, dropped, or punted to the RP. The crypto engine is responsible for IPsec packet processing, such as encryption, decryption, and header manipulation.

The GETVPN solution provides the redundant cooperative KS functionality, and therefore the GM registration and the group policy management on the KS are already HA-capable. However, for the IPsec data path, the platform implements the HA support. Currently, the IPsec implementation on the ASR 1000 supports only ESP-to-ESP HA and no RP HA. The GETVPN feature follows the same approach.

In the GETVPN solution, one group SA is used by all group members for sending IPsec packets, and there is no easy way to synchronize the sequence number among the multiple senders. So, the IPsec standard sequence number-based antireplay protocol will not work well for the group environment if the sequence number cannot be synchronized correctly. Instead of tackling the synchronization of the sequence number, the GETVPN solution uses a time-based antireplay mechanism to provide loose antireplay protection as an alternative to the sequence-number-based antireplay protection.

The time-based antireplay (TBAR) uses a time stamp in IPsec packets to perform replay protection. When a group member sends an IPsec packet, it inserts the current time stamp in the IPsec packet. When a group member receives an IPsec packet, it compares the time stamp in the packet with its current time to determine whether the packet is within the antireplay time window. If the packet is not within the window, the packet is treated as a replay and will be dropped. The base pseudo time (as opposed to real time based on a network timing source) is maintained by the primary KS via a clock that does not synchronize to any particular real clock. The KS clock is periodically advanced in tick, and the length of a tick is globally defined as 10 ms.

Table 14-4 shows the work split between the QFP and crypto engine.

Table 14-4 *GETVPN Tasks Performed by the Crypto Engine and QFP*

GETVPN Tasks	Crypto Engine	QuantumFlow Processor
Copy inner IP to outer IP	Yes	—
Insert pseudo time stamp into packet	—	Yes
Handle custom header	Yes	—
TBAR check	—	Yes
Enforce receive-only SA semantics	—	Yes
Enforce passive SA semantics	—	Yes
SPI and destination IP range lookup	—	Yes
Pseudo clock for TBAR	—	Yes
Packet encryption and decryption	Yes	—

GETVPN Configuration Overview

As noted previously, the ASR 1000 as a GDOI group member will work with any Cisco router that is capable of serving as a KS (for example, a Cisco 7200VXR router) but will not perform the KS function itself. The steps for local policy configuration on GM are as follows:

Step 1. Define the GDOI group:

crypto gdoi group *group_name*

  identity {address ipv4 *ip* **| number** *n***}**

  [no] passive

  server { address ipv4 *ks_ip* **| hostname ipv4** *ks_hostname***} (*)**

Step 2. Define the GDOI crypto map:

crypto map *cm_name seq* **gdoi**

  set group *group_name*

  match address *gm_acl*

  qos pre-classify

Cisco ASR 1000 Memory, Performance, and Scaling

GETVPN features on the ASR 1000 have a relatively small memory footprint. The memory increase is proportional to the number of GDOI groups supported with the ASR 1000 being a GM. The memory increase is roughly the multiple of the number of GDOI groups and the per-group memory usage.

Both on packet per seconds and on packet processing overhead there is no degradation when doing GETVPN on the ASR 1000 over IPsec baseline. For a GM, the main scaling factor is number of group SAs that the router can handle. This number is determined by the number of groups and the number of ACEs in a group (or KS) ACL. For IOS XE 2.3, the ASR 1000 supports up to 20 GDOI groups within a system as GM and 100 ACE lines in a KS ACL.

Note Twenty GDOI groups is not a hard limit, but rather a tested recommendation for deployment with 100 ACEs in each GDOI group. It is also to be noted that 20 GDOI groups per GM meets the requirements of most deployments.

The GETVPN features supported by the Cisco ASR 1000 are as follows:

- IPsec tunnel mode with IP header preservation
- GDOI group ACL
- GDOI GM ACL
- GDOI group IPsec SA
- Unicast GDOI IPsec SA rekey
- Multicast GDOI IPsec SA rekey
- Receive-only IPsec SA mode
- Passive IPsec SA mode
- Time-based antireplay (TBAR)
- Fail open / fail close interface mode
- Explicit passive mode IPsec SA

Note The ASR 1000, as of IOS XE 2.3, supports all the GETVPN features that are present in Cisco IOS Software Release 12.4(22)T except the following:

- VPN Routing and Forwarding (VRF) Lite support on GM
- KS support

Caveats and Limitations

When planning a GETVPN deployment, keep the following caveats in mind:

- An additional router (other than an ASR 1000) is needed to function as the KS; in general, a GM cannot be configured as a KS at this time in Cisco IOS.
- Key servers and group members behind Network Address Translation (NAT) are not supported because of the needed preservation of source and destination addresses.
- DMVPN can be used where NAT is needed with a partial mesh.
- Policies defined in the KS are downloaded to all GMs even if no multicast source or receiver is connected or active for that GM.
- It is also suggested to avoid using counter-based SAs, and to expand the antireplay window accordingly if any post-crypto QoS shaping/queuing is involved.

Cisco ASR 1000 GETVPN Deployment Models

There are two principal types of deployments for GETVPN GMs in the enterprise networks today: data center and branch. There can be numerous variations of these deployments. The sections that follow focus on a large GM (at the data center [DC]) and a medium GM (at the branch office).

DC Design

The Cisco ASR 1000 brings a lot of consolidation to the existing GETVPN design recommendation for GMs, especially in the DC, where both WAN aggregation and GM functionality can be combined under one physical router. Multiple GMs can be used to achieve redundancy goals commonly needed in the DC, while still leveraging the integration available in the Cisco ASR 1000 router.

Figure 14-6 shows a separate pair of ASR 1000s used for WAN aggregation, along with GMs in a *distributed* fashion where they can scale as needed.

Figure 14-7 shows a single pair of ASR 1000s used for WAN aggregation, along with GMs in an *integrated* fashion, most appropriate for small- to medium-sized DC deployments and enabling extremely power-friendly usage.

Branch Design

For branches with backup technologies (EasyVPN, DMVPN, and VTI are all supported on the ASR 1000 since IOS XE Release 2.1) or without backup, the Cisco ASR 1000 series router adds value by bringing the high level of services integration and software modularity.

Figure 14-8 shows how multihomed branch offices can be connected primarily via GETVPN and backed up using multiple Cisco Secure WAN technologies that are all supported on the ASR 1000 (via the Internet).

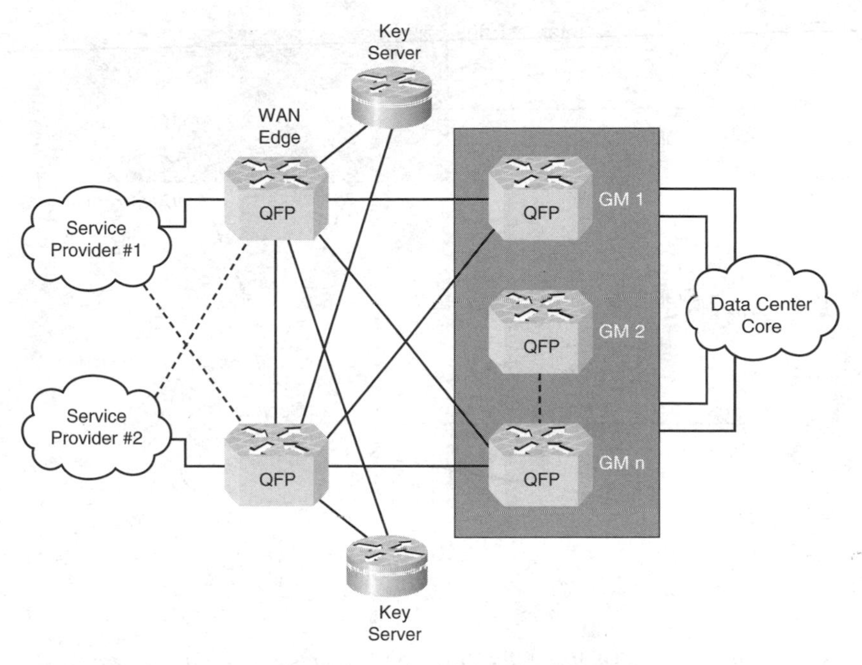

Figure 14-6 *ASR 1000 used as a large GM at the DC locations.*

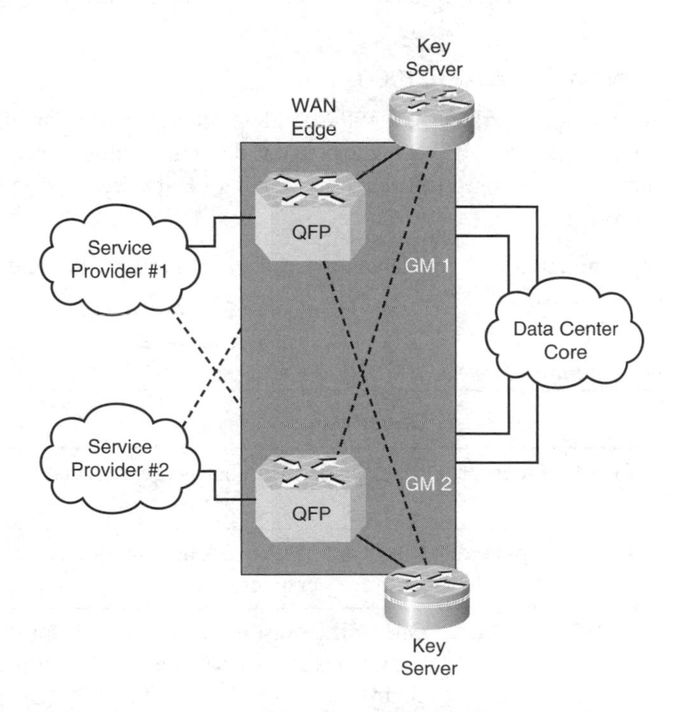

Figure 14-7 *Converged WAN edge and GETVPN GM role in a single ASR 1000 router.*

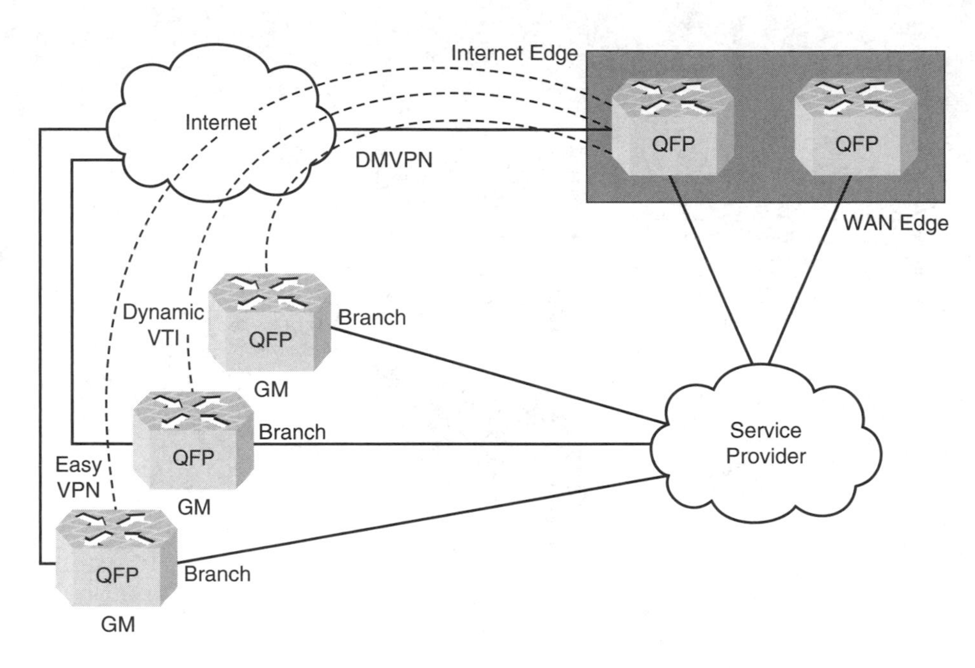

Figure 14-8 *Branch office sites (smaller GETVPN GMs) provisioned with backup Internet access and DMVPN or EasyVPN for encryption over the public Internet.*

Troubleshooting GETVPN on Cisco ASR 1000

From a user experience perspective, the Cisco ASR 1000 is another platform running Cisco IOS. This does not change for GETVPN implementation. In fact, most Cisco IOS **show** and **debug** commands can be used to troubleshoot and look at different crypto-related statistics on the router.

Table 4-5 describes the commands that enable you to display counter statistics and various lower-level data-plane statistics.

Table 14-5 show/debug *Commands for the ASR 1000 Platform*

Command	Description
show platform hardware qfp active feature ipsec	Displays platform hardware information
show platform software ipsec isakmp-sa all	Displays ISAKMP SA information from a platform perspective
show platform software ipsec f0 encryption-processor	One of the most useful commands for displaying various statistics related to the crypto engine
debug platform software ipsec	Displays platform-related crypto debugging

Integrated Threat Control Solutions

Cisco IOS has a host of solutions under the integrated threat control umbrella, including the IOS Firewall, intrusion prevention systems (IPS), content and endpoint security, and so on.

This section discusses only the Cisco IOS zone-based firewall, which is what is supported in both Cisco IOS Software Release 12.4T and IOS XE for the ASR 1000.

Cisco IOS Firewall provides a number of benefits, including the following:

- Integrated firewall, reducing the number of devices required (thus lowering hop count and latency)
- Integrated firewall (with routing), simplifying the overall deployment both at headquarters and branch offices
- Helps achieve regulatory compliance (Sarbanes-Oxley [SOX] or Payment Card Industry [PCI])
- Improves the interoperability with unified communications-related transport, such as Session Initiation Protocol (SIP) and H.323, using both firewall and NAT for pinholing to let return traffic come back through, protocol conformance, and application/payload translation

Introduction to Threat Control Solutions on the ASR 1000

IOS Firewalls before the ASR 1000 have been supported only on software-based routers (c800 to c7200VXR), which have no special hardware to accelerate the firewall function. The Cisco ASR 1000 uses QFP, which has the native capability to accelerate the firewall and provide throughput of 5 Gbps to 20 Gbps for Layer 4 TCP or UDP inspection and millions of sessions. Because of this performance and scale increase, IOS zone-based firewalls using the ASR 1000 becomes an attractive proposition. This opens up the option where you don't have to make separate system choices when it comes to carrier class routing and scalable security solutions.

Cisco IOS zone-based firewalls use the concept of zone, which is nothing but a set of interfaces that belong to a given security level. Zone pairs tie different zones together to enforce various actions that can be taken by IOS Firewalls (such as inspect, drop, log, or a combination) when a packet traverses between zones.

Figure 14-9 shows the basic IOS zone-based firewall concept.

Table 14-6 outlines the benefits of both IOS Firewall solutions and ASR 1000 platform specifics.

Figure 14-10 shows the basic IOS zone-based firewall logic and how a packet traverses various stages while in the firewall engine.

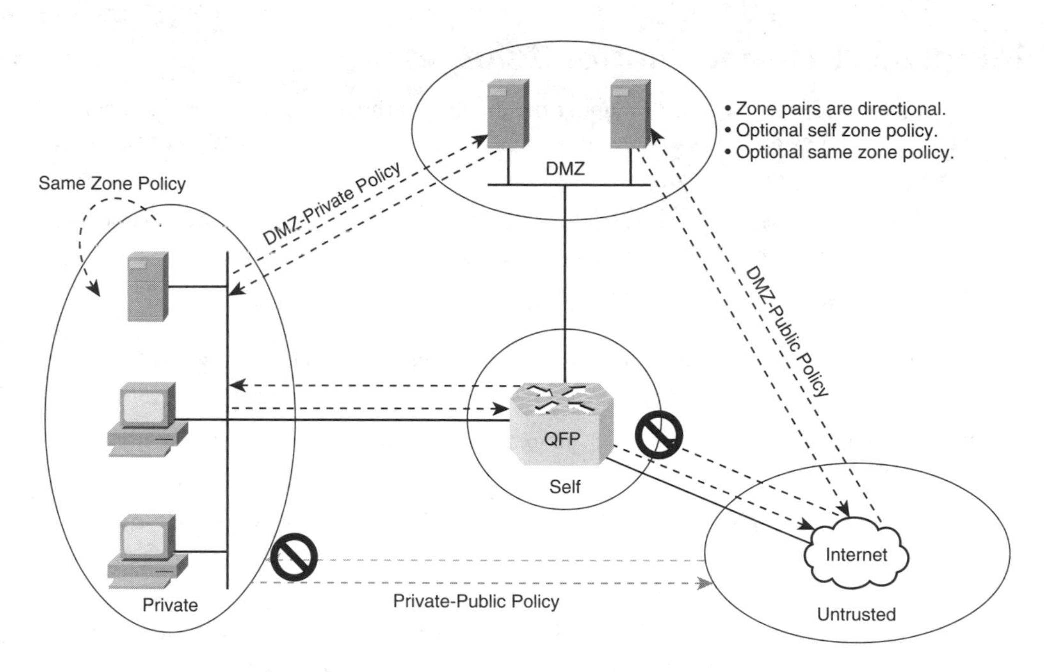

Figure 14-9 *IOS zone-based firewall.*

Table 14-6 *Combined Benefits of Deploying Cisco ASR 1000 with a Cisco IOS Firewall*

Cisco ASR 1000 Platform Benefits	Cisco IOS Zone-Based Firewall Benefits
Native multigigabit and multimillion packets per second throughput and forwarding for firewall	Integrated firewall engine with routing
Support for up to 20-Gbps firewall with ASR1000-ESP20 in a single chassis	End-to-end security for voice, video, and data traffic
Support for up to 2M firewall concurrent sessions	Capability to provide native pinholing for all VoIP protocols
Combines the firewall solutions with NetFlow event logging for higher logging scale	Consistent firewall syntax/CLI across all IOS-based platforms
Full firewall processing done inside the ESP, including at L7	Centralized policy control and integration with IOS VPN solutions
Instant turn-on via IOS firewall "right to use" license (requiring no additional hardware)	Centralized provisioning using single Cisco Security Monitor platform v3.3 or later

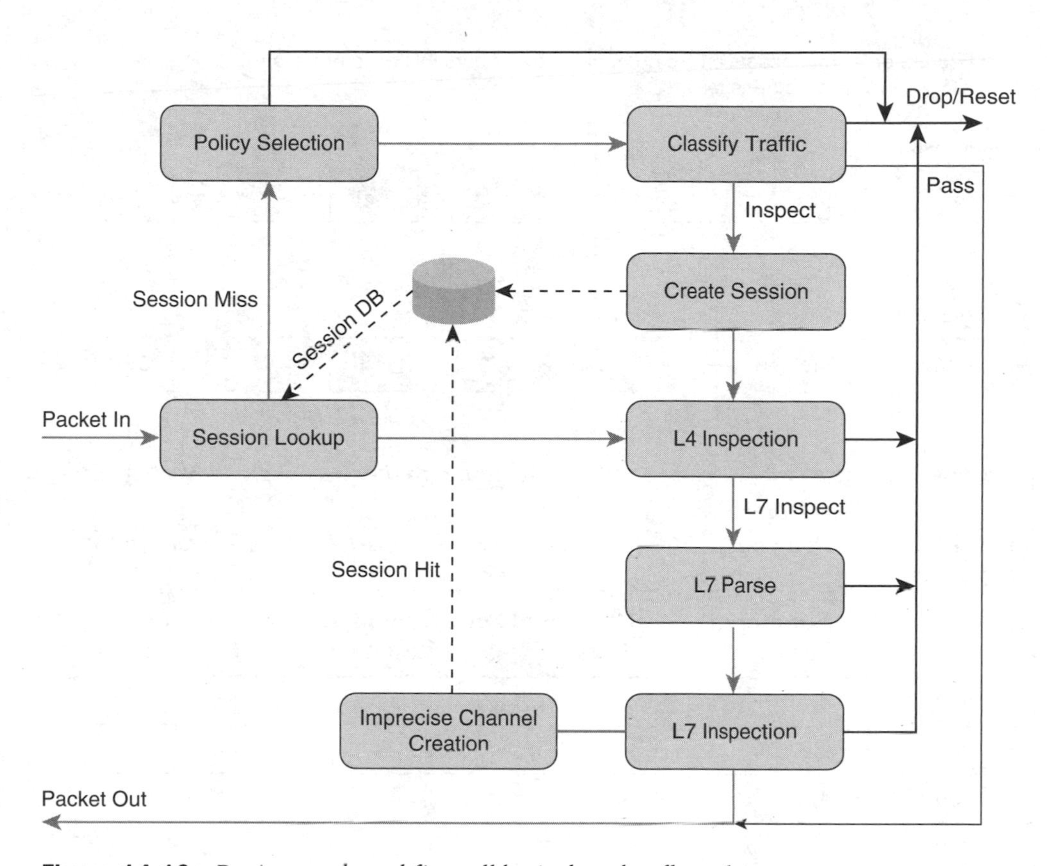

Figure 14-10 *Basic zone-based firewall logical packet flow chart.*

Using In-Built Firewall High Availability

An IOS Firewall implementation on the ASR 1000 not only provides the higher throughput and scale, but also adds stateful in-box failover to it. Both system RP and ESP failover are stateful (much like NAT) on the ASR 1000; so in case of a component failure, existing firewall sessions will not be torn down and re-created from scratch.

As soon as a session becomes established (Layer 4 only), the active ESP sends the session data to the standby ESP.

A Cisco IOS Firewall is an egress feature, and is handled likewise by the QFP processor.

Figure 14-11 shows the feature order of operation for firewalls and NAT in a Cisco ASR 1000.

IOS Firewall Zone/Zone Pair Scale

Table 14-7 shows the firewall configuration related scale for various ESPs supported by the ASR 1000 as of IOS XE 2.3.

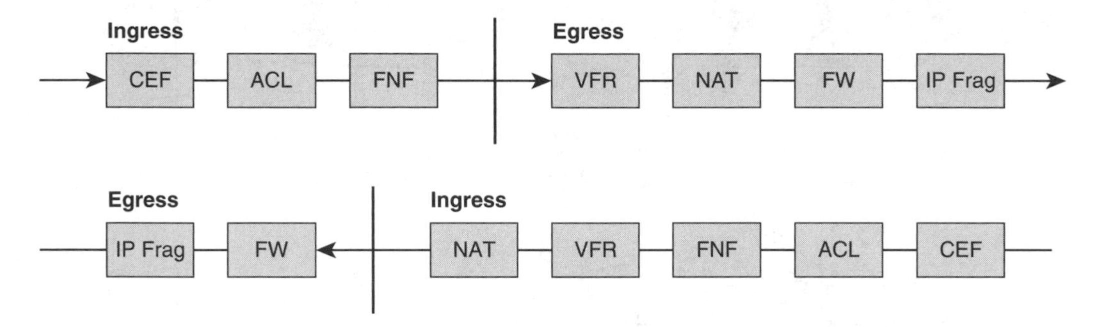

Figure 14-11 *Firewall/NAT feature order of operation in the Cisco ASR 1000.*

Table 14-7 *IOS Zone-Based Firewall Scale for Cisco ASR 1000 Series Routers and Respective ESPs*

ESP	Number of Zones	Number of Zone Pairs	Number of Matches/Class	Number of Policy Maps
ASR1000-ESP5	4K	2K	16	4K
ASR1000-ESP10	4K	4K	16	4K
ASR1000-ESP20	4K	4K	16	4K

Scalable Multigigabit Router Firewall at the Internet Edge: Use Case

For this use case, the first thing to identify is the number of zones required. A security zone should be configured for each region of relative security within the network so that all interfaces assigned to the same zone are protected with a similar level of security:

- One interface connected to the public Internet
- One interface connected to a private LAN that must not be accessible from the public Internet

For the Internet edge scenario, each zone might hold only one interface. If an additional interface is added to the private zone, the hosts connected to the new interface in the zone would be able to pass traffic to all hosts on the existing interface in the same zone. In addition, the hosts' traffic to hosts in other zones would be similarly affected by existing policies.

Typically, the example network will have two main policies:

- Private zone connectivity to the Internet
- Internet zone connectivity to demilitarized zone (DMZ) hosts (optionally, if there is one)

The following procedure can be used to configure a zone-based policy firewall in the above scenario where the ASR 1000 is being used as a demarcation point between inside-private and outside-public Internet networks:

Step 1. Define class maps that outline the traffic that needs to have policy application as traffic crosses between zones.

Step 2. Define policy maps to apply action to previously identified traffic.

Step 3. Define zones and zone pairs.

Step 4. Apply a policy map to zone pairs.

Step 5. Assign interfaces to zones. This must be the last step, and configuration should be verified before assigning interfaces to zones.

The sequence of steps is not crucial, but some steps must be completed in a particular order. For example, you must configure a class map before you assign a class map to a policy map. Similarly, you cannot assign a policy map to a zone pair until you have configured the policy.

If you try to configure a portion that relies on another one, the router will respond with an error message.

Example 14-2 shows an Internet edge zone-based firewall policy.

Example 14-2 *Configuration Steps for Cisco IOS Zone-Based Firewall*

```
ASR1000(config)# class-map type inspect INT-EDGE
 ASR1000(config-cmap)# match protocol ftp
 ASR1000(config-cmap)# match protocol tcp
 ASR1000(config-cmap)# match protocol udp
ASR1000(config)# policy-map type inspect my-map
 ASR1000(config-pmap-c)# class type inspect INT-EDGE
ASR1000(config-pmap-c)# inspect log
! this will cause traffic inspection and logging
ASR1000(config)# zone-pair security private-to- public source private destination
public
 ASR1000((config-sec-zone-pair)# service-policy type inspect my-map
ASR1000(config)# interface TenGigabitEthernet0/0/0
ASR1000(config)-if# zone-member security private
ASR1000(config-if)# interface TenGigabitEthernet1/0/0
ASR1000(config-if)# zone-member security public
! If NetFlow Event Logging is needed, configure the following:
ASR1000(config)# parameter-map type inspect global
 ASR1000(config-profile)# log flow-export v9 udp destination collector-IP
  collectorport
 ASR1000(config-profile)# log flow-export template timeout-rate 30
 ASR1000(config-profile)# log dropped-packets
```

Note With NetFlow event logging, audit trail messages are not rate-limited at all (unlike usual syslog). However, drop messages are rate-limited every 10 ms to protect the firewall and system from causing self-inflicted denial of service (DoS).

Summary

This chapter discussed the various VPN and IOS firewall solutions in detail, and examined use cases detailing the following ASR 1000 implementations:

- DMVPN hub with H-QoS for per-spoke policy
- GETVPN GM for data center and large branch
- Internet edge firewall

Chapter Review Questions

1. What is the penalty of doing H-QoS on Cisco ASR 1000, and how does this compare with a software-based router?
2. How does the ASR 1000 handle the usual issue of dropping IP multicast packets at crypto engine Rx (receive) ring?
3. Does the ASR 1000 require any services modules for NAT, firewalls, or IPsec.
4. What are the limits on the number of zones, zone pairs in the Cisco ASR 1000?

Answers

1. Because of native QFP acceleration, there is almost no penalty of doing QoS, even when you are actively shaping traffic. The ASR 1000 is one of the rare platforms where you can schedule the overall system bandwidth. Software-based routers, simply due to lack of purpose-built hardware acceleration for QoS, do not scale well with active QoS tasks such as shaping.

2. ASR 1000 uses what can be termed as a full circle of backpressure between the QFP's traffic manager (where packets wait before coming to crypto engine) and the crypto engine itself. This allows the system to deal with any form of quasi-instantaneous oversubscription, such as seen during multicast encryption when a burst of packets comes to encryptor and some of that ends up getting dropped at the Rx ring.

3. The ASR 1000 does not require any services modules, and this is one of the most distinguishing aspects of the platform, that it can natively accelerate almost all Cisco IOS services. Notable benefits include the following:

   a. Day one, you get hardware that has everything you need to accelerate most of the basic services (such as NAT, firewalls, IPsec, and so on).

   b. You can use those services without having to wait for the module to arrive (via software licenses where applicable; note that NAT doesn't require a license).

   c. Lower total cost of ownership (TCO). Service modules procured later on increase the overall TCO over the product's lifetime.

   d. You save precious IO slots/density of the platform and so can use the I/O slots for the purpose of bringing traffic of various types into the platform.

   e. Debugging and troubleshooting are easier. After all, no complex packet paths exist; it is just a centralized engine (QFP in case of the ASR 1000) that all packets traverse.

4. The ASR 1000 supports 4000 zones on all ESPs, whereas the number of zone pairs varies from 2000 to 4000, depending on the ESP used.

Further Reading

GETVPN Design and Implementation Guide, document: http://tinyurl.com/nk4a8h

QoS and DMVPN Design Guides, documents: http://tinyurl.com/ny9et6

Network Security Features for ASR 1000 Series Routers, document: http://tinyurl.com/yoaee8

Internet Gateway Router Design Using ASR 1000 Series Routers, document: http://tinyurl.com/l6nbcp

NAT and Firewall ALG Support on Cisco ASR 1000 Series Routers, document: http://tinyurl.com/lcw584

Chapter 15

WAN Optimization Services Use Cases

Whereas data center consolidation is on the rise, an ever-increasing number of file and application servers are now being centralized at regional or main data center locations. Another trend is the increasing number of remote users connecting from across the globe, especially for organizations with an international footprint.

Data and infrastructure consolidation to a few locations does solve security, compliance, backup, and many other issues that result from employees turning on and running local file servers scattered throughout the branches. However, data consolidation raises its own challenges. The most obvious ones are bandwidth limitation and increased latency, because branch offices have relatively slower data rate connections, and now all file and application traffic has to traverse the WAN to get to the branch office. Increasing bandwidth at all branch office locations usually is not an option.

This is where Cisco Wide Area Application Services (WAAS) comes into play. Cisco WAAS provides the LAN-like experience in the branches. It centralizes data, video, and applications hosted at the data center, and essentially bridges the traffic-optimization gap between centralized servers and distributed users.

This chapter focuses on how the Cisco ASR 1000 can be used for both data and voice WAN optimization using Cisco WAAS and Cisco IOS Real-Time Protocol (RTP) compression, respectively.

Introduction to WAN Optimization Solutions on the Cisco ASR 1000

Cisco ASR 1000 uses Web Cache Control Protocol (WCCP) Version 2 to provide the data redirection to WAAS (or similar WAN optimization) appliances up to 10 Gigabit Ethernet line rates.

Originally created as a component of IOS, the sole purpose of WCCP (or WCCPv1) was to intercept HTTP traffic traversing a router and to redirect that traffic to a local cache engine, with the goal of reducing access times to websites and conserving wide-area link upstream bandwidth.

With the introduction of WCCPv2, the scope of the protocol widened to include traffic types other than HTTP, allowing the protocol to be used as a more general interception mechanism.

In WCCPv2, clients specify the nature of the traffic to be intercepted and forwarded to external devices, which are then in a position to provide services based on the traffic type, such as WAN optimization and application acceleration.

Figure 15-1 shows the basic usage of WCCP for redirecting HTTP traffic.

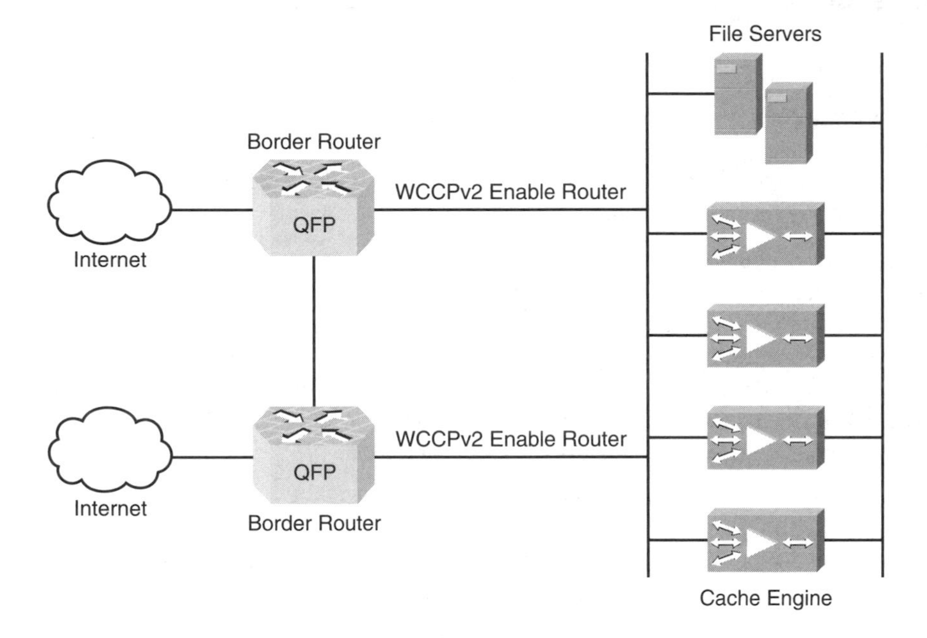

Figure 15-1 *Deployment of ASR 1000 for web caching.*

Using WCCPv2 for Web Caching

WCCPv2 transparently redirects a variety of traffic types, specified by protocol (TCP or UDP) and port. End users do not know that the page came from the cache engine rather than from the originally requested web server.

The protocol has the following specifications:

- Routers and WCCPv2 clients interact to form service groups (all routers/WCCPv2 clients in a cluster running the same service) such as 61 and 62 (TCP promiscuous mode)
- Up to 32 routers per service group

- Up to 32 WCCPv2 clients per service group
- Each service group established and maintained independently
- Number of service groups implementation dependent
- Protocol allows the negotiation of either generic routing encapsulation (GRE) or Layer 2 return

Table 15-1 shows the ASR 1000 and WCCPv2 mutual benefits.

Table 15-1 *WCCPv2 and ASR 1000 Benefits*

Cisco ASR 1000 Platform Benefits	WCCPv2 Protocol Benefits
Multigigabit and multimillion packets per second throughput and forwarding	Fault tolerance of the service cluster
Support for both GRE and L2 redirect and return for complete deployment flexibility	Multiple router support in one service group
GRE return handled in the data plane (Embedded Services Processor [ESP]), no punts to system Route Processor (RP), and hence performance boost	Message digest algorithm 5 (MD5) authentication between router and service cluster
Provides interoperability with Cisco IOS Firewalls for Cisco WAAS	Multiple service groups
WCCPv2 supported in all IOS types starting from IP BASE	Fault prevention; packet-return feature (overload and bypass)
No IOS XE feature license required	Load distribution using mask or hash mode

Interaction of WCCPv2 with Other IOS Features

Various IOS features interact with WCCPv2, including the following:

- **Policy Based Routing (PBR):** In all software-based platforms (c800 to c7200VXR), traffic matching WCCPv2 is exempted from the PBR path decision and traffic is redirected to the WCCPv2 client. Traffic not matching WCCPv2 will follow the PBR policy. Cisco ASR 1000 WCCPv2 implementation preserves this IOS behavior.
- **Network Based Application Recognition (NBAR):** Many NBAR classifiers will not function if packets are redirected to WAAS and it gets applied first. The workaround is to classify packets on the inbound interface.
- **Firewalls:** Firewalls in general have two issues:

  WAAS discovery failure is caused by resetting the TCP options bits.

WAAS modifies the TCP sequence number space, which causes firewalls to drop the session (because they track it). The workaround for this issue is to use a Cisco IOS firewall fix-up for complete WAAS awareness (also supported in IOS XE Release 2.2 and later). The fix-up is enabled in Cisco IOS XE by default; hence, no IOS CLI is needed.

The Cisco ASR 1000 series provides two ways to redirect packets to WAAS appliances:

- WCCPv2 (preferred method)
- PBR (an option, but lacks the sophisticated load-sharing algorithm present in WCCPv2)

The Cisco ASR 1000 can transparently integrate with a WAAS appliance (or any appliance that supports WCCP) via WCCPv2. Transparency ensures compliance with critical network features to provide the industry's only holistic and secure optimization, visibility, and control solution.

Cisco IOS XE Release 2.2 supports the following WCCPv2 features:

- **WAAS/IOS FW interoperability:** The **ip inspect waas enable** command is needed to turn on the interoperability between WAAS and Cisco IOS Firewalls in 12.4T. The command enables firewall inspection to tolerate TCP sequence number manipulation indicative of the application of WAAS. It is enabled by default on Cisco IOS XE.
- **WCCPv2 applied as an input feature:** WCCPv2 can be applied only as an inbound feature on ASR 1000; outbound support might be introduced in the future releases.
- **Forwarding and return method (GRE and L2):** WCCPv2 redirect and return methods could either use Layer 3 (very useful if WAE devices are Layer 3 hops away) or Layer 2 (when they are Layer 2 adjacent) to WCCPv2 client routers.
- **Assignment method (mask mode only):** Assignment method is used for load distribution between the WCCPv2 client and WAE devices. ASR 1000 currently supports only mask mode.
- **Service group authentication password:** WCCPv2 provides optional authentication that enables you to control which routers and cache engines become part of the service group with shared passwords and the HMAC MD5 hash standard.

Note The Cisco ASR 1000 does not support stateful switchover (SSO) for Route Processor (RP)-to-RP (or IOS daemon [IOSD]-to-IOSD), as opposed to ESP (Embedded Services Processor)-to-ESP, failover with WCCPv2 configuration.

WAN Optimization Through WAAS Integration

You can deploy the Cisco ASR 1000 at the campus WAN headend, WAN distribution, and in large branches. The sections that follow describe the different variations of those deployments.

Figure 15-2 begins with the end-to-end topology that captures various positionings of ASR 1000 along with the Cisco WAAS solution. Figure 15-2 shows the packet flow paths before and after WAAS optimization

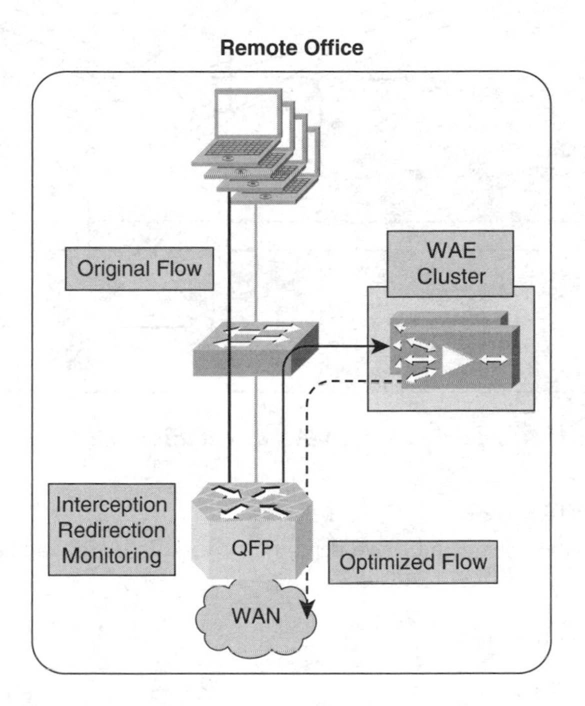

Figure 15-2 *ASR 1000 positionings within a Cisco WAAS solution.*

Campus WAN Headend Deployment

The Cisco ASR 1000 can be used at the unified WAN edge in the campus with WCCPv2 along with IOS firewalls, virtual private networks (VPN), and other features. In this deployment, the ASR 1000 combines all those functions into a single device and reduces the overall total cost of ownership (TCO) while providing optimized power and space footprints.

When deploying with IOS Firewalls, be sure to turn on and use the WAAS fix-up in IOS Firewalls, which is disabled by default in 12.4T. The IOS Firewall recognizes TCP sequence number modification during the TCP handshake as a possible attack. The following command enables the interoperation of WAAS optimization with IOS Firewalls for generic routing encapsulation (GRE)-returned packets.

```
C7200VXR(config)# ip inspect waas enable
```

Figure 15-3 shows the ASR 1000 deployed at the WAN distribution or headend and peering with the WAAS appliances at the WAN access or branch offices.

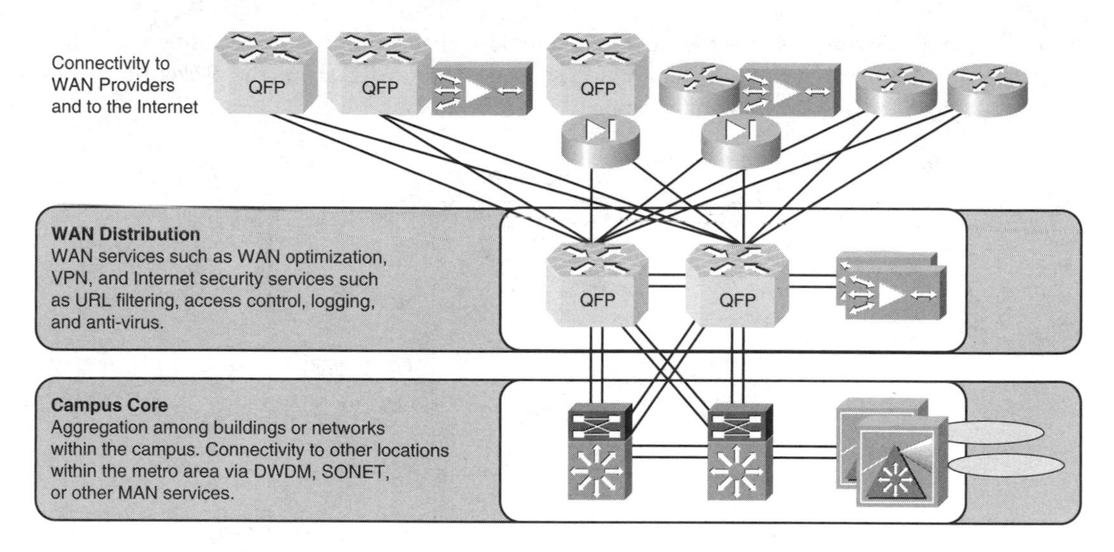

Figure 15-3 *ASR 1000 deployed at the WAN distribution end.*

Branch Deployment

On the branch side, there can be two deployment variations, depending on size of the branch, as illustrated in Figure 15-4:

- Single-router branch
- Dual-router branch

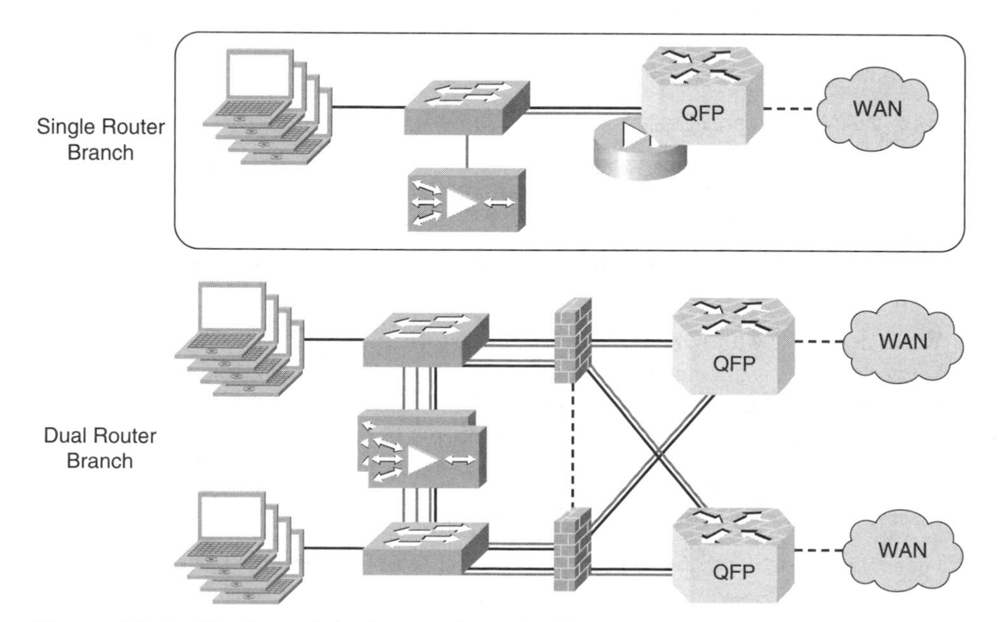

Figure 15-4 *Single- and dual-router branch office scenarios.*

WAN Headend and IronPort's WSA Appliance

The Cisco ASR 1000 can integrate with Web Security Appliance (WSA) or IronPort appliances using WCCPv2. WSAs provide web and email security. More specifically, they can provide antispam, antivirus, and content security. This applies to both S and C series appliances.

The Cisco ASR 1000 can be used both in headquarters and in the branches alongside with these appliances. Figure 15-5 illustrates a Cisco ASR 1000/WSA deployment at the headend to provide email security

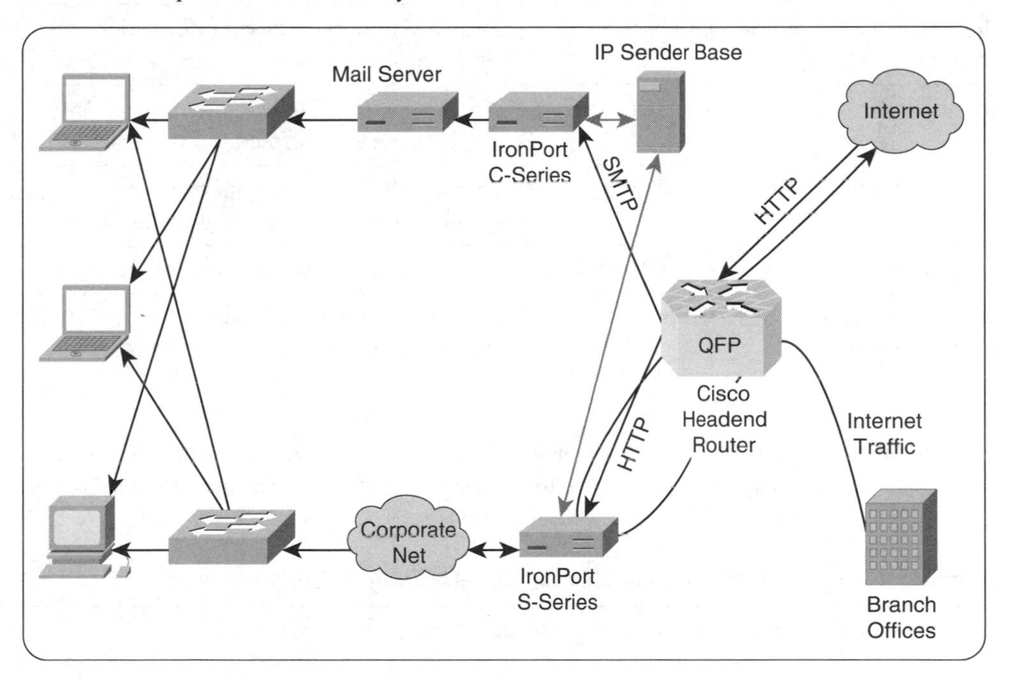

Figure 15-5 *ASR 1000 deployed at the headend.*

Troubleshooting WCCPv2 on Cisco ASR 1000

From the user perspective, the Cisco ASR 1000 is another platform running Cisco IOS. This does not change for WCCPv2 implementation.

Table 15-2 shows the ASR 1000 platform-specific WCCPv2 commands.

Table 15-2 *ASR 1000 WCCP-Related Commands*

ASR 1000 Command	Description
show platform software wccp fp active	Displays the Flow Processor (FP), forwarding manager information
show platform software wccp rp active	Displays the RP information
show platform software wccp interface counters	Displays the total number of redirected packets by interfaces
sh platform software wccp web-cache counters	Displays the service group information and drop statistics
show platform so wccp *service Id* **counters**	Checks the redirected counter for a given WCCP service (an often used command)
show platform so interface F0 brief	Displays the low-level (data-plane) QuantumFlow Processor (QFP) information
show platform software wccp f0 interface	Displays the low-level (data-plane) information
debug platform software wccp configuration	Displays debug information about the WCCP configuration

The output from the various forms of the **show wccp** command will show zero counter values, which is expected. To be able to see the real values, you need to use the **show platform** equivalent of the command, as demonstrated in Example 15-1.

Example 15-1 *Displaying Service Group and Associated Counter Values*

```
ASR1000# show platform software wccp 61 counters
 Service Group (1, 61) counters
        Unassigned count = 0
        Dropped due to closed service count = 0
        Bypass count = 0
        Bypass failed count = 0
        Denied count = 0
        Redirect count = 8192000 ‹ Total Count

  CE = 1.1.1.2, obj_id = 51, Redirect Packets = 1024000
  CE = 2.1.1.2, obj_id = 52, Redirect Packets = 1024000
  CE = 3.1.1.2, obj_id = 53, Redirect Packets = 1024000
  CE = 4.1.1.2, obj_id = 54, Redirect Packets = 1024000
  CE = 5.1.1.2, obj_id = 55, Redirect Packets = 1024000
  CE = 6.1.1.2, obj_id = 56, Redirect Packets = 1024000
  CE = 7.1.1.2, obj_id = 57, Redirect Packets = 1024000
  CE = 8.1.1.2, obj_id = 58, Redirect Packets = 1024000
```

Voice Header Compression Using Cisco IOS cRTP

At this point in the chapter, you've seen the WAN optimization for data traffic that uses WAAS. For voice, you will just bypass traffic by excluding it from the redirect access control lists (ACL) so that the voice traffic does not get redirected to WAAS appliances. (Because, at this point, WAAS does not provide any WAN optimization for UDP traffic.)

However, Cisco IOS has a feature called compressed Real-Time Protocol (cRTP) that enables you to compress the voice header down to 2 to 4 bytes of UDP.

The Cisco ASR 1000 supports interface-based application of cRTP and can literally compress thousands of voice sessions going over a WAN connection, thereby reducing the overall WAN utilization.

Configuring IP RTP compression is pretty straightforward. Use the following command to configure cRTP on both sides of peer-to-peer (p2p) WAN link.

```
ASR1000(config-if)# ip rtp header-compression cisco
```

This configuration can prove quite useful on low-/high-speed serial links and is supported for almost all varieties of WAN encapsulation (PPP, Frame Relay, High-Level Data Link Control [HDLC], and so on).

Note No IOS license is required to turn on cRTP, and up to 2000 VoIP sessions (or 4000 contexts) are supported.

Chapter Review Questions

1. ASR 1000 specifically addresses which problems that usually happen in WAAS/WCCPv2 scenarios?
2. Does the ASR 1000 support hash mode?
3. Is the ASR 1000 appropriate for both WAN headend and branch office WAAS deployments?
4. Can I use the **show wccp** command to view WCCP-related counters?
5. Can I use WAAS for voice optimization? If not, what are some other options?
6. Is there any hard limit on the cRTP sessions on ASR 1000 hardware?

Answers

1. ASR 1000 uses the same WCCPv2 implementation that exists in other platforms (in concept); however, the implementation is optimized for QFP hardware, and therefore the performance of WCCPv2 redirect is in multiple gigabits. THE Cisco ASR 1000 also supports GRE return in hardware, which makes it deployable in flexible environments where the cache engine can be multiple Layer 3 hops away. Because the ASR 1000 uses a single IOS XE binary for all chassis, you can use an ASR 1006 at the headend and an ASR 1002 at the large branch office, which reduces product qualification cycles while keeping the consistency end to end.
2. No, at the time of this writing, IOS XE does not support hash mode. Mask mode, which is supported, is something that is preferred to be run in hardware. Having said that, hash mode will likely come in the future.
3. Yes, because of its scalable and flexible WCCPv2 feature set, the ASR 1000 is appropriate for both small and large WAAS deployments.
4. No, the **show wccp** command does not show the counter values. That information is available via the **show platform wccp** command.
5. No, you cannot use WAAS for voice optimization. However, you can use Cisco IOS cRTP on the ASR 1000 to compress a large number of voice sessions. cRTP literally reduces the optimized UDP packets down to 2 to 4 bytes.
6. There is no hard limit, but the minimum supported count is about 4000.

Further Reading

IOS NAT Order of Operation, document: http://tinyurl.com/8vrj

Enterprise Data Center Wide Area Application Services (WAAS) Design Guide, document: http://tinyurl.com/ca9ag8

Cisco WSA Guides, documents: http://ironport.com/resources/guides.html

Configuring RTP Header Compression, document: http://tinyurl.com/lzjbxt

Chapter 16

Unified Communications Services Use Cases

Cisco Unified Communications is about making the communication experience for customers, partners, vendors, and employees more personal, efficient, effective, secure, and productive. To sum it up, it is about realizing the total potential of network investment in making business more successful.

The focus of this chapter is on Cisco unified communications elements that are supported on Cisco ASR 1000 series routers, namely distributed and unified Session Border Controller (SBC) and the WebEx Node Shared Port Adapter (SPA). This chapter refers to unified SBC as *CUBE for SP* (Cisco Unified Border Element for service provider). CUBE (Enterprise Edition) is what Cisco supports today on Integrated Services Routers (ISR), 7200VXR, and AS5400 series routers.

Introduction to Unified WAN Solutions on Cisco ASR 1000

CUBE (SP Edition) is a carrier-grade highly available and scalable version of a typical unified SBC function. An existing ASR 1000 deployed as an Internet edge router, for example, can even be repurposed for SBC functionality (and thus extend the value-add routing services present in IOS XE). CUBE is used to interconnect either SP to SP, SP to enterprise, or SP to residential gateway. The SBC function makes perfect sense to be incorporated in a router at the border of the network for both enterprises and SPs.

WebEx is well known for providing an advanced and feature-rich online meeting, collaboration, and remote desktop sharing toolset. It is delivered as Software as a Service (SaaS), and so people (even on different operating systems) joining the collaboration session can be anywhere in the world and still expect the same experience. All users, either connecting from within the enterprise or connecting from the public Internet, have to go to WebEx data centers.

With the ASR 1000 WebEx Node module, enterprises and SPs can provide a complete WebEx experience by locally terminating the WebEx sessions on this module. The WebEx Node service module serves as the local replication device for all WebEx content (VoIP, video, and data). Major benefits of this approach include the following:

- Savings of enterprise uplink Internet bandwidth for all internal users (because all WebEx sessions up to the service module limit can be served locally)
- Faster and quicker response (because of local hosting of the WebEx service)
- Capability to go through any firewall/NAT (Network Address Translation) device

The chapter examines each solution in more detail later.

Figure 16-1 shows the overall pieces of the Cisco unified communications solution set.

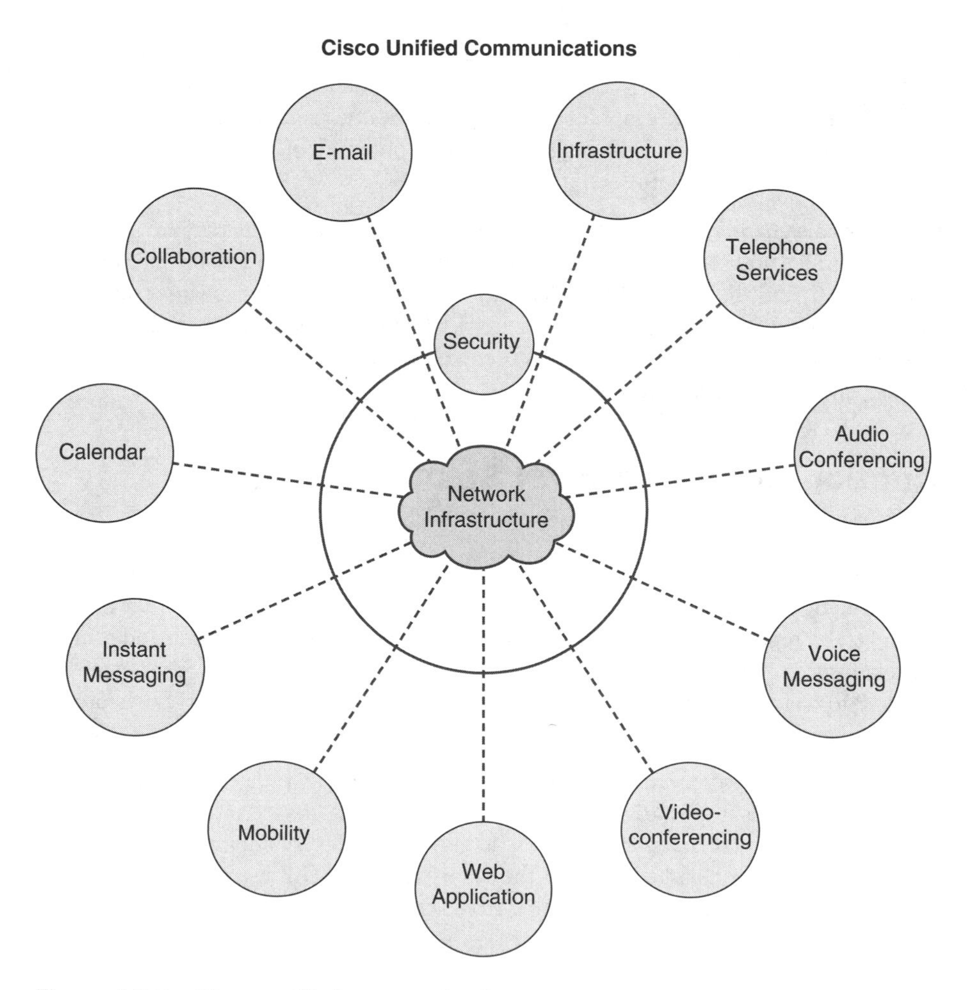

Figure 16-1 *Cisco unified communications components.*

Using Integrated CUBE

By offering a truly scalable version of CUBE functions integrated within the router, the Cisco ASR 1000 router promises a multitude of benefits.

Table 16-1 shows the SBC functional benefits and how they add to the ASR 1000 platform benefits.

Table 16-1 *SBC and ASR 1000 Benefits*

General SBC Benefits	Cisco ASR 1000 Benefits
Allows for seamless interconnection for different multimedia device interconnection	Tighter integration of SBC function along with the routing function configurable via the IOS command-line interface (CLI).
Provides demarcation in the guise of topology hiding, call accounting, and separation of fault domains	All router benefits such as high availability (HA), quality of service (QoS), and in-service software upgrade (ISSU) are provided by a single device.
Protocol interworking: Session Initiation Protocol (SIP) to SIP, SIP to H.323, H.323 to SIP	Faster services add-on using QuantumFlow Processor (QFP).
Billing and call detail record (CDR) functions	All security benefits such as IPsec, NAT, and firewalls are available for SBC or general VoIP protocol inspection.
Media interworking: codecs, Real-Time Protocol / Real-Time Control Protocol (RTP/RTCP)	Supporting both voice and video (Telepresence).
Session management via QoS and service level agreement (SLA)	Native acceleration for QoS in ASR1000-ESP.
Usually deployed as an “appliance sitting next to border” router	Reduced power and space footprint with integrated routing versus an appliance-based solution.

Note The ASR 1000, in IOS XE 2.4, supports only SIP trunks; internetworking with H.323 will be introduced later.

The Cisco ASR 1000 offers both unified and distributed versions of SBC models for complete flexibility in deployments. The SBC functionality can be divided into two functional areas:

- Signaling Border Element (SBE), also known as signaling proxy
- Data Border Element (DBE), also known as media proxy

The SBE is supported on the ASR 1000 Route Processor (RP) to handle the signaling part, whereas the DBE function is implemented on the Embedded Service Processor (ESP) that is in the data plane within the QFP for native hardware acceleration for media handling.

SBE provides services such as the following:

- Call admission control (CAC) and routing
- Billing
- Policy-based call routing

DBE (implemented on QFP/ESP) provides services such as the following:

- Flow identification
- Per flow rate
- Packet marking
- Packet statistics

Figure 16-2 shows the SBE and DBE architectural elements within the ASR 1000 platform architecture.

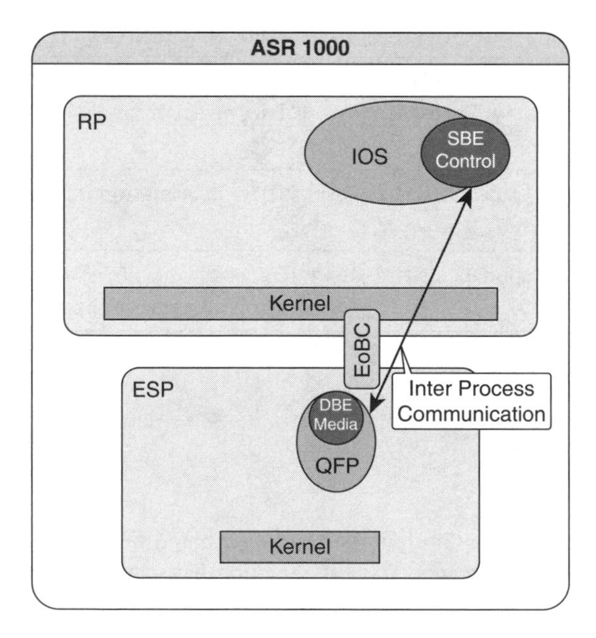

Figure 16-2 *SBE and DBE architectural elements.*

Starting with IOS XE 2.4, the ASR 1000 allows configuration of either distributed or unified SBC via the IOS CLI. In the case of distributed SBC function, the network needs to host an out-of-the-box SBE device that interfaces with the ASR 1000 via an H.248 standard interface. With the unified SBC variation, the SBE function is directly collapsed within IOS running on the RP, and therefore no external H.248 communication is needed. The ASR 1000 uses the built-in Ethernet Out of Band Channel (EOBC) to carry the Inter Process Communication (IPC) between the SBE and DBE elements.

Note Supported beginning with IOS XE 2.4, CUBE (SP) implementation is consistent and interoperable with the SBC functionality in the Cisco 7600 and 12000. Before IOS XE 2.4, the ASR 1000 supported only the distributed SBC function.

Full RP and ESP stateful failover are supported for both SBE and DBE functions, thus virtually eliminating the hit to the unified SBC service in a fully hardware redundant system such as the ASR 1006.

Before delving into the deployment architectural details, refer to Table 16-2 and Table 16-3, which provide the details of each component supported under the SBE and DBE functional umbrella.

Table 16-2 shows the details for the SBE functionality.

Table 16-3 shows the details for the DBE functionality.

Note In IOS XE 2.4 and later releases, the ASR 1000 can be configured as DBE only or as a unified SBC supporting both SBE and DBE functions.

Tables 16-2 and 16-3 do not provide a complete list of functions but capture the most prominent ones. Refer to the documents listed in the "Further Reading" section at the end of the chapter for further information.

Table 16-2 *SBE Functions Supported on Cisco ASR 1000 Series Routers, Starting with IOS XE 2.4*

SBE Function	Description
CAC	QoS, security
Signaling scrubbing	Signaling message normalization across different signaling protocols
Call routing	Dialing plans
Registration/authentication	Registration relay
Identity hiding	L3–L7 header changes
Topology hiding	L3–L7 header changes
Protocol conversion	Signal/protocol version interworking

Table 16-3 *DBE Functions Supported on Cisco ASR 1000 Series Routers, Starting with IOS XE 2.1*

DBE Function	Description
Bandwidth allocation, CAC, and SLA monitoring	Configured on SBE, and signaled to DBE
Policing, marking (differentiated services code point [DSCP]), and rate limiting	Configured on SBE, and signaled to DBE (QoS functions)
Firewall (media pinholes)	Media protocol pinholing
Security functions	Bandwidth protection, and unexpected source alerting
NAPT (Network Address Port Translation) traversing (header translation)	Network/Port Address Translation (NAT/PAT) for media packets
Topology hiding	DBE invoking address insertion
Quality monitoring and statistics gathering	Billing, troubleshooting purposes

CUBE (SP) Deployment Scenarios

There are at least three major scenarios where SBCs are being deployed today:

- SP-to-SP peering
- SP-to-managed enterprise and residential SIP trunking
- Business-to-business Telepresence

The sections that follow describe these different deployments.

SP-to-SP Peering

When two SPs peer with each other, usually over a SIP trunk, this allows both SPs and enterprises to carry originating or terminating calls over VoIP rather than time-division multiplexing (TDM). The advantages of using this technique are as follows:

- End-to-end delay is reduced because there is no need to perform VoIP to TDM and back packetization. This improves call quality and reduces the infrastructure costs. This is not limited to just VoIP. Calls can also be video or Telepresence in this scenario. With TDM, this flexibility is not available.

- Multiple benefits of just using CUBE (SP) here, such as topology hiding and enhanced security. Topology hiding brings the extra security by providing an option to use a dedicated set of IP addresses or subnet with the other party.

Figure 16-3 shows the SP-to-SP peering scenario.

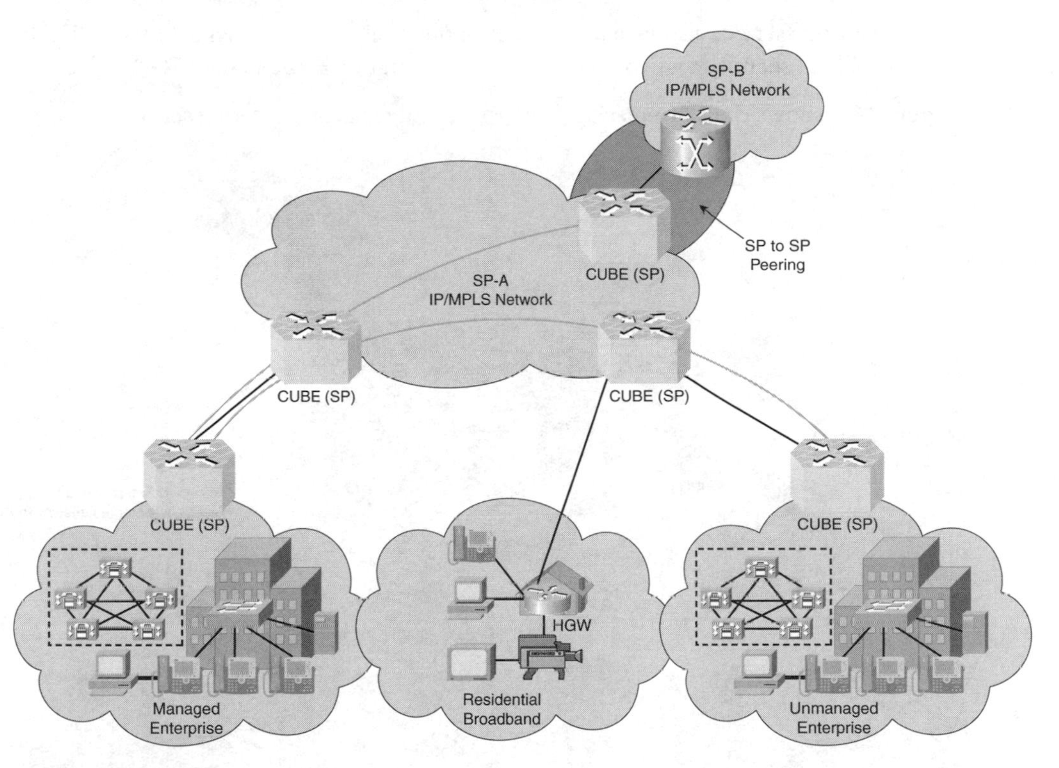

Figure 16-3 *SP-to-SP peering.*

SP-to-Managed Enterprise and Residential SIP Trunking

SP-to-managed enterprise and residential SIP trunking is where either the managed enterprise or residential home gateway is connecting to an SP via CUBE (SP). Because this connection is over a SIP trunk, this also allows residential gateway to carry their voice, video, and data (triple-play) traffic via a unified border router (ASR 1000 in this case) and save public switched telephone network (PSTN) charges. This is already deployed by some of the large SPs to thousands of households via their bundled broadband services.

SPs have been offering a number of managed services such as network-based security services for a long time. Because of the increasing amount of VoIP traffic, there is a clear need for it to be offered as a managed service. Managed services basically relieve enterprises from dealing with a plethora of protocol or standard interoperability issues. Where they can provide such a service, doing so opens up a new stream of revenue for SPs.

Benefits of this service also include the various functions that are provided by CUBE (SP), such as billing, security, and voice/Telepresence integration at the unified WAN edge.

Figure 16-4 shows the SP-to-managed enterprise and residential peering scenario

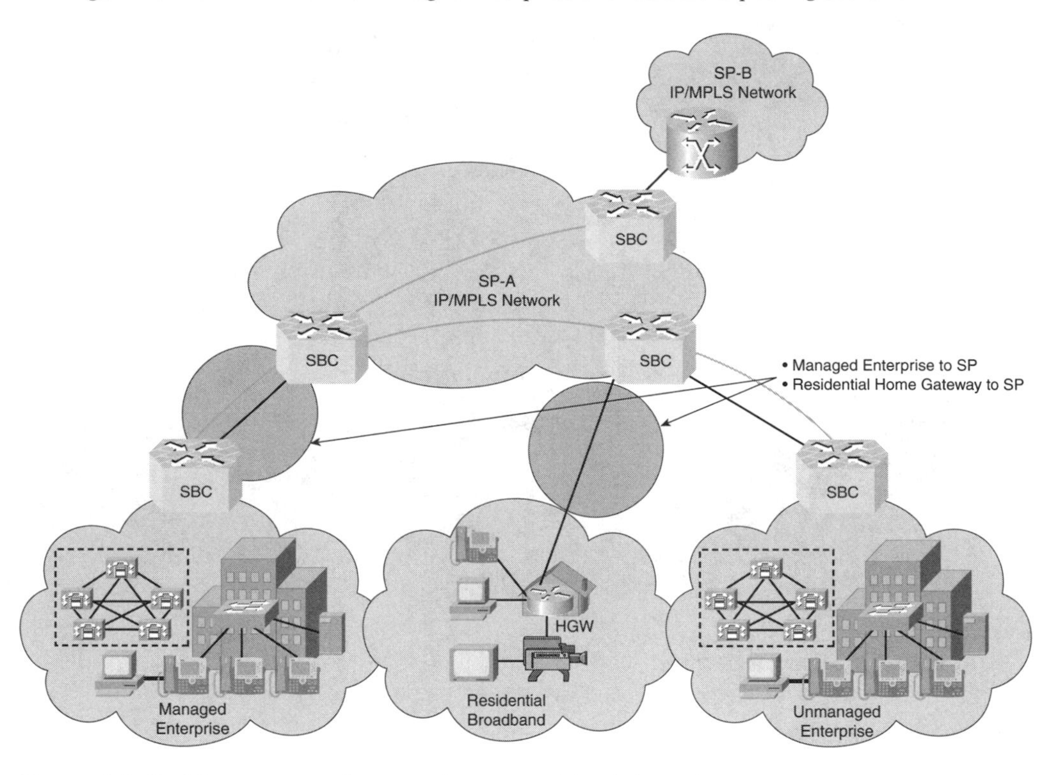

Figure 16-4 *SP-to-managed enterprise and residential peering.*

Business-to-Business Telepresence

Cisco TelePresence is an intracompany and intercompany collaboration medium with advanced visual and audio technology that delivers a face-to-face interaction experience between people across geographies. Intercompany Telepresence enables a huge opportunity for SPs where they can provide connectivity across companies and perhaps their high-touch customers, partners, and vendors. CUBE (SP) can provide support for Cisco TelePresence calls across different networks.

SPs can position the CUBE (SP) on their extranet, and because CUBE (SP) is VPN Routing and Forwarding (VRF)-aware, it can provide connectivity across the customer address spaces while still preserving the demarcation for all other traffic.

Figure 16-5 shows the business-to-business (enterprise A and B) Telepresence scenario.

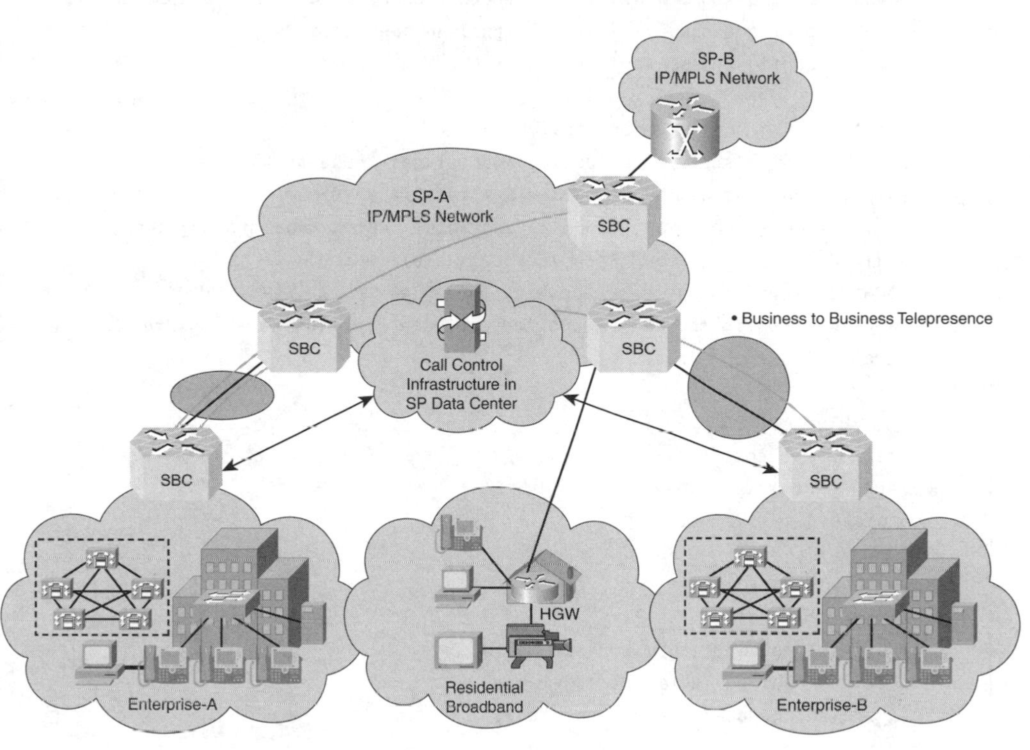

Figure 16-5 *Business-to-business Telepresence.*

Example 16-1 shows a typical configuration of a CUBE (SP) SBE function.

Example 16-1 *SBE Configuration*

```
ASR1000(config)# interface SBC1
ASR1000(config-if# ip address 50.0.0.1 255.0.0.0
!
ASR1000(config)# sbc global
ASR1000(config-sbc)#sbe
 ASR1000(config-sbc-sbe)# secure-media
 ASR1000 (config-sbc-sbe)# adjacency sip CUCM1
    ASR1000 (config-sbc-sbe-adj-sip)# preferred-transport tcp
    ASR1000 (config-sbc-sbe-adj-sip)# signaling-address ipv4 22.1.10.1
    ASR1000 (config-sbc-sbe-adj-sip)# signaling-port 5060
    ASR1000 (config-sbc-sbe-adj-sip)# remote-address ipv4 11.1.0.0 255.255.0.0
    ASR1000 (config-sbc-sbe-adj-sip)# signaling-peer 11.1.201.1
    ASR1000 (config-sbc-sbe-adj-sip)# attach
   ASR1000 (config-sbc-sbe)# adjacency sip CUCM2
    ASR1000 (config-sbc-sbe-adj-sip)# preferred-transport tcp
    ASR1000 (config-sbc-sbe-adj-sip)# signaling-address ipv4 21.1.10.1
    ASR1000 (config-sbc-sbe-adj-sip)# signaling-port 5060
```

```
    ASR1000 (config-sbc-sbe-adj-sip)# remote-address ipv4 21.1.0.0 255.255.0.0
    ASR1000 (config-sbc-sbe-adj-sip)# signaling-peer 21.1.201.2
    ASR1000 (config-sbc-sbe-adj-sip)# attach

   ASR1000 (config-sbc-sbe)# cac-policy-set 1
    ASR1000 (config-sbc-sbe- cacpolicy)# first-cac-table srtp1
    ASR1000 (config-sbc-sbe- cacpolicy)# cac-table srtp1
    ASR1000 (config-sbc-sbe- cacpolicy-cactable)# match-type src-adjacency
     ASR1000 (config-sbc-sbe- cacpolicy-cactable)# entry 1
      ASR1000 (config-sbc-sbe- cacpolicy-cactable)# match-value CUCM1
      ASR1000 (config-sbc-sbe- cacpolicy-cactable)# action cac-complete
      transport srtp allowed
     entry 2
      match-value CUCM2
      action cac-complete
      transport srtp allowed
    complete

   active-cac-policy-set 1
   call-policy-set 1
    first-call-routing-table src-acc-table
    first-reg-routing-table src-acc-table
    rtg-src-adjacency-table src-acc-table
     entry 1
      action complete
      dst-adjacency CUCM2
      match-adjacency CUCM1
     entry 2
      action complete
      dst-adjacency CUCM1
      match-adjacency CUCM2
     entry 3
      action complete
      dst-adjacency NETWORK1
      match-adjacency NETWORK2
     entry 4
      action complete
      dst-adjacency NETWORK2
      match-adjacency NETWORK1
    complete
   active-call-policy-set 1
!

ASR1000((config-sbc)# media-address ipv4 50.0.0.1
 port-range 17000 27000 any
activate
```

```
ASR1000((config)# interface GigabitEthernet0/0/0
ASR1000((config-if)# ip address 22.1.10.1 255.255.0.0

ASR1000((config-# interface GigabitEthernet0/0/1
ASR1000((config-if)#ip address 21.1.10.1 255.255.0.0
```

Note For resources that provide detailed SBC configuration, refer to the "Further Reading" section at the end of this chapter.

Troubleshooting CUBE

You can use various platform-specific CLI commands to collect a wealth of data to understand the inner workings of CUBE or to troubleshoot an unexpected behavior.

Table 16-4 outlines CLI **show** and **debug** commands to troubleshoot CUBE.

Table 16-4 *CUBE Troubleshooting Commands*

Command	Description
show platform software sbc esp forwarding-processor active tables	Displays the SBC table summary from the ESP
show platform hardware qfp active feature sbc global	Displays a lot of platform information, such as media forwarder, dropped and punted packets, and so on
show platform software sbc rp route-processor active tables	Displays the SBC table summary from the RP
show sbc global dbe addresses	Displays SBC controllers and associated media addresses, and so on
show sbc global dbe controllers	Displays DBE status
show sbc global dbe media-flow-stats	Displays global DBE media flow statistics
show sbc global dbe signaling-flow-stats	Displays global DBE signaling flow statistics
show sbc global dbe forwarder-stats	Displays SBC media forwarder messaging statistics
debug sbc *name* **mpf all**	Displays real-time SBC MPF-related flow info and error information
debug sbc *name* **high-availability all**	Displays real-time SBC HA-related information
debug platform hardware qfp active feature sbc [**sbe** | **dbe**]	Displays real-time QFP-related information for SBE (packet filter, fast register) or DBE (QFP client or data path) functions

Using the WebEx Node Services Module

Cisco WebEx Meeting applications deliver web conferencing through Software as a Service (SaaS), as discussed previously, meaning hardware and software is hosted by Cisco through the Cisco WebEx Collaboration Cloud and delivered to end users on demand through a web browser. The SaaS model delivers a host of benefits, including rapid deployment, global scaling, and low total cost of ownership (TCO).

Because this service is offered from a globally hosted cloud, the natural trade-off to these benefits is that enterprise Internet bandwidth requirements are increased, especially in a large enterprise environment with widescale adoption of web conferencing. For example, an all-hands meeting could be a worst-case scenario, where hundreds of internal enterprise users all connect into the WebEx cloud and end up putting a huge demand on the Internet uplink during the conference duration. This increased demand will have to compete with all other usual Internet access needs within the organization and will essentially require either a permanently increased bandwidth to the Internet or an on-demand provisioning to accommodate the extra bandwidth used during WebEx conference load. The former will increase the overall circuit cost, whereas the latter will limit the WebEx usage only to conferences planned in advance.

The Cisco WebEx Node for the ASR 1000 series is a Shared Port Adapter (SPA). The full-height adapter is easy to install and can function seamlessly as a part of the WebEx Collaboration Cloud.

Figure 16-6 shows the WebEx Node services module that functions as local gateway for internal WebEx users.

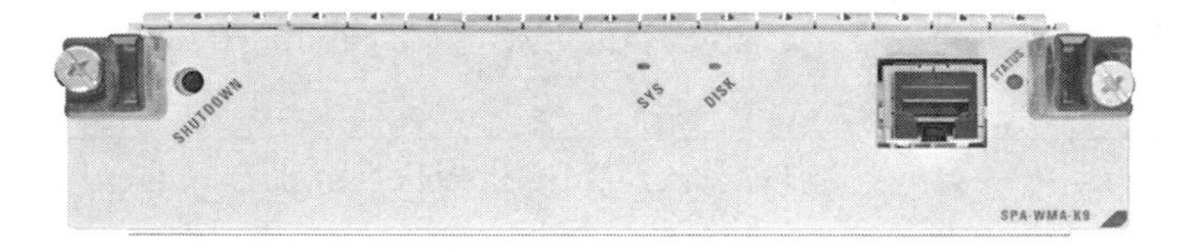

Figure 16-6 *ASR 1000 WebEx Node SPA module.*

Hardware configuration requirements for the WebEx Node SPA include the following:

- Multicore network processor with built-in encryption engine
- 4-GB DRAM
- 256-GB hard drive

Note The WebEx Node SPA is supported in IOS XE Release 2.4 or later and comes as a subpackage, which means that the IOS XE must be running in subpackage mode (versus consolidated package mode).

Please note that even with the WebEx Node, enterprises will still need a WebEx subscription.

The WebEx Node SPA is supported on all ASR 1000 systems, and because it's a full-height SPA, you can have up to five, three, and one SPAs in the ASR 1006, ASR 1004, and ASR 1002 chassis, respectively. For the ASR 1004/1006, the one full-height is reserved for network connectivity because there are no built-in Gigabit Ethernet (GE) ports (unlike the ASR 1002). Multiple WebEx Node SPAs can be used as a means to survivability within the enterprise, so if a WebEx Node SPA fails, the WebEx client can rehome to another SPA within the same system or another SPA locally located on the enterprise network in another ASR 1000 chassis.

The WebEx Node service module provides the following benefits:

- **Bandwidth savings:** Enterprise uplink bandwidth is reduced to a single control/media (voice/video or presentation) session per conference.
- **Local acceleration for WebEx:** Because of local replication of traffic, delay and latency are extremely small (and therefore the WebEx session is more responsive).
- **Enhanced security:** All traffic except a single session for data/voice/video goes to the centralized WebEx cloud data center for recording, monitoring, and billing purposes. This session is also sent over a Secure Sockets Layer (SSL)-encrypted tunnel with an Advanced Encryption Standard (AES) 256-bits key length.
- **Overflow of WebEx users and failure protection:** In case of any of these events, the traffic is forwarded over to the WebEx cloud.

Note The WebEx Node does not provide replacement for full SaaS functionality. Traffic for external clients (connecting via the Internet) goes directly to the WebEx data center rather than through the WebEx Node.

The WebEx Node can function in either one of the two modes:

- **Web presentation:** The maximum capacity per WebEx Node is 500 attendees.
- **VoIP/video solution:** The maximum capacity per WebEx Node is roughly 600 attendees, although this capacity is determined by the type of VoIP and video calls involved.

The function is selected by downloading the IOS XE subpackage from Cisco.com and is mutually exclusive.

WebEx Node Deployment Architecture

The WebEx Node is deployed in the ASR 1000 that is sitting at the Internet edge in the form of a full-height SPA. Therefore, the basic deployment is simple and can be explained by showing the before and after changes.

Figure 16-7 shows the WebEx conference before the WebEx Node is deployed.

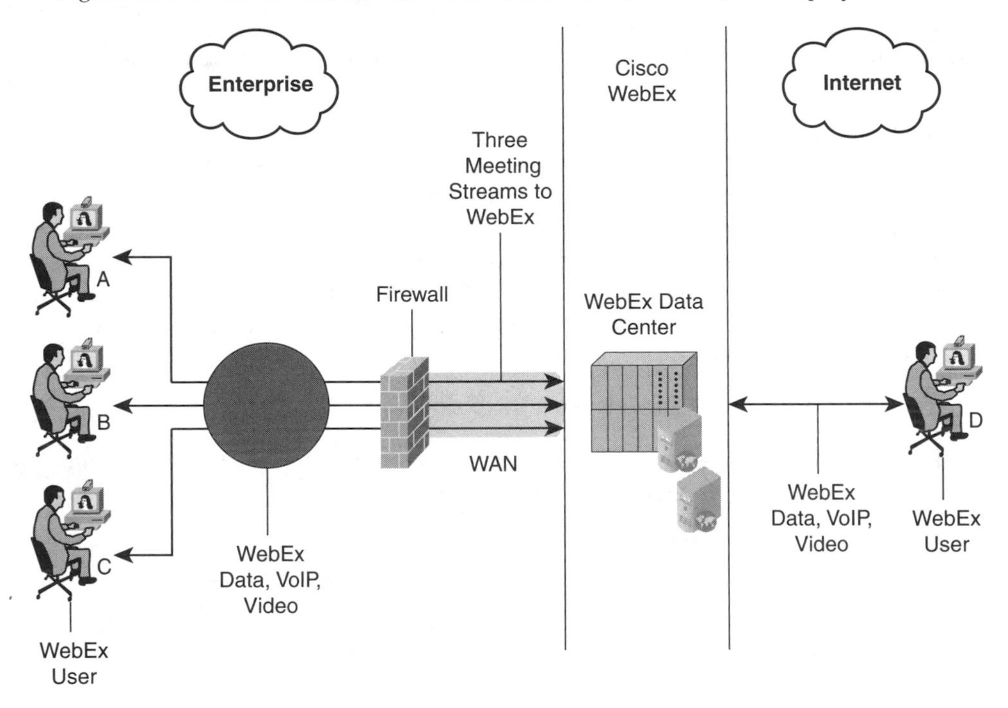

Figure 16-7 *WebEx conference before deployment of the WebEx Node.*

Figure 16-8 shows the WebEx conference after the WebEx Node is deployed.

Deployment Considerations

When deploying the WebEx Node, keep the following caveats in mind:

- Attendees connect to the closest WebEx Node onsite or offsite (based on smallest round-trip delay).
- Overflow and failover work regardless of the location of the WebEx Node (overflowed sessions are handled by the WebEx data center cloud).

- The WebEx Node works behind NAT/firewalls, and does not require any configuration for this to happen.
- The WebEx Node can be deployed on the ASR 1000 serving other functions, such as firewall, IPsec termination, NetFlow, or even CUBE.
- WebEx clients automatically find the WebEx Node; no configuration is required for this to happen.
- The ASR 1000 must be running in IOS XE subpackages mode before the WebEx Node subpackage can be applied to the SPA bay.

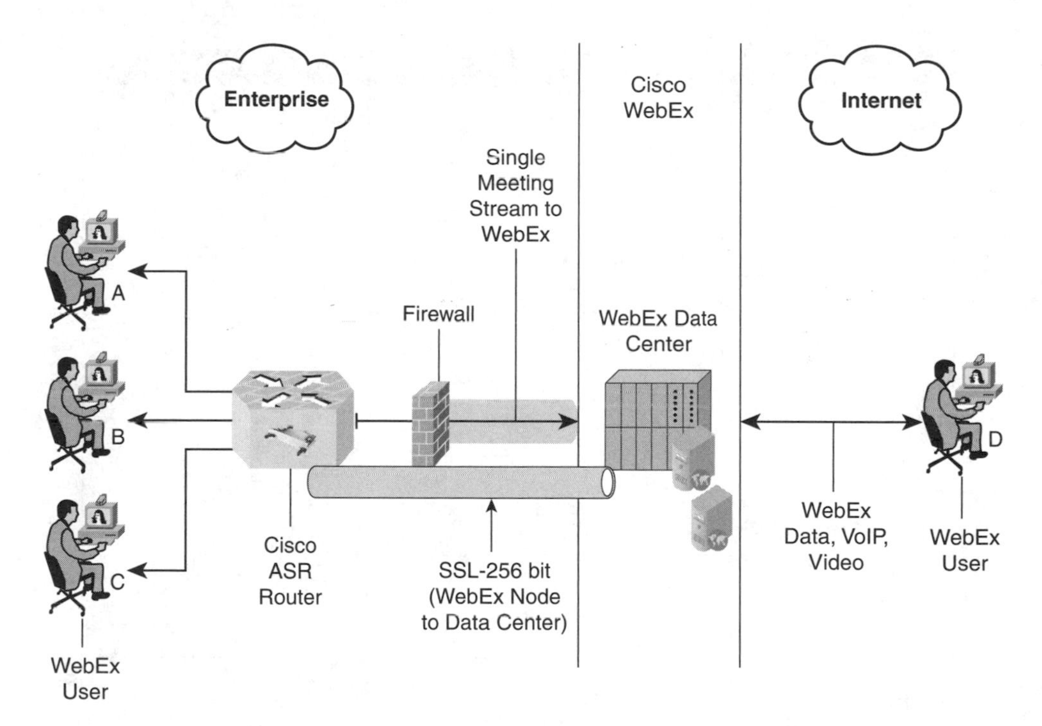

Figure 16-8 *WebEx conference after deployment of the WebEx Node.*

Installation Steps

The steps for installing the WebEx Node module are straightforward and can be followed without requiring any special understanding of WebEx intricacies:

Step 1. Install the WebEx Node module in the ASR 1000 chassis (can be installed in any vacant full-height SPA bay).

Step 2. Download the WebEx Node subpackage. There are two subpackages: one for web presentation, and one for a VoIP/video solution.

Step 3. Install the WebEx SPA subpackage using the **request platform** command or the legacy **issu** command.

```
ASR1006# request platform software package install rp <0-1> file
<filesystem>:<webex-subpackage>
```

You need to repeat this for standby RP as well for ASR1006 systems.

Step 4. Log in to the WebEx Service GUI, and configure the WebEx Node.

Figure 16-9 shows the WebEx Service GUI and the parameters that must be configured through the HTML form.

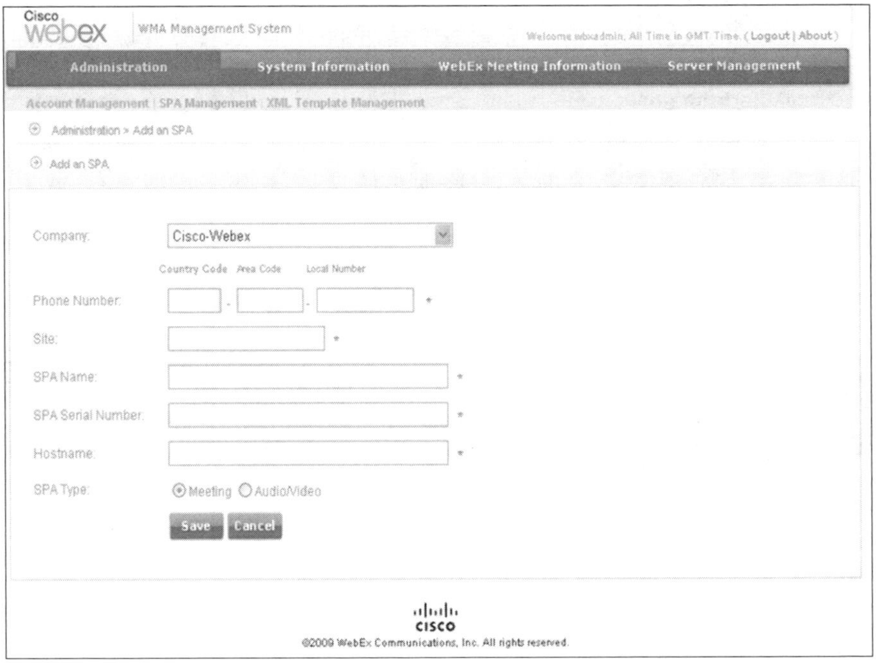

Figure 16-9 *WebEx Service GUI.*

Step 5. Once the form is submitted, a few parameters will be downloaded into the WebEx Node SPA.

Now the WebEx Node is ready to be configured.

Example 16-2 shows the only configuration steps required for direct configuration of the WebEx SPA with IOS XE 2.4.0 and later.

Example 16-2 *WebEx SPA Configuration*

```
ASR1000(config)# interface Service-Engine1/0/0
  ASR1000(config-if)# ip address 172.16.1.1 255.255.255.0
  ASR1000(config-if)# service-engine ip address 172.16.1.2 255.255.255.0
  ASR1000(config-if)# service-engine default-gateway 172.16.1.1
  ASR1000(config-if)# service-engine nameserver 210.90.1.2 211.90.1.2
  ASR1000(config-if)# service-engine hostname spa cisco.com
  ASR1000(config-if)# service-engine wma-url https://spa.webex.com/getconfig
  ASR1000(config-if)# service-engine wma-token 123456
  ASR1000(config-if)# service-engine wma-passcode ciscospa 123456
```

When you complete the configuration, WebEx Node is ready to host meetings.

Summary

This chapter covered unified communications topics as they relate to ASR 1000 routers. The chapter focused on two major topics:

- Cisco Unified Border Element (CUBE)
- WebEx Node service module

CUBE comes in two flavors: SP and Enterprise Edition. Cisco ASR 1000, starting with IOS XE 2.4, supports CUBE SP, which includes both SBE and DBE function in the form of highly scalable unified SBC for very large deployments. The current feature set mostly focuses on SIP, but is expected to include H.323 in the future.

The WebEx Node service module is a revolutionary product in that it provides most of the hosted WebEx experience locally via a full-height SPA. This chapter discussed in detail the various deployment models, caveats to keep in mind, and configurations for both CUBE (SP) and the WebEx Node.

Review Questions

1. What are the two flavors of CUBE?
2. How is CUBE (SP) different from unified SBC?
3. What is WebEx Node?
4. What are the two modes in which the WebEx Node can function?
5. What happens if the WebEx Node fails in a given network and there is no other node to take the load?
6. What is the upper limit number of attendees for a WebEx Node running in web presentation mode?

Answers

1. There are two types of Cisco Unified Border Element (CUBE): CUBE enterprise and CUBE service provider.
2. The main difference lies in the feature set and scale of each implementation. CUBE enterprise offers SIP/H.323, but at low scale because lack of any specialized hardware acceleration. CUBE (SP), on the other hand, provides carrier-grade SBC implementation on ASR 1000, 7600, and 12000 series routers at very high scale.
3. WebEx Node is a service module for the ASR 1000 family of routers and comes in a full-height SPA form factor. It enables enterprises to host meetings locally while still using the hosted WebEx service for billing, recording, and monitoring purposes.
4. WebEx Node can be configured in either web presentation mode or VoIP/video mode. These are two mutually exclusive modes and are determined by the IOS XE subpackage loaded on the ASR 1000, which in turn downloads the respective software into the WebEx Node SPA.
5. If no WebEx Node SPA is present in a failure scenario, the WebEx front end will simply fall back to the WebEx cloud.
6. The upper limit number of attendees for a WebEx Node running in web presentation mode is 500.

Further Reading

Cisco IOS XE Integrated Session Border Controller Configuration Guide for the Cisco ASR 1000 Series Aggregation Services Routers, document:
http://tinyurl.com/msqspd

SBC and SIP Functions, document:
http://en.wikipedia.org/wiki/Session_Border_Controller

Cisco IOS XR Session Border Controller Configuration Guide, Release 3.4, document:
http://tinyurl.com/l3jmkl

Index

Symbols

7200VXR (QoS scaling guidelines), 216

A

active ESP, 220

active RP, 220

adoption, time to (WAN architectures), 24, 26

aggregating

- policies, 215
- SIP traffic, ESP Interconnect Scheduler, 213

application mobility, virtualization and, 20

arrival processing (transit packets), ASR 1000 series routers, 88–90

ASR 1000 GUI (Graphical User Interface)

- configuring, 142
- usage examples, 143, 146
- views of, 141–142

ASR 1000 series routers, 43–44

- availability, 46
- bootflash, ISSU, 117
- booting, 103
  - *ROMMON, 104–106*
  - *valid configurations, 103*
- branch aggregation, 50
- BRAS, 53–54
- carrier-class routing, 57
  - *BITS reference clocks, 60*
  - *chassis design/modularity, 57*
  - *integrated QoS, 59*
  - *ISSU, 58*
  - *LAN interfaces, 60*
  - *nonstop router management, 60*
  - *operating system modularity, 57*
  - *oversubscription, 59*
  - *plane separation, 58–59*
  - *WAN interfaces, 60*
- configuring, 107, 109
- control plane, 177–178
- CPE, 54
- CWDM/DWDM, 196

DBE, 274
embedded services, 56
ERSPAN support, 184
Ethernet frame capture/transport across Layer 3 clouds, 184–186
ESP, 79, 103, 106
chassis manager, 87
crypto engines, 82–83
displaying insertion/uptime, 166–167
DRAM, 79
ESP subpackages, 135–136
forwarding manager, 86
initializing, 81
interconnect ASIC, 79
packet handling, 81
QFP software, 86
system board, 80
TCAM, 80
file system structure, 109–110
hardware components
chassis options, 61
chassis slot naming/numbering, 62
ESP, 63
RP, 62
SIP, 63
hidden costs of, 49
Internet gateway/edge routers, 193
Internet gateways, 49–50
IOS XE software, 98
releasing, 99
IP services case studies, 205
high-speed logging via NetFlow, 223–225
scalable hierarchical QoS, 216–217, 219
scalable IPv4/IPv6 multicast acceleration via QFP, 219–221
scalable multigigabit NAT, 221–223
scalable multigigabit NBAR/FPM, 225, 227–228
scalable QoS via QFP Traffic Manager, 206–215
ISSU, 114, 117
consolidated packages on fully redundant 6RU, 117
impact on subpackages, 114–115
ISSU on 6RU system for IOSD, 118–123
running dual IOSD on 2/4RU systems, 137–138
subpackage ISSU on fully redundant 6RU, 124–131
upgrading ESP subpackages, 135–136
upgrading RP subpackages, 132–134
upgrading SIP/SPA subpackages, 131
life span of, 49
modular operation, 87
multicast HA, 220–221
multicast replication on ESP, 221
operational savings, 49
packet handling
arrival processing, 88–90
egress processing, 91
ingress processing, 88
partitioning, 68
data plane, 68
I/O plane, 68
routing plane, 68

PQ
  conditional policing, 214
  unconditional policing, 214
QFP, 56, 106–107
  displaying QFP PPE utilization information, 167–168
QoS, 48, 207
QoS scaling guidelines, 216
reliability, 46–47
remote user aggregation, 50
ROI, 49
RP, 71, 103
  bootflash, 73
  chassis manager, 85
  CPU tasks, 85
  displaying insertion/uptime, 166–167
  DRAM, 73
  forwarding manager, 86
  front panel, 72
  hardware-assisted control-plane protection, 78
  HDD, 74
  initializing, 75
  interconnect ASIC, 74
  interface manager, 86
  legacy protocol traffic, 78
  packet handling, 75, 77
  RP subpackages, 132–134
RR, 191–192
SBC, 271
SBE, 273, 277–278
scalability, 48
security headends, 50
security services case studies, 231
  Cisco Self-Defending Network schema, 0, 231
  DMVPN hub design, 239–241
  GETVPN, 242, 244–248, 250
  IKE initiation requests, 235
  integrated threat control solutions, 251, 253–256
  IOS firewalls, 251, 253–256
  IPsec HA, 236
  IPsec multicast encryption, 236–237
  IPsec packet flow (egress), 235
  IPsec packet flow (ingress), 235
  IPsec-based VPN solutions, 232, 234
  QoS scalable encryption, 237, 239
segmentation, MPLS over GRE, 187, 189
SIP, 83–84, 103, 106
  chassis manager, 87
  displaying insertion/uptime, 166–167
  displaying SPA status in SIP, 163
  interface manager, 87
  SIP subpackages, 131
  SPA drivers, 87
software components
  ESP software, 65
  IOS XE, 63
  IOSD, 67
  Linux kernels, 67
  ROMMON, 68
  RP software, 63, 65
  SIP software, 66
SPA
  displaying SPA status in SIP, 163
  displaying SPA-level statistics, 164
  SPA subpackages, 131

subpackages
- *ISSU impact on subpackages, 114–115*
- *subpackage ISSU on fully redundant 6RU, 124–131*
- *upgrading ESP subpackages, 135–136*
- *upgrading RP subpackages, 132–134*
- *upgrading SIP/SPA subpackages, 131*

system redundancy/modularity, 68

traffic encryption over EoMPLS Pseudowire at Layer 2 via TrustSec, 198, 200–203

traffic manager priority queues, 213–215

troubleshooting
- *debug commands, 150–153, 168–174*
- *displaying drop statistics, 164–165*
- *displaying front-panel LED status via show platform hardware command, 163*
- *displaying interface-level feature binding, 165*
- *displaying IPv4-related drops for active QFP, 155–156*
- *displaying processors, 154–155*
- *displaying QFP memory statistics for IRAM/DRAM/SRAM usage, 156–157*
- *displaying QFP memory statistics on per-IOS feature/internal-usage basis, 157–161*
- *displaying QFP PPE utilization information, 167–168*
- *displaying RP/ESP/SIP insertion/uptime, 166–167*
- *displaying SPA status in SIP, 163*
- *displaying SPA-level statistics, 164*
- *memory utilization, 154–155*
- *show commands, 150–153, 169–174*
- *tracking command output via monitor command, 162*
- *tracking control CPU usage from Linux shell, 161–162*
- *"Warning: Filesystem Is Not clean" error messages, 174–175*

unified communications services case studies, CUBE, 269, 271, 273–279

virtualization, 190

voice header compression via cRTP, 267

VPN
- *SP L2 VPN, 51*
- *SP L3 VPN, 51*

WAAS, 262
- *WAN optimization, 262–265*

WAN aggregation, 49

WAN optimization, 262
- *branch deployments, 264*
- *campus headend deployments, 263*
- *IronPort appliances, 265*
- *WSA, 265*

WCCPv2, 259
- *troubleshooting, 265–266*
- *web caching, 260–262*

WebEx Node services module, 269, 280–283, 285

"ASR1000_PEM-3-PEMFAIL: The PEM in Slot 0 Is Switched Off or Encountering a Failure Condition" error message, 175
audit trail messages, NetFlow event logging, 256
automation (policy-based), encapsulation and, 20
availability
ASR 1000 series routers, 46
HA
NSF, 179, 181–183
SSO, 179, 181–183
multicast HA, ASR 1000 series routers, 220–221

B

bandwidth
excess bandwidth, examples of, 214
minimum bandwidth, examples of, 214
WAN architectures, bandwidth commoditization in, 22–23, 25
WebEx Node services module, 281
benchmarking routers, 40
data-plane performance/scale, 41
routing-plane performance/scale, 41
BITS (Building Integrated Timing Source) reference clocks, ASR 1000 series routers, 60
bootflash
ASR 1000 series routers, ISSU, 117
ASR 1000 series RP, 73
IOS XE software, 96
booting
ASR 1000 series routers, 103
ROMMON, 104–106
valid configurations, 103
IOS XE software, 96, 98
nonmodular boot procedure, 97
RP, "Warning: Filesystem Is Not Clean" error messages, 174–175
branch aggregation, ASR series routers, 50
branch deployments, WAN optimization via WAAS integration, 264
branch WAN aggregation, 2
connectivity options table, 4
feature requirements table, 5
secure WAN technologies table, 5
SLA requirements, 5
BRAS (broadband aggregation systems), ASR series 1000 routers, 53–54
buffering
egress SIP buffering, 211–212
GPM, 208
ingress SIP buffering, 207–208
multicast packets, 210
packet buffer DRAM (QFP Traffic Manager), 208–209
packet buffering (QFP Traffic Manager), 209–210
punt packets, 210
unicast packets, 210
business drivers, WAN architectures
bandwidth commoditization, 22–23, 25
carbon footprint reduction, 23, 26
infrastructure consolidation, 19, 25
regulatory compliance, 24, 26
reliability, 22, 25
security, 22, 25
segmentation/virtualization, 20–21, 25

service awareness/integration, 18, 25
time to adoption, 24, 26
time to understanding, 24, 26
troubleshooting, 24, 26

C

campus headend deployments, WAN optimization via WAAS integration, 263
carbon footprint reduction
Enterprise Edge platforms, 31–32
WAN architectures, 23, 26
carrier-class routing
ASR series 1000 routers, 57
Enterprise Edge platforms, 29
chassis manager
ESP software, 65
ASR 1000 series routers, 87
RP software, 64
ASR 1000 series routers, 85
SIP software, 66
ASR 1000 series routers, 87
Cisco Self-Defending Network schema, 231
compliance (regulatory), WAN architectures, 24, 26
conditional policing, PQ (ASR 1000 series routers), 214
configuring
ASR 1000 GUI, 142
ASR 1000 series routers, 103, 107, 109
consolidation (infrastructure), WAN architectures, 19, 25
control plane (ASR 1000 series routers), 59, 177–178
convergence times (DCI), 195
cooling systems, WAN architectures, 23, 26
CoPP (control-plane policing) feature, 78
CPE (customer premises equipment), ASR series 1000 routers, 54
cRTP (compressed Real-Time Protocol), voice header compression, 267
crypto engines
ASR 1000 series router ESP, 82–83
GETVPN, 245
multicast encryption, 236
QoS scalable encryption, 237, 239
CUBE (Cisco Unified Border Element for service provider), 269
business-to-business telepresence deployment scenario, 276–278
integrated CUBE, 271, 273
SP-to-managed enterprise and residential SIP trunking deployment scenario, 275–276
SP-to-SP peering deployment scenario, 274
troubleshooting, 279
CWDM/DWDM, ASR 1000 series routers, 196

D

dark fiber transport (DCI), 195
data plane, ASR 1000 series routers, 59
partitioning, 68
DBE (Data Border Elements), 272
ASR 1000 series routers, 274
DCI (data center interconnects), 10
convergence times, 195
dark fiber transport, 195

feature requirements table, 11–13
loop prevention, 195
redundancy, 195
scalability, 195–196
traffic encryption over EoMPLS Pseudowire at Layer 2 via TrustSec, 198, 200–203

DDoS (distributed denial of service), self-inflicted, 256

debug commands (ASR 1000 series routers), troubleshooting, 150–153, 168–174

DM VPN (Dynamic Multipoint VPN), 7
hub design, ASR 1000 series routers, 239–241
multipoint GRE tunnels, 239
NHRP, 239

DRAM
ASR 1000 series router ESP, 79
ASR 1000 series RP, 73
QFP memory statistics, displaying for, 156–157

drop messages, NetFlow event logging, 256

dual IOSD, running on 2/4RU systems, 137–138

dual IOSD failovers, ESP, 193

E

egress processing (transit packets), ASR 1000 series routers, 91

egress SIP buffering, 211–212

embedded services, ASR series 1000 routers, 56

encapsulation, virtualization and, 20

encryption
EoMPLS Pseudowire at Layer 2 using TrustSec, 198, 200–203
multicast encryption, ASR 1000 series routers, 236–237
scalable encryption, ASR 1000 series routers, 237, 239

Enterprise Edge platforms
carbon footprint reduction, 31–32
carrier-class routing, 29
feature velocity, 31
flexible system architectures, 30
industry standard compliance, 32
interface diversity/density, 31
QoS, 30
service integration, 29
system investment protection, 31
test plans, writing, 32
functional tests, 35
load testing methodology, 35
longevity testing methodology, 35
negative testing methodology, 35
performance tests, 35
positive testing methodology, 35
scale tests, 35
stress testing methodology, 35
test case details, 36
test entry/exit criteria, 35
test resources, 34
test results reporting, 36
test schedules, 36
test scope/objective, 34
test setup/topology, 34

Enterprise Private WAN, segmentation, 187, 189

environmental concerns
Enterprise Edge platforms, 31–32
WAN architectures, 23, 26

EoMPLS Pseudowire, traffic encryption at Layer 2 using TrustSec, 198, 200–203

error messages

"ASR1000_PEM-3-PEMFAIL: The PEM in Slot 0 Is Switched Off or Encountering a Failure Condition" messages, 175

"Warning: Filesystem Is Not Clean" messages, 174–175

ERSPAN (Encapsulated Remote SPAN)

ASR 1000 series router support, 184–186

packet capturing, 184–186

ESP (embedded service processors), 220

active ESP, 220

ASR 1000 series routers, 63, 79, 103, 106

displaying RP insertion/uptime, 166–167

DRAM, 79

ESP chassis manager, 87

ESP crypto engines, 82–83

ESP forwarding manager, 86

ESP initialization, 81

ESP packet handling, 81

ESP subpackages, 135–136

interconnect ASIC, 79

QFP software, 86

system board, 80

TCAM, 80

IOS zone-based firewalls, 193

IOSD failovers, 193

IPsec, 193

ISO XE software, 94–95

LED color and description table, 79

multicast replication, 221

NetFlow, 193

software, ASR 1000 series routers, 65

ESP Interconnect Scheduler, aggregating SIP traffic, 213

Ethernet

frame capture/transport across Layer 3 clouds, 184–186

Metro Ethernet, 4

event logging (NetFlow)

audit trail messages, 256

drop messages, 256

F

feature velocity, Enterprise Edge platforms, 31

FIB (Forwarding Information Base), 183

firewalls

high-speed logging via NetFlow, 223–225

IOS zone-based firewalls, 251

ESP, 193

HA, 253

scalable multigigabit router firewalls, 254–256

zone pair scale, 253

WAAS, 261

WCCPv2, 261–262

flexibility, Internet edge routers, 193

flexible system architectures, Enterprise Edge platforms, 30

forwarding manager

ESP software, 66

ASR 1000 series routers, 86

RP software, 65

ASR 1000 series routers, 86

FPM, scalable multigigabit, 225, 227–228
front-panel LED, status of, displaying via show platform hardware command, 163
front panels, ASR 1000 series router RP, 72
functional tests, Enterprise Edge platforms, 35

G

gateways (Internet), ASR series routers, 49–50
GDOI (Group Domain of Interpretation), 242
  GM registration, 244
GET VPN (Group Encrypted Transport VPN), 7
  ASR 1000 series routers, 242, 244–246
    branch design deployment model, 248
    DC design deployment model, 248
    limitations in, 248
    memory, 247
    supported features, 247
    troubleshooting, 250
  crypto engine, 245
  GDOI, 242
    GM registration, 244
  GM, 242
    registering, 244
  key servers, 242
  QFP, 245
GM (group members), GETVPN, 242
  registering in, 244
GPM (global packet memory), 208
GR (graceful restarts), 179
GRE (generic routing encapsulation)
  MPLS over GRE, segmentation, 187
  multipoint GRE tunnels, 239
  p2p GRE inside IPsec, 7
  p2p GRE tunnels, WAN edge routers, 190
GRE over IPsec, 236

H

HA (high availability)
  IOS firewalls, 253
  IOS XE software, 94
  IPsec, ASR 1000 series routers, 236
  multicast HA, ASR 1000 series routers, 220–221
  NSF, 179, 181–183
  SSO, 179, 181–183
hardware-assisted control-plane protection, ASR 1000 series RP, 78
HDD (hard disk drives)
  ASR 1000 series RP, 74
  RP, IOS XE software, 95–96
HQF (Hierarchical Queuing Framework), ASR 1000 series router QoS, 207

I-J

I/O (input/output) plane, ASR 1000 series routers, partitioning, 68
IKE (Internet Key Exchanges), initiation requests, ASR 1000 series routers, 235
industry standard compliance, Enterprise Edge platforms, 32

infrastructure consolidation, WAN architectures, 19, 25
ingress processing (transit packets), ASR 1000 series routers, 88
ingress SIP buffering, 207–208
initializing
ASR 1000 series router ESP, 81
ASR 1000 series RP, 75
injected packets
defining, 74
displaying, 77
installing WebEx Node services module, 283, 285
integrated QoS (Quality of Service), ASR 1000 series routers, 59
integrated threat control solutions, ASR 1000 series routers, IOS firewalls, 251, 253–256
interconnect ASIC (application-specific integrated circuits)
ASR 1000 series ESP, 79
ASR 1000 series RP, 74
interface diversity/density, Enterprise Edge platforms, 31
interface manager
RP software, 65
ASR 1000 series routers, 86
SIP software, 66
ASR 1000 series routers, 87
Internet edge role
feature requirements table, 9–10
router functionality table, 8–9
Internet edge routers, scalability/flexibility of, 193
Internet gateway/edge routers, 193
Internet gateways, ASR series routers, 49–50
IOS
CoPP feature, 78
troubleshooting, 169–174
IOS firewalls, 251
HA, 253
scalable multigigabit router firewalls, 254–256
zone pair scale, 253
IOS XE, ASR 1000 series routers, 63
IOS XE software, 93
ASR 1000 series routers, packaging, 98
benefits of, 94
bootflash, 96
booting, 96, 98
nonmodular boot procedure, 97
components of, 93
ESP, 94–95
feature support, 94
HA, 94
IOSD, 93
licensing, 100
Linux 2.6.x kernel, 94
middleware processes, 94
modularity, 94
packaging, 96–98
subpackages of, 94–95
QFP software, 94
redundancy, 98
releases, overall release plan, 99
RP, 94–95
HDD file system structure, 95–96
security, 94
SIP, 94–95
UMI, 94

IOS zone-based firewalls, ESP, 193

IOSD (IOS daemon), 93

ASR 1000 series routers, 67

dual IOSD, running on 2/4RU systems, 137–138

IOSD failovers, ESP, 193

IP, DCI transport, 195

IP routing

DCI

scalability, 195–196

traffic encryption over EoMPLS Pseudowire at Layer 2 via TrustSec, 198, 200–203

Internet edge routers, scalability/flexibility of, 193

NetFlow, 184

packet capturing, ERSPAN, 184–186

RR, 191–192

segmentation, MPLS over GRE, 187, 189

IP services, 205

high-speed logging via NetFlow, 223–225

IPv4/IPv6 scalable multicast acceleration via QFP, 219

multicast HA, 220–221

multicast replication on ESP, 221

scalable hierarchical QoS, 216–217, 219

scalable multigigabit NAT, 221–223

scalable multigigabit NBAR/FPM, 225, 227–228

scalable QoS via QFP Traffic Manager, 206–207

aggregating SIP traffic, 213

egress SIP buffering, 211–212

ingress SIP buffering, 207–208

packet buffering, 209–210

priority queues, 213–215

IPsec, 7

ESP, 193

GRE over IPsec, 236

HA, ASR 1000 series routers, 236

multicast encryption, ASR 1000 series routers, 236–237

p2p GRE inside IPsec, 7

packet flow (egress), ASR 1000 series routers, 235

packet flow (ingress), ASR 1000 series routers, 235

VPN, ASR 1000 series routers, 232, 234

IPv4, scalable multicast acceleration via QFP, 219

multicast HA, 220–221

multicast replication on ESP, 221

IPv6, scalable multicast acceleration via QFP, 219

multicast HA, 220–221

multicast replication on ESP, 221

IRAM, QFP memory statistics, displaying for, 156–157

IronPort appliances, WAN optimization, 265

ISSU (in-service software upgrades)

ASR 1000 series routers, 58, 114, 117

consolidated packages on fully redundant 6RU, 117

ISSU impact on subpackages, 114–115

ISSU on 6RU system for IOSD, 118–123

running dual IOSD on 2/4RU systems, 137–138

subpackage ISSU on fully redundant 6RU, 124–131

upgrading ESP subpackages, 135–136
upgrading RP subpackages, 132–134
upgrading SIP/SPA subpackages, 131
benefits of
business benefits, 114
operational benefits, 113
issu acceptversion command, 118, 122
issu commitversion command, 118, 133, 135
issu loadversion command, 118–119, 131, 135
issu runversion command, 118, 121
issu set rollback-timer command, 118

K

key servers, GETVPN, 242

L

LAN (local area networks), ASR 1000 series routers, 60
large branch WAN (wide area networks), office deployment requirements table, 13–14
Layer 3 clouds, Ethernet frame capture/transport, 184–186
LED, displaying status of via show platform hardware command, 163
licensing IOS XE software, 100
Linux
ASR 1000 series routers, 67
control CPU usage, tracking from Linux shell, 161–162
Linux 2.6.x kernel, IOS XE software, 94
LLQ (low-latency queuing), ASR 1000 series routers, 83
load testing methodology, Enterprise Edge platforms, 35
logs
high-speed logging via NetFlow, 223–225
NetFlow event logging, 256
longevity testing methodology, Enterprise Edge platforms, 35
loop prevention, DCI, 195

M

management plane, ASR 1000 series routers, 59
MEC (Multichassis EtherChannel), 195
memory, ASR 1000 series routers, 154–155
GETVPN, 247
Metro Ethernet, 4
MFIB, 219
middleware, IOS XE software, 94
mobility (applications), virtualization and, 20
modular control plane (ASR 1000 series routers), 177–178
modularity, IOS XE software, 94
momentary packet loss, 220
monitor command, command output, tracking via, 162
MPLS
DCI transport, 195
MPLS over GRE, segmentation, 187
MRIB, 219
multicast encryption, ASR 1000 series routers, 236–237

multicast HA (high availability), ASR 1000 series routers, 220–221
multicast packets, buffering, 210
multipoint GRE tunnels, 239

N

NAT (Network Address Translation)
high-speed logging via NetFlow, 223–225
scalable in-built multigigabit NAT, 221–223
NBAR (Network Based Application Recognition)
scalable multigigabit NBAR, 225, 227–228
WCCPv2, 261
NDR (non drop rates), 35
negative testing methodology, Enterprise Edge platforms, 35
NetFlow, 184
ESP, 193
event logging, 256
firewalls, high-speed logging, 223–225
NAT, high-speed logging, 223–225
NHRP (Next-Hop Resolution Protocol), 239
nonmodular boot procedure, IOS XE software, 97
nonstop router management, ASR 1000 series routers, 60
NSF (nonstop forwarding), 179
HA, 179, 181–183
NSR (nonstop routing), 179

O

optimized WAN aggregation, 2
oversubscription, ASR 1000 series routers, 59

P

p2p GRE inside IPsec, 7
p2p GRE tunnels, WAN edge routers, 190
packet buffer DRAM (QFP Traffic Manager), 208–209
packet buffering, QFP Traffic Manager, 209
multicast packets, 210
punt packets, 210
unicast packets, 210
packet capturing, ERSPAN, 184
Ethernet frame capture/transport across Layer 3 clouds, 184–186
packet handling
ASR 1000 series router ESP, 81
ASR 1000 series RP, 75, 77
transit packets
arrival processing, 88–90
egress processing, 91
ingress processing, 88
packets, momentary packet loss, 220
partitioning ASR 1000 series routers, 68
PBR (Policy Based Routing), WCCPv2, 261
performance
data-plane performance (benchmarking routers), 41

routing-plane performance (benchmarking routers), 41
tests, Enterprise Edge platforms, 35
policy aggregation, 215
policy-based automation, virtualization and, 20
positive testing methodology, Enterprise Edge platforms, 35
power usage
Enterprise Edge platforms, 31–32
WAN architectures, 23, 26
PQ (priority queuing), ASR 1000 series routers, 214
private WAN aggregation, 2
connectivity options table, 4
feature requirements table, 5
secure WAN technologies table, 5
SLA requirements, 5
Pseudowire, traffic encryption over EoMPLS Pseudowire at Layer 2 using TrustSec, 198, 200–203
punt packets, buffering, 210
punted traffic
defining, 74
displaying, 75, 77

Q

QFP (QuantumFlow Processor), 78
ASR 1000 series routers, 56, 106–107
ASR 1000 series router ESP, 86
GETVPN, 245
IOS XE software, 94
IPv4-related drops, displaying for, 155–156
Ipv4/IPv6 scalable multicast acceleration, 219
multicast HA, 220–221
multicast replication on ESP, 221
memory statistics
displaying for IRAM/DRAM/SRAM, 156–157
displaying on per-IOS feature/internal-usage basis, 157–161
QFP utilization information, displaying, 167–168
Traffic Manager
packet buffer DRAM, 208–209
packet buffering, 209–210
scalable QoS via, 206–215
QoS (Quality of Service)
7200VXR, QoS scaling guidelines, 216
ASR 1000 series routers, 48, 207
QoS scaling guidelines, 216
Enterprise Edge platforms, 30
integrated QoS, ASR 1000 series routers, 59
QoS preclassify, 237
scalability
hierarchical QoS, 216–217, 219
QFP Traffic Manager, 206–215
scalable encryption, ASR 1000 series routers, 237, 239

R

redundancy
ASR 1000 series routers, 68
DCI, 195
IOS XE software, 98
RP subpackages, ASR 1000 series routers, 134

reliability
- ASR 1000 series routers, 46–47, 49
- WAN architectures, 22, 25

remote user aggregation, ASR series routers, 50

remote-access VPN (virtual private networks), 7

replay protection via TBAR (time-based antireplay), 245

ROI (return on investment), ASR 1000 series routers, 49

ROMMON, ASR 1000 series routers, 68, 104–106

routers
- ASR 1000 series routers, 43–44
  - *availability, 46*
  - *bootflash, 117*
  - *booting, 103–106*
  - *branch aggregation, 50*
  - *BRAS, 53–54*
  - *carrier-class routing, 57–60*
  - *configuring, 107, 109*
  - *control plane, 177–178*
  - *CPE, 54*
  - *CWDM/DWDM, 196*
  - *DBE, 274*
  - *embedded services, 56*
  - *ERSPAN support, 184*
  - *ESP, 79, 81–83, 86–87, 103, 106, 135–136, 166–167*
  - *Ethernet frame capture/transport across Layer 3 clouds, 184–186*
  - *file system structure, 109–110*
  - *hardware components, 61–63*
  - *hidden costs of, 49*
  - *IKE initiation requests, 235*
  - *Internet gateway/edge routers, 193*
  - *Internet gateways, 49–50*
  - *IOS XE software, 98–99*
  - *IP services case studies, 205–217, 219–225, 227–228*
  - *ISSU, 114–115, 117–138*
  - *life span of, 49*
  - *modular operation, 87*
  - *multicast HA, 220–221*
  - *multicast replication on ESP, 221*
  - *operational savings, 49*
  - *packet handling, 88–91*
  - *partitioning, 68*
  - *QFP, 56, 106–107, 167–168*
  - *QoS, 48, 207*
  - *QoS scaling guidelines, 216*
  - *reliability, 46–47*
  - *remote user aggregation, 50*
  - *ROI, 49*
  - *RP, 71–73, 75, 77–78, 85–86, 103, 132–134, 166–167*
  - *RR, 191–192*
  - *SBC, 271*
  - *SBE, 273, 277–278*
  - *scalability, 48*
  - *security headends, 50*
  - *security services case studies, 231–232, 234–237, 239–242, 244–248, 250–251, 253–256*
  - *segmentation, 187, 189*
  - *SIP, 83–84, 87, 103, 106, 131, 163, 166–167*
  - *software components, 63, 65–68*
  - *SP L2 VPN, 51*
  - *SP L3 VPN, 51*
  - *SPA, 131, 163–164*
  - *subpackages, 114–115, 124–136*

system redundancy/modularity, 68
traffic encryption over EoMPLS Pseudowire at Layer 2 via TrustSec, 198, 200–203
traffic manager priority queues, 213–215
troubleshooting, 150–175
unified communications services case studies, 269, 271, 273–279
virtualization, 190
voice header compression via cRTP, 267
WAAS, 262–265
WAN aggregation, 49
WAN optimization, 262–265
WCCPv2, 259–262, 265–266
WebEx Node services module, 269, 280–283, 285
benchmarking, 40
data-plane performance/scale, 41
routing-plane performance/scale, 41
characteristics of, 39–40
choosing, 39–40
DCI feature requirements table, 12–13
Internet edge role
feature requirements table, 9–10
router functionality table, 8–9
Internet edge routers, scalability/flexibility of, 193
Internet gateway/edge routers, 193
nonstop router management, ASR 1000 series routers, 60
WAN edge routers, p2p GRE tunnels, 190

routing plane (ASR 1000 series routers), partitioning, 68
RP (Route Processors), 220
active RP, 220
ASR 1000 series routers, 62, 71, 103
bootflash, 73
displaying RP insertion/uptime, 166–167
DRAM, 73
front panel, 72
hardware-assisted control-plane protection, 78
HDD, 74
initializing RP, 75
interconnect ASIC, 74
legacy protocol traffic, 78
packet handling, 75, 77
RP chassis manager, 85
RP CPU tasks, 85
RP forwarding manager, 86
RP interface manager, 86
RP subpackages, 132–134
booting, "Warning: Filesystem Is Not Clean" error messages, 174–175
IOS XE software, 94–95
HDD file system structure, 95–96
LED color and description table, 72–73
RP software, ASR 1000 series routers, 63, 65
RR (route reflection), 191–192

S

SBC, ASR 1000 series routers, 271
SBE (Signaling Border Elements), 272
ASR 1000 series routers, 273, 277–278

scalability
ASR 1000 series routers, 48
DCI, 195–196
Internet edge routers, 193
IPv4/IPv6 scalable multicast acceleration via QFP, 219–221
multigigabit FPM, 225, 227–228
multigigabit NAT, 221–223
multigigabit NBAR, 225, 227–228
QOS
hierarchical QoS, 216–217, 219
QFP Traffic Manager, 206–215
scalable control plane (ASR 1000 series routers), 177–178
scalable encryption (ASR 1000 series routers), 237, 239
scale tests (Enterprise Edge platforms), 35
schedulers, ESP Interconnect Scheduler, aggregating SIP traffic, 213
secure WAN aggregation, 2
security
IOS XE software, 94
WAN architectures, 22, 25
WebEx Node services module, 281
security headends, ASR series routers, 50
security services, 231
Cisco Self-Defending Network schema, 231
crypto engines, multicast encryption, 236
DMVPN
ASR 1000 series routers, 239–241
hub design, 239–241
GETVPN, ASR 1000 series routers, 242, 244–248, 250
integrated threat control solutions, ASR 1000 series routers, 251, 253–256
IOS firewalls, 251
HA, 253
scalable multigigabit router firewalls, 254–256
zone pair scale, 253
IPsec
GRE over IPsec, 236
HA, 236
multicast encryption, 236–237
packet flow (egress), 235
packet flow (ingress), 235
VPN, 232, 234
QoS, scalable encryption, 237, 239
SPD, 235
segmentation
Enterprise Private WAN, 187, 189
MPLS over GRE, 187
WAN architectures, 20–21, 25
self-inflicted DDoS (distributed denial of service), 256
service awareness, WAN architectures, 18, 25
service integration
Enterprise Edge platforms, 29
WAN architectures, 18, 25
show commands, troubleshooting ASR 1000 series routers, 150–153, 169–174
show inventory command, 64
SIP (SPA interface processors), 220
aggregating traffic, ESP Interconnect Scheduler, 213

ASR 1000 series routers, 63, 83–84, 103, 106
displaying SIP insertion/uptime, 166–167
SIP chassis manager, 87
SIP interface manager, 87
SIP subpackages, 131
SPA drivers, 87
egress SIP buffering, 211–212
ingress SIP buffering, 207–208
SPA, displaying status in SIP, 163
IOS XE software, 94–95
SIP software, ASR 1000 series routers, 66
SLA (Service Level Agreements), branch/private WAN aggregation, SLA requirements for, 5
SP L2 VPN (Service Provider Layer 2 VPN), ASR series 1000 routers, 51
SP L3 VPN (Service Provider Layer 3 VPN), ASR series 1000 routers, 51
SPA
ASR 1000 series routers, SPA subpackages, 131
SIP, displaying SPA status in, 163
SPA-level statistics, displaying, 164
SPA drivers
SIP, ASR 1000 series routers, 87
SIP software, 66
SPAN (Switch Port Analyzers), ERSPAN
ASR 1000 series router packet capturing, 184–186
ASR 1000 series router support, 184
packet capturing, 184–186
SPD (security policy databases), 235
SRAM, QFP memory statistics, displaying for, 156–157
SSO (stateful switchovers), 179
HA, 179, 181–183
stress testing methodology, Enterprise Edge platforms, 35
switches, DCI feature requirements table, 12–13
system investment protection, Enterprise Edge platforms, 31
system redundancy, ASR 1000 series routers, 68

T

TBAR (time-based antireplay), GETVPN, 245
TCAM (tertiary content-addressable memory), ASR 1000 series ESP, 80
test plans, writing for Enterprise Edge platforms, 32
functional tests, 35
load testing methodology, 35
longevity testing methodology, 35
negative testing methodology, 35
performance tests, 35
positive testing methodology, 35
scale tests, 35
stress testing methodology, 35
test case details, 36
test entry/exit criteria, 35
test resources, 34
test results reporting, 36
test schedules, 36
test scope/objective, 34
test setup/topology, 34
Traffic Manager (QFP)
packet buffer DRAM, 208–209
packet buffering, 209

multicast packets, 210
punt packets, 210
unicast packets, 210
transit packets (ASR 1000 series routers)
arrival processing, 88–90
egress processing, 91
ingress processing, 88
troubleshooting
ASR 1000 series routers
debug commands, 150–153, 168–174
displaying drop statistics, 164–165
displaying front-panel LED status via show platform hardware command, 163
displaying interface-level binding, 165
displaying IPv4-related drops for active QFP, 155–156
displaying processors, 154–155
displaying QFP memory statistics for IRAM/DRAM/SRAM usage, 156–157
displaying QFP memory statistics on per-IOS feature/internal-usage basis, 157–161
displaying QFP PPE utilization information, 167–168
displaying RP/ESP/SIP insertion/uptime, 166–167
displaying SPA status in SIP, 163
displaying SPA-level statistics, 164
memory utilization, 154–155
show commands, 150–153, 169–174
tracking command output via monitor command, 162
tracking control CPU usage from Linux shell, 161–162
"Warning: Filesystem Is Not Clean" error messages, 174–175
CUBE, 279
GETVPN, ASR 1000 series routers, 250
IOS, 169–174
methodology of, 149
WAN architectures, 24, 26
WCCPv2, 265–266
TrustSec, traffic encryption over EoMPLS Pseudowire at Layer 2, 198, 200–203

U

UMI (unified management interfaces), IOS XE software, 94
unconditional policing, PQ (ASR 1000 series routers), 214
understanding, time to (WAN architectures), 24, 26
unicast packets, buffering, 210
unified communications services
CUBE, 269
business-to-business telepresence deployment scenario, 276–278
integrated CUBE, 271, 273
SP-to-managed enterprise and residential SIP trunking deployment scenario, 275–276
SP-to-SP peering deployment scenario, 274
troubleshooting, 279

WebEx Node services module, 269, 280
bandwidth, 281
deploying, 282
installing, 283, 285
security, 281
VoIP/video solution mode, 281
web presentation mode, 281
upgrades
ESP subpackages, ASR 1000 series routers, 135–136
ISSU
ASR 1000 series routers, 58, 114–115, 117–136
benefits of, 113–114
issu acceptversion command, 118, 122
issu commitversion command, 118, 133, 135
issu loadversion command, 118–119, 131, 135
issu runversion command, 118, 121
issu set rollback-timer command, 118
RP subpackages, ASR 1000 series routers, 132–134
SIP subpackages, ASR 1000 series routers, 131
SPA subpackages, ASR 1000 series routers, 131
users, remote user aggregation, ASR 1000 series routers, 50

V

virtualization
application mobility and, 20
ASR 1000 series routers, 190
encapsulation and, 20
WAN architectures, 20–21, 25
voice header compression, cRTP, 267
VoIP/video solution mode (WebEx Node services module), 281
vPC (virtual port channels), 195
VPN (virtual private networks)
DM VPN, 7
ASR 1000 series routers, 239–241
hub design, 239–241
multipoint GRE tunnels, 239
NHRP, 239
GET VPN, 7
ASR 1000 series routers, 242, 244–248, 250
crypto engine, 245
GDOI, 242, 244
GM, 242, 244
key servers, 242
QFP, 245
IPsec, ASR 1000 series routers, 232, 234
remote-access VPN, 7
SP L2 VPN, ASR series 1000 routers, 51
SP L3 VPN, ASR series 1000 routers, 51
VPNv4 routes, RR, 191–192
VSS (Virtual Switching Systems), 195

W-Z

WAAS (Wide Area Application Services), 259
ASR 1000 series routers, 262
WAN optimization, 262–265
firewalls, 261
WCCPv2, 259

WAN (wide area networks)
ASR 1000 series routers, 60
aggregation, 49
branch WAN aggregation, 2
connectivity options table, 4
feature requirements table, 5
secure WAN technologies table, 5
SLA requirements, 5
DCI, 10
feature requirements table, 11–13
edge routers, p2p GRE tunnels, 190
Enterprise Private WAN, segmentation, 187, 189
Internet edge role
feature requirements table, 9–10
router functionality table, 8–9
large branch WAN, office deployment requirements table, 13–14
private WAN aggregation, 2
connectivity options table, 4
feature requirements table, 5
secure WAN technologies table, 5
SLA requirements, 5
WAN architectures
business drivers
bandwidth commoditization, 22–23, 25
carbon footprint reduction, 23, 26
infrastructure consolidation, 19, 25
regulatory compliance, 24, 26
reliability, 22, 25
security, 22, 25
segmentation/virtualization, 20–21, 25
service awareness/integration, 18, 25
time to adoption, 24, 26
time to understanding, 24, 26
troubleshooting, 24, 26
evolution of, 17
WAN optimization, 262
branch deployments, 264
campus headend deployments, 263
IronPort appliances, 265
WSA, 265
"Warning: Filesystem Is Not Clean" error messages, 174–175
WCCPv2 (Web Cache Control Protocol version 2), 259
firewalls, 261–262
NBAR, 261
PBR, 261
troubleshooting, 265–266
web caching, 260–262
web caching, WCCPv2, 260–262
web interfaces, ASR 1000 GUI
configuring, 142
usage examples, 143, 146
views of, 141–142
web presentation mode (WebEx Node services module), 281
WebEx Node services module, 269, 280
bandwidth, 281
deploying, 282
installing, 283, 285
security, 281
VoIP/video solution mode, 281
web presentation mode, 281
WSA (Web Security Appliances), WAN optimization, 265

ciscopress.com: Your Cisco Certification and Networking Learning Resource

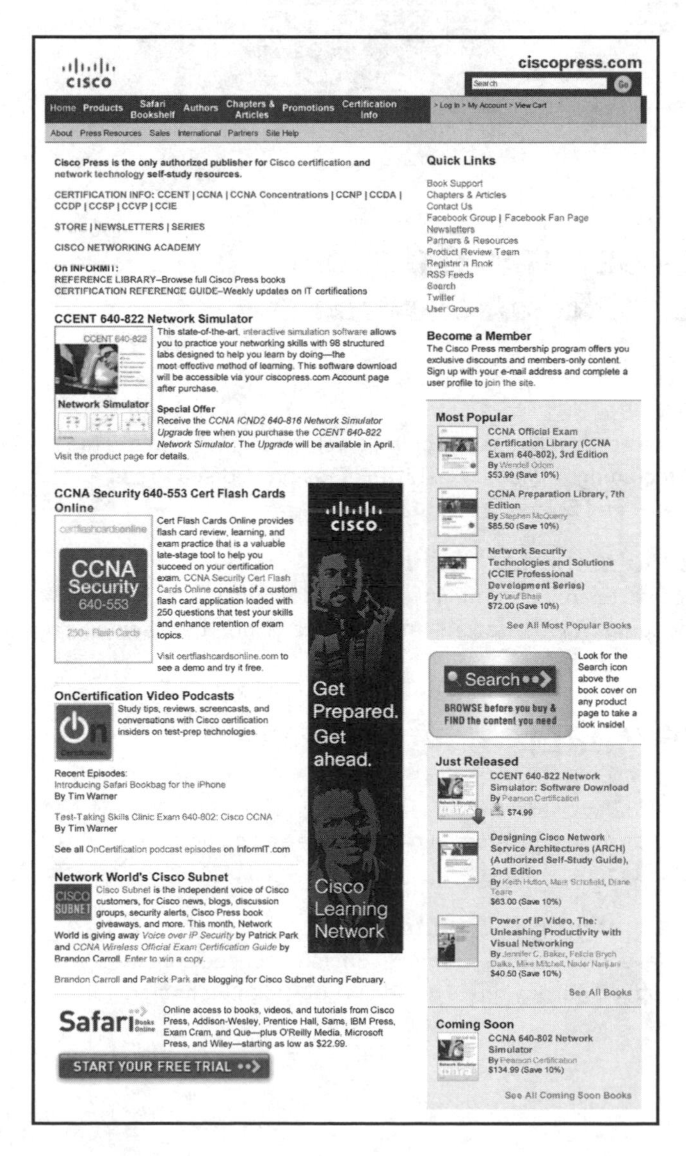

Subscribe to the monthly Cisco Press newsletter to be the first to learn about new releases and special promotions.

Visit **ciscopress.com/newsletters.**

While you are visiting, check out the offerings available at your finger tips.

–Free Podcasts from experts:
- OnNetworking
- OnCertification
- OnSecurity

View them at **ciscopress.com/podcasts**.

–Read the latest author **articles** and **sample chapters** at **ciscopress.com/articles**.

–Bookmark the Certification Reference Guide available through our partner site at **informit.com/certguide**.

Connect with Cisco Press authors and editors via Facebook and Twitter, visit **informit.com/socialconnect**.